MOUNTAINS AT RISK
Current Issues in Environmental Studies

MOUNTAINS AT RISK
Current Issues in Environmental Studies

Edited by
NIGEL J.R. ALLAN

Manohar
New Delhi

ISBN 81-7304-133-4

First Published 1995

© Nigel J.R. Allan, 1995

Published by
Ajay Kumar Jain
Manohar Publishers & Distributors
2/6 Ansari Road, Daryaganj
New Delhi - 110002

Lasertypeset by
AJ Software Publishing Co., Pvt. Ltd.
305, Durga Chambers, 1333, D.B. Gupta Road,
Karol Bagh, New Delhi - 110005

Printed at
Print Perfect
Mayapuri
New Delhi - 110064

Contents

Preface vii
Contributors ix
Acknowledgements xiii
Introduction xv

Part One: FOUNDATIONS

1. Human Aspects of Mountain Environmental Change, 1889-1992
   Nigel J.R. Allan — 3

2. Mapping Vegetation in the Himalaya
   Ulrich Schweinfurth — 27

3. The Protective Role of Mountain Forests
   Lawrence S. Hamilton — 49

Part Two: NEW ISSUES

4. Climate Change and Mountain Ecosystems
   Martin F. Price and John R. Haslett — 73

5. Hazards and Disaster in Mountain Environments: Problems in the Geography of Risk
   Kenneth Hewitt — 98

6. Havens on High? The Fate of Biodiversity in Mountain Agriculture
   Karl S. Zimmerer — 129

7   Reclamation of a Mountain Coal Mine:
    Designing Habitat for Bighorn Sheep
    Norma Beth MacCallum and Valerius Geist   152

Part Three: MOUNTAINS AND LEISURE

8   Patterns of the Development of Tourism in
    Mountain Communities
    Martin F. Price   199

9   Outdoor Recreation and Tourism in Mountain
    Environments
    Herbert G. Kariel and Dianne L. Draper   220

10 Mountains, Nations, Parks, and Conservation:
    A Case Study of the Mt. Everest Area
    Daniel Taylor-Ide   238

11 National Parks and Nature Reserves in Mountain
    Environments of the World
    Jim Thorsell and Jeremy Harrison   255

    Index   290

Preface

Compilation of this volume was stimulated by two events at the end of the 1980s. In 1989 I was fortunate to receive a research fellowship at the Environment and Policy Institute at the East-West Center in Honolulu, Hawaii. During that all too brief summer I had time to reflect on my own work on mountain societies and habitats of the past decade and that of colleagues. In that same period I was exposed to the ideas and accomplishments of other fellows at the EWC who had worked on environmental issues in Asia. Larry Hamilton was the guiding light there, and the interaction with Terry Rambo, Jeff Fox, Michael Dove and other permanent and temporary sojourners from Asia at the EWC was most fruitful.

On another front, a former colleague, and co-founder of *Ecological Economics*, Herman Daly, suggested that I prepare for public consumption a document that could be used as a mountain environment reference for the United Nations Environment Programme's "Earth Summit" scheduled for Rio de Janeiro in 1992. With the stimulus of the East-West Center experience and the anticipation of the Rio Earth Summit, I solicited the cooperation and assistance of mountain experts in creating a volume that would summarize the contemporary knowledge and debates about mountain environments. This volume is the product of that effort.

The chapters in this volume were not designed to be an exhaustive collation of material on mountains nor were all mountains of the world included in the volume. That regional perspective is provided in a book edited by Peter Stone, published in conjunction with the Earth Summit. The focus of this volume is on stocktaking—a retrospective look at the academic and some applied information generated during the previous decade. At the start of the 1980s grandiose claims were made about the environmental status of the world's mountains, especially those in Asia. Early in the decade field researchers raised their voices to question the universal statements of the prophets of doom and gloom concerning ecological disaster and hazards in the world's mountains. This volume assesses the most recent thoughts on issues relating to mountain environments after the 1980s decade. Many of the chapters are derived from the contents of a special issue of *GeoJournal*. Grateful acknowledgment is made here to Jeffrey Smith, Vice-President, Kluwer Academic Publishers USA, Petra van Steenbergen and Wolf Tietze of Kluwer, Dordrecht, Netherlands, for encouragement to publish revised versions of these papers for an Asian edition. Additional chapters have been added to complete the existing coverage of mountain environments.

My thanks to the authors of the book chapters who were very generous with their time, talent, and advice. The entire volume was processed in Times Roman Font by Lisa Morse from my Word Perfect draft manuscripts. Jon Barbour formatted the book in Aldus Pagemaker, prior to printing. Their patience and fortitude in coordinating all the disparate material, in addition to resolving software and hardware problems, is greatly appreciated.

It is to be hoped that this Asian edition will enable local resource managers and indigenous stewards of the mountains to accommodate the desires and demands of a burgeoning population to the environmental integrity of the mountains.

August 1994   NIGEL J.R. ALLAN
Leh, Ladakh
India

Contributors

Nigel J. R. Allan is Professor of Geography and Chair of the Geography Department at the University of California at Davis. A native of Scotland he began his South Asian mountain field research in Uttarakhand and Nepal in 1966 with USAID. Since that time he has done field research in Tajikistan, Afghanistan, Pakistan, Xinjiang and Tibet in China, and further work in Nepal. His principal interests are in mountaim society and habitat. He has published *North Pakistan: Karakorum Conquered* and *Human Impact on Mountains*.

Dianne L. Draper is Associate Professor of Geography at the University of Calgary. She teaches in the fields of Human Geography, Tourism and Recreation, and Environmental Issues and Resources Management. Her research and field study interests encompass tourism and recreation planning, development, and impact studies; coastal zone and fisheries management; water resources; and policy-making in environmental issues including forestry, recreation, parks, and other natural environments, principally within Canada. She is the co-author of *Relevance and Ethics in Geography* and other publications in the tourism and resource management fields.

Valerius Geist, Professor and program director for Environmental Science, Faculty of Environmental Design, has been involved in research on large herbivorous mammals since 1959. Geist is a long-standing member of the IUCN/SSC specialist groups, being involved with the caprid, deer and sustainable utilization of wildlife groups. He has been twice honored by the Wildlife Society for his work and once by the American Association for the Advancement of Science. He has written or edited seven technical and popular books, 115 refereed papers and over 150 popular articles and encyclopedia entries.

Lawrence S. Hamilton is Co-Director of Islands and Highlands Consultancy in Vermont, USA. For twelve years, at the East-West Center in Hawaii, he worked in various countries of Asia and the Pacific on topics of forest watershed planning and management, protected areas, mountain development and conserving tropical ecosystems on small islands. He was born in Canada and received his initial forestry training at the University of Toronto. He received a doctoral degree from the School of Natural Resources at the University of Michigan in 1963. He was named Vice-Chair for Mountains in IUCN's Commission on National Parks and Protected Areas in 1992.

Jeremy Harrison is responsible for management of information on protected areas of the World Conservation Monitoring Centre (WCMC) in Cambridge, England, where he has been based for twelve years. Information from the WCMC Protected Areas Database has been used in a wide range of publications, most recently in the four volume *Protected Areas of the World* prepared for the World Parks Congress in Caracas. WCMC is also responsible for management of information on natural World Heritage sites and on biosphere reserves designated under the UNESCO MAB program.

John R. Haslett was trained as an ecologist and has spent the last ten years working on terrestrial ecosystems in the Austrian and German Alps. His special interests include animal/plant interactions, the complexity of mountain habitat mosaics and the effects of human activities, particularly winter tourism, on mountain ecosystems. He is based at the University of Salzburg in Austria and has published a number of scientific papers on different aspects of mountain ecology. He is presently writing a textbook on "Alpine Ecology".

Kenneth Hewitt is Professor of Geography at Wilfrid Laurier University, Canada. For over thirty years he has completed a wide array of mountain studies throughout the world, both physical, as in geomorphology, glaciology, and hydrology, and human, especially in the geography of risk, hazard, and catastrophe. He has also published on the intellectual history of mountain research and exploration. Among his recent books are *Interpretations of Calamity*, and *Spartan Walls*.

Herbert G. Kariel is Professor of Geography at the University of Calgary, Canada. A native of Germany, he has conducted field research in New Zealand, North Africa, Mexico, the Himalaya, Alps, and the Rocky Mountains of the United States and Canada. He is co-author of *Explorations in Social Geography*, and *Alpine Huts in the Rockies, Selkirks, and Purcells*, and has authored publications in his research interests that include noise and its perception, tourism, and communicaton flows.

Norma Beth MacCallum is a professional biologist consultant in Alberta,

Canada. Prior to operating her own consulting practice she was a wildlife biologist with the Alberta Provincial Fish and Wildlife Division. She has designed and carried out many wildlife inventories, breeding bird surveys, and small mammal studies. Most recently her specialty is wildlife inventory related to reclamation planning and environmental impact assessment. Her Master's thesis, done under the supervision of Val Geist was "Bighorn Sheep: Use of an Open Pit Coal Mine in the Foothills of Alberta."

Martin F. Price has worked on the interactions of permanent and visiting human populations with mountain ecosystems that began in the late 1970's, with his M.Sc. work in Banff National Park, Canada. His book, *Mountain Forests as Common Property Resources*, was a comparative study of the sources, implementation, and effects of forest management in the Colorado Rockies and the Swiss Alps. A more recent focus of his work, particularly at the National Center for Atmospheric Research (Colorado, USA), has been the implications of global climate change for mountain ecosystems and communities. He is presently a Research Scientist at the Environmental Change Unit of the University of Oxford.

Ulrich Schweinfurth was Professor and head of the Department of Geography, South Asia Institute, at the University of Heidelberg in Germany. His geoecological research has taken him to the Himalaya, Sri Lanka, Australia, New Zealand, and Oceania. In addition to his role as editor of the *Geoecological Research* series since 1972 and his early research cited herein, he has published two monographs in the Bonner Geographische Abhandlungen series, *Studien zur Pflanzengeographie von Tasmanien* and *Neuseeland and Beobachtungen und Studien zur Pflanzengeographie und Oekologie der antipodischen Inselgroppe*. His latest book is *Neue Forschungen im Himalaya* published in the Erkundliches Wissenschaften series in 1993.

Daniel Taylor-Ide is Director, Population and Environment Scientific Group for the Johns Hopkins University Institute for International Programs in Baltimore, USA. In 1972 he founded and then directed for twenty years the Woodlands Mountain Institute in the Appalachia Mountains of West Virginia, USA. He initiated and led the international support for creating the Qomolangma Nature Preserve on the north side of Mount Everest and the Makalu-Barun National Park and Conservation Area in contiguous Nepal.

Jim Thorsell is IUCN's Senior Advisor on Natural Heritage and coordinator of its Mountain Protected Area initiative based in Gland, Switzerland. He has worked in national parks planning and management since he began as a ranger in Banff, Alberta in 1962. He has authored and edited many books, articles and reports on conservation; recently published books include *Managing Protected Areas in Tropics, Parks on the Borderline: Experience in Transfrontier Conservation,* and *World Heritage Twenty Years Later.*

Karl S. Zimmerer is Associate Professor of Geography at the University of Wisconsin, Madison. He is interested in the geography of agricultural biodiversity in mountain environments. His other research interests include the impact of economic development on soils and non-crop biological resources in peasant and indigenous societies in the Himalaya and the Andes. Currently, he is at work on a study of soil erosion and agricultural change in the Bolivian Andes.

Acknowledgements

Chapters appearing with minor or major revisions by permission are derived from: Nigel J.R. Allan, "Mountain Environments: An Assessment," *GeoJournal* 27 (1992) : 5-11; L.S. Hamilton, " The Protective Role of Mountains Forests," *GeoJournal* 27 (1992) : 13-22; Kenneth Hewitt, "Mountain Hazards," *GeoJournal* 27 (1992) : 47-60; Kariel and D.L. Draper, "Outdoor Recreation in Mountains," *GeoJournal* 17 (1992) : 95-104; N.B. MacCallum and V. Geist, " Mountain Restoration: Soil and Surface Wildlife Habitat," *GeoJournal* 27 (1992) : 23-46; M. Price, "Patterns of Tourism in Mountain Environments," *GeoJournal* 27 (1992) : 87-96; U.Schweinfurth, "Mapping Mountains: Vegetation in the Himalaya," *GeoJournal* 27 (1992): 73-83; D. Taylor-Ide, "Mountains, Nations, Parks, and Conservation: A Case Study of Mt. Everest Area," *GeoJournal* 27 (1992) :105-112; J. Thorsell and J. Harrison, "National Parks and Nature Reserves in Mountain Environments," *GeoJournal* 27 (1992): 113-126; K. Zimmerer, "The Loss and Maintenace of Native Crops in Mountain Agriculture," *GeoJournal* 27 (1992) : 61-72.

Introduction

Much of the world's attention is increasingly focussed on mountains, not just mountains in the Western world but mountains around the world. The reasons for this attention are manifold. Mountain environments have, during the last two decades, been seen to be vulnerable to a host of environmental ills, including deforestation, increasing sedimentation of mountain rivers, peasant exploitation of fragile soils for short gain agriculture, floral and faunal depletion due to mining and hunting, loss of habitat caused by increasing human settlement on steep slopes for extended leisure in Western countries and for arable land extensification in non-Western countries. These perceptions have caused the public to believe that mountains are at risk.

While the issue of "risk" in mountains is fully explored by Hewitt, *infra*, the key idea in this book is an understanding that risk, vulnerability and its associated problems in mountains are strongly associated with human agency and that the mountain environment is also subject to short and long term biophysical environmental perturbation. So much of the concern about mountains is riveted on the biophysical properties, but too little emphasis is focussed on the properties that are associated with the social, economic, or political pressures on the mountain environment. This situation is being ameliorated on a worldwide basis by several new initiatives (Blaikie et al. 1994; Kirby 1990; Waterstone 1992; Wisner 1994).

The focus of the book is on the period following the United Nations Conference on the Human Environment, held in Stockholm in 1972. Another pertinent event was the UN Environment Programme report on mountain environments issued in 1980. At that time other United Nations agencies were exhibiting their concern about the mountains. Foremost among them was UNESCO with its Man and the Biosphere Project 6, focussing on mountains. Another term that one frequently encounters is "stress." When the Swiss merged some of their everyday planning activities into the UNESCO Man and the Biosphere Project 6 program (Messerli, Messerli 1980), they envisioned integration of practitioners of social and natural sciences towards solving planning problems. Joint projects in the Swiss national research program were entitled "Socio-Economic development and the limits of ecological stress in mountain regions." As Ernst Winkler (1980) has reported, these titles engendered a confidence that might lead to the resolution of problems in national planning but he cautions that the information derived from "the experience of Swiss national and environmental planning will hopefully be accepted critically." Some chapters in this book clearly suggest that "ecological stress" and similar concepts are quite elusive in nature and application.

Our knowledge of what is occurring in mountains is too often circumscribed by the donor agencies who have a small stake in the outcome. All the calamities afflicting mountains that are mentioned above may or may not be present in the mountains. Donor agencies, whether bureaucracies within the governments of countries or multinational or binational agencies, many times seek to "invent" calamities and associated risk. It behooves these organizations to portray mountain environments as at risk in order to maintain their existence. This "calamity" existence is not confined to agencies. Despite entreaties about mountains for over a decade, for example by John Lall in India, scientists and commentators of the common polity have not critically examined the issues relating to mountains. The linkages between natural and social scientists are tenuous to say the least. Natural scientists who have examined the mountain environment with instrumentalist approaches neglect the human population as actors in the mountain environment. Social scientists fare little better because their approach too often has been to assign ecological models to human phenomena. Furthermore, the vast amount of studies have been conducted at the microscale, for example those using only a handful of survey sites, thereby creating a body of knowledge with little application to surrounding places outside the immediate survey sites, not to mention application to other mountain environments.

These "scientistical" efforts aimed at creating a theoretical or conceptual unity within mountain environments so that mountains can be examined as a "whole" ecosystem or natural region are not new—they are derived from statements made in Europe a century ago and have antecedents in the dark reaches of antiquity. This book departs from that tradition by emphasizing the *in situ* contextual nature of mountain studies. To use Thomas Kuhn's term, a paradigm shift has occurred in the study of mountains—one which has moved away from the technocratic, deterministic solutions to perceived mountain problems, like natural hazards, that typified much of the UNESCO MAB-6 work. The chapters in this book critically examine the received wisdom as they probe for soft spots in the positions and arguments that have been made about mountains. It is this emphasis on skepticism that marks the chapters in the book. No chapter author advocates a particular doctrine; instead the authors dissect current views about mountains and present recent evidence to compel everyone concerned about mountains to think again.

All authors of the chapters in this book possess an awareness of the necessity of linking natural and social sciences in the examination of mountain environments. This facility avoids confounding the bipolar views of mountains. The optimistic view is to see mountains as relatively unpopulated, often in an Arcadian delight far removed from the grinding urban squalor and poverty that confronts every visitor to cities, whether they are Euro-American or scattered around the world. This vision is perpetuated because urban residents perceive mountains as subliminal places to recreate. It also confers upon mountain residents the aura of purity of existence; to be a mountain peasant is seen as a noble calling. Much of this perception derives from generous contemporary welfare systems enacted by Alpine countries to provide transfer payments to small landholdings occupied by their own part-time farmers. The pernicious effect of this imagery is the promotion of disguised self-sufficiency that is then transferred to non-Western countries where the mountain farmers are seen lacking in facilities that prevent them from attaining self-sufficiency in a marginal environment. Development agencies, their staffs and consultants, prefer to live in places that are enjoyable with high leisure amenities. This perception clouds the actual conditions that may actually exist in marginal mountain environments.

The opposite viewpoint is to see mountain environments as places of great risk in the biophysical sense. A concern with hazards dominates this viewpoint. The gloomy assessment of mountains and their populations is similar to that which existed prior to the Enlightenment when Europeans changed their minds about mountains. Topics that dominate this latter modern view include a preoccupation with avalanches, floods, deforestation, earthquakes, and soil erosion. The eco-doomsters, as they are labelled, are aggrieved by this situation, notwithstanding the fact that normal physical processes in mountains confirm the Biblical injunction in Isaiah 40:4, "...every mountain and hill shall be made low." Despite the natural physical processes at work in mountains, too many natural scientists ascribe to the mountain environment a quality of stability, as viewed in ecology, that does not exist. Orville Freeman, a former American Secretary of Agriculture, remarked that he had been a farmer for eighteen years and only two years out of that time were considered average in terms of weather and income. Weather in mountains is notoriously fickle and those who wrest a living from the land in mountains learn to accommodate to yearly and seasonal environmental perturbations.

Despite the proliferation of its advocates who like to use ecology based terms (Purrington 1984), "adaptation" to the mountain environment by a local population remains questionable. Mountain populations are chronic migrants, whether seasonal or permanent. A sampling of mountain populations around the world from Staszewski's (1957) *Vertical Distribution of World Population*— the only source on this subject in the past half century — does not reveal any abnormal population increase in rural mountains. Even mountain towns, those for example in the Alps like Grenoble, Innsbrueck, and Bozen, have not grown in size commensurate to cities elsewhere in the lowlands or forelands.

Contrary to popular imagery, the argument can be made that humans appear maladapted to mountains. Birth rates are high and land availability or intensification is inelastic; consequently mountaineers have migrated to the lowlands in large numbers to become new settlers or urban residents. An "adaptation" to the marginal resource base among mountaineers is the participation in commodity exchange with other higher highland or lowland places, such as the Tibetan plateau or the Altiplano in the Andes. Long distance trading with men absent from the community for weeks or months may have had ripple effects such as inducing polyandry or polygynandry. These marital systems might be a product not, as one often hears, of a limited resource base or encapsulated communities, but as a result of long distance trading. By imposing nation-state borders in mountainous areas the centralized state increasingly marginalized mountain communities, thereby causing an increased use —often overuse—of the local resources. In recent times foreign "experts" involved in development of peripheral areas have failed to recognize historical processes in mountain communities that reveal geographies extending far beyond the confines of a farm, community or even valley. The urban mentality of domocentric life, of living in one place, has overlooked the peripatetic, egocentric life that often characterized a mountain dweller. It is no wonder, then, that the rise of the nation state has imperiled mountain people by placing an increasing burden on the shackled mountain farmer. Such limitations have created a mountain population that is now maladapted to the mountain environment. Marginality in the state polity sense has resulted in marginality of a minority in an increasing marginal environment.

The book is divided into three parts, the first part being concerned with some fundamentals: how did we reach this state of knowledge and what are the positions of the major disputants about the conditions of mountain environments. In Chapter 1, I have discussed the contemporary situation from a personal perspective, one which has been tempered by almost thirty years of experience in the highest mountains of the world but one that exhibits the disaffection, perhaps even cynicism, of the instrumentalist approach to the condition of mountains. My initial chapter is not meant to be exhaustive but to detect some of the major trends among the examiners of mountains during the past two decades. Chapter 1 proposes a paradigm shift in mountain studies and is therefore adversarial. When I published an early draft two years ago I fully

Introduction

expected an informed response in the literature; as yet none has appeared. Schweinfurth and Hamilton perform a great service by telling us about the effort expended over time and terrain to document the vegetation of a mountain area that rims South Asia. In addition, they document exactly what a mountain forest does in the environment. Despite the facile generalizations about the forests of the Himalaya, Schweinfurth alerts us to the fact that much is incomplete in our knowledge about mountain vegetation, but perhaps more importantly, he informs us by documenting the difficulties in mapping the actual and not predicted vegetation found in the Himalaya. Mountain forests are believed to have extrafloral properties, according to some popular environmental commentators, but Hamilton dissolves these myths by delineating the role of forests in mountains. Chapters 2 and 3 provide an environmental template upon which other chapters are placed.

Part Two is directly concerned with topical issues that concern mountain scientists. Climate change, hazards, biodiversity, and wildlife protection are issues that pervade discussions about mountains. Price and Haslett, both residing in Europe, portray, in a range of scenarios, the consequences of climate change upon mountains. Not the least of the effects of climate change is the modelled impact of climate change upon European mountains, which contains dire consequences for local mountain economies dependent on winter and summer tourists, especially skiing in the winter.

Hewitt dissects the literature about mountain hazards. While he acknowledges the existence of mountain hazards in the geophysical sense in his role as a geomorphologist, the major contribution of Hewitt, in his adopted role as a humanist, is to spell out the alien human induced hazards upon mountain environments, the notions of calamity, hazard, and risk (Hewitt 1982, 1988, 1992). These, he judges, are much more common and dangerous and life threatening than are hazards and risks connected to the geophysical properties of mountains. Hewitt's philosophy on this topic extends far beyond mere mountains to include a consideration of war and impoverishment at the periphery.

Agropastoralism dominates mountain life. A feature that is bewildering to the development officer stationed in mountain communities is the refusal of local cultivators to adopt new seed varieties that have been tried and proven elsewhere. These cultivars are frequently propagated for specific *in situ* conditions, as Zimmerer discusses. Their value for posterity should be maintained through local conservation and use instead of relying on distant crop germplasm centers. Zimmerer's chapter clearly demonstrates that mountain agriculture has evolved within the context of the local agrosystem.

Mining has always been a part of mountain life because the geological structure of the earth exposes minerals deemed valuable to human use. The recent emergence of "Oetzi," the Bronze Age man, from a glacier at the head of the Oetz valley south of Innsbrueck reveals early use of minerals. Much furor exists over the extraction of minerals but as MacCallum and Geist demonstrate, a thorough knowledge of mountain animal behavior can assist in the rehabilitation of the mining site by fitting the human sculpted geomorphology to the behavioral traits of indigenous mountain fauna. The Alberta case described by the authors forces us to rethink our preconceived notions about the behavior of mountain animals in close proximity of machinery and humans.

Chapters in Part Three tackle the twentieth century phenomenon of human use of mountains by an external population. Price, Kariel, and Draper, with a wealth of experience from around the world, highlight the impacts upon mountains of mass tourism and the more vigorous recreation by visitors. Much of this tourism is the product of enhanced forms of accessibility, whether road, rail or air transport.

Large portions of mountains are now being set aside for protected areas, a somewhat strange situation to a Scotsman as Scotland is the only modern, industrialized country in the world without a national park. Scots, with the sanction of law, have long had access to the countryside, which is a right denied citizens of most countries. While the concept of national parks to the Scots therefore seems redundant, this is not the case elsewhere in the mountain world. The highest mountain on earth, Mt. Everest on the border of China and Nepal, has seen a tremendous influx of outsiders, now 9000 per year into the nearby south side of Khumbu Himal. The popularity of this destination has placed enormous pressures on the cultural and environmental integrity of the region. As we can see from Taylor-Ide's contribution in Chapter 10, there are many lessons to be learned from integrating the long-term benefits accruing to the local population from enhanced incomes with long-term bio-physical conservation. The Everest experience allows protected area planners the luxury of hindsight as planning is now underway for the creation of a Karakorum National Park and proposed World Heritage Site in the greatest collection of high mountains in the world. With the experience of indigenous formal rights of access to mountains as in the case of Scotland, and the informal common property rights in the Sagarmatha National Park, the planners of the proposed Karakorum National Park have well established precedents for dealing with indigenous property rights.

The last chapter in the book summarizes for the first time all the mountain protected areas in the world. This gargantuan task, under the direction of Thorsell and Harrison, is the product of the World Data Center of the International Union for the Conservation of Nature and Natural Resources. Forty-two per cent of the area of all protected areas in the world is in mountains. This large proportion reflects the concern of governments and people about

Introduction

their mountain environments, a genuine concern shared by all the contributions to this volume. It is to be hoped that this book's contents, like that of the recently published volume by the IUCN Commission on National Parks and Protects Areas, (Hamilton et al. 1993), will alert the reader to the contemporary issues surrounding mountain environments.

REFERENCES

Blaikie, Piers, Terry Cannon, Ian Davis, Ben Wisner. 1994. *At Risk: Natural Hazards, People's Vulnerability and Disaters*. New York: Routledge.
Beaver, Patricia D. and Burton L. Purrington, editors. 1984. *Cultural Adaptation to Mountain Environments*. Athens: University of Georgia Press.
Hamilton, Lawrence S., Daniel P. Bauer, and Helen Takeuchi. 1993. *Parks, Peaks, and People*. Honolulu: East-West Center.
Hewitt, Kenneth. (ed.). 1982. *Interpretations of Calamity*. London: George Allen and Unwin.
Hewitt, Kenneth. 1988. "The Study of Mountain Lands and People: A Critical Overview." In *Human Impact on Mountains*, edited by Nigel J. R. Allan et al., 6-23. Totowa, NJ: Rowman and Littlefield.
Kirby, Andrew. (ed.). 1990. "Toward a New Risk Analysis." In *Nothing to Fear: Risks and Hazards in American Society*, edited by A. Kirby, 281-298. Tucson: University of Arizona Press.
Messerli, Paul, and Bruno Messerli. 1978. "Wirtschaftliche Entwicklung und oekologische Belastbarkeit im Bergebiet." *Geographica Helvetica* 33:203-210.
Staszewski, Josef. 1957. *Vertical Distribution of World Population*, Polish Academy of Sciences Geographical Studies No. 14. Warsaw: State Scientific Publishing House.
Waterstone, Marvin. 1992. "Introduction: The Social Genesis of Risks and Hazards." In *Risk and Society: The Interaction of Science, Technology, and Public Policy*, edited by M. Waterstone, 1-12. Dordecht: Kluwer
Winkler, Ernst. 1980. "Current Problems of Swiss National Planning and Geography." In *Geography in Switzerland*, edited by F. Mueller, L. Bridel, and E. Schwabe, 179-183. Zurich: Commission on Geography, SAS.
Wisner, Ben. 1994. "Disaster Vulnerability: Geographical Scale and Existential Reality." In *Worlds of Pain and Hunger*, edited by Hans-Gorg Bohle, 13-52. Saarbrueken: Breitenbach.

Part One
FOUNDATIONS

CHAPTER 1

Human Aspects of Mountain Environmental Change, 1889-1992

NIGEL J. R. ALLAN

Introduction

The Greater Himalaya, that long mountain arc stretching from the Hindukush mountains in Afghanistan to the Hengduan mountains in China, is now being thoroughly scrutinized by residents, neighbors and others from afar.. Both the east-west dimension and the south-north dimension exhibit a precipitation cline from wet to dry. The Himalayan biotic environment reflects this range but the humans populating the Himalaya exhibit such a diversity that their distribution cannot be connected with climate zone, or terrain, or altitude. The mountains contain, in the words of one veteran ethnographer, an ethnic zoo. Yet in spite of the staggering complexity of the biophysical environment and the human occupants, there is a great temptation among scientists and others to characterize this huge area by the most simplistic generalized statements. I seek to elucidate the statements made about mountains in general and the Himalaya in particular, and to scrutinize them with a considerable degree of skepticism, because science, at its basal level, is skepticism.

The models and generalized statements about the Himalaya that we have are largely the product of Eurocentric minds, as one might expect given Friedrich Ratzel's dominance when geography emerged as an ideographic discipline in the past century. Ratzel set forth his ideas on models of mountain habitat in his essay "Hoehengrenzen and Hoehenguertel" published in the *Zeitschrift des Deutschen und Oestereichischen Alpenvereins* (Ratzel 1889). His ideas formed the dominant paradigm of mountain society and habitat until recently. For many recent statements about the models of mountain landscapes, if they are not of European origin then they are made by indigenous, but

Western trained scientists. Since many of the ideas about mountains concern the European Alps, the Eurocentric Alpine perspective dominates the literature on much of the world's mountain research, especially the Himalayan research. Anyone who examines my own past record shall see that I am as culpable as many others for adopting this perspective (Allan 1984). But it is time to take stock of where we are going, how we shall proceed in examining mountain environments in the future, and, most importantly, what can we learn from the past, especially the past two decades of field research. In this spirit of inquiry I offer an appraisal—a very personal appraisal—of what has transpired since Ratzel's essay on mountains in 1889, but more specifically, since the June 1972 UN Conference on the Human Environment held in Stockholm (United Nations 1973).

For scientists interested in mountains the question can be raised by them: can mountains and their populations be studied as an independent entity divorced from every day life in other biomes? Is there something specific that sets "Mountain Habitat and Society," as I call it, apart from other environments? Ecologists have a way of subsuming every environment under the banner of ecology, but can we say that mountains are a separate entity, perhaps an ecosystem or bioregion as conceived by an ecologist, as discrete as river plains, coastal marshes, or deserts? This dispute about the topical field clearly sets mountains in a category by itself. Much of the problem defining mountain as a distinct entity was caused by the United Nations agencies that used Miklos Udvardy's (1975) map of biotic realms of the world for defining "natural regions" (Parsons 1985). Mountains, because they contained numerous biomes, did not emerge as a coherent entity. The geographers of old made a clear distinction that mountains were a separate "natural region." Europeans were not united in their definitions, but in the English language, Peattie (1936) had one, Troll (1988) another, while a contemporary international, IUCN, definition, authored by Thorsell and Harrison (*infra*) has just emerged for identifying mountain protected areas. Hewitt in the opening chapter of *Human Impact on Mountains*, the first general book since Peattie's about humans in mountains (Allan et al. 1988), critically reviews the various definitions. For models of mountains, Uhlig (1984) gives an excellent, exhaustive review of traditional altitudinal zonation models that he prepared for a conference in Bavaria. In a new journal exclusively devoted to mountain affairs, *Mountain Research and Development*, and elsewhere, several authors have commented on the contemporary revisions to the traditional models of mountains. I give an example in an early discussion of my altitudinal zonation model (Allan 1984). The French mountain scholar Veyret (1972) diverges significantly from the Germanic mode by offering a model devoid of the deterministic implications.

Since the United Nations Conference on the Human Environment was held

Human Aspects of Mountain Environmental Change   5

in Stockholm, 5-16 June 1972, much attention has been focussed on the mountain human environment. Chapter 2 of the 1973 *Report of the United Nations Conference on the Human Environment* promulgated an "Action Plan for the Human Environment." The plan called for environmental assessment and management and supporting measures. Topics in the environmental assessment portion included evaluation and review, research, monitoring and information exchange. Among the 109 formal recommendations were several that focussed specifically on environments, for example forests, deserts, aquatic and marine resources. Mountains were not specifically mentioned. A forerunner of UNEP's interest in mountains prior to the 1992 Earth Summit was a report published in 1980 entitled *The Major Problems of Man and Environment Interactions in Mountain Ecosystems*. This report presaged the evaluative research on the Himalaya done by Michael Thompson and his collaborators on a UNEP project in the International Institute for Applied Systems Analysis (IIASA) facility in Laxenburg, Austria during 1980-84 (Thompson et al. 1986). Now that the United Nations Conference on Environment and Development was held in 1992 in Rio de Janeiro twenty years after the Stockholm Conference and ten years after the United Nations Environment Programme sponsored reports on mountain environments, it is a propitious time to take a retrospective look at the major themes and issues that have occurred in the research of habitat and society in mountains.

Although the time frame for this review is a century, I focus on the past twenty years because this period coincides with the revisions of our thinking about mountain environments. Several stages of investigation into the mountain human environment on a world wide basis can be recognized. These are discussed first. The major shift has occurred from a focus on biophysical models and methods of inquiry that are applied generally to all mountains, to a contemporary inquiry into culture and site specific features found in places in the mountain world. This shift moves from the (environmental) deterministic Ratzel era idea that later formed the basis for the landscape ecology paradigm of Carl Troll, through its interpretation into geoecology and related notions of the primacy of system or structure of "mountain ecosystems", to a contemporary situation wherein human agency, cast as an ensemble of nature-culture within a regional setting, is paramount (Allan 1992, Hewitt 1988).

Some of the audience may lack a perspective of mountain environments. A comprehensive English language treatment of the mountain physical environment can be found in Larry Price's *Mountains and Man*—the mountain portion is the best physical introduction—while a contemporary source for humans in mountains is *Human Impact on Mountains* containing contributions on themes found in mountain areas around the world. The editors of that volume represented field expertise in Asia, the Andes, and the Alps and archival facility in a number of languages. After a discussion of the historical view of mountains, the second part of this chapter addresses the immediate concerns germane to the Himalaya: first, images of the Himalayan environment; second, the evidence and counter evidence for arguments about the condition of the Himalayan habitat; and third, tourism in its several manifestations.

Generalized Biophysical Models of Mountains

The altitudinal zonation relationship between humans and the mountain environment was summarized a century ago by Ratzel's (1889) article "Hoehengrenzen und Hoehenguertel." Ratzel's general geography writing in *Anthropo-geographie* was supplemented by some acute observations on the mountain environment that were summarized in an altitudinal form drawing heavily on Alexander von Humboldt's observations early in the nineteenth century. These observations, in turn, had their origins in the ancient Greek notions about mountains.

In contrast to the German language literature, the French geographers such as Vidal de la Blache (1911), Arbos (1922) and later Blanchard (1938-56) and Veyret (1972), firmly established the idea that mountain environments exhibited great diversity in culture and resource exploitation. If there was an environmentalist bias it appeared more in the work of French historians like Braudel (1972) rather than the geographers. French mountains located close to northern Europe, the Atlantic, and the Mediterranean had populations that were predisposed to a variety of strategies for wresting a living from the mountains and from the contiguous lowlands world. Nevertheless, our dominant paradigms and concepts relating to mountains remain Germanic constructions of the conditions in mountains around the world.

The ideas of Humboldt and Ratzel about mountains were firmly grounded in the biophysical model of mountain vegetation that was itself the product of climatic controls. This paradigm is at the core of all the German terms such as *hoehengrenzen* and *hoehenstufen*, as Groetzbach (1985) and others (Jentsch, Liedtke 1980) have explained, and what we know in English as altitudinal zonation or verticality.

Geoecology

Foremost among geographers working in the mountains was the German biogeographer Carl Troll. Unlike American biogeographers who developed ecology and founded the *Journal of Ecology* early this century, only to abandon a consideration of humans by 1920, German biogeographers such as Troll had an initial interest in the local folk in the area of their field research. Troll's forays into the high mountains of East Africa, the Andes, and the Himalaya, wherein he analyzed the relationships between geology, climate and biology, induced him to proclaim his field method in 1938 as "landscape ecology"(1988). During the next twenty five years Troll, like so many other physical geographers, concentrated on the physical processes involved in mountain geography while neglecting the characteristics of the local population. By 1965, a paradigm shift became evident when Troll replaced his term "landscape ecology," which had included a contingent consideration of human modification of the landscape, with "geoecology," a term that placed less emphasis on human interaction with the biophysical properties of climate, geology, and biology.

Geoecology was the rubric for scientists working on largely physical processes in mountains. It became a shibboleth for anything related to mountain research in much the same manner as ecosystem embraced myriad field research projects. For mountain scientists the word appeared in the title of many works produced by conferences and commissions (Ives 1992). The mountain tenor of the geoecology paradigm reinforced the environmentalist notion implicit in its application. Many field studies, symposia, and publications reflect this shift in conception of mountain geography.

GERMAN MOUNTAIN GEOGRAPHY STUDIES

Three symposia organized by the Commission on Mountain Geoecology have been held in Mainz during the past quarter century. The Commission, founded by Carl Troll, produced the *Geo-ecology of the Mountainous Regions of Eurasia* after the 1969 symposium, in 1974, the *Geoecological Relations between the Southern Temperate Zone and Tropical Mountains* and in 1983, *Natural Environment and Man in Tropical Mountain Ecosystems*. These volumes, all in the geoecology paradigm of mountain environment, in the later volumes make liberal use of Heinz Ellenberg's (1975) notion of the ecosystem in mountain environments.

In the same year (1983) that the last Mainz symposium was held, a conference entitled "Probleme der vergleichenden Kulturgeographie von Hochgebirgen" (Groetzbach, Rinschede 1984) was convened in Eichstaett in Bavaria. This conference marked a departure from the geoecology format of previous meetings because papers focussed more on the specific society and habitat context of mountain environments rather than on the (biophysical) geoecological aspects. There had been predecessors, namely the 1970 Mainz conference "Comparative Cultural Geography of the High Mountain Regions of Southern Asia," the aforementioned Mueller-Hohenstein "International Workshop on the Development of Mountain Environment" in Munich in 1974, and the Innsbrueck 1975 meeting of German geographers that focussed on

"Comparative Geography of High Mountains." A symposium on a related topic on "Height Limits on High Mountains," was held in Saarbrucken in 1979 at the instigation of Christoph Jentsch (1974), who had made an earlier foray into the relationships between mountain habitat and society by proposing a model of comparative cultural geography in mountains.

The above conferences sought to identify cultural and ecological adaptation in mountains. Theory and comparative contributions elucidated the differences in settlement, land use and spatial organization. A feature of the Eichstaett conference was the challenge to the geoecology paradigm that had for so long dominated the mountain literature. Uhlig's (1984) review article of the Ratzel inspired altitudinal zonation models implicit in the geoecology paradigm that dominated thinking about mountain environments for so long represents the encyclopedic work on this topic. Humans were placed at the forefront of the Eichstaett conference by some participants, with the physical properties included where appropriate. Lichtenberger's (1984) introductory chapter summarizes the shifts in European alpine research and relates contemporary studies to existing models of human use of mountain environments. Her acknowledgement of new ways of examining mountains, such as the accessibility model based on the rapidity with which wheeled traffic modified mountain life, was portentous in that it introduced revisions in the traditional models of mountain society and habitat. Harald Uhlig and Willibald Haffner (1984) give an exhaustive, excellent review of the German language literature of the comparative geography of high mountains. The fifty page bibliography compiled by Hertz and Pohle (1984) in this volume can be regarded as the benchmark of the study of mountain environments.

Although so much of the early application of geoecology was originally concerned with vegetation, the term became closely allied with geomorphological processes in mountains. The environmental "crisis," as construed by some scientists, was an opportunity for the application of a comparative paradigm for universal application in the mountains (Goudie 1981; Ives, Pitt 1988). Much of the literature was associated with mountain "hazards" seen in the form of landslides, glacial lake outbursts, floods, and mass wasting. A common thread throughout so much of this literature is that these physical processes were viewed as a response to reckless use of the mountain environment by the indigenous inhabitants. Hewitt (*infra*), in a critical review of all mountain hazard literature, sees the problem as one concocted by the technocratic Eurocentric mind and of the industrial dominant core in general. Much of the mountain "hazard" literature is a product of the past two decades. For the Himalaya, the Rieger et al. (1976) report on the Himalaya was an example of this perceived "crisis" and its recommended management. This clamor was joined by sensationalist public media members, like Erik

Human Aspects of Mountain Environmental Change

Eckholm, a former science editor of the *New York Times*, who wrote of the apparent public anguish about the purported human induced erosion in mountains (Eckholm 1975). Some of this fervor continues today. These "crisis" projects that arose in the 1970s had wide international concern and support. The concern spawned a number of studies, including those falling under the umbrella of UNESCO's Man and the Biophere Project - 6 "Human Impact on Mountain and Tundra Ecosystems" programmes (Ives 1975, 1977). The rationale for these projects lay in the "natural hazards" notion that was widespread in geography in the 1960s.

The evaluation of much of this literature, its purported factual base and the "doom and gloom" scenario, but more importantly, the underlying assumptions of the argument, have been discussed by Thompson, Warburton, Hatley (1986), Hewitt (1988, 1992), and Allan (1992) in their reviews of mountain society and habitat.

Topics of Mountain Research

Methods and styles of research have not been merged into a coherent statement about the mountain environment. Colloquia, however, have been held and attempts in the literature made to summarize the advances in the study of mountain habitat and society. These contributions fall under two types: those using ecology as an underlying notion for organization, and a second group using a habitat-society approach, incorporating a large number of studies conducted in mountains but without any attempt to integrate these particularistic field studies into the general thematic literature.

ECOLOGY STUDIES

A major emphasis on using "ecology" or the "ecosystem" paradigm was provided by the creation of the UNESCO Man and the Biosphere Project - 6, Human Impact on Mountain Ecosystems," the progression of which Ives (1992) has summarized. Much of the early literature has an alarmist tone to it. Moreover, many practitioners had little experience of field research in mountains outside their own temperate regions of the world, invariably Europe or North America. In many instances their field research skills were limited to nonreactive research. An example of this design and methodology was done in the Austrian village of Obergurgl, in which extensive surveys were made by a variety of ecologists and like minded scientists (Bunnell 1975, Moser 1975). Moser and Moser (1986) and Moser and Peterson (1988) summarize the case study field research.

At a time when the rationale for many economic development projects was being questioned, the German Foundation for International Development sponsored an *International Workshop on the Development of Mountain Environments* in which Ellenberg (1975) proposed the concept of the ecosystem as a heuristic device to be used for successful development in the mountains. The final report by Klaus Mueller-Hohenstein (1975) enumerates the underlying reasons why ecology as a discipline should be the guiding rationale for development in mountains. Included in this new focus of development were considerations of altitude, geology and vegetation. Ellenberg's (1979) advocacy of the ecosystem ended with a plea for sample sites, which use this form of inquiry, to be incorporated into the MAB-6 program.

The culmination, perhaps, of the technocratic, environmentalist movement was the above mentioned German report on Nepal by Hans-Christoph Reiger and his colleagues. The claims of this group stimulated numerous other alarmist predictions about the fate of Nepal, thereby promoting many studies on the Himalaya. At the instigation of Jack Ives, who had earlier commented about the degraded condition of the Himalaya (Ives 1981; Ives, Pitt 1988), the Mohonk Mountain Conference in 1986 was convened in New York State to examine this issue. Mountain experts from around the world debated the condition of the Himalaya. The overall conclusion (dare we call it the "Mohonk Manifesto?") of these conference participants (with some dissenters), synthesized and amplified by Ives and Messerli (1989), is that fifteen years after this perceived calamity we now realize that the "doom and gloom" scenario throughout the entire Himalaya cannot be substantiated by the available evidence. But here and there, major problems are recognized. Other investigators, including Europeans and North Americans, at the end of the 1980s decade had already reached a similar conclusion (Bruijnzeel 1989, Rogers et al. 1989).

Further advocacy of the ecology paradigm as the key to "ecologically sound development" was provided by di Castri and Glaser (1979) in their influential paper "Ecology and the Development of Mountains and Islands." The section on the Alps concludes that "decision makers and the local populations concerned realize that the trend in the changing human-use systems of the Alps is towards instability of the systems...." (diCastri and Glaser 1979:9). These remarks seem odd to anyone who has read anything of the very unstable history of the Alps, its wars, decimation of wildlife, emigration, grazing and forestry practices, all of which have occurred in past centuries.

Another avenue of research was probed by the incorporation of ecosystem modelling in the Obergurgl test area in Oetztal, Austria. The Alpine Areas Workshop in 1974 sponsored by the International Institute for Applied Systems

Analysis (IIASA) incorporated a Holling (1980) simulation model to reduce all factors in the test area to a common denominator. As in so many similar studies various hypotheses and scenarios were developed and the report concluded with a list of priorities that should be accomplished by someone else.

"Stability" (and its opposite, instability) as a term seemed to be the precursor of the "sustainability" issue that now has great currency. Both of these ideas are derived from the academic discipline of ecology. Rhoades and Thompson (1975) made an early plea for ecology based studies in anthropology. Rhoades' (1992) latest effort is a further example of this nomothetic approach. The deterministic use of ecosystem that characterized the Mueller-Hohenstein report is not confined to scientists in Europe. In the United States a similar trend was encountered in Neustadtl's "Montology: The Ecology of Mountains" (1977), which reported on a Cambridge, Massachusetts conference on the mountain environment that met to discuss the perceived crisis in the mountains. Their manifesto called upon the academic and research scientific community to give advice immediately.

The Swiss effort at using the ecosystem concept is noted not for any major theoretical advances over the Obergurgl model but in the financial and personnel commitment to the analysis of four locations, Grindelwald, Pays d'Enhaut, Aletch and Davos representing a cross-section of Swiss mountain landscapes (P. Messerli 1983). These studies, underlain by a tradition of regional planning and land use zoning, were conducted under the aegis of the UNESCO MAB-6 program and represent intensive application of the ecosystem paradigm. The reports are profuse with flow model diagrams so beloved by system analysts. Heino Apel's (1982) theoretical and model publication "Dynamische Simulation eines Bergoekosystems", for example, provides a comprehensive treatment of the concepts and methodology employed in this elucidation of the inner workings of Swiss mountain villages. Quite often field researchers leave themselves open to charges that a small number of sample sites, four, means that in fact this microscale work constitutes an example of the universal fallacy—generalizing from a few observations (the four locations) the characteristics of all mountain villages. M. Price (1994) gives an extensive review of the Swiss and other MAB-6 mountain activities including site selection criteria. Twelve potential areas were originally identified from which four areas were eventually studied.

To his credit, Apel (1982:9) discusses the problem "Mikro-Makro" but does not mention the meso level characteristics that are constituent parts of any alpine regional planning exercise. Unfortunately the reader has little idea of the level of representation that the four test locations offered (Brugger, Furrer, Messerli, Messerli 1984). Had Apel's report amplified the MAB methodology in detail, the reader would be more confident in the selection of these four test locations. Price (1994) now recapitulates and explains the MAB-6 Alpine efforts in detail.

The Swiss efforts are characterized by acute concern for mountain environments but theoretically, conceptually and methodologically they are considerably removed from the conditions elsewhere in the mountain world, especially in the Greater Himalaya. Their enthusiasm for mountain studies is matched by their willingness to fund international research, for example, the International Center for Integrated Mountain Development (ICIMOD) in Kathmandu, the journal *Mountain Research and Development*, and projects using the geoecology paradigm.

A more modest but very worthwhile contribution to the ecological literature using the ecosystem paradigm was achieved by the IUCN (World Conservation Union) booklet *Ecological Guidelines for Balanced Land Use, Conservation and Development in High Mountains* (Dasmann, Poore 1979). This useful IUCN booklet outlined precautions and recommendations for consideration when planning for further activities in mountain areas. It obtained worldwide distribution that far exceeded any other document and, therefore, is the most influential guideline for the South Asian mountain rimland. The document omitted the polemics that characterize so much of the literature related to similar topics. A new completely revised version edited by Duncan Poore (1992) and published by IUCN, differs from the original in that much greater attention is given to the indigenous cultural characteristics of the population that may be residing in the protected areas.

Following up their earlier reports for UNEP, Hatley and Thompson (1985), in a probing essay about research and development, point out a serious problem in using "ecology" to discern perceived problems of conservation in mountain environments. In a section entitled "The Appliance of the Wrong Science," they discuss the dichotomy between an academic subject like ecology that divorces the human economy from the environment and applied sciences of agriculture and forestry. As Hewitt, himself an eminent alpine geomorphologist, points out, too much time is spent examining mountain solifluction lobes and not enough time meshing ideas about the physical environment with the human economy of mountain populations.

HABITAT AND SOCIETY STUDIES

Most of the efforts in using the ecosystem model for elucidating mountain environments have been unsuccessful because they attempted to find a simple solution to the very complicated habitat and society in mountains. The ecosystem concept did, however, provide a working hypothesis for numerous studies around the mountain world.

Among field research that could be singled out for achievement are the numerous publications associated with the "Man and the Andes" studies of physical anthropologists in the altiplano of Nunyoa, Peru. Paul Baker (1976) and his colleagues established a laboratory in this highland (largely a plateau instead of a mountain location) village. A focus was on food intake, often labelled the "caloric obsession" by detractors, but the field research made noticeable contributions in human biology of high altitude populations. The location was, however, highland and not mountain, and the contingent conditions of the wider population largely ignored. Published models of the local population and resource base were subjected to severe criticism upon scrutiny (Burnham 1982, Thomas 1988). The principal contributions of the Nunyoa research were to the discoveries of physiological capabilities of the local population rather than adaptation to an actual mountain environment. With MacArthur's (1977) critique of Rapaport's early study in the mountains of New Guinea, energetic studies declined rapidly during the 1980s.

The pioneering fieldwork by Paul Baker's student Cynthia Beall, in the human biology of high altitude populations of the Altiplano in the Andes, has now been extended to the Changtang Plateau of Tibetan Autonomous Region of China. Beall and Goldstein (1993) identify the physiological and behavioral concomitant of a culturally caused seasonality of dietary intake that results in a very low summer but high winter food energy intake among nomads in Tibet. The paradox is that summer food energy intake may be only a quarter of that energy consumption in winter, but despite this low food energy intake during the summer season of high activity the sample of Changtang nomads studied do not become malnourished during this period. Apparently there must be a seasonally adjusted basal metabolic rate. This field research may answer some of the general observations of mountain researchers from abroad who continually observe high rates of human energy expenditure among mountain residents who appear to subsist on bread and tea and not much else.

Under Franco-American cooperation a successful series of symposia charted the human physiological adaptation of high altitude populations. This was truly a comparative effort with many contributions from the Andes and the Himalaya (Jest, Baker 1977; Baker, Jest 1981).

Images of the Himalayan Environment

Several studies give us an idea of how European images of mountains have affected the indigenous people. South Asians from the plains, just as much as Europeans, do this about mountains and their inhabitants too. In Fisher's edited book *The Indo-Tibetan Interface,* and in another essay, the famous Indologist, Agehananda Bharati (1978, 1988), wrote about the divergence between the plains Hindu perception of the Himalaya with that of the Himalayan resident. The plains Indian traditionally viewed the Himalaya with fear, and even loathing, and did not really have mental images of mountains. This traditional view has now been superceded by the middle class Indian family who follow Eurocentric behavior and take summer holidays in the mountains, many of them at the old British hill stations. Recently trekking and climbing interest among Indians has induced the access into hitherto prohibited and border areas of India with China. This action has followed the similar practice of the Chinese and Pakistani governments a decade ago.

Traditional sacred pilgrimage patterns have also been altered by the mass media. At one time Rishikesh and Hardwar were the foci, but with enhanced accessibility masses now travel to the source points of India's holy rivers in the western Himalaya. The profane sites are now included with side trips to the Bhakra Nangal dam, for example. Other instances elsewhere in the Himalaya are documented (Stevens 1988).

For the European, new books like Pratt's (1992) *Imperial Eyes: Travel Writing and Transculturation*, and Peter Bishop's (1989) *The Myth of Shangri La* on the European social construction of Tibet, provide a fresh perspective on mountain society and habitat. The 19th century exploration of the Himalaya exhibited a divergence between British exploration and continental European exploration. Hewitt (1989), in an illuminating essay, charts the exploration and writing of the early Europeans in the Karakorum and demonstrates how the British placed a priority on political and military objectives while the continental Europeans had a more scientific view of their efforts. Hewitt's scrutiny of the writing of these explorers, like that of Pratt's, demonstrates how the South Asia mountains and their inhabitants were constructed according to Eurocentric fashion of the day.

The casual reader need only read the "coffee table" picture books of the Himalaya that spew forth every year to get a glimpse of the social construction of the mountains. Not only do the Europeans remake the Himalaya in their minds but Indians, too, have changed their perspective.

The Notion of Himalayan Degradation

Hewitt, *infra*, examines the notion of mountain hazards as it is generally conceived and how it applies to the Himalaya. Hewitt sees that this environmental theme in geography that gained so much popularity in the 1960s is a concoction of the Eurocentric technocratic/deterministic scientific mind. He finds suspect the perceived "objectivity" of the foreign and domestic scientists who have conducted "hazard" research and the related question of perceived "environmental degradation."

What is being examined here is the legitimacy of the questions and answers. For the Himalaya, Michael Thompson (1986) and his colleagues, based on their IIASA work, phrased this condition, *Uncertainty on a Himalayan Scale*. In a less direct way, I have documented how the idea of Himalayan degradation was associated with idealistic notions of ecology, especially as ecology emerged in the 1970s as the paradigm for Himalayan research. In retrospect, it seems that the conceptual base and the methodologies employed in so much of environmentally based Himalayan research were never placed in the context of the locations specified in the Himalaya. Not only was the spatial dimension omitted but the time dimension was neglected as studies favored synchronic application. The question of what constitutes degradation was rarely posed. If Blaikie and Brookfield's (1987) definition is used, then much that was viewed as environmental degradation for the Himalaya would be considered as appropriate land use.

In a series of articles (Mahat, Griffin, Shepherd 1986a, 1986b, 1987a, 1987b) in *Mountain Research and Development* and elsewhere (Gilmour 1991, Hamilton 1992) the authors generally thought that the environmental perturbation in the Himalaya was a product of long standing use and on occasion, abuse, and that it was quite specific to certain areas. The mere conversion of forest land to agricultural land could not be described as degradation. In addition, the continued expansion of agricultural land could not be substantiated. In some places where detailed studies were carried out, such as those by Miehe (1982) and Schmidt-Vogt (1990) (who were students of Schweinfurth—a longtime observer of Himalayan vegetation), it was found that local conditions of forest use were highly variable, that high agricultural land was being abandoned but forest fodder use might be more intense due to urban demand for yak crossbreed butter.

Tourism in the Mountains

Many UNESCO MAB-6 studies were created using the notion of ecology as a guiding principle to solve tourist generated conditions in mountains. Much of this early thinking was charted by Moser (1975) at a conference of the Club of Munich. Despite the emphasis on systems analysis with its comparative generalizations to other alpine places, P. Moser and W. Moser (1986), in a frank retrospective look at what they and their colleagues had wrought on the Austrian tourism village of Obergurgl, reverted to a contextual appraisal of their work by stressing the contributions of 100 scientists to the people of Obergurgl. In addition to the Obergurgl case study the Swiss studies appeared to be a response to pressure from tourism. P. Messerli (1983:22) outlines a design for Swiss research on integrated management. The initial design emphasized a study rooted in the context of a single community and regional decision making to resolve differences. But the design is only operational in four locations designated as test areas. Such a design has limited application to elsewhere in the mountain world if the conditions remain unknown. Such "ecological" studies are often divorced from the "economic" realities of Switzerland where Swiss farmers receive eighty per cent of their income in transfer payments from the state. Little, if any, of this MAB-6 "exercise" information can be used in a location outside the Western world, for example the Himalaya, where such transfer payments are unknown.

A byproduct of the United States Department of Defense spatial digital landuse research in the early 1960s was Geographical Information Systems. Designed at Rome (New York State) Air Development Center to make topographic maps upon demand in South Vietnam warfare, GIS is now used to display the phenomena present in mountains. An early enterprising attempt at applying geocoding to the issue of tourism was Bodo Degenhardt's (1980) dissertation that investigated the tourist potential of the same Oetz valley that contains the Obergurgl MAB-6 study site. Designed during the infant days of public rather than military GIS, Degenhardt's cartograms contain a series of geocoded scaled variables that can be compared with one another. The cartograms avoid the conceptual problems of flow diagrams that omit the critical criteria of scale and resolution absent in many MAB-6 alpine studies and rely entirely on the empirical data. In this rudimentary study the pixel was set on a square with 250 m sides, a degree of resolution that is surpassed by contemporary imagery, but Degenhardt's study was portentous in its application of raster data to mountain studies.

A major transition has now occurred in tourism from a consideration of mass tourism such as one finds in the European Alps to what is called adventure tourism or ecotourism (Boo 1990) that is carried out in remote mountain locations. The favorite place for these recreational activities are Khumbu and the Annapurna circuit in Nepal, highland Himachal Pradesh, Kashmir with special attention focussed on Ladakh, and the Karakorum in Pakistan. Two Trans Himalaya locations with favored locales are the northern flanks of the Everest area in Tibet and western Pamirs in Tajikistan (MacDonald 1995, Swift 1990, Zurick 1992).

Adventure tourism in the Himalaya is characterized by individuals or small groups usually calling themselves trekkers, travellers, climbers, or mountaineers. Although these people fervently believe that they are involved in ecotourism they often disrupt the rather narrow resource base accessible to mountain dwellers. For example, 56 climbing parties were granted permission to climb in the Karakorum during 1990. MacDonald has documented how this huge influx of people has had an adverse impact on the local welfare. While the local income may have increased on the whole, a new dependency relationship—some might say neo-colonialism—has been created between the local inhabitants and the European dependent local brokers organizing porters and other suppliers and the tourists (MacDonald 1994).

Many mountain geographers disdain, for academic reasons, studies on mountain tourism but tourists cannot be ignored because they have such an impact on mountain life. I attempted one of these studies some years ago in the Karakorum. I counted foreign tourism registrations in Gilgit District in the Karakorum for "adventure travellers." For the less athletically inclined people, travel by bus along these "Highways to the Sky," as I called the four major roads through the Himalaya, often satiates the adventurous appetite. I found that this initial interest in a remote mountain area can be stimulated by reprinted old books or travelogues, stories of hunters—usually colonialists—later military or political emissaries, then "ancient" adventure travellers like climbers and explorer. Finally, we have today glossy large format photo books of climbing expeditions or mountain climbing accounts that are sold throughout the world. Much of the appeal lies not in the local travel itself but in the images conjured up during the months prior to the actual tourism. My experience in the Karakorum is duplicated by other researchers throughout the Himalaya. Bishop's (1989) timely book on the European creation of "Tibet" helps us to understand how such images are constructed.

Conclusion

In this personal review of issues that have concerned scholars and managers in the mountain environment, a history of development over the past century has been given with special systematic attention to the developments of the two decades and regional attention given to the Himalaya. As a paradigm for investigating the mountain environment, the biophysicalist model, dubbed here as the Ratzel/Troll model, has given way recently to investigating the human agency in mountains that is rooted in space and time. This perspective requires that there should be a variety of investigations in mountains at several scales; for example, village studies are of use in examining the inner dynamics of the village itself, but contribute little to the understanding of valleys or regions because their causal features are not enumerated in the wider context. Similarly, the watershed has been advanced as the ideal unit of study, but that scale and model work only if hydrology is being investigated. It does not make much sense to use the watershed for an investigation of Highland-Lowland Interaction systems because physical boundaries do not inhibit the mobility of local mountain population. One could make the argument that rivers divide and river dendrograms are not replicated by the circulation patterns of local people (Allan 1985).

A major dilemma for future research in mountains is the position of the biophysicalist "mountain characteristics" in investigating mountain habitat and society. Proponents of "sustainable development" in mountains like Bandyopadhyay (1992), Ives (1992), Jodha (1992) and Rhoades (1992), see the biophysical or geoecological (as they are sometimes called) characteristics of mountains as paramount. I would join Hewitt (1988) and Knapp (1992) in saying that the biophysical characteristics played a larger role in the past than now. The academic contention between these two positions can have a positive outcome by promoting studies of both an academic and applied nature that fully incorporate concepts and methodologies of both perspectives. Unfortunately, adversarial government agencies and non-government organizations working in mountains do not wish to engage in this debate because it is inimical to their very existence.

At the present it is of little use to make generalizations about regions of the "Himalaya" because there is so little information available from which to make generalizations. Only one book on the Himalaya in recent years has come close to being a regional study and that is Bishop's (1990) widely acclaimed monograph on Karnali Region in western Nepal.

Several challenges loom on the horizon. First of all, who will carry out the research? We still do not have any analysis of the vast array of information available for Indian Himalayan villages in the western Himalaya similar to that done by David Sopher (1980) for the patterning of culture and ecology of India. Despite the cheap availability of automated cartography no Indian scholars have used published decennial census village data for a number of villages in tehsils or districts, nor have they investigated them using the techniques of exploratory data analysis. We still do not know the role of ethnicity or of caste complexes in determining the mountain agrosystem. The xenophobia of the Indian government since 1969 about foreigners conducting field research in the Indian Himalaya has meant that a generation of Indian scientists, albeit urban oriented Indian scientists, have been omitted from the international intellectual discourse about mountain environments. Indian scientists display many of the foibles of their Eurocentric antecedents. They, too, are often strangers in a foreign land when they are in the Himalaya (Sutherland 1993).

Too many generalizations about the Himalaya are derived from Nepal. The willingness of the Nepalese government to permit foreign scientists to wander almost at will over their country has meant that the sheer volume of international published research skews the perspective. Nepal, in fact, is probably atypical of the Himalayan environment in that the exposure of its citizens, outside a few cities, to the transformation of modernizing influences is much less than elsewhere in the Himalaya, with Bhutan being the exception. Highly limited road accessibility in Nepal means that Nepalese and Bhutanese lack the highland-lowland perspective that is so typical elsewhere in the South Asian mountain rimland. What is very encouraging is the enhanced access through international borders. Although India still forbids access to Gyantse up the traditional Chumbi Valley route pilgrims now travel to Mt. Kailash from Kumaon. In Nepal there is permanent access via the "Friendship" bridge with TAR. Pakistan has opened the Karakorum Highway over the Khunjerab pass since 1986 and is now constructing another northerly access route over the Dorah Pass into Badakhshan. Local commerce and age old communication patterns are being stimulated by these events. One can only hope that these tentative steps by the centralized nation-states will be expanded. No event has had such a devastating effect on the mountain economies and welfare than the creation and imposition of nation-state boundaries in the twentieth century (Lamb 1964, 1966, 1989, 1991). Much of the social dislocations and environmental perturbation that has occurred from the closure and realignment of traditional agropastoral patterns was brought about by externally defined geopolitical boundaries like the McMahon Line and the Durand Line and by the enduring hostilities between the aggressive nation-states, none of whom have the interests of the local population at heart.

One successful route towards enhancing the welfare of the local mountain residents and reducing cross-border tension is the establishment of mountain protected areas in border areas (Thorsell, Harrison *infra*). The Sagarmatha/ Chomolungma Park is a prototype for further transborder protected areas in the Himalaya (Taylor-Ide *infra*).The proposed Karakorum World Heritage Site is another example. One already sees in the international literature an agreement about the fundamental rights and cultural integrity that is inherent in mountain populations taking precedence over the biophysicalist determination of mountain protected areas. This movement is spurred, not by the Himalayan countries, but by the foreigner from both East and West, and is symptomatic of the concern for indigenous mountain inhabitants who are the keepers and protectors of the Himalaya.

Despite all the clamor at the Earth Summit in Rio about environment and development it appears that the environment issue is being treated more fully than development. For mountain environments and the people dwelling in them there has been very little development. There is no mystery to development. One need only look at the transformation after World War II of east Asian countries like South Korea, Taiwan, and Japan to see that land reform with formalized indigenous property rights and wealth in the countryside was the first priority in developing these nations. Total land reform provided the basis for the amazing transformation of China with so much of its industrial wealth located in rural areas. China, with one fifth of the world's population on nine per cent of its cultivable land, is now at the economic level South Korea was in 1970. In the Trans-Himalaya, in TAR, one sees relatively high levels of rural food intake and nutrition, health care, education, and quality of life when compared to similar places in the Hindukush-Himalaya. The keys to unlocking the wretchedness of so many people in mountains are changes in the structure in land holding, creation of formal property rights, raising of rural incomes through comparative advantage, encouragement of savings, removal of subsidies, and above all, decentralization in decision making in the bureaucracy. Minorities, Fourth World people, usually live in the mountains: centralized Third World bureaucracies would do well to devolve power to these marginalized minorities on the periphery.

Acknowledgements

Most of this chapter was originally prepared for presentation at the 27th Congress of the International Geographical Union held in Washington D. C., 12 August 1992, Section 340 (B) "Human-Induced Environmental Stress: Part II." Portions appeared concurrently in Allan (1992).

REFERENCES

Allan, Nigel J.R. 1984. "Accessibility and Altitudinal Models of Mountains." *Journal of Himalayan Studies and Regional Development* 8:11-18.
———. 1985. "Periodic and Daily Markets in Highland-Lowland Interaction Systems: Hindukush-Western Himalaya." In *Integrated Mountain Development,* edited by T.V. Singh and J. Kaur, 239-256. New Delhi: Himalayan Books.
———. 1986. "Accessibility and Altitudinal Models of Mountains." *Mountain Research and Development* 6:185-194.
———. 1986."Highways to the Sky: The Impact of Tourism on South Asian Mountain Culture." *Tourism Recreation Research* 13:11-16.
———. 1992. "Mountain Environments: An Assessment." *GeoJournal* 27:5-11.
———. et al. (eds.). 1988. *Human Impact on Mountains*. Totowa NJ: Rowman and Littlefield.
Apel, H. 1982. *Dynamische Simulation Eines Bergoekosystems (Testgebeit*

Grindelwald): TheoretischerAnsatz undModellenwurf. MAB-Information no. 13. Bern

Arbos, Paul, 1922. *La vie pastorale dans les Alpes francaises.* Paris: A. Colin.

Baker, Paul and Michael Little (eds.). 1976. *Man in the Andes. A Multidisciplinary Study of the High Altitude Quechua.* Stroudsburg PA: Dowden, Hutchinson, and Ross.

Baker, Paul and Corneille Jest (eds.).1981. *L'Homme et son Environment a Haute Altitude,* Paris: CNRS.

Bandyopadhyay, Jayanta. 1992. "On the Perception of Mountain Characteristics." *World Mountain Network Newsletter* 7:5-7.

Beall, Cynthia M. and Melvyn C. Goldstein 1993. "Dietary Seasonality Among Tibetan Nomads." *Research and Exploration* 9:477-479

Bharati, Agehananda. 1978. "Actual and Ideal Himalayas: Hindu Views of the Mountains." In *Himalayan Anthropology: The Indo-Tebetan Interface,* edited by J.F. Fisher, 77-83. The Hague: Mouton.

――――. 1988. "Mountain People and Monastics in Kumaon Himalaya, India." In *Human Impact on Mountains,* edited by N.J.R. Allan, 83-95. Totowa NJ: Rowman and Littlefield.

Bishop, Barry C. 1990. *Karnali Under Stress:Livelihood Strategies and Seasonal Rhythms in a Changing Nepal Himalaya.* Chicago: University of Chicago Department of Geography.

Bishop, Peter. 1989. *The Myth of Shangri La.* Los Angeles: University of California Press, 1989.

Blaikie, Piers and Harold C. Brooksfield, 1987. *Land Degradation and Society.* New York: Methuen

Blanchard, Raoul. 1938-56. *Les Alpes Occidentales.* 7 vols. Grenoble: B. Arthaud.

Boo, Elizabeth. 1990. *Ecotourism: The Potentials and Pitfalls,* vols. 1 and 2. Washington: World Wildlife Fund.

Braudel, Fernand. 1972. *The Mediterranean and the Mediterranean World in the Age of Philip II.* New York: Harper & Row.

Brugger, Ernest, Gerhard Furrer, Bruno Messerli, Paul Messerli, eds. 1984. *The Transformation of the Swiss Mountain Regions.* Bern: Paul Haupt.

Bruijnzeel, L.A. 1989. *Highland-Lowland Interactions in the Ganges Brahmaputra River Basin.* Occasional Paper no. 11. Kathmandu: ICIMOD.

Bunnell, Fred et al. 1975. "The Obergurgl Model: A Microcosm of Economic Growth in Relation to Limited Ecological Resources." *Nature and Resources* 11/2:10-21.

Burnham, Paul. 1982. "Energetics and Ecological Anthropology," In *Energy and Effort,* edited by G.A. Harrison. London: Taylor and Francis.

Dasmann, Raymond F. and Duncan Poore. 1979. *Ecological Guidelines for*

Balanced Land Use, Conservation, and Development in High Mountains. Gland: UNEP, IUCN, WWF.

Degenhardt, Bodo. 1980. "Das Touristische Potential des Hochgebirges und Seine Nutzung: Untersucht am Beispiel des Gurgler Tales Oetztal/Tirol." Dissertation, Free University of Berlin.

di Castri, Francesco and Gisbert Glaser. 1975. "Ecology and the Development of Mountains and Islands." *Nature and Resources* 15/3:8-16.

Eckholm, Erik. 1975. "The Deterioration of Mountain Environments." *Science* 189:189.

Ellenberg, Heinz. 1975. "The Ecosystem as a Basis for Practical Development Aid in Mountains Regions." In *International Workshop on the Development of Mountain Environments:Final Report*, edited by Klaus Mueller-Hohenstein, 155-166. Munich: German Foundation for International Development.

─────────. 1979. "Man's Influence in Tropical Mountain Ecosystems in South America." *Journal of Ecology* 67:401-416.

Gilmour, Donald A. 1991. "Trends in Forest Resources and Management in the Middle Mountains of Nepal" In *Soil Fertility and Erosion Issues in the Middle Mountains of Nepal,* edited by P.B. Shah, H. Schreier and K.W. Riley, 33-46. Ottawa: IDRC.

Goudie, Andrew. 1981. "Fearful Landscape of the Karakorum." *Geographical Magazine* 53:306-312.

Groetzbach, Erwin F. 1985. "Hoehengrenzen und Hoehenstufen." *Geographische Rundschau* 37:339-344.

Groetzbach, Erwin F. and Gisbert Rinschede (eds.). 1984. *Beitraege zur vergleichenden Kulturgeographie der Hochgebirge*. Regensberg: Frierich Pustet.

Hamilton, Lawrence S. 1992. "The Protective Role of Mountain Forests." *GeoJournal* 27:13-22.

Hatley, Thomas and Michael Thompson. 1985. "Rare animals, Poor People, and Big Agencies: A Perspective on Biological Conservation and Rural Development." *Mountain Research and Development* 5:365-377.

Hertz, Claudia and Perdita Pohle. 1984. "Bibliographie." In *Entwicklung der Vergleichenden Geographie der Hochgebirge,* edited by H. Uhlig and W. Haffner,493-544. Darmstadt: Wissenschaftliche Buchgesellschafte

Hewitt, Kenneth. 1988. "European Science in High Asia: Geomorphology in the Karakorum Himalaya to 1939." In *History of Geomorphology from Hutton to Hack,* edited by Keith J. Tinkler, 165-203. Boston:Unwin Hyman.

─────────. 1988. "The Study of Mountain Lands and Peoples." In *Human Impact on Mountains,* edited by N.J.R. Allan et al., 6-23. Totowa NJ:

Rowman and Littlefield.

———. 1992. "Mountain Hazards." *GeoJournal* 27:47-60.

Ives, J.D. 1977. "Regional Meeting on Integrated Ecological Research and Training Needs in the Southern Asian Mountain Systems, Particularly the Hindu Kush-Himalayas: Final Report." MAB Report Series no. 34. Paris: UNESCO.

———. 1981."The Natural Environment and Human Use Problems in Nepal: An Overview." In *Environment and Human Population Problems at High Altitude*, 27-31. Paris: CNRS

———. 1992. "Institutional Frameworks for the Study of Mountain Environments and Development." *GeoJournal* 27:127-129.

Ives, Jack D. and Anne Stites. (eds.). 1975. *MAB-6 Proceedings of the Boulder Workshop, July 1974, Final Report.* Boulder:INSTAAR.

Ives, Jack D. and Bruno Messerli. 1989. *The Himalayan Dilemma:Reconciling Development and Conservation.* London: Routledge.

Ives, Jack D. and David Pitt. (eds.).1988. *Deforestation: Social-Dynamics in Watersheds and Mountain Ecosystems.* New York: Routledge.

Jentsch, Christof. 1974. "Fuer Eine Vergleichende Kulturgeographie der Hochgebirge." *Mannheimer Geographische Arbeiten* 1:57-71.

Jentsch, Christoph and Herbert Liedtke. (eds.). 1980. *Hochengrenzen and Hochgebirgen.* Arbeiten aus dem Geographischen Institutder Universtaet des Saarlandes, Vol. 29. Saarbrueken: Union Druck und Zeitungsverlag.

Jest, Corneille and Paul Baker. (eds.). 1977. *Ecologie et Geologie de l'Himalaya.* Colloques internationaux no. 268. Paris: CNRS.

Johda, Narpat. et al. (eds.). *Sustainable Mountain Agriculture*, 2 vols. New Delhi: Oxford and IBH.

Lamb, Alistair. 1964. *The China-India Border: The Origins of Disputed Boundaries.* New York: Oxford.

———. 1966. *The McMahon Line: A Study in Relations between India, China, and Tibet.* Toronto: University of Toronto Press.

———. 1989. *Tibet, China and India, 1914-1950: A History of Imperial Diplomacy.* Hertingforbury (England): Roxford.

———. 1991. *Kashmir: A Disputed Legacy, 1846-1990.* Hertingfordbury (England): Roxford.

Lauer, Wilhelm. (ed.). 1984. *Natural Environment and Man in Tropical Mountain Ecosystems.* Erdwissenschaftliche Forschung, vol. 18, Stuttgart: Frans Steiner

Lichtenberger, Elizabeth. 1984. "Comparative Research into High Mountain Areas: A Few General Remarks." In *Beitraege zur vergleichenden Kulturgeographie der Hochgebirge.* Eichstaetter Beitraege no. 12, edited by E. Groetzbach and G. Rinschede, 11-30. Regensberg:Friedreich Pustet.

MacDonald, Kenneth. 1995. "Of Coolies and Sahibs: 'Exploration', Adventure Travel and the Place Colonization of Baltistan." *In North Pakistan: Karakorum Conquered.* New York: St. Martin's Press (forthcoming)

Mahat, Tirtha B.S., David M. Griffin and K.R. Shepherd. 1986, 1987. "Human Impact on Some Forests of the Middle Hills of Nepal: Parts I, II, III, IV." *Mountain Research and Development* 6:223-232, 325-34; 7:53-70, 111-134.

McArthur, Margeret. 1977. "Nutritional Research in Melanesia: A Second Look at the Tsembaga." In *Subsistence and Survival: Rural Ecology in the Pacific*, edited by T. Bayliss-Smith and A. Feachem, 91-128. Cambridge: Cambridge University Press.

Messerli, Paul. 1983. "The Design and Implementation of Swiss Research on Integrated Mountain Management." In *Contribution Suisse al la Conference sur L'Exposition Internationale "L'Ecologie en Action."* MAB-6 Information No. 14, Bern.

Miehe, Georg. 1990. *Langtang Himal: Hora und Vegetation als Klimazeiger im Himalaya.* Stuttgart: J. Kramer.

Moser, Paul and Walter Moser. 1986. "Reflection and the MAB-6 Obergurgl Project and tourism in an Alpine Environment." *Mountain Research and Development* 6:101-118.

Moser, W. 1975. "Experience with Tourism in the Alps—the Ecosystem of Obergurgl." In *International Workshop on the Development of Mountain Environment: An Interdisciplinary Approach for a Future Strategy*, edited by K. Mueller-Hohenstein, 77-95. Munich: German Foundation for International Development.

Moser, Walter and Jennie Peterson. 1988. "Limit's to Obergurgl's Growth: An Alpine Experience in Environmental Management." In *Human Impact on Mountains*, edited by N.J.R. Allan et al., 201-212. Totowa NJ: Rowman and Littlefield.

Mueller-Hohenstein, Klaus. (ed.). 1975. *International Workshop on the Development of Mountain Environments, December 1974, Final Report.* Munich: German Foundation for International Development.

Neustadtl, S.J. 1977. "Montology: the Ecology of Mountains." *Technology Review* 79/8:64-66.

Parsons, James J. 1985. "On Bioregionalism and Watershed Consciousness." *Professional Geographer* 37:1-6.

Peattie, Roderick. 1936. *Mountain Geography* New York: Greenwood Press.

Poore, Duncan. 1992. *Guidelines for Mountain Protected Areas.* Gland:IUCN.

Pratt, Mary Louise. 1992. *Imperial Eyes: Travel Writing and Transculturation.* New York: Routledge.

Price, Larry. 1981. *Mountains and Man.* Berkeley: University of California Press.

Price, Martin. 1994. *Mountains in Europe: An Overview of MAB Research from the Pyrennees to Siberia.* MAB Book Series No. 14. Paris: UNESCO/ Parthenon.

Ratzel, Friedrich. 1889, "Hoehengrenzen und Hoehenguertel." *Zeitschrift der Deutschen und Oestereichischen Alpenvereins* 21:62-84.

Reiger, Hans. C., F. Bieri, H. Eggers, W. Goldschalt and J. Steiger. 1976. "Himalayan Ecosystems Research Mission: Nepal Report." Heidelberg: South Asia Research Institute.

Rhoades, Robert. 1992. "Thinking Globally, Acting Locally: Technology for Sustainable Mountain Agriculture." In *Sustainable Mountain Agriculture:Perspective and Issues.* Vol 1, edited by N.S. Johda et al., 253-272. New Delhi: Oxford & IBH.

Rhoades, Robert and I. Stephen Thompson. 1975. "Adaptive Strategies in Alpine Environments: Beyond Ecological Particularism." *American Ethnologist* 2:535-551.

Rogers, Peter Lydon. P. and D. Seckler. 1989. "Eastern Waters Study: Strategies to Manage Flood and Drought in the Ganges-Brahmaputra Basin." Washington DC: USAID.

Schmidt-Vogt, Dietrich S. 1990. *High Altitude Forests in the Jugal Himal (Eastern Central Nepal).* Stuttgart: Steiner.

Sopher, David E. (ed.). 1980. *An Exploration of India: Geographical Perspectives on Society and Culture.* Ithaca: Cornell University Press.

Stevens, Stanley. 1988. "Sacred and Profaned Himalaya." *Natural History* 97:26-35.

Stone, Peter. 1992. *The State of the World's Mountains: A Global Report.* London: Zed Books, 1992

Sutherland, Peter. 1993. "Book Review: *Social Economy of a Tribal Village* by R. Swarup and R. Singh." *Mountain Research and Development* 13:111-113.

Swift, Hugh. 1990. *Trekking in Pakistan and India.* San Francisco: Sierra Club Books.

Taylor-Ide, Daniel, Alton C. Byers III and J. Gabriel Campbell. 1992. "Mountains, Nations, Parks and Conservation." *GeoJournal* 27:105-112.

Thomas, R. Brooke. 1988. "Simulation Models of Andean Adaptability and Change." In *Human Impact on Mountains*, edited by N.J.R. Allan et al., 165-184. Totowa NJ: Rowman and Littlefield.

Thompson, Michael, Michael Warburton and Thomas Hatley. 1986. *Uncertainty on a Himalayan Scale.* London, Ethnographica.

Thorsell, James and Jeremy Harrison. 1992. "National Parks and Nature Reserves in Mountain Environments." *GeoJournal* 27:113-126.

Troll, Carl and Wilhelm Lauer. (eds.). 1978. *Geoecological Relations Between the Southern Temperate Zone and the Tropical Mountains.*

Erdwissenschaftliche Forschung, vol. 11, Wiesbaden: Franz Steiner.
Troll, Carl. 1939. "Das Pflanzenkleid des Nanga Parbat. Begleitworte zur Vegetationskarte der Nanga Parbat Gruppe (Nordwest-Himalaya) 1:50,000." *Wissenschaftliche Veroeffentlichungen des Deutschen Museums fuer Landerkunde zu Leipzig* 7:149-193.

—————. 1972. *Geoecology of the High-Mountain Regions of Eurasia.* Wiesbaden: Franz Steiner.

—————. 1988. "Comparative Geography of the High Mountains of the World from the View of Landscape Ecology." In *Human Impact on Mountains,* edited by N.J.R. Allan et al., 36-56. Totowa NJ: Rowman Littlefield.

Udvardy, Miklos D.F. 1975. *A Classification of the Biogeographical Provinces of the World.* Occasional Paper 18. Gland: IUCN.

Uhlig, Harald and Willibald Haffner. 1984. *Zur Entwicklung der vergleichenden Geographie der Hochgebirge,* Wege der Forschung, vol. 223, Darmstadt. Wissenschaft Buchgesellschaft

Uhlig, Harald. 1984. "Die Darstellung von Geo-Oekosystemen in Profilin und Diagrammen als Mittel der vergleichenden Geographie der Hochgebirge." In *Beitraege zur vergleichenden Kulturgeographie der Hochgebirge,* edited by E. Groetzbach and G. Rinschede, 93-152. Regensberg: Friedreich Pustet.

UNEP. 1980. *The Major Problems of Man and Environment Interactions in Mountain Ecosystems: A Review.* UNEP Report no. 2, Nairobi: Unipub.

—————. 1992. *Agenda 21.* New York: UNEP.

United Nations. 1973. *Report of the United Nations Conference on the Human Environment.* New York: UNEP.

Veyret, Paul. 1972. *Les Alpes.* Paris: Presses universitaires de France.

Vidal de la Blache, Paul. 1911. "Les genres de vie dans la geographie humaine." *Annales de Geographie* 20:193-212, 289-304.

Zurick, David N. 1992. "Adventure Travel and Sustainable Tourism in the Peripheral Economy of Nepal." *Annals, Association of American Geographers* 8: 608-628.

CHAPTER 2

Mapping Vegetation in the Himalaya

ULRICH SCHWEINFURTH

Introduction

There is nothing more fundamental to comprehending a country than a study of its vegetation because vegetation is the result of the interaction of all factors operating in a given area. Vegetation, therefore, is the best indicator of environmental conditions and to learn about vegetation means to try to understand a habitat: it is also an introduction into understanding a country's basic resource.

Hence, to understand a mountain system as diverse, complex, and complicated as the Himalaya, means, first of all, to try to find out about its vegetation cover. Therefore, vegetation research is fundamental to Himalaya research—and vegetation mapping is the basic documentation of the environmental inventory of such a mountain system. This was the guiding principle when I first set out to work on the vegetation map of the Himalaya and this basic conviction has been confirmed ever since.

My vegetation map (Figure 1) of the Himalaya (Schweinfurth 1957) represents a first effort to convey an overall idea of the distribution of the vegetation in the Himalayan mountain system. The idea owes its origin to Carl Troll's 1937 visit to various parts of the Himalaya including his exploits around Nanga Parbat, a brief visit to Dehra Dun and its surroundings and a trip from Darjeeling to the Natu La, a pass on the Sikkim-Tibet border.

Troll (1939) subsequently published the 1:50,000 vegetation map of the Nanga Parbat massif, based on the cartographical achievements of the 1934 German Nanga Parbat Expedition. A detailed description of his journey from the Punjab plains across the Vale of Kashmir to Nanga Parbat, kept in his

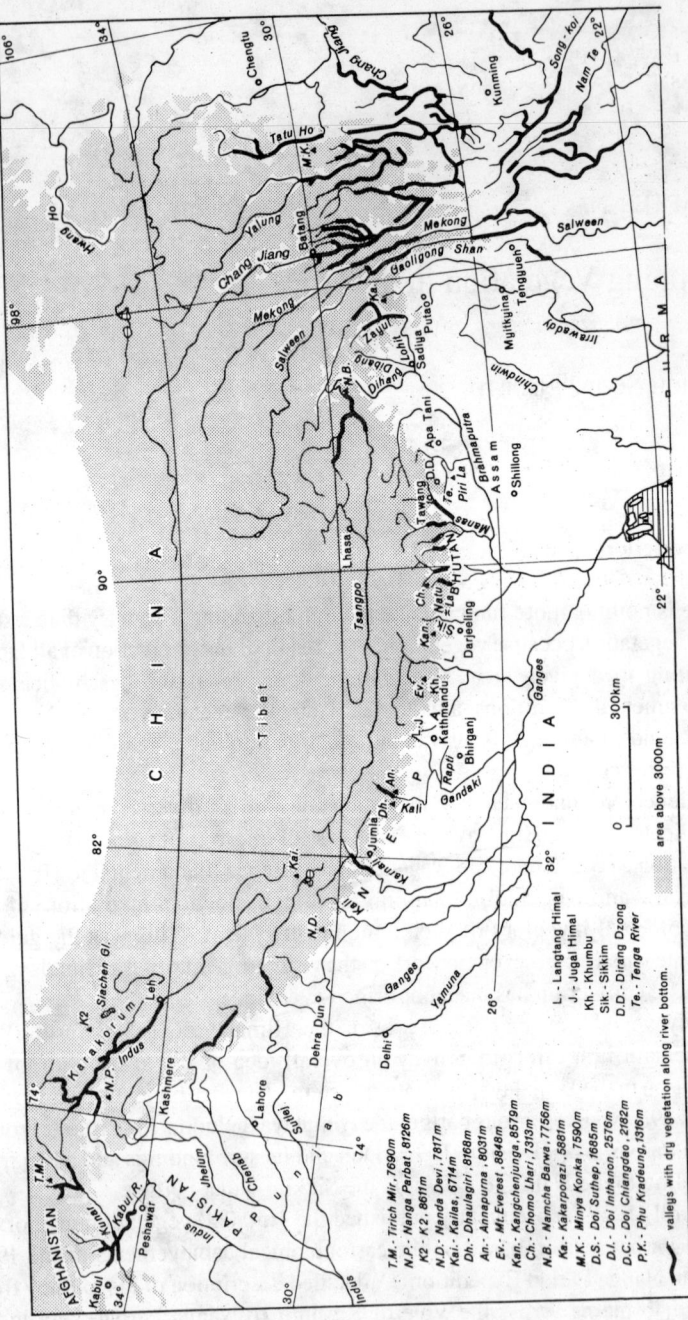

The Greater Himalaya

Mapping Vegetation in the Himalaya

diaries, was never published, nor were his notes from Dehra Dun and the trip in Sikkim. Troll was struck by the differences he noticed during these three incursions along the Himalayan System and, immediately, his imagination was fired by the thought of the transitions that must take place "along" or, rather, "within" the mountain ranges between these very different observations.

War intervened and in its aftermath the rebuilding of the department in Bonn claimed first priority, so that Troll's ambition to delve again into the Himalayan problems had been stalled until the summer of 1952 when he proposed the distribution of the vegetation in the Himalaya as a topic for a doctoral dissertation to be written by me. I embraced this idea with enthusiasm and determination.

Naturally, the vegetation map of Nanga Parbat presented itself as the one reliable pillar to build upon. In various sessions Carl Troll opened up the contents of his diaries of the access to Nanga Parbat, his stay around Dehra Dun, and the ascent of Natu La, written in a now out-of-date shorthand that needed Carl Troll's own interpretation. A lot of personal reminiscences gave even more color to the narrative. Beyond that, it was, to begin with, a search for observations hidden in a mass of papers, short accounts, and travel logs, which by their varied nature were not easy to evaluate until a certain experience had been gained.

Troll, right from the beginning, imagined a vegetation map of all the Himalaya to be the final result of the exercise. To me it was soon obvious that Troll's notion, or rather, conception of total coverage, would be impossible to achieve because of the lack of information available for certain parts of the Himalaya and the varied nature of the mountain system in general. This state of affairs was brought home convincingly during the course of the research when I confronted Troll with the findings for the central part of the Himalaya as shown by the "range of colors" depicting vegetation types west of the Nepal border (Kali River) and those of the Singalilah Range in the east of Nepal. Perhaps more troublesome were the few local "patches" of color applicable over the entire 800 km range of the territory of Nepal from west to east. The consequence was compelling and supported my intention to indicate on the map by color only those areas that were appropriately scaled and reported botanically reliable. This decision proved to be a sound foundation for continuing with the map work, even though it meant abandoning Troll's erstwhile cherished idea of a complete map, but it assured for the "rest" the necessary degree of reliability that, at the time of publication of the map Troll and I agreed to the statement, "the white patches of the map are the most important achievement of the entire enterprise!" These "blank patches," or voids on the map do not at all preclude the appreciation of the general distribution of vegetation, rather, they demonstrate the necessary caution applied to the project.

The vegetation map of 1957 embraces the mountain ranges from Kabul in the west to the Chang Jiang in the east although it is all called "the Himalaya," it was not meant to introduce a new definition of the Himalayan system. The map incorporated the so-called "Hengduan" (Ch=transverse gorges) mountains in Sichuan. The delimitations developed out of the "research in progress." To the west, vegetation was documented roughly as far west as "forest" could be traced. The forest disappears because of increasing dryness—whereas to the east, the various, and not always succinct, observations regarding the "climatically dry valleys," led the research to include those sections of the gorges of Salween, Mekong, and Chang Jiang (27°30'-30°N) that lay in the "possible" extension of the main Himalayan Range to the east. These river gorges would yield more pertinent clues that the author anticipated for understanding the complex phenomenon of the climatically dry valleys.

Within this West-East range, the "Himalaya" represents, more or less, the "southern rim" of High or Inner Asia (Jessen 1948: "Randschwelle"). The 1957 vegetation map, then, displayed for the first time, a comprehensive, overall view of the distribution of the vegetation from west to east, south to north and with altitude portrayed in a three-dimensional arrangement of the vegetation along and within this "southern rim" of High Asia. The trained eye is able to imagine from the two-dimensional map the "reliefwise" arrangement to give the map representation its full meaning. I recollect with pleasure the day when the Department of Geography in Bonn, under Carl Troll's directorship, was able to acquire a relief representation of the Nanga Parbat massif in 1:50,000, to which, subsequently, the colors of Troll's vegetation map of the mountain massif were applied conveying a superb idea of the three-dimensional arrangement of the vegetation within the massif.

In addition to the three-dimensional framework, special unexpected, features emerged from the 1957 map. These "nonconformities" or deviations from the general rules of distribution were represented by the "inner valleys." Two types can be distinguished, first are valleys more or less arranged West-East, that are roughly within the general "lay-out" of the mountain system, and called "inner valleys" sensu stricto, and second, valleys running perpendicular to the prevailing ranges cutting through the ranges, more or less north to south, which were later called "climatically dry valleys."

A careful choice of colors adds to the immediate comprehension not only of the vegetation in its distribution, but also to some climatic concept involved, for example bright red and yellow shades for desert-like and drier climates, and green and blue shades for the humid wet types. Therefore, the vegetation map conveys some general ideas about basic climatic conditions as well as the vegetation being the visible result of all environmental factors combined. It

Mapping Vegetation in the Himalaya

also communicates an idea of the landscape pattern—the regional arrangement of habitats—in short, the "landscape structure" of this complex mountain world. If one recollects the state of knowledge prior to the construction of the map, it was a maze of ranges, peaks, valleys—a virtual confusion of details with no apparent order—the progress to order and to insight is apparent.

More than thirty years after the publication of the 1957 map, it can be said that the map has stood the test of time, or to be more precise, "the first thirty years." It would be preposterous not to allow for amendments made necessary by further research and more detailed knowledge.

Recent Modifications and Additions

What has been the development since this first stock-taking took place? The innocent may have expected an immediate rush towards filling the white gaps glaring so invitingly from the map. Unfortunately, this is not the case. Political tension about the demarcation of boundaries escalated into war in some places or intervened in many areas of particular botanical interest. It has been only in Nepal that real progress has been achieved in filling the gaps in our vegetation map. We are still far from success in achieving the ultimate goal of complete knowledge of the vegetation in the Himalaya.

Since the publication of the 1957 vegetation map, the Himalaya have not been an "area of peaceful research"—rather, the contrary exists! Decolonization in Asia has changed the political map of Asia and the emergence of a new central power in China after decades of disintegration has had its repercussions throughout the Himalayan world. By the nature of things, especially accidents of history, political centers, more often than not, are situated in low-lying plains or even at or near the coast, while as a consequence of historical events spheres of influence extended inland and reached their limits in less easily accessible mountain regions, which—as a consequence—became the areas where various spheres of influence meet.

Western Himalaya

After the Second World War, and especially since the 1947 independence for the Indian subcontinent, political disputes have been carried far into the mountain world and even the most remote places have suddenly gained headline status. With independence for the subcontinent, Pakistan came into being and the process of dividing the subcontinent and its northern mountain rimland began. The establishment of territorial boundaries between India and

Pakistan resulted in a demarcation line through the northwest-Himalaya in 1948, which was supposed to be provisional but it is still "operational," that is, no permanent agreement save the one concerning the current one has been reached. Locally, the status quo seems to stimulate some minor periodical shooting activities, as illustrated by the glacier skirmishes high up in the Karakorum on and around the Siachen Glacier. These often take place during the summer, which is the only time of the year when such activities seem to be "practical" at altitudes above 5000 m.

Because of the civil war in Afghanistan, and the consequent refugees in Pakistan that have affected the forests in the Hindukush (Allan 1987) the westernmost forests of the Himalayan system have been ravaged. As yet there is no estimate of the damage done during the past ten years of civil war.

Chinese-Pakistan cooperation forced the Karakorum Highway through the seemingly inaccessible Indus Gorge from Nanga Parbat down to the Punjab Plains. This was "beyond" Troll's Nanga Parbat map. "Indus Kohistan," as the area was called during the Imperial days, was left unadministered by the British Raj—perhaps wisely so, as the tribes there had proved to be very recalcitrant—with the sad effect, as far as knowledge of vegetation is concerned, that even scientific expeditions did not gain permission to enter this region. The result has been a large white void on the 1957 vegetation map. It is, however, deplorable to note that the completion of the Karakorum Highway has not yet changed the situation. There is still no vegetation survey of this area. The completion of the map here would be a comparatively easy affair, because Troll's Nanga Parbat map would serve as a guideline and a vegetation survey would follow principles expounded there (Schweinfurth 1983).

Nepal

It has already been indicated that Nepal deserves pride of place insofar as the expansion of our knowledge of the Himalayan system since publication of my 1957 map is concerned. In Nepal, all the enumeration and plotting of vegetation started from zero. In comparison to other areas in the Himalayas, the progress in our knowledge has been quite remarkable and very encouraging. French scholars committed themselves to a project that covered the entire country with vegetation maps. This goal was achieved in the mid-1980s with the completion of eight maps at 1:250,000 scale. Two additional maps at 1:50,000 were drafted for the special development areas of Jiri and Trisuli. If one recollects the dearth of data shown on the 1957 map as far as Nepal was concerned the progress in our knowledge about the vegetation of the Himalaya is indeed substantial.

The French Center National de la Recherche Scientifique maps (Dobremez 1976) include "Carte écologique du Nepal" of the following areas: Annapurna-Dhaulagiri, 1:250,000, 1974; Jiri-Thodung, 1:50,000, 1974; Kathmandou-Everest, 1:250,000, 1974; Region Terai central, 1:250,000, 1974; Biratnagar-Kangchenjunga, 1:250,000, 1977; Ankhou Khola-Trisuli, 1:50,000, 1977; Jumla-Saipal, 1:250,000, 1980; Dhangarhi-Api, 1:250,000, 1984; Butwal-Mustang, 1:250,000, 1984; Nepalganj-Dailekh, 1:250,000.

In addition, some detailed local work has been carried out in central Nepal, for example, Schmidt-Vogt's (1990) study of the Jugal Himal. His objective was a detailed analysis of the high altitude montane forests that were the only remaining forests in the area, and simultaneously, a thorough study of human interference in these remaining forests. The results of Schmidt-Vogt's analyses provide us with better ideas about the floristic composition and age structure of the high altitude forests as well as an insight into what people do to these forests that seemingly are not within easy reach of settlements. After reading his work one should refrain from talking about "natural" forests and "natural" vegetation. There may be some satisfaction gained from the knowledge that forest is regaining areas that humans relinquished because of unprofitability, for example, high cultivated terraces. These lands became cultivated under pressure from Kathmandu during the days of the Rana dynasties; the moment they are no longer cultivated, forest advances to regain these habitats. Conversely, development activities that build new roads into an area to, supposedly, facilitate better access to markets leading to expanding economic activities, that is, promoting more livestock grazing especially above timberline, often aggravate the pressure on the higher altitude areas thereby creating deleterious effects in these ecologically sensitive areas.

Schmidt-Vogt's observations reveal some of the less obvious ecological forces at work in high altitudes—like pip-crake—the occurrence, at least occasionally, of a freeze-thaw cycle, that is so conducive to weakening the top soil-layer. Pip-crake and the normally prevailing weather forces, like rain, snow, and high winds, together with grazing and trampling of cattle, are in their combination absolutely detrimental to the stability of the exposed parts of these ridges above timberline. They are also disastrous in their effects on the upper parts of the montane forests because they lead to a gradual retreat of the timberline.

Another example of detailed research devoted to a specific area in a particularly interesting part of the Himalayan system is Miehe's (1982) thesis on the vegetation in the Dhaulagiri and Annapurna Himal, or, more precisely, Thak Khola in the Kali Gandaki Gorge. It is interesting to note that Miehe calls his thesis "Vegetationsgeographische Untersuchungen im Dhaulagiri—und Annapurna-Himalaya," whereas in his regional section (Vol.II) he prefers to focus on the Thak Khola gorge between these mountain ranges without even mentioning Dhaulagiri and Annapurnal Himal in his discussion!

The gorge of the Thak Khola—Kali Gandaki can be regarded as a valley that is centrally located in the Himalayan system. That this valley occupies a central topographical position is borne out by the fact that vegetation types from the West meet and intermingle with those from the East. This situation can be deduced from the 1957 map where the vegetation arrangement is presented on the basis of Nakao's (1955) material, which included the first reliable observations from this area. The overall importance of the Kali Gandaki Valley insofar as the arrangement of the vegetation is concerned became obvious through Nakao's reports, which proved crucial to our understanding of the distribution of the vegetation in the entire mountain system. In 1954, they provided the cornerstone for the "edifice" of the vegetation map and spurred further enthusiasm for the entire enterprise (Nakao 1955). Miehe's thesis, in its detailed approach, now reveals the intricate pattern of vegetation distribution and conveys a clear idea with a vegetation map at 1:100,000. It may be compared with Troll's vegetation map of Nanga Parbat at 1:50,000. In the one case a valley is the focus of interest, in the other, a mountain massif of more than 8000 m altitude.

In 1982, Miehe turned further east and carried out research in the Khumbu on the southern slopes of Mt. Everest and compiled, on the basis of the topographical maps of Erwin Schneider, a vegetation map at 1:50,000 (1991). More recently, Miehe has been active in the Langtang Himal (1990).

Haffner has concerned himself more specifically with the vertical arrangement of the vegetation in Eastern and Central Nepal (1967, 1979) concentrating on Khumbu and the Valley of Kathmandu as well as the foothill areas of Bhirganj and the Rapti Dun.

Bhutan

Will Bhutan also suffer the accompanying problems of "development" when it occurs there one day? It is to be hoped that the example of similar situations, in particular Nepal, will serve as a warning and temper the understandable desire "not to lag too far behind." The country with its many unexplored corners badly needs basic field research and, in addition, certain problems need to be addressed, for example, the climatically dry valleys could be studied in Bhutan to great advantage.

Since the 1957 vegetation map was published, the diaries of Ludlow and Sheriff have been published posthumously (Fletcher 1975). These accounts are a welcome addition to our knowledge of the country, although the book does not provide many more observations "to be put on the map," either because locations are not sufficiently enough described or because of the lack of reliable maps for the country. It is encouraging to hear of recent Japanese vegetation research in Bhutan that was initiated by M. Numata who is following in the footsteps of Sasuke Nakao, and whose work is now carried on by Ohsawa (1987).

The Bhutan climatically dry valleys, which were first shown on the 1957 map as a result of the vegetation analysis, are of particular interest. These valleys are, in varying degrees, the most characteristic features of the various "valley-chambers" (Ger.=Talkammern), that constitute the country. It appears that the climatically dry valleys in Bhutan present ideal examples for elucidating the mechanism of the local wind systems leading to specific local dryness, because all the "valley-chambers" of Bhutan are clearly defined, well-circumscribed areas. In addition, they offer the opportunity of comparison with contiguous areas. Unfortunately one needs to get permission to do the field research, which out of necessity has to be done on the spot. Again, we see that political conditions, in this case the understandable caution of the Government of Bhutan, are not wholly conducive to research. It would be, however, a fascinating research prospect if one could examine one valley after the other right up to the main range and thereby fill in the "white parts" of the 1957 map that Bhutan still presents, and, at the same time, to come to grips with the dry valley problem.

Assam Himalaya

In 1962, as a result of the postcolonial dispute, the Chinese Government decided "to teach Nehru's India a lesson" by penetrating, in a surprise action, the Assam Himalaya in at least two sections, via Tawang-Dirang Dzong, and the Lohit valley (Zayul) in the East. Perhaps only the initiated were able to recognize this remarkable feat of military enterprise. For reasons of their own, the Chinese soldiers retreated after the demonstration of military power. The territorial dispute, however, remains unresolved. Meanwhile, the Indian government, as far as it is known (Nanda 1982), pays more attention to the infrastructure of the Assam Himalaya, but there are as yet no references to botanical research in this vast, unexplored area—a situation to be regarded as deplorable. Consequently, there have been no advances in filling the gaps on the 1957 map for the whole area east of Bhutan to especially the Lohit Valley in the east.

The Assam Himalaya presents a prime example of how political squabbles have obstructed field research. During the colonial days, the combination of difficult terrain, "atrocious" climate, "impenetrable jungle" and the unpredictability of the tribes led the British Government in India to avoid this area almost entirely. Independent India followed the Imperial example. The emergence of a new central power in Beijing and the reassertion of China's territorial claims changed the situation. As far as vegetation is concerned this is exemplified by the Vegetation Map of China (Hou 1979). This 1:4,000,000 vegetation map of China is a great achievement for the country in general; but it does not stand up to close scrutiny in special areas. Because the political concept of the vegetation map of China seems to have been to show all Chinese claimed territories covered solidly by color—whether actually botanically known or not—the Chinese obviously took recourse to analogy, which is an unreliable procedure in a mountain country as full of surprises as the Himalaya. Misconceptions can arise from this procedure. An illustration is the Tenga Valley, an "inner" valley of the Assam Himalaya. The "inner valleys" in the Himalaya are often incongruous when compared to the expected conditions for that part of the mountain system in which they are situated. The Tenga Valley lies to the north of the Piri La, that is, in the rainshadow of the foothills: it, therefore, contains specific conditions reflected in the vegetation. Because the Assam Himalaya is still poorly known, no parallel development or similar occurrence can as yet be quoted, although the Apa Tani Valley further east may bear some resemblance, and beyond that, other "inner valleys" of the Assam Himalaya may still harbor more surprises. The misrepresentation of the Tenga Valley on the Chinese map could have been avoided easily by consulting Bor's (1938) lucid description of the Tenga Valley and its surroundings or the 1957 vegetation map of the Himalaya, where the Tenga Valley is represented according to Bor, who is the only authority for this area. Therefore, doubts may remain about other parts of the 1979 China vegetation map, where again, analogy or some other means of expediency might have been applied to achieve completeness for political reasons. "Inner valleys" in the Himalayas have to be treated with caution, they are more often than not, likely to offer surprises and ought to be divorced from expedient analogy!

Transverse Gorges

On the northern side of the borderline, Chinese botanists have been active on and around Namcha Barwa, according to Chen Weilie who was a research fellow during 1982 and 1983 in my department. One achievement was the establishment of a detailed vertical sequence of the vegetation of this prominent mountain massif that towers above the gorge of the Tsangpo-Dihang-Brahmaputra, but thus far no publication has been produced. According to

Mapping Vegetation in the Himalaya 37

Chen Weilie the Chinese have material enabling them to compile a detailed vegetation map of the area, perhaps on the lines of Troll's Nanga Parbat map at 1:50,000. It would be a great achievement to have a comparable vegetation map of Namcha Barwa published, thereby facilitating comparison of the two extreme positions of Nanga Parbat in the West and Namcha Barwa in the East, where the former mountain massif towers above the desert gorge of the Indus, and the latter, Namcha Barwa, rises out of the soaking, near-tropical vegetation of the Tsangpo gorge. The 1957 map indicates the extremes thereby stimulating interest in having a comparable vegetation map of Namcha Barwa published.

A special note at this juncture seems appropriate to emphasize our absolute lack of information relating to the vegetation of the Dibang system, that section of the Himalayan mountains extending east of the course of the Dihang, which is the part of the Tsangpo-Brahmaputra where the river actually cuts through the mountain ranges. Apart from a few remarks by Bailey (1957), we lack any information whatsoever. We may safely assume a very wet, near-tropical vegetation in general, but what about the conditions in some inner valleys?

The great river courses of Salween, Mekong and Chang Jiang are of particular interest in that they lead from tropical or near-tropical seas right up into the heart of Asia. Thus far it is not possible to form a clear and well-documented idea how the transition of vegetation in these valleys progresses from mouth to source, although we now know about the conditions along their courses within Chinese territory. For example, the extent of climatically dry valley bottoms, as shown on the 1957 map for the sections between 27°-30°N only, are now indicated on the 1979 Vegetation Map of China. The northernmost extension of these dry valley areas seem to be limited by forest as shown on the 1979 vegetation map. But our interest in these valleys does not end there. On the contrary, it is of great interest to know how "forest" penetrates further up the valleys into the very heart of the continent in all the three valleys (and respective side valleys), and in which way timberline presents itself under the extraordinary conditions prevailing there. Finally, from a floristic point of view, the entire sequence of vegetation, from mouth to source, along these prominent river courses is of particular interest because they reflect on the conditions in transition from the periphery of Asia into the heart and on the "top" of the continent. The vegetation map of 1957 tries to summarize the situation as far as could be gleaned from literature up to 1956 for the sections limited roughly by 27°-30°S (Schweinfurth 1956, 1957, 1972, 1986, 1987).

The climatically dry valleys are, perhaps, the most striking example of what such a map making venture and vegetation evaluation might produce. These valleys' existence as topographical features may have been known but their particular characteristics became apparent bit by bit only out of the evaluation of the literature where their particular character remained hidden in details just waiting to be put together for representation on the map. As far as the "climatically dry valleys" in the Himalaya that were discovered while compiling the 1957 vegetation map, the 1979 vegetation map of China (scale permitting) now presents the most striking confirmation showing within the boundaries of China the vegetation of certain river valleys by the same color and based on the same floristic composition as on the Himalayan map of 1957 (Schweinfurth 1957: 1:2,000,000; Hou 1979: 1:4,000,000). Both these maps are congruent in the part of the river gorges of the Salween, Mekong, Yangtsekiang represented on the 1957 map, i.e. for a sector roughly 27°-30°N.

The 1957 Himalayan map and the 1979 China map, together show climatically dry valleys as a distinct phenomenon all along the South Asian mountains rimland from the Kabul River in the West all the way through to the East and into Tatu Ho in Sichuan Province wherever certain preconditions for their development are met. Comparatively long, straight courses, deeply cut in and providing extended slopes are preconditions to the full development of the climatically dry valleys. A summary of the situation along this rimland with reference to the climatically dry valleys was published recently (Schweinfurth 1987).

There are still some valleys that seem to be prominent candidates to be included in this category, ones like Chenab and Sutlej, but thus far, nothing has been done to find out more about this phenomenon. For the Sutlej, there is the basic description of Gorrie (1933) available dealing with the forests of the valley from a silvicultural point of view, but it relates sufficient observations to make this valley a serious pretender. For the Chenab, there is, as yet, no such treatment available.

Is this situation a purely academic question? Perhaps it is when seen from a distance but a closer look, however, will reveal that the peculiar climatic conditions of these dry valleys will be of great local importance. Chinese scholars now seem to have become aware of the specific situation in these valleys and for reasons of better management and development, they have differentiated between dry-hot, dry-warm, and dry-temperate stretches in these valleys (Zhang 1992).

While at Heidelberg during 1982 and 1983, Chen Weilie also reported on Chinese botanical explorations in Tibet and, in particular, in the upper gorge country of Salween, Mekong, and Chang Jiang. It was not, however, possible at that stage to form a clear idea of the cartographic results of this field research. There is now, perhaps, the answer to these problems, unfortunately published only in Chinese. Chiang King Wai published a map of the Vegetation of Xizang (Tibet) in 1988 but as is often the case, there is no English language translation next to a table of contents—not even a summary in English attached. My evaluation is restricted to intelligent interpretation of Latin botanical names,

Mapping Vegetation in the Himalaya

photographs, diagrams, and maps which is a fascinating, although not entirely satisfying procedure. The most important item is the colored vegetation map of Tibet at 1:3,000,000 scale. This is a superb achievement for Tibet and by virtue of its scale perhaps preferable to the treatment of Tibet in the 1979 Vegetation Map of China, although the English translation of the legend to the 1979 China map is, when comparing the two maps, helpful. My plea is now for a speedy English translation of the Vegetation of Tibet to see whether it answers all our questions!

Further south is the Gaoligong Shan, another area of great interest, which was discussed in more detail while Chen Weilie stayed in Heidelberg. This mountain range runs North-South to the West of the Salween between 27°30'-25°N. In this case, it was possible with the field observations supplied by Chen Weilie to compile a vegetation cross section of this range while following the 1957 vegetation analysis of the Himalaya South into the Southeast Asian Peninsula. The material seemed to be sufficient to elaborate a schematic cross section West-East, but it was by no means adequate to sketch a vegetation map, because the period of field work in the area according to Chen Weilie, was only three months (Schweinfurth and Chen Weilie 1984).

The importance of this cross-section lies in the fact that the evidence available helps to bridge the gap existing in the area of the Shan States between the vegetation map of the Himalayas to the North, the vegetation map of China to the East and research about vegetation conducted in mountainous Northern Thailand to the South.

Southeast Asia

Moving in our coverage into the Southeast Asian Peninsula, an early interest in Pinus, originating from the Himalayan research, served as a guiding line. In the Himalayan system, various species of Pinus appear in ecologically interesting places for example, at the "dry" edge of forest in general. An illustration is in the Indus Valley in the Nanga Parbat area or in the upper Tsangpo Valley in the Namcha Barwa region to name only two prominent parts of the system. The same holds true for the Sutlej and Kali Gandaki Valley. At the same time, Pinus is often prevalent where human enterprise impinges on the forest, thereby making it virtually impossible to distinguish between whether Pinus occurs here naturally or whether its presence is helped or made possible by man, for instance, using fire, periodic or otherwise, for keeping competition at bay. The 1957 vegetation map shows many examples of this, and the climatically dry valleys offer further evidence, for instance, in the Lohit Valley of Zayul.

The occurrence and status of Pinus further East and South, as seen from the

Himalaya, has always been of interest to me (Schweinfurth 1988). Having, for instance, in mind the situation in Zayul (Lohit Valley), it was interesting to examine the few observations available from some valleys of Upper Burma (Ward 1949, Stanford 1945) suggesting quite similar conditions, although information from Upper Burma is scarce and local information from the Shan States non-existent, although the occurrence of Pinus in similar, comparable positions is reliably known.

Further south, Northern Thailand promised better information (Kuechler and Sawyer 1967; Robbins and Smitinand 1966). Contact with Smitinand over the years finally resulted in the secondment of T. Santisuk for a year at Heidelberg to work on the problems of vegetation in Northern Thailand. Santisuk's predominantly floristic account was subsequently published in 1988, and in further pursuit of the problems of the Pinus forests in Northern Thailand, their distribution and status, Werner (1993) conducted field work in Northern Thailand.

The distribution of Pinus sp. within the Southeast Asian Peninsula proves a topic of absorbing interest (Schweinfurth 1988). It seems that the genus extends, from a supposed center of origin somewhere in Southwest China which is well-known for its abundance of species (Cheng 1939), probably in all possible directions along the Himalayan system, into China, and into the Southeast Asian Peninsula where the North-South running valleys and ranges may have served as guidelines in the distribution. At one time, the area of Mt. Kerintji in Sumatra situated at 2° South was regarded as the southernmost "natural" habitat. However, recent evidence of Pinus being planted by local people makes it possible to believe that even "earlier" man was instrumental in the expansion of the genus "further south"! Today, there are plantations of Pinus in southern Sumatra and in Java where there is a tendency towards large-scale propagation, at least, in the Asian tropics (Armitage, Burley 1980; Cooling 1975), which in a modern way makes the differentiation between "natural" and "man-made," or "human-induced" and "influenced" habitats quite unrealistic.

In this connection, some early evidence of man's interest in Pinus leading to "plantations," however small in size, is of particular interest. The Apa Tanis in the Assam Himalaya provide a classic example. Because they are surrounded by hostile tribes and virtually enclosed in a small valley they had to come to terms with the available resources so they turned to planting Pinus (excelsa?) and bamboo (Fuerer-Haimendorf 1955). Sir Dietrich Brandis, while conservator of forests in Upper Burma, noticed local people's ingenious way of combining swidden with planting trees, including Pinus (insularis?), and subsequently decided to implement this ecologically sound local approach into forestry practice (Hesmer 1975). Stein (1978) observed Pinus (merkusii) planted by local people in the vicinity of Lake Toba as part of their land use activities.

There is no doubt that there will be more examples of Pinus sp. being accepted and cultivated by local people. and, at the same time, propagated and promoted in their distribution.

There is, of course, another interest in these practices, now commonly summarized under the term "agroforestry," and that is the question, whether the planting and cultivation of trees points to a developed or developing sense of tree and, further, forest consciousness. The Apa Tanis, being confined to a small, well-circumscribed and limited valley habitat may have felt the need to have their particular important resources, Pinus and bamboo, ready at their disposal, without being forced to go out into the forest exposing themselves to ambush by hostile neighbors. This is not, per se, what we mean by forest-consciousness, but it may lead to it. However, the idea of forest-consciousness, a sense for the value of trees and forest, may be worthwhile to pursue and it is on these lines that Schmidt-Vogt is going to investigate the relationship of different types of secondary vegetation developing in swidden habitats under different management by different tribes in Northern Thailand, or basically, the interrelationships of land use, vegetation, and tribal concepts of resource management. The basic idea is that the differences in swidden-management can be deduced from the secondary vegetation developing on the plots, especially specific secondary vegetation that may be attributed to a specific tribe and its specific land use management. The importance given to trees in these activities may shed some light on the possible existence of a forest consciousness in a wider concept of environmental awareness beyond pure "tree consciousness," which, in the first instance, may be based on the assessment of particular values of a tree species among local people. The Southeast Asian Peninsula with its enormous variety of habitats and people, many still in places barely known, promises rewarding field research in contrast, for instance, to China proper, where Pinus is found prolifically along the fringe of forest towards cultivation, but, as it seems, more often than not fire-supported by man.

Vegetation Map Construction

Troll's vision for mapping the entire mountain system was stimulated after his fieldwork on Nanga Parbat by two further short visits to other parts of the Himalaya, which revealed the changes along the foot of the hills going east. These experiences of Troll in 1937 led to a thesis on the distribution of vegetation in the Himalayan system resulting in the 1957 vegetation map of the Himalaya, which fulfilled Troll's idea in establishing the three-dimensional framework for the changes in the vegetation and of climatic conditions and landscape ecology from West to East, South to North, and with altitude. But the effort yielded, much more than could be expected in the beginning. By conscientiously avoiding the traps of "completeness," that is, by avoiding vegetation mapping by analogy, the resulting map lacked "the completeness" that Troll had visualized at the beginning, but by its white gaps the map reduced the inevitable pitfalls of mis-interpretation and, on top of that, stimulated further research. Beyond everything else and not withstanding the apparent gaps, the 1957 vegetation map revealed for the first time an overall idea of the landscape pattern of the Himalayan system or, in short "the country." The preceding pages dealt with the endeavors to fill in the gaps since the publication of the 1957 map and described in detail some local studies introducing the next phase, which is local in-depth research (see Miehe 1982, Schmidt-Vogt 1990). The 1957 map framework also encourages new methods dealing with the distribution of other phenomena within the Himalayan system. One obvious topic would be the geopony or landuse, which is a daunting task, but a fascinating project if the geographical entity of the South Asia mountain rimland representing the transitional zone between the southern Asian northern periphery and Inner Asia is taken seriously. A great deal of material is available, which deserves to be put together within the context of the mountain system to demonstrate the enormous variety met with in this three-dimensional framework.

An interesting case in testing the framework offered by the 1957 vegetation map for explaining the distribution of other phenomena is Kleinert's thesis of housetypes and settlements in the Central Himalayas; the particular value of his analysis here lies in the fact that Kleinert performed his fieldwork without any preconceived ideas about the vegetation distribution in the 1957 vegetation map. Only later, while working on his material, did he come across the 1957 map, which provided the answer to many of his observations, especially the "order" to the distribution phenomena he had observed in the field. This was a most welcome confirmation, in that the three-dimensional framework, as established by the vegetation, might serve as a guideline and explanation to the distribution pattern of other phenomena as well.

The 1957 vegetation map brought to light the "inner valleys" and the information discovered adds greatly to our perception of the wealth of conditions and the potential for differentiation a mountain world of the size and extent of the Himalaya offers.

The experience I gained in dealing with the "inner valleys" of the Himalaya was applied to a survey of possible "inner valleys" in the vast area of transition between the Tibetan Plateau and China proper, that is, the zone of transition between Sichuan and Inner Asia. I perused the 1979 vegetation map of China, along with a considerable bulk of observations related by plant hunters and other travellers, thereby adding greatly to our perception of local conditions within the eastern rampart of High Asia (Schweinfurth 1965, 1982, 1986).

Finally, out of the 1957 vegetation map, the climatically dry valleys emerged as a particular and quite unexpected feature and with the evidence gleaned from the Vegetation Map of China (Hou 1979) we gained an excellent idea about the distribution of such valleys all along the southern rim of High Asia from the Hindukush to the Basin of Sichuan (Schweinfurth 1987). The evidence I assembled has now stimulated my interest into more detailed research of the climatically dry valleys within the boundaries of China, where the greatest variety of conditions was to be expected (Zhang Rongzu 1992), and also in Bhutan (Ohsawa 1987), where detailed research may be of particular value to our concept of the mechanism involved.

Like the 1979 vegetation map of China 1:4,000,000, the recent Chinese language publication of the vegetation of Tibet (Chang 1988) together with a vegetation map at 1:3,000,000, will help greatly to extend our knowledge of the country "beyond the main range" once this publication will be available in English.

Moving from the Himalaya to the South, the material provided by Chen Weilie allowed the establishment of a cross section of the vegetation of the Gaoligong Shan (Schweinfurth, Chen 1984), which is step forward in closing the gap that still exists towards the South comprising more or less, the Shan States until one enters in Northern Thailand botanically better known areas. Santisuk's (1988) monograph summarizes the floristic situation. The intense interest in the ganus of Pinus leads right into the vegetation problems of the Southeast Asian Peninsula. A detailed investigation of the pine forests in Thailand was performed by Werner (1993) as well as an analysis of the different vegetation types following different ways of swidden management by different hill tribes in Northern Thailand (Schmidt-Vogt 1991). This latter project may lead into an assessment of certain ways of "agroforestry" and may, in the final analysis, produce an insight into the tribal folks' ways of thinking, or at least appreciating their values of certain trees. At the same time, their appreciation of forests in general, what I previously called environmental consciousness—their mental attitude—is an improvement in people's attitudes towards their environment. There is a great need for further field work on these lines, but let it be said again: political boundaries and their associated disputes over territory still keep some of the most interesting areas for field research closed.

Knowledge of vegetation is basic to understanding a country, a habitat, or an ecosystem, because vegetation represents the combination of all ecological factors present in specific area we just have to "read" the "template" to learn to interpret the vegetation pattern.

It lies in the nature of things of that the human impact will be compared with, for instance, the evidence available in 1957. In the case of Nepal, it suffices to point to the vast inroads made into the terai forests by timber contractors for road building or to the impact created by trekking in areas frequented by tourists. One could also stress the impact of political decisions again: the results from the closure of Nepal-China border by the influx of refugees from Tibet and of their herds. Previously seasonally using pastures on the Tibetan plateau, but now aggravating pressures on forest and vegetation in certain parts of Nepal.

Here and there, human impact may be obvious, in other cases not; but the arbitary distinction between "natural" and "human influenced" vegetation still flourishing in geographical parlance, and better be avoided. Furthermore with increasing human enterprise and technical ability, it will be difficult to point out a single area on the globe that is not yet visited or "used" by man, that is, places not yet influenced by human beings, directly or indirectly.

Out of all this follows that to avoid further dangerous environmental developments, knowledge of vegetation is a basic necessity and requires a clear grasp of the vegetation cover of an area. Vegetation mapping is an absolute precondition for analysis. It would be promising step forward if this principle would be taken to heart in all the current activities to "better the world." Documenting the one basic, all life supporting asset, instead of starting from some peripheral phenomena, however, eye-catching they may be, is fundamental contribution. Concurrently, one could investigate the idea of trees or forest consciousness amongst the local population as a social awareness, on which, gradually, an environmental consciousness could be developed.

After more than thirty years, which is an adequate period of judgement and hindsight, it shows quite clearly where essential basic research has been impeded by politics and political events. The "territorial imperative" is still rampant in the Himalaya! But to impede basic research any further will be to the detriment of the countries concerned. Therefore it seems appropriate to conclude this survey on vegetation and Himalayan research with the urgent plea to lift the curtains obstructing scientific progress and let research work proceed. In the case of vegetation research, the first step is to complete the vegetation map of the highest mountain system in the world.

Conclusion

Himalayan research in vegetation is traced back to Carl Troll's 1937 exploits around Nanga Parbat and his 1939 vegetation map of the Nanga Parbat massif. Troll's experience in the field led to his suggestion that I write a doctoral dissertation on the distribution of the vegetation in the Himalaya. This effort culminated in the publication of 1957 vegetation map of Himalaya.

The 1957 vegetation map shows the change of vegetation within the

Himalayan system from west to east, south to north, and with altitude. Despite considerable voids, left white, indicating areas that are botanically unknown, and by careful choice of colors, the map provides for the first time a three-dimensional framework of the distribution of the vegetation. It also offers for the first time a vegetation-based insight into the landscape ecology of this complex mountain world, in short "the country". Furthermore, some unexpected features were elicited for the first time. Foremost among these are the "inner valleys."

Inner valleys sensu stricto, lie more or less in the general West-East trend of the mountain ranges, but they also present conditions of their own. Other valleys, more or less running North-South, are characterized by climatically dry valley bottoms. Both of these features add considerably to the enormous variety of conditions of Himalayan system offers. Since the publication of the 1957 map, the elimination of vegetation "voids" has been successful on a large scale for Nepal (Dobremez et al. 1976), and in a few in-depth studies (Miehe 1982, Schmidt-Vogt 1990). Furthermore, the 1957 map proved its worth in explaining the distribution of phenomena other than vegetation as, for instance, in the types of houses and settlements (Kleinert 1983).

Prior to the publication of the 1957 map little was known about the country "beyond the main range". Now this area has been investigated by chinese botanists, in Tibet, the climatically dry valley in the Hengduan (transverse gorge) region, and the Gaoligong Shan. In the case of the climatically dry valley, the 1979 vegetation map of China shows together with the 1957 vegetation map of the Himalaya, these valleys as a definite feature of the entire southern rim of high Inner Asia from Afghanistan to Sichuan.

The study of the vegetation is basic is understanding one of a country's basic resources and, in particular, how complicated the mountain world of the Himalayan system is. Today there will be few areas left where man has not been active changing either directly or indirectly, the vegetation over. Finding out about his influence on vegetation is fundamental for gaining insight into man's attitude towards vegetation, and in particular towards trees and forest. A possible tree and forest consciousness, or rather, general environmental awareness—a mental attitude central to all sensible endeavors towards development—is desired if we are to preserve human habitat. Vegetation mapping provides the basic documentation in this enterprise.

REFERENCES

Allan, Nigel J.R. 1987. "Impact of Afghan Refugees on the Vegetation Resources of Pakistan's Hindukush-Himalaya." *Mountain Research and Development* 7:200-204.

Armitage, F.B. and J. Burley (eds.). 1980. *"Pinus kesiya Royle ex Gordon* (syn. *P. Khasya Royle; P. insularis Endlicher)."* Tropical Forest Paper No. 9. Oxford: Commonwealth Forest Institute.

Bailey, F.M. 1957. *No Passport to Tibet.* London: Rupert Hart-Davis.

Bor, N.L. 1938. "A Sketch of the Vegetation of the Aka Hills." *Assam Indian Forest Records, New Series.* "Botany" 1/4, 10:103-221.

Zhang, Qing Wai. 1988. *Vegetation of Xizang (Tibet).* (in Chinese). Beijing: Academia Sinica.

Cheng, W.C. 1939. *Les forêts du Se-Tchouan et du Sikang Oriental.* Toulouse: Faculte des Sciences.

Cooling, E.N.G. 1968. *"Pinus merkusii.* Fast Growing Timber Trees of the Lowland Tropics." Paper no. 4. Oxford, Commonwealth Forest Institute.

Dobremez, J.F. 1976. *Le Népal—Écologie et biogéographie.* Paris: CNRS.

Fletcher, H.R. 1975. *A Quest of Flowers: The Plant Explorations of Frank Ludlow and George Sheriff.* Edinburgh: Edinburgh University Press.

Fuerer-Haimendorf, C. von. 1955. *Himalayan Barbary.* London: John Murray.

Gorrie, R.M. 1933. "The Sutlej Deodar, Its Ecology and Timber Production." *Indian Forest Records (*Silviculture Series*)* 17/4:1-140.

Haffner, W. 1967. "Ostnepal—Grundzuege des vertikalen Landschaftsaufbaus." *Khumbu Himal* 1/5:389-426.

―――――. 1979. *Nepal Himalaya: Untersuchungen zum vertikalen Landschaftsaufbau Zentral- und Ostnepals.* Erdwissenschaftliche Forschung 12. Wiesbaden: Steiner Verlag.

Hesmer, H. 1975. *Leben und Werk von Dietrich Brandis (1824-1907).* Abhandlungen Rheinisch-Westfaelische Akademie der Wissenschaften, Opladen: Westdeutscher Verlag.

Hou, Hsioh-Yu. 1979. "Vegetation Map of China, 1:4,000,000." Beijing: Academia Sinica.

Jessen, O. 1948. "Die Randschwellen der Kontinente." *Petermanns Geographische Mitteilungen* 241:1-205.

Kleinert, C. 1983. *Siedlung und Umwelt im zentralen Himalaya.* Geoecological Research 4. Wiesbaden: Steiner.

Kuechler, A.W. and J.O. Sawyer. 1967. "A Study of the Vegetation near Chiangmai, Thailand." *Transactions, Kansas Academy of Sciences* 70:281-348.

Miehe, G. 1982. *Vegetationsgeographische Untersuchungen im Dhaulagiri und Annapurna Himalaya.* Dissertationes Botanicae, vol. 66, Part 1 and 2. Vaduz: J. Cramer.

―――――. 1990. *Langtang Himal.* Dissertation Botanical 158, Berlin: Stuttgart: J. Cramer.

―――――. 1991 "Die Vegetationskarte des Khumbu Himal (Mt. Everest-

Suedabdau) 1:50,000." *Erdkunde* 45:81-94.
Nakao, S. 1955. "Ecological Notes." In *Fauna and Flora of Nepal Himalaya; Scientific Research of the Japanese Expedition to Nepal Himalaya, 1952-1953*, vol. I, 278-290. Kyoto: Fauna and Flora Research Society, Kyoto University.
Nanda, N. 1982. *Tawang*. New Delhi: Vikas.
Ohsawa, M. (ed.). 1987. *Life Zone Ecology of the Bhutan Himalaya*. Vol. 1 (1992 Vol. 2). Chiba: Laboratory of Ecology, Chiba University.
Robbins, R.G. and T. Smitinand. 1966. "A Botanical Ascent of Doi Inthanond." *Natural History Bulletin Siam Society* 21: 205-227.
Santisuk, T. 1988. *An Account of the Vegetation of Northern Thailand*. Geoecological Research Vol. 5. Stuttgart: Steiner.
Schmidt-Vogt, D. 1990. *High Altitude Forests in the Jugal Himal (Eastern Central Nepal): Forest Types and Human Impact*. Geoecological Research no. 6. Stuttgart: Steiner.
―――――. 1991. "Schwendbau und Pfzanzensukzession in Novd-Thailand." *A.v. Humboldt-Swiftung, Mitteilungen* 58:21-32.
Schweinfurth, U. 1956. "Ueber klimatische Trockentaeler im Himalaya." *Erdkunde* 10:297-302.
―――――. 1957. "Die Horizontale und Vertikale Verbreitung der Vegetation im Himalaya." *Bonner Geographische Abhandlungen* 20:1-375.
―――――. 1965. "Der Himalaya—Landschaftsscheide, Rueckzugsgebiet und politisches Spannungsfeld." *Geographische Zeitschrift* 53/4: 241-260.
―――――. 1972. "The Eastern Marches of High Asia and the River Gorge Country." *Erdwissenschaftliche Forschungen* 4:276-287.
―――――. 1982. "Der innere Himalaya—Rueckzugsgebiet, Interferenzzone, Eigenentwicklung." *Erdkundliches Wissen* 59:15-24.
―――――. 1983. "Mensch und Umwelt im Indus-Durchbruch am Nanga Parbat (NW-Himalaya)." *Beitraege zur Sued Asien Forschung* 86:536-559.
―――――. 1986. "Zur Landschaftsgliederung im chinesisch-tibetischen Uebergangsraum." *Berliner Geographische Studien* 20:237-249.
―――――. 1987. "Climatically Dry valleys in the Himalayas and Further East." In *Explorations in the Tropics*, edited by R.L. Singh, 20-25. Poona: Department of Geography, University of Poona.
―――――. 1988. "*Pinus* in Southeast Asia." *Beitraege zur Biologie der Pflanzen* 63:253-269.
Schweinfurth, Ulrich, and Chen Weilie. 1984. "Vegetation und Landesnatur im suedlichen Gaoligong Shan (West-Yunnan)." *Erdkunde* 38:278-288.
Smitinand, T. 1966. "The Vegetation of Doi Chiang Dao, a Limestone Massif

in Chiang Mai, Northern Thailand." *Natural History Bulletin of Siam Society* 21:93-128.

Stanford, J.K. 1945. *Far Ridges*. London: C. & J. Temple.

Stein, N. 1978. *Coniferen im westlichen Malayischen Archipelago.* Biogeographica 11. The Hague: Dr. W. Junk.

Troll, Carl. 1939. "Das Pflanzenkleid des Nanga Parbat: Begleitworte zur Vegetationskarte der Nanga-Parbat-Gruppe (NW-Himalaya) 1:50,000." *Wissenschaftliche Veroeffentlichungen des Deutschen Museums fuer Laenderkunde.* New Series, 7:151-180.

Ward, F. Kingdon. 1949. *Burma's Icy Mountains*. London: Jonathan Cape.

Werner, W. 1993. *Pinus in Thailand*. Geoecological Research 7. Stuttgart: Steiner.

Zhang Jing-Wei. 1988. Vegetation of Xizang (Tibet). Beijing: Academia Sinica (in Chinese).

Zhang Rongzu, et al. 1992. *The Dry Valleys of the Hengduan Mountains Region.* Beijing: Science Press (in Chinese, summary in English).

CHAPTER 3

The Protective Role of Mountain Forests

LAWRENCE S. HAMILTON

Introduction

Mountain forests yield various direct products, have an array of ecological functions, and provide a number of indirect, intangible benefits and environmental services. In Rwanda they are required habitat for the endangered mountain gorilla and in Nepal for the red panda. The mountain forests in Yunnan's Xishuangbanna are revered and protected as the dwelling of the spirits of the ancestors. They are a source of needed fuelwood and of livestock feed from fodder-lopping in Pakistan, and a backdrop for recreational skiing and hiking in the Alps and the Caucasus. The role of mountain forests throughout much of the world seems to be shifting from one where direct economic production was paramount, to one that emphasizes the social, cultural and ecological service function complex. Other chapters in this volume allude to some of these "products" of mountain forests. This chapter will be confined to the *protective* role of mountain forests, and to what happens to that role as forests are altered or replaced by other uses. The protective role will be confined to those *forest influences relating to water and soil.*

The positive role of forests in affording a measure of protection from natural hazards such as avalanches, torrents and landslides has long been recognized. There are allusions to the relationship in Greek, Hebrew and Roman literature. A Chinese print from the 16th century hanging on my office wall, depicts a large-scale tree restoration project following deforestation of a mountainous landscape in the interests of "river conservancy" (sic). Among the earliest regulations with respect to mountain protection forests (and mountain grazing) were rules for the Alps in the 1850s which were codified into a law in Switzerland in 1872 (Zwerman and Richard 1959). At about this same time, a major portion (all the state-owned land representing some 1,021,500 hectares) of New York State's Adirondack Mountains in the northeastern United States was recommended for protection as a Forest Reserve with the justification of safeguarding the headwaters of New York State's navigable rivers (Hamilton 1983a). This protection was incorporated into the state constitution in 1895 in words that captured the prevailing public sentiment in an era of widespread forest exploitation: the lands were to be "kept forever wild ...They shall not be leased, sold or exchanged...nor shall the timber thereon be sold, removed, or destroyed" (New York State 1895). A nostrum for the current concern about deforestation in the tropics could hardly be expressed more forcibly than those words written almost one hundred years ago.

Deforestation Impacts Re-visited

Up until the last decade, policymakers have seemingly had the assurance that mountain forests fulfilled a protective role that would prevent soil erosion and therefore mountain degradation; keep sediment from reducing the storage capacity of lakes and reservoirs; control catastrophic floods in the lowlands and provide more water in the dry season, thus giving fully "regulated" rivers to the plains; eliminate avalanches, local torrents and landslides; induce more rainfall; and maintain springs and wells. Conversely "deforestation" (usually taken to mean the alteration of the forest, as by logging or fuelwood cutting, or the conversion of forest to another use) resulted in the reverse effects. This "reasonable" view of the impacts of deforestation was articulated in compelling manner as recently as the mid-seventies for Nepal by Eckholm (1975, 1976). It is widely accepted today as an ecocatastrophe scenario. While developed as a characterization of the crisis in Nepal, it has been applied to the entire Himalayas, and to other developing country mountain regions. One finds some elements of this degradation scenario in recent descriptions for instance of the situation in the Carpathians (Golubets et al. In press) and the Caucasus (Anisimov, In press). There is no question but what there has been severe anthropogenic mountain land degradation, especially as "flatlanders" have influenced development (Plate 1). At issue is the real versus perceived causes, and the linkage of the mountains and the lowlands in terms of effects (Hamilton 1987). Ives and Messerli (1989) have characterized the deforestation/population growth scenario as the "Theory of Himalayan Environmental Degradation." Through their book *The Himalayan Dilemma* they have thrust into the development policy arena a new scrutiny of the old paradigm about direct cause and effect relationships, and are helping thereby to guide donors, technical assistance agencies, governments, and resource management professionals toward a deeper understanding of the role of forests in sustainable mountain land use and the highland-lowland interaction. This chapter will attempt to summarize my current understanding of what we know and do not know in this arena.

Forests and Rainfall

It has been popularly suggested that mountain (and other) forests be protected, not only from conversion to agriculture or grazing, but from wood harvesting and low intensity shifting cultivation, because such interventions will result in decreased rainfall, causing droughts and even creating deserts (Sharp and Sharp 1982, Rao 1989). This age-old myth, like many myths, has a kernel of truth in the special case of the Amazon Basin (Salati and Vose 1984, Shukla et al. 1990), but in general there is no good scientific evidence that removal of forests on mountains reduces rainfall nor that reforestation increases rainfall. Perhaps, however, it was the kernel of truth that induced the perceptive spiritual leader of the Chipko (tree hugging) Movement in the Himalayas to claim that cutting of forests results in drought and that planting of trees has the reverse effect (World Water 1981). But unfortunately that extrapolation cannot be made.

Mountains themselves through their orographic effect induce rainfall. They are the water-capture landforms of the world. But the additional increase in height provided by upper forests would be of little consequence on this effect. Most research on the effects of forests on rainfall has not been done in mountain areas. Some Russian work, cited and summarized by Shpak (1968) showed approximately 10 percent more rain in forest areas as opposed to adjacent open areas. Shpak goes on, however, to point out precipitation measuring problems that invariably allow forest gauges to catch more rain. He concludes that "the considerable increase (found by some authors) ... is usually overstated ... the problem of the effect of forest on precipitation remains open at present." An early study in the United States following large scale "deforestation" by smelter fume injury, showed small (14 percent) but significantly greater precipitation in the forest area compared with the denuded area (Hursch 1948). A subsequent analysis of those experimental procedures by Lee (1978), however, indicated that when catch differences were accounted for (mainly from wind effects), the differences were less than 0.5 percent, well within experimental error. In the tropics, Bernard (1953) found no evidence of any influence of forests on rainfall. He speculated, however, that forest clearing, by increasing the heat reflectance might introduce some instability into weather patterns. For most hydrometeorological situations (the Amazon Basin excluded), it is likely that Pereira's (1973) summary is still valid: "There is no corresponding evidence as to any effects of forests on the occurrence of rainfall."

The major exception for mountain forests is where frequent wind-driven clouds provide horizontal or "occult" precipitation that is most effectively captured by forest cover with its multitude of intersecting surfaces (Zadroga 1981, Juvik and Ekern 1978). The "cloud" or "mossy" forests of the windward side or summits of many mountains (for example Mauna Loa in Hawaii, Mount Kinabalu in Sabah, and the many volcanic mountains of Central America) can add substantial effective water to the system above that received from normal vertical precipitation (Plate 2). For instance on an Hawaiian mountain, Ekern (1964) measured an increase of 760 mm of occult precipitation in addition to the non-forested 2,600 mm of rainfall. Removal of the forest loses this water; restoring forests will again recapture it. Keeping cloud forests intact makes good hydrological sense as well as preserving areas of unusual biotic character (Hamilton 1986; La Bastille and Poole 1978). The most recent review of these important montane forests has been provided by Stadtmuller (1987).

Forests and Erosion

Popular wisdom insists that having trees will prevent erosion and that removing trees, per se, results in drastic erosion leading to land degradation. Trees, and particularly trees in forest stands, do indeed generally reduce the amount of erosion, and conventional wisdom does coincide with proven effects. Soil erosion under dense natural humid and seasonally humid forest is usually less than one ton per hectare per year (UNESCO/UNEP/FAO 1978). Hurni (1988) also gives annual soil loss estimates of 1 tonne per hectare for the Ethiopian Highlands, the lowest for 7 categories of mountain land use. However, substantial surface erosion can occur in undisturbed forest (Lal 1983), as can large landslips and debris avalanches on forested unstable slopes (Lin 1984). Nonetheless, the undisturbed mountain forest is excellent watershed cover from the erosion standpoint, but it is more appropriate to speak of forests as having *low* erosion rather than *no* erosion; and when putting forest back on mountain land to talk about erosion *reduction*, rather than *prevention*. To be more precise it is also necessary to separate two classes of erosion: (1) *surface* (sheetwash, rills, and gullies); and (2) *mass wasting* (landslips, slumps, debris flows, etc.).

Surface Erosion

Advocates sometimes talk about the benefits of having a tree canopy interposed between the falling rain and the bare soil to reduce splash erosion (detachment of particles by raindrop impact, and then movement downslope). Actually, splash erosion can be greater under trees if the soil is bare because drop sizes are larger. Coalescing raindrops on large-leaved species (such as teak), falling from a high canopy may be more damaging to the soil than the rain itself. For instance, *Albizia falcataria* (now *Paraserianthes falcataria*) with canopy height of 20 m yielded raindrops with an erosive energy 102 percent of rain in the open, but for the *Anthocephalus chinensis* with its large leaves at only 10 m canopy height, this figure was 147 percent (Lembaga Ekologi, 1980). Larger drops falling from canopies tall enough so that terminal velocity is reached, have greater kinetic energy per drop. Moreover Mosley (1982) working in a mountain beech forest in New Zealand showed that the kinetic energy of water drops *per unit area* was greater under forest than in the open. Repeated results of surface erosion studies in forests have shown that it is the leaf litter and low understory rather than the tall tree canopy that impart erosion protection. If this surface protection is removed for fodder and/or fuel, or if livestock are turned in to graze, or fire occurs, the presence of trees will not minimize surface erosion on slopes. Wiersum (1984) has synthesized much of the research literature on erosion under various forest and tree crop systems and presented an interesting table of averages (lumping all data, even though derived from different slopes and soils — Table 1). Note that as soon as the litter is removed by cultivation, weeding or burning, the erosion rate increases substantially.

The importance of the low vegetative cover and leaf litter in reducing splash erosion and resulting sheet erosion (which channelizes and develops into rills, in the absence of barriers, and then into gullies) should focus concern on such traditional mountain forest land use practices as grazing, burning and leaf litter collection. In reality, lopping twigs for fodder or cutting branches and whole trees for fuel or other wood products, is of lesser concern from the standpoint of surface erosion, than are practices that leave the ground bare of cover or that remove the near-ground canopy. In general for mountainous lands in agriculture and forest uses, the most severe surface erosion problems and productivity degradation are on over-utilized open-access grazing and forested land where the individual has no motivation for improving management (Carson 1985) and on lands repeatedly damaged by fires for whatever reason. Compared with these situations, the soil conservation regime can even be better where shifting agriculture of the long-fallow, traditional type prevails (Nye, Greeland 1960), or where well-constructed and well-maintained terraces characterize the cultivated land (Carson 1985). However, it is well-recognized

TABLE 1. EROSION IN VARIOUS TROPICAL MOIST FOREST AND TREE CROP SYSTEMS (TON/HA/YEAR).

	Minimal	Median	Maximal
Multistoried tree gardens (4/4)1	0.01	0.06	0.14
Natural forests (18/27)	0.03	0.30	6.16
Shifting cultivation, fallow period (6/14)	0.05	0.15	7.40
Forest plantations, undisturbed (14/20)	0.02	0.58	6.20
Tree crops with cover crop/mulch (9/17)	0.10	0.75	5.60
Shifting cultivation, cropping period (7/22)	0.40	2.78	70.05
Taungya cultivation (2/6)	0.63	5.23	17.37
Tree crops, clean-weeded (10/17)	1.20	47.60	182.90
Forest plantations, burned/litter removed (7/7)	5.92	53.40	104.80

1(x/y)
where x = no. locations, and y = no. treatments or observations
From Wiersum (1984)   KB:4:4/23/90

that in many parts of the world's mountain environment, forest removal has been followed by grazing and cropping practices that do not employ soil conservation measures. For instance in Africa, the consequences have been documented for the Mbeya Highlands of Tanzania by Mashalla (1988), the Ethiopian Highlands by Hurni (1988) the Moroccan Atlas Mountains by Bencherifa (1983).

In wood harvesting also, it is not so much the cutting of the trees for logs or fuelwood that should concern us from the standpoint of surface erosion. This should concern us, of course, if we care about fauna habitat, composition of the vegetation and biological diversity. Rather it is the way the material is removed from the forest. Again, it is disturbance to the soil cover by dragging, skidding, hauling, roading, and poor location of landings that are the villains in the erosion drama (Hamilton 1983b). Logging in mountain forests must be very carefully carried out in order to minimize erosion, and many mountain forests are located on such erodible sites that even with aerial logging systems, this use must be carefully planned and monitored.

Mass Erosion

In mountain forest planning and management, slopes which are prone to mass wasting merit special attention as "critical areas." Megahan and King (1985) have made suggestions for identifying areas with high hazard for mass erosion. Land use allocations and management policies for landslide-prone areas should be based on the degree of climatic, topographic, and edaphic hazard. In the case of deep-seated slides this is indicated simply by whether or not slides occur or have occurred in the area (i.e., "hazardous" or "not hazardous"). For shallow slides, the degree of hazard can be assessed, and stratified, for different levels of care. The criteria for the hazard rating are based on storm rainfall intensity and duration, and on slope gradient and shape. Megahan and King summarized the literature and suggested that shallow landslips are limited to slopes greater than 45 to 55 percent, with a maximum frequency of occurrence at about 70 percent. Landslips also are correlated with slope concavities and convergences that concentrate water. Phillips and Pearce (1984) have illustrated terrain stability zoning in New Zealand using somewhat different criteria, more related to geologic and geomorphic factors.

Sites that are prone to shallow landslips, are given greater stability by tree roots. These roots impart shear strength to the soil. Loss of this shear strength following tree cutting or tree removal and subsequent greater incidence of slope failures has been reported for mountain country in New Zealand, Alaska, Japan and western North America by O'Loughlin and Ziemer (1982).

Where stumps coppice, so that the root systems remain alive, there is no problem. Thus, in short-rotation fuelwood plantations of fast-growing coppicing species, the root systems would continue their beneficial function. Where this is not the case, loss of soil shear strength depends on the rate of root decay following cutting, compared to the growth of new roots from uncut trees or forest reproduction. Because of this, in the northern Rocky Mountains of the United States, in mountainous Japan, and in Alaska, post cutting landslide hazards did not peak until 2 to 10 years after logging (Bishop and Stevens 1964,

Megahan el al. 1978, Nakano 1971) (see Plate 3). If the forest is cleared for conversion to grazing or cropping, the root systems of the grasses and annual crops provide much less shear strength compared to forest, and therefore this conversion may accelerate landslide activity. Trustrum et al. (1984) in New Zealand's steeplands have documented this phenomenon, and shown its magnitude in major storm events such as cyclones (see Plate 4).

While Swanston (1981) stated that deep-seated landslides are only slightly, if at all, reduced by vegetative cover, O'Loughlin (1984) suggested that there may be some beneficial effects. Road construction involving embankments, excavation, and changes in slope drainage often have dramatic impact on such deep-seated mass movements (Plate 5). The magnitude of the problem of landslides associated with mountain roads has been shown for an area in Garhwal, Lesser Himalaya by Haigh (1979). He found in one survey area an average of ten mid-size landslides per kilometer of road. Areas prone to such mass erosion should be avoided if possible in planning roads. The cross-island mountain highway in Taiwan initiated spectacular and persistent landslides.

If forested, mass movement prone areas should be maintained in forest, for such vegetation tends to involve less intensive use and disturbance under the heavy pressure placed on land in developing countries. Any forest harvesting in these sensitive areas must be done with extreme care. If timber is sufficiently valuable, logging might be accomplished by helicopter or balloon, though there is little or no experience with these "high-tech" methods in the mountains of developing countries. If fuelwood is required, transporting should be done by hand or by animal power without road construction. Non-wood forest product harvesting would appear acceptable. In many cases these steep areas might well be allocated to forest preserve status or to park status, if there are appropriate national patrimony values.

Sediment

The major negative off-site consequence of erosion processes is sediment, whether in rivers, lakes, reservoirs, or estuaries. Sediment can: harm or kill valuable aquatic life (including fisheries and mangrove resources); impair water quality for drinking, other domestic uses, and industrial processes; reduce reservoir capacity for important flood, hydropower, or irrigation storages; shorten the useful life of hydroelectric turbines and water pumps; interfere with navigation; and aggrade river channels, thus aggravating flooding. Most of these unwanted effects of sediment are in the downstream portions of watersheds where most of the wealth, political power and population of a drainage basin usually reside (e.g., Calcutta and Dhaka). The link between mountain land erosion and downstream sediment problems has been recognized by these affected people, and there are increasing levels of action being called for to stop or reduce harmful sedimentation through better upper watershed management. It should be recognized, however, that where the upper watersheds are mountainous, the greater part of the sediment is probably due to natural forces, involving mass erosion, rather than to agriculture or forest land use and surface erosion. Carson (1985) makes this conclusion for the Nepalese Himalaya, and it seems to be generally applicable, at least in other young or tectonically active mountain systems, e.g., Papua New Guinea (Blong 1986). Shroder (1989), in assessing hazards in the Himalaya, states:

"Probably the most common catastrophic mass movement in the Himalaya is the debris flow, in which surface debris is mobilized by rain or snowmelt. Waves of this slurry rush down gullies, destroying bridges and devastating fields. Debris flows have blocked some of the largest rivers and overwhelmed major structures as a result of intense storms or breakout floods."

Human activity, however, in developing infrastructure such as roads, power lines and storage reservoirs can substantially increase land instability and mass erosion in mountainous forest areas.

On the local scene, in small watersheds, erosion due to land use may have a direct link to local sediment problems. And at this scale, anthropogenic sediment may be the problem of concern rather than sediment from natural erosion processes that locals can do little about. Moreover, when considering small, steep watersheds, for instance in such mountainous islands as Hawaii or Fiji, the pipeline of effects is much shorter and more direct. Yesterday's erosion from housing construction or logging in the upper watershed forest is today's sediment blanketing the near shore waters and reef.

Forests and Floods

There is a widespread belief that forest covered upper watersheds will prevent floods on the mainstem downstream reaches of major rivers, and that cutting of forests will cause catastrophic floods in the lowlands. For instance Sharp and Sharp (1982) for China, Openshaw (1974) for India and Corvera (1981) for the Philippines all support this contention. How this belief can influence policies was dramatically demonstrated in early 1989 when, following disastrous 1988 flooding and sediment damage in Southern Thailand, all logging in Thailand's forests was halted, since logging was supposedly responsible for the flooding

(The Nation 1989). What had happened is that this area had received 1,022 mm of rainfall in three days and the greatest damage was caused by widespread and spectacular landslips resulting from conversion of forest to agriculture and young rubber plantations on steep slopes. In spite of these revelations, the logging ban from the great flood remains in force. Parenthetically, one should remember that much good for the remaining natural forest of Thailand may result from this dramatic action, for Thailand's fledgling system of protected areas is getting some respite. One consequence, however, is increased logging of the neighboring mountain forests of Burma and its impact on tribal peoples of those hills.

Unfortunately forests are visualized as behaving like a sponge, whose roots "suck up" water in times of excess (a storm event) and then release it during the post-storm or post-monsoon season to augment the dry-season flow (Myers 1983, Spears 1982). This root-sponge concept is slow to fade from popular thinking. Roots actually operate more like a pump than a sponge.

What water storage is available on-site is in the soil, and the potential storage is largely a function of soil depth and texture/structure. If a soil has only the capacity to accept 50 mm of rain and 150 mm falls, there is going to be rapid sub-surface and overland flow contributing to streamflow, whether forest covered or not. Unfortunately mountain soils tend not to be very deep, and not to have large soil water storage capacity. Whether a rainfall event can be accommodated also depends on antecedent water in storage. During monsoon seasons, unfortunately, soils may be near saturation for prolonged periods. Forests are more effective than other types of land cover in reducing antecedent water. Partly because of their deep root system and tall, rough canopy, they exhibit greater evapo-transpiration than other vegetation, hence, comparatively speaking, leaving the soil storage capacity in more receptive state for the next rainfall event. Pearce and Rowe (1979) in New Zealand have shown the great importance of interception evaporative loss from forests as a factor in the hydrologic cycle and the water yield. This would seem to account for the usual results of experiments, that show in streams emanating from the forest: smaller stormflow volumes, lower peak flows and somewhat later peaks than from non-forest or recently cut forests (Reinhart et al. 1963; Douglass and Swank 1975; Pearce et al. 1980). However, if soil water storage is already occupied from antecedent rains, this result generally does not show in significant manner (Douglass and Swank 1975). Moreover as the area of concern about large stormflows (those that produce flooding) moves further down the watershed, any beneficial effects in flood reduction become proportionately less, because so many other influences materialize with increasing size of drainage basin. These influences include: the mosaic of land uses with differing effects, the increasing variability in soil depth and geology, the morphometry of the basin, the nature and intensity of the precipitation and the way it moves across the basin, the amount of rain falling directly on the water surface, the increasing amount of non-absorbing surface for urban and transportation purposes, and human constriction of the river channels. Hewlett (1982) examined the evidence worldwide from forest watershed research and reported that there was no cause-effect relationship between forest cutting in the headwaters and floods in the lower basin. Taking a cue from Hewlett, Hamilton (1983b, 1987, 1988) extended the scenario to interventions or conversions of forest land other than forest cutting and has argued that the catastrophic floods of the lower basin flood plains of major rivers cannot be blamed on peasant land-use practices in the mountain headwaters.

The June 1985 flood disaster in India affecting six lower basin states, killing 237 persons and destroying 400,000 homes was attributed by many to mountain deforestation (Reuter 1985). This is nonsense when one considers that in those states some areas received 414 mm of rain in 24 hours in the monsoon season when soils were already saturated. Similarly the Great Bangladesh floods of August to September of 1988 were not caused by forest use, or even abuse in the Himalayas (Hamilton 1988).

That is not to say that intact forest and forest soils are not effective in flood reduction at a smaller scale. Where soils are deep, and for the frequent, lower intensity, short duration storms, intact forest compared with cutover forest or non-forest land can reduce the occasions and severity of overbank flow in streams close to the area in question. Such benefits may be very substantial to local people who face flooding damage to fields and their shelters, and washouts of roads, tracks and bridges. The difference in benefits depends also on to what extent sound soil and water conservation practices are in place on the cropland, grazing land or the forest harvesting operation. Abusive agriculture and poor logging practices may increase local flood frequency and extend in these common rainfall events, because of compaction and reduced infiltration capacity, and therefore greater subsurface and overland flow on steep mountain slopes. However, for the rarer, high intensity and/or long duration storms, the flood reduction benefit dwindles proportionately, even at the local level. When one moves to a consideration of large basins and to assessment locations or receiving points far removed from the mountain headwaters, the effects are dwarfed by natural forces and characteristics. It is all too common, unfortunate, and mistaken, for flood-affected lower basin populations to look for scapegoats, and find them in the mountain land use practices of cultural minorities or citizens of another country. Much of the problem and the solution lies with the lower basin flood plain dwellers themselves (Hamilton 1988; Ives and Messerli 1989).

Forests and Dry-Season Water Availability

Conventional wisdom insists that those same forests that soaked up the water in the wet season (or during a single storm) to prevent floods release that water slowly during the dry season (or after the storm), thus evening out the flow of streams and rivers, and maintaining springs and wells. While this sponge concept is nonsense, there is much murkiness that prevents an unambiguous picture.

There can be no gainsaying the overwhelming evidence from reliable watershed research around the world, summarized by Bosch and Hewlett (1982). In all forty-four cases it would seem that tree roots were behaving more like pumps than sponges, for water yields in streams from the study catchments increased when the trees were removed, and these increases generally occurred throughout the year — wet season and dry season alike. A typical result from one of these experiments for a clearcut mountain watershed in the Southern Appalachians of the United States is shown in Figure 1. Note the increase following cutting in every month of the year, and the greater proportional increase in the dry season streamflow (Douglass and Swank 1972). These increases are due to a reduction in the evapo-transpirational losses, which are higher for tall canopy forests with deep root systems than for other kinds of vegetation or land use. Although these substantial increases in streamflow may

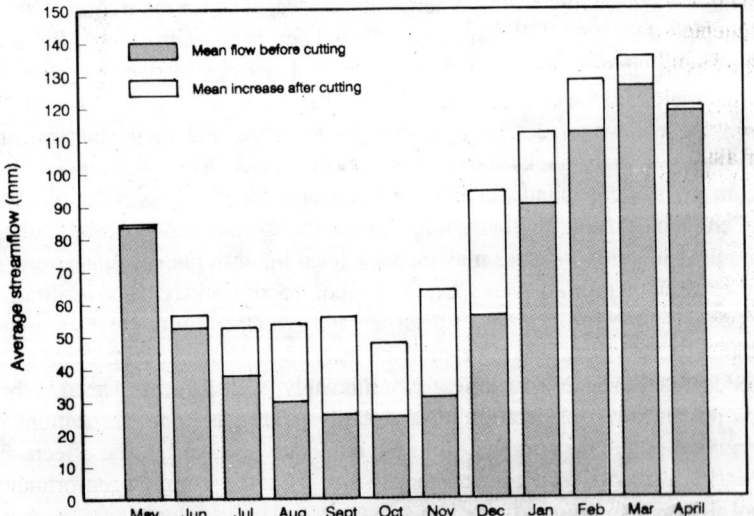

Figure 1: Average monthly streamflow and the increase in flow during 7 years of annual recutting of deciduous forest on Watershed 17, Coweeta, USA (after Douglass and Swank, 1975)

be partly attributable to the deep soils in the experimental catchment, monthly increases have also been obtained from experiments on mountain watersheds with thinner soils in Taiwan (Hsia and Goh 1983); Japan (Nakano 1967); New Zealand (Pearce et al. 1980); and Australia (Gilmour 1977). Even when forest watersheds have been converted to another cover or land use, such as grassland, shifting cultivation, tea or annual crops (Edwards and Blackie 1981, Mueller-Dombois 1973) increased water availability is the rule from small watershed studies. Yet the conventional concept persists—and some is folk wisdom that should not be dismissed out-of-hand. This suggests that the reduced low-flows being actually experienced in many rivers is due to loss of mountain forests, and that water that once infiltrated forest soils to provide a base flow in the dry season now runs off because of abusive land use, and is not recharging the base-flow sources. This is a seductive theory. It is necessary to remember, however, that there is a great deal more water being removed from the system for both domestic and irrigation use, by the many more people now inhabiting these watersheds and intensifying their agriculture. This consumptive use could well account for any real decrease in water availability, as well as precipitation vagaries. Similarly the springs and wells that are no longer adequate could be the result of increased population and higher per capita use, rather than loss of forests.

Bruijnzeel (1988) has reviewed the research and observations with regard to forest removal and dry season flow in the tropics (not high mountains, and no snow conditions) and concluded that there was conflicting evidence, even though most well-documented cases showed increased streamflow water following forest removal. Hamilton (1986) speculated earlier that there were indeed countervailing processes operating, in that while forest removal reduced the evapo-transpirational losses, this might be counterbalanced by a reduced infiltration capacity from a subsequent land use, resulting in less water recharge to provide baseflow for the dry season although there were no experimental results that conclusively showed this. Bruijnzeel (1988), in reviewing five research projects in Australia, Malaysia, Tanzania, and Indonesia felt that the two Indonesian studies (neither of them of the paired-catchment type) did suggest that in the real world of tropical land use (rather than in small catchment experiments) dry season flow could be lower through reduced infiltration more than compensating for evapo-transpirational gains in the non-forested watersheds. In view of the infiltration research in Nepal by Gilmour et al. (1987), I remain somewhat skeptical, except for those watersheds with a substantial amount of totally non-absorbing surface such as roads, buildings, villages, and livestock yarding areas. There is not enough research, over a wide range of situations, to settle this question. Indeed for the Himalayas, Bruijnzeel (1989) reviewed the literature and came up with an ambiguous answer because of the complexity of the factors. He presented the prudent precaution that maintaining infiltration capacities in the subsequent land use, when forests are replaced, is a good insurance against decreases in low season flow. On the other hand all evidence from reliable studies of the effects of *re-establishing* mountain forests on dry season flows showed decreases (Bruijnzeel 1989, Hamilton and Pearce 1987). Apparently the increased water consumption of new forest outweighs any improvement in infiltration and nurturing of base flows.

The situation is even more complex where there is snowfall and snow accumulation in mountain forests, and streams are dependent largely on winter snow to carry them into the dry summer. Closed forests (often coniferous) can intercept snow on the canopy, and re-evaporate back to the atmosphere substantially larger amounts of water than other vegetation. On the other hand the insulating effect of the forest canopy can maintain longer what snowpack is accumulating under the canopy during the warmer temperatures when the snowpack melts. Thus in regions of dry summer/wet winter (in the form of snow) and where the dry warm season flow has a high value (e.g., Rocky Mountains of U.S.A.), forest manipulation has been practiced to increase snowmelt water yields (Troendle 1983). This management consists of reducing forest densities or creating openings within the forest, and has been shown to increase snowpack and resulting streamflow by 7 to 111 percent (Ffolliott et al. 1989). Too much opening up, i.e. clearing, would not prolong the streamflow as much. Whether or not such management is applicable in other mountain forests depends on the precipitation regime, the value of water, accessibility, and technical expertise available.

Re-establishing Mountain Forests

This discussion has mainly dealt with the effects of alteration or removal of mountain forests with respect to soil and water. Mountain environments everywhere are undergoing rapid changes in land use. Projects of restoration of degraded mountain environments are involving re-establishment of forests in abandoned or degraded lands from the Ethiopian Highlands to the Andes. The effects of reforestation are in general the opposite of forest removal. One might expect locally, within a few years: reduced surface erosion; fewer and smaller shallow landslips; no change in debris flows and major landslides; reduced total water yield; somewhat lower storm peaks and stormflow volumes in the short or low-intensity storms especially where there are deep soils, but little change in these phenomena for the infrequent major storms especially during the rainy season; reduced dry season flows (Hamilton and Pearce 1987).

It is not likely that once-dry springs will flow again nor that water levels will rise in wells, as has often been claimed. Nor will the rainfall be increased.

Conclusion

Mountain forests, whether original remnants that have escaped "mountain development," or artificially established ones that are planted to correct past mistakes or meet changed social objectives, have many values and functions other than the hydrologic and erosion related aspects covered in this paper. Moreover, the functions are inter-related. While the promise of additional water yield in the dry season might suggest logging of mountain forests, the erosion and sediment generated by inappropriate ground disturbance in wood extraction especially by poorly located, designed and maintained roads may far outweigh any benefit. One must consider the overall results of actions on all processes and all values.

When considering the off-site effects of forest alteration or removal on soil and water, one must also put matters into a spatial scale perspective. The writer has never heard this matter so well stated as it was by Bruno Messerli at the Mohonk (New York State) conference on mountain environments in 1986, and that was subsequently paraphrased by Hamilton (1987). It is worth repeating herein:

- At the local level (<50 km^2) sediment load is strongly influenced by human activity, stream discharge characteristics are much less, but that on the whole, for flood and sedimentation problems in the Himalaya, human activity has less impact than natural factors.

- At the medium level (50-20,000 km^2) downstream of the catchment receiving the impact, we are still uncertain of the quantitative effects of human activity, but the high variability of natural factors dominates stream discharge and sediment load.

- At the macro-level (>20,000 km^2) in large basins, one postulates that human impacts in the upper watershed are insignificant on lowland floods, low flow, and sediment, but that these effects can be significantly influenced by human activity in the lower reaches of the river.

This concept has been supported by some data, and elaborated in somewhat more detail in *The Himalayan Dilemma: Reconciling Development and Conservation*, by Ives and Messerli (1989). It seems appropriate to other mountain systems as well. Not only size but geology, relief and shape of catchment will influence the highland/lowland interaction within a given climatic regime. Because of this variability, it is prudent to refrain from sweeping generalizations about the protective role of mountain forests.

REFERENCES

Anisinov, Vladimir I. 1989. "Natural-Anthropogenic Factor in the Degradation of Mountain Ecosystems (the case of Checheno-Ingush, Armenian S.S.R.)." Presented at Conference Transformation of Mountain Environments: Regional Development and Sustainability; Consequences for Global Change held at Tsahkadzor, Armenian S.S.R. In press.

Bencherifa, A. 1983. "Land Use and Equilibrium of Mountain Ecosystems in the High Atlas of West Morocco." *Mountain Research and Development* 3:273-279.

Bernard, A.E. 1953. "L'evapotranspiration annuelle de la foret equatoriale Congolaise et son influence sur la pluviosite." In *Comptes Rendus,* 201-204. Rome: IUFRO Congress.

Bishop, D.M. and M.E. Stevens. 1964. "Landslides on Logged Areas in Southeast Alaska." Research Paper NOR-1. Portland: USDA Forest Service.

Blong, R.J. 1986. "Natural Hazards in the Papua New Guinea Highlands." *Mountain Research and Development* 6:233-246.

Bosch, J.M. and J.D. Hewlett. 1982. "A Review of Catchment Experiments to Determine the Effect of Vegetation Changes on Water Yield and Evapotranspiration." *Hydrology* 55:3-23.

Bruijnzeel, L.A. 1988. "(De)forestation and Dry Season Flow in the Tropics: a Closer Look." Konto River Project Working Paper 27. Malang, Indonesia: DHV Consultants.

Bruijnzeel, L.A. with C.N. Bremmer. 1989. *Highland-Lowland Interactions in the Ganges Brahmaputra River Basin: A Review of Published Literature.* ICIMOD Occasional Paper 11. Kathmandu: International Centre for Integrated Mountain Development.

Carson, Brian. 1985. *Erosion and Sedimentation Processes in the Nepalese Himalaya.* Occasional Paper No 1. Kathmandu: International Centre for Integrated Mountain Development.

Corvera, A. 1981. "What Caused the Great Agusan Flood?" *Weekend,* March 1, 12-13.

Douglass, J.E. and W.T. Swank. 1972. "Streamflow Modification Through Management of Eastern Forests." Southeastern Forest Experiment Station

Research Paper SE-94, Asheville, NC: U.S.D.A. Forest Service.
———. 1975. "Effects of Management Practices on Water Quality and Quantity: Coweeta Hydrological Laboratory, North Carolina." In *Municipal Watershed Management Symposium Proceedings*. General Technical Report NE-13, 1-13. Asherville: USDA Forest Service.
Eckholm, Erik. 1975. "The Deterioration of Mountain Environments." *Science* 189:764-770.
———. 1976. *Losing Ground*. New York: W.W. Norton.
Edwards, K.A. and J.R. Blackie. 1981. "Results of the East African Catchment Experiments, 1958-1974." In *Tropical Agricultural Hydrology*, edited by R. Lal and E.W. Russell, 163-188. New York: Wiley.
Ekern, P.C. 1964. "Direct Interception of Cloud Water on Lanaihale, Hawaii." *Proceedings Soil Science Society of America* 28:417-421.
Ffolliott, P.F., G.J. Gottfried and M.B. Baker, Jr. 1989. "Water yield from forest snowpack management: research findings in Arizona and New Mexico." *Water Resources Research* 25:1999-2007.
Gilmour, Donald A. 1977. "Effect of logging and clearing on water yield and quality in a high rainfall zone of northeast Queensland." Hydrology Symposium Proceedings, Institute of Engineers, Brisbane, 156-160.
Golubets, M.A., Y.P. Odinak and I.I. Dozak. 1989. "Anthropogenic Transformation of the Biogeocenotic Cover in the Carpathian Region." Paper presented at Conference Transformation of Mountain Environments: Regional Development and Sustainability; Consequences for Global Change held at Tsahkadzor, Armenian SSR, In press.
Haigh, Martin J. 1979. "Landslide Sediment Accumulations on the Mussoorie-Tehri Road, Garhwal Lesser Himalaya." *Indian Journal Soil Conservation* 7:1-4.
Hamilton, Lawrence S. 1983a. "Water Resources Development and the Emerging Concept of Environmental Protection in the United States." In *Water Management and Environmental Protection in Asia and the Pacific*, edited by I. Kato, N. Kumamoto, W.H. Matthews, and R.T.M. Sutamihardja, 149-162. Tokyo: University of Tokyo Press.
———. 1986. "Towards clarifying the appropriate mandate in forestry for watershed rehabilitation and management." In *Strategies, Approaches and Systems in Integrated Watershed Management*, 33-51. Conservation Guide 14, Rome: UN/FAO.
———. 1987. "What are the Impacts of Himalayan Deforestation on the Ganges-Brahmaputra Lowlands and Delta? Assumptions and Facts." *Mountain Research and Development* 7:256-263.
———. 1988. "The Recent Bangladesh Flood Disaster Was Not Caused by Deforestation Alone." *Environmental Conservation* 15:369-370.

Hamilton, Lawrence S. with P.N. King. 1983b. *Tropical Forested Watersheds: Hydrologic and Soils Response to Major Uses of Conversions.* Boulder, CO: Westview Press.

Hamilton, Lawrence S. and A.J. Pearce. 1987. "What Are the Soil and Water Benefits of Planting Trees in Developing Country Watersheds?" In *Sustainable Development of Natural Resources in the Third World*, edited by D.D. Southgate and J.D. Desinger, 39-58. Boulder, CO: Westview Press.

Hewlett, J.D. 1982. "Forests and Floods in the Light of Recent Investigation." Publication No. 20548, 543-560. Ottawa: National Research Council of Canada.

Hsiah, Y.J. and C.C. Goh. 1983. "Water Yield Resulting From Clearcutting a Small Hardwood Basin in Central Taiwan." In *Hydrology of Humid Tropical Regions*, edited by R. Keller, 215-220. Publication No. 140, Washington D.C.: International Association of Hydrologic Sciences.

Hurni, Hans. 1988. "Degradation and Conservation of the Resources in the Ethiopian Highlands." *Mountain Resources and Development* 8:123-130.

Hursch, C.R. 1948. "Local Climate in the Copper Basin of Tennessee as Modified by the Removal of Vegetation." Circular 774, Washington: U.S. Department of Agriculture.

Ives, J.D. and B. Messerli. 1989. *The Himalayan Dilemma: Reconciling Development and Conservation.* London: Routledge.

Juvik, J.O. and P.C. Ekern. 1978. "A Climatology of Mountain Fog on Mauna Loa, Hawaii Island." Technical Report 118, Honolulu: Water Resources Research Center, University of Hawaii.

LaBastille, A. and D.J. Poole. 1978. "On the Need for a System of Cloud-forest Parks in Middle America and the Caribbean." *Environmental Conservation* 5:183-190.

Lal, R. 1983. "Soil Erosion in the Humid Tropics with Particular Reference to Agricultural Land Development and Soil Management." In *Hydrology of Humid Tropical Regions*, edited by R. Keller, 221-239. Publication No. 140, Washington D.C.: International Association of Hydrologic Sciences.

Lee, R. 1978. *Forest Microclimatology.* New York: Columbia University Press.

Lembaga Ekologi. 1980. "Report on study of vegation and erosion in the Jatiluhur catchment, 1980." Bandung: Institute of Ecology.

Lin, Y.L. 1984. "Status of Forest Hydrology Research in Taiwan." In *Country Papers on Status of Watershed Forest Influence Research in Asia and the Pacific*, edited by L. Hamilton, M. Bonell and E. Mercer, 238-96. Working Paper, Honolulu: East-West Center.

Mashalla, S.K. 1988. "The Human Impact on the Natural Environment of the

Mbeya Highlands, Tanzania." *Mountain Research and Development* 8:283-288.

Megahan, W.F., N.F. Day and T.M. Bliss. 1978. "Landslide Occurrence in the Western and Central Northern Rocky Mountain Physiographic Province in Idaho." In *Forest Soils and Land Use*, edited by C.T. Youngberg, Proc. Fifth Northern American For. Soils Conf., 116-39. Fort Collins: Colorado State University.

Megahan, W.F. and P.N. King. 1985. "Identification of Critical Areas on Forest Lands for Control of Nonpoint Sources of Pollution." *Environmental Management* 9:7-18.

Mosley, M.P. 1982. "The Effect of a New Zealand Beech Forest Canopy on the Kinetic Energy of Water Drops and on Surface Erosion." *Earth Surface Processes and Landforms* 7:103-107.

Mueller-Dombois, D. 1973. "A Non-adapted Vegetation Interferes with Water Removal in a Tropical Rainforest Area in Hawaii." *Tropical Ecology* 14:1-18.

Myers, Norman. 1983. "Tropical Moist Forests: Over-exploited and Under Utilized?" *Forest Ecology and Management* 6:59-79.

Nakano, H. 1967. "Effects of Changes of Forest Conditions on Water Yield, Peak Flow and Direct Runoff of Small Watersheds in Japan." In *International Symposium on Forest Hydrology*, edited by W.E. Sopper and H.W. Lull, 551-564. Oxford: Pergamon.

—————. 1971. "Soil and Water Conservation Functions of Forest on Mountainous Land." Government Forest Experiment Station (Japan), Tokyo: Forest Influences Division.

New York State: New York State Constitution, Article XIV, Section 1, 1895.

Nye, P.H. and D.J. Greenland. 1960. "The Soil Under Shifting Cultivation." Technical Communication No. 51, Farnham UK: Commonwealth Agricultural Bureau.

O'Loughlin, C. and R.R. Ziemer. 1982. "The Importance of Root Strength and Deterioration Rates Upon Edaphic Stability in Steepland Forests." In *Carbon Uptake and Allocation; a Key to Management of Subalpine Ecosystems*, edited by R.H. Waring, 70-78. Corvallis: Oregon State University.

Openshaw, K. 1974. "Woodfuels in the Developing World." *New Scientist* January 31, 271-272.

Pearce, A.J. and L.K. Rowe. 1979. "Forest Management Effects on Interception, Evaporation, and Water Yield." *Journal of Hydrology* (New Zealand) 18:73-87.

Pearce, A.J., L.K. Rowe, and C.L. O'Loughlin. 1980. "Effects of Clearfelling and Slash-burning on Water Yield and Storm Hydrographs in Evergreen

Mixed Forests, Western New Zealand." In *Influence of Man on the Hydrological Regime with Special Reference to Representative and Experimental Basins*, 119-127. Publication No. 130, Washington D.C.: International Association of Hydrologic Sciences.

Pereira, H.C. 1973. *Land Use on Water Resources in Temperate and Tropical Climates.* Cambridge: Cambridge University Press.

Phillips, C. J. and A.J. Pearce. 1984. "Terrain Stability Zoning of the Makamako Block of Tokomaru State Forest." Bulletin No. 91, Rotorua: New Zealand Forest Research Institute.

Rao, R. 1989. "Water Scarcity Haunts World's Wettest Place." *Ambio* 18:300.

Rao, Y.S. 1988. "Flash Floods in Southern Thailand." *Tigerpaper* 15:1-2.

Reinhart, K.G., A.R. Eschner and G.R. Trimble Jr. 1963. "Effect on Streamflow of Four Forest Practices, in the Mountains of West Virginia." Research paper NE-1. Syracuse: USDA Forest Service.

Reuter. 1985. "Rain leaves 237 Dead in India."

Salati, E. and P.B. Vose. 1984. "Amazon Basin: a System in Equilibrium." *Science* 225:129-138.

Sharp, D. and T. Sharp. 1982. "The Desertification of Asia." *Asia 2000* 1: 40-42.

Shpak, I.S. 1968. "Effect of Forest on Water Balance Components of Drainage Basins." Kiev, 137-43. Academy of Sciences of the Ukraine SSR. (Translated from Russian, 1971). Jerusalem: Israel Program for Scientific Translations.

Shroder, J.F. 1989. "Hazards of the Himalaya." *American Scientist* 77:564-575.

Shukla, J., C. Nobre and P. Sellers. 1990. "Amazon Deforestation and Climate Change." *Science* 247:1322-1325.

Spears, J. 1982. "Rehabilitating Watersheds." *Finance and Development* 19:30-33.

Stadtmuller, T. 1987. "Cloud Forests in the Humid Tropics." Tokyo: United Nations University.

Swanston, D.N. 1981. "Creep and Earthflow Erosion from Undisturbed and Management Impacted Slopes in the Coast and Cascade Ranges of the Pacific Northwest, USA." In *Erosion and Sediment Transport in Pacific Rim Steeplands*, edited by T.R.H. Davies and A.J. Pearce, 76-91. Publication No. 132, Washington D.C.: International Association of Hydrologic Sciences.

Trustrum, N.A., V.J. Thames and M.G. Lamber. 1984. "Soil Slip Erosion as a Constraint to Hill Country Pasture Production." *Proceedings New Zealand Grassland Association* 45:66-76.

UNESCO/UNEP/FAO. 1978. "Tropical Forest Ecosystems." *Natural Resources*

Research XIV. Paris: UNESCO.

Wiersum, K.F. 1984. "Surface Erosion Under Various Tropical Agroforestry Systems." In *Symposium on Effects of Forest Land Use on Erosion and Slope Stability*, edited by C.L. O'Loughlin and A.J. Pearce, 231-239, Honolulu: East-West Center.

World Water. 1981. "How Trees Can Combat Droughts and Floods." *World Water* 4:10, 18.

Zadroga, F. 1981. "The Hydrological Importance of a Montane Cloud Forest Area of Costa Rica." In *Tropical Agricultural Hydrology*, edited by R. Lal and F.W. Russell, 59-73. New York: Wiley.

Zwerman, P.J. and F. Richard. 1959. "Protective Forestry in Switzerland." *Soil and Water Conservation* 14:220-223.

Part Two
NEW ISSUES

CHAPTER 4

Climate Change and Mountain Ecosystems

MARTIN F. PRICE AND JOHN R. HASLETT

Introduction

Over the past decade, the issue of climate change has risen rapidly to an important position on international scientific and political agendas. A number of key events in this process may be identified, beginning with the 1988 Conference on "The Changing Atmosphere" (World Meteorological Organization 1989), and the consequent establishment of the Intergovernmental Panel on Climate Change (IPCC). The three Working Groups of the IPCC presented their first reports (Houghton et al. 1990; Tegart et al. 1990; IPCC Working Group III 1990) to the Second World Climate Conference in 1990 (Jaeger and Ferguson 1991), which provided a major impetus to the formulation of a Framework Convention on Climate Change. This was signed by the heads of state of most of the world's nations at the 1992 UN Conference on Environment and Development. Yet, although mountains occupy a considerable part of the world's land surface and are directly or indirectly vital for a significant proportion of the global population, little explicit attention has been given to the possible implications of climate change for mountain ecosystems. Only one international meeting, held in 1992 in Davos, Switzerland, has been entirely devoted to this topic (ProClim 1992).

For those who make decisions concerning the future of mountain regions, recognition of the likelihood of rapid climate change leads to some of the greatest uncertainties they are likely to face. The purpose of this chapter is to outline the complexities and implications connected with climate change and its potential results for mountain areas. This chapter considers, first, climate change and mountain climates; second, potential changes in mountain ecosystems — particularly their vegetation — resulting from climate change; and, third, methods for assessing these changes. It concludes with a discussion of some of the long-term implications to be considered by those responsible for managing mountain protected areas.

Climate Change and Mountain Climates

Climate is usually described, for convenience, in terms of long-term (typically 30-year) averages of a range of parameters. It varies continuously, at all scales of time and space; the variation at daily and local scales we call the weather. Both climate and weather are ways of describing the variety of states of the Earth's atmosphere, which is a non-linear (chaotic) system (Gleick 1987). The atmosphere's chaotic nature represents one of the greatest problems in climatology. While recognition of this problem means that specific predictions of the rate and degree of future changes in climate are not possible, it does not prevent projection of a range of likely future climates and the study of the responses of ecosystems to these.

There is now a general consensus within the scientific community that the global climate — and therefore its regional components, including mountain climates — is likely to change over coming decades, at rates unprecedented in human history (Houghton et al. 1990, 1992, Schneider 1989b). This means that, at any point on Earth, over the next few decades, significant changes in long-term averages (e.g., temperatures, rainfall, sunshine) and in frequencies of extremes (e.g., floods, droughts, storms) may occur. It appears likely that the global average temperature will rise to the highest level of the past 100,000 years, during which most mountain ecosystems have evolved (Huntley and Webb 1988; Schneider and Londer 1984). Yet, even if the average global temperature rises, there may be — at least for some decades — places where average temperatures will stay the same, or even decrease. In addition, it is very unclear how the projected increase in average global temperature would affect patterns of rainfall, snowfall, and soil moisture (Mitchell et al. 1990).

The definite identification of climate change will be based on a certainty that significant changes have been, and are occurring over all parts of the globe over a period of many years. Yet, for a number of interlinked reasons, it is not possible to specify whether a period of rapid climate change has begun. Even though available data show an upward trend in average global temperature, these data neither extend far enough back in time, nor do they provide adequate coverage around the Earth, to allow the conclusion that statistically-significant changes in the global climate are occurring (Folland et al. 1992, Wigley and

Barnett 1990). Nevertheless, three undeniable facts suggest that an era of climate change is likely in the near future, if it has not already arrived (Shine et al. 1990, Watson et al. 1990). The first fact is that two independent types of research show that atmospheric concentrations of a number of gases are increasing. Polar ice sheets include air bubbles that record the chemical composition of air trapped for many millennia. Ice cores from these glaciers show that concentrations of carbon dioxide (CO_2), nitrous oxide (NO_2), and methane (CH_4) have increased over the past three centuries. For the past two to three decades, these upward trends have been corroborated by analysis of air samples collected at isolated locations far from centers of population or industrialization. These data show increasing concentrations of not only CO_2, NO_2, and CH_4, but also man-made chlorofluorocarbons (CFCs). The second fact is that laboratory experiments show that the addition of any of these gases to a volume of air permits it to absorb additional infrared radiation. The third fact is that the Earth emits infrared radiation. Added together, these facts suggest that, as the atmospheric concentrations of these gases increase, the energy balance of the Earth-atmosphere system is likely to change, so that the atmosphere as a whole will warm — the phenomenon described as "global warming."

The principal causes for the increasing concentrations of the infrared-absorbing gases (or "greenhouse gases") are found not in natural processes, but in human activities (Watson et al. 1990). The combustion of fossil and organic fuels releases CO_2 and NO_2. During the production and distribution of fossil fuels, the cultivation of wetland rice, and the raising of livestock, CH_4 is released. All three gases are released as a consequence of forest clearing and agricultural activities. Finally, CFCs are released from leaking refrigerators and air conditioners and during the manufacture of electronic components. Thus, the precursors to likely climate change — increasing concentrations of greenhouse gases — derive not only from industrial processes and the use of fossil-fuelled transport, but also from the daily activities of all of humankind: growing, harvesting, preserving, and cooking food; and heating and cooling homes and workplaces.

It is inconceivable for human populations to cease these daily activities. There are however, technological, economic, and policy solutions that may be used to limit emissions of greenhouse gases, and therefore likely rates of climate change. The identification and implementation of such solutions are a major focus of current developments in global environmental policy (Andresen and Wettestad 1992). Given the likely implications of climate change for protected mountain areas, those concerned with the management of these areas should consider how they might contribute to the creation and implementation of policies to limit emissions of greenhouse gases.

For mountain climates and the likely implications of climate change in mountain regions, one should note that these climates are characterized by marked diurnal and seasonal cycles, with high variability at all spatial scales. In any mountain region, the diverse relief, aspect, and slope further increase both temporal and spatial variability (Barry 1986, 1992b). The availability of long-term year-round climatological data for mountain regions is highly variable (Barry 1992a), and such data tend to be available more readily from settlements close to the mountains or in valleys than from mountain sides and peaks. Consequently, even when data are available, they often do not provide a good overall description of the climate of an entire mountain area, because relationships between climatic variables in mountains and neighboring areas are highly complex (Barry 1990).

Some mountain areas contain quite dense networks of meteorological stations at many altitudes. Such networks, however, often record only data for part of the year (e.g., winter, for providing information useful for predicting avalanches), and measurement at individual sites may not have taken place for long enough to provide a statistically valid — or useful — description of the local climate. Very small changes in the location of measurement sites can result in considerable changes in the data collected. To summarize, it is evident that there are considerable difficulties in describing mountain climates even under current conditions. Yet, research on possible future climates requires baseline descriptions of current climates from which projections can be made.

Apart from the chaotic nature of climate, there are other reasons, of more regional importance, why scientific projections of global climate are not likely to be available in the foreseeable future. These reasons are all more pronounced in heterogeneous regions, such as mountains. The first has already been noted: the lack of climate data sets for locations around the globe over an adequately long time period. Clearly, this problem is particularly difficult in mountain areas, though it also applies to much of the world's oceans (Folland et al. 1990). A second is the inadequate knowledge of the interactions of the atmosphere and the Earth's other systems, particularly with regard to the roles of clouds and vegetation in influencing the Earth's radiation balance and of the oceans in absorbing heat (Cusbach and Cess 1990, Gates et al. 1992). Both of these cause problems in constructing climate models from which projections could be drawn. Yet another reason relates specifically to the computers in which such models are constructed. These models are known as GCMs: General Circulation Models or Global Climate Models, depending on their history and who is describing them.

GCMs require immense computational capacity. For example, a state-of-the-art GCM that portrays the Earth's surface and atmosphere as a grid of cells spaced at 4.5° latitude and 7.5° longitude (about 500 by 640 km at 40° latitude), with nine vertical levels, has 17,280 cells. To calculate a year of climate statistics for all of these cells at realistic intervals (thirty minutes), using one of the most powerful current supercomputers, which can add nearly a billion numbers a second, requires ten hours (Schneider 1989a). In more concrete terms, each cell in this model is approximately the size of Colorado, which has an altitudinal range of nearly 3000 m. and a great diversity of landscapes including deserts, mountains, and plains. Yet Colorado's great variety of climates is, because of the model's constraints, described by a single set of statistics. To create GCMs with a finer spatial resolution will require far more powerful computers. Even if the power of computer processing continues, however, to increase as fast as in recent years, it is improbable that the spatial resolution required for projections relevant to mountain regions will be attained this century.

A number of additional problems remain to be addressed before GCMs would be able to produce information useful for assessing the potential effects of climate change in mountain regions. First, GCMs are typically used to produce outputs which represent a new equilibrium climate resulting from an atmospheric concentration of CO_2 which is double that of the pre-industrial era. Although some scientists foresee the possibility of sudden change as a result of global warming (Broecker 1987), and abrupt changes in regional climates have occurred in the past (Dansgaard et al. 1989), the general consensus is that climates will change gradually. "Transient" model investigations of gradual changes are a relatively new area of research (Gates et al. 1992), and suffer from all of the problems described above. A final problem is that the statistical outputs of GCMs are typically in the form of average values. For many ecosystems and their components, including people, extreme values are often more important. To provide such values would require considerable reconceptualization of the design and use of GCMs (Katz 1988).

In summary, given the non-linearity of the climate system, the considerable research needed to provide basic understanding of the complex interactions between its different parts, the problems of GCMs, and the great variability of mountain climates over both space and time, computer models will remain exploratory tools for defining potential future mountain climates for the time being. This applies not only to GCMs, but also to new approaches, such as the "nested models" being developed for the western United States and the Alps (Giorgi 1990, Giorgi et al. 1990). However, this does not mean that projections of possible future mountain climates cannot be constructed. The primary alternative approach is to develop scenarios: internally consistent descriptions of future climatic conditions over space and time. These may be derived from the output of GCMs, from geological, historical, or current analogies, or through the application of exfungi (e.g., O'Neill et al. 1987); and other soil organisms (Whitford 1992). To summarize, it appears likely that, even though the possible effects of CO_2 enrichment on mountain ecosystems may be very important, only a very generalized understanding of these effects will be available for a long time to come.

Direct Physical Responses to Climate Change

This section discusses the interactions of climate and the various components of ecosystems. It uses the chapter on natural tent phases. It is beyond the scope of this paper to discuss in detail potential changes in all of these components. Initial assessments for glacial, geomorphological, and hydro-systems, in particular, were prepared for conferences in 1989 in the Netherlands (Rupke and Boer 1989) and Armenia (Barry 1990, Kotlyakov et al. 1991, Luckman 1990, Slaymaker 1990) and the International Conference on Mountain Environments in Changing Climates, held in Davos, Switzerland in 1992 (ProClim 1992). This section concentrates on the vegetation of natural and semi-natural ecosystems, bearing in mind the comment of IPCC Working Group II that, for the reasons shown in Table 1, "...assessing the ecological and socioeconomic consequences of climatic changes for natural terrestrial ecosystems is a highly speculative endeavor" (Street and Semonov 1990).

Mountain ecosystems may be affected by climate change in two ways: first, by the increased concentrations of CO_2 available for photosynthesis (i.e., physiological responses); and second, by the actual changes in climate (i.e., physical responses). These two types of response are very closely interlinked, since physiological processes such as photosynthesis and respiration are closely influenced by temperature, water availability and, in the case of photosynthesis, sunlight. A basic assumption of assessments of the potential impacts of climate change on species is that, for each, there is an optimum range — and also threshold values — of climatic parameters for growth and reproduction and that, as climates change, species will be able to follow this optimal "climatic zone" with a lag from years to centuries. Physiological or behavioral adaptation, however, or even genetic adaptation, to changing climate are also possible.

PHYSIOLOGICAL RESPONSES TO CO_2 ENRICHMENT

Before considering how changes in climate might affect the distribution of plant and animal species, it is essential to briefly consider the potential effects of increasing atmospheric concentrations of CO_2 that would be partly responsible for these changes.

Very many experiments on the potential effects of CO_2 enrichment on

TABLE 1: SHORTCOMINGS OF APPROACHES FOR ASSESSING ECOLOGICAL EFFECTS OF CLIMATE CHANGE ON NATURAL ECOSYSTEMS (BASED PRIMARILY ON STREET AND SEMENOV 1990).

Direct transfer function approach

(analysis of current bioclimatic distribution of assemblages of flora and fauna to assess future distributions in response to climate change)

1) Species respond individually to climate change:
   •current assemblages will not move
   •**key species (pollinators, symbionts etc.)** may be absent
2) Responses to CO_2 will probably alter responses to climate
3) interactive effects of climate change are not considered:
   wildfire frequency, air pollution, herbivory, pathogenicity
4) Impacts of barriers to migration are not considered

Historical approach

(Inferences from past and present distributions of plant and animal species sensitive to critical levels of heat and moisture)

1) Climate change may evoke genetic responses, creating divergent races of species to take over newly evolving niches
2) Rates of climate change affect rates and degree of response
3) Range shifts in response to climate change depend on dispersal strategy
4) Individual species may respond differently to climate change in different ecosystems

Paleoreconstruction

1) Projected amount/rate of climate change is unprecedented
2) CO_2 variations in the past did not drive climate change
3) Dating uncertainties
4) Mean temperatures of past eras are only rough estimates
5) Projected climate change will occur with other pressures without precedent in previous eras:
   air/water pollution, human population growth
-> Paleo-based scenarios for species migration may give indications of mechanisms and patterns of dispersal, but not rates

Simulation models

1) Do not examine interactions at the landscape level:
   migration, dispersal, substrate change, spread of fire, pests, pathogens
2) Do not incorporate interactive effects of changes in:
   fire frequency, air quality, greenhouse gas concentrations, pest potential
   on multispecies perennial communities

Ecophysiological understanding

1) Long-term effects of increased temperatures and greenhouse gas concentrations are unknown
2) Inability to account for interactive effects:
   competition, herbivory, etc.

vegetation have been performed. Most have taken place under highly artificial conditions, however, often using only one species, usually seedlings; avoiding extremes of temperature and light; without limitations of water and nutrients; and excluding herbivores and pathogens. There have been few studies of complete ecosystems: none has been in a mountain environment (Koerner 1992b, Street and Semonov 1990). The results of the experiments show that responses to CO_2 enrichment are very species-dependent (Melillo et al. 1990). These responses include changes in photosynthesis, respiration, water use efficiency, reproduction, growth rate, form, nutritional quality (for herbivores), and ratios of roots:shoots and of seed production:vegetative growth (Curtis et al. 1990, Strain and Cure 1985). In real-world situations, all of these changes will be relevant, but many interactive processes will also come into play: between plants (e.g., competition, symbiosis, mycorrhizal infection); between plants and animals (e.g., herbivory, pollination); and between plants and microbes (e.g., disease, decomposition) (Street and Semonov 1990).

Reviewing the literature, Koerner (1992b) concludes that, because of diverse negative feedback processes, long-term responses of plant canopies to increased levels of CO_2 will be markedly different from the immediate responses of leaf photosynthesis. He proposes a hierarchy of criteria for delineating the differential sensitivity of different types of vegetation to increased CO_2. This approach leads to the initial conclusions that the effects of CO_2 enrichment are likely to be much greater for high-altitude plants than for most low-altitude plants, and that alpine plants are likely to be particularly sensitive. These hypotheses are now being tested at an altitude of 2500 m. near the Furka Pass, Switzerland, using open-top chambers in the most common alpine vegetation type (*Caricetum curvulae*) of the Central Alps (Koerner 1992a).

For forests, which compose a large proportion of mountain vegetation, the likely direct effects of increased atmospheric CO_2 concentrations are also unclear (Eamus and Jarvis 1989, Fanta 1992, Gale 1986, Peterson et al. 1990). These effects have been described as "the factor which is most difficult to evaluate in forest ecosystems" (Fischlin 1991). While research in subalpine forests in the western United States concluded that radial growth was enhanced in response to increasing CO_2 concentrations (LaMarche et al. 1984), similar research in the Alps found only vague relationships (Kienast and Luxmoore 1988). The possibility of conducting experiments to resolve this question is restricted by very substantial resources that would be required to construct experimental areas to provide statistically-valid data, by the long life-times of trees, and the myriad interactive processes of forest ecosystems.

A final important, but almost unknown, group of responses of mountain ecosystems to CO_2 enrichment involves their below-ground components.

These include the below-ground parts of plants, which comprise a large proportion of the biomass of many mountain communities (Billings 1974b, Klug-Puempel 1989); their associated mycorrhizal fungi (e.g., O'Neill et al. 1987); and other soil organisms (Whitford 1992). To summarize, it appears likely that, even though the possible effects of CO_2 enrichment on mountain ecosystems may be very important, only a very generalized understanding of these effects will be available for a long time to come.

Direct Physical Responses to Climate Change

This section discusses the interactions of climate and the various components of ecosystems. It uses the chapter on natural terrestrial ecosystems in the report of IPCC Working Group II (Street and Semonov 1990) as a primary source, with specific discussion of the implications for mountain ecosystems wherever possible.

The component of climate change on which most attention has been focussed is increasing temperature. There are a number of reasons for this. First, it is the most obvious change, which would result in other changes (e.g., soil moisture, evapotranspiration, fire frequency and severity). Second, it is the change for which there is the greatest agreement between GCMs. Third, it is the change that can be most easily assessed for past (paleo-) and recent climates, from which parallels for future climates can be drawn. Fourth, there is a large literature on the influences of temperature on the distribution of species and on ecological processes. This last point also applies to water; and the distribution of vegetation types can be treated as determined by the interaction of temperature and water regimes (Ellenberg 1988, Holdridge 1964, Ozenda 1988). Furthermore, for the distribution and survival of many flora and fauna, temperature may be a less important factor than moisture (Billings 1974a, Woodward 1992). Yet, while water is crucial in all ecosystem processes and interactions, the outputs of GCMs vary greatly in their projections of changes in precipitation and soil moisture, as noted above.

Like any climatic variable, temperature can be described in a number of ways: means, ranges, extremes, etc. As mentioned above, GCMs primarily provide information about possible changes in means, and assessments of future distributions of flora and fauna have primarily been based on such information. Yet, for many animal and plant species, both actual extremes and the length of the period over which organisms experience them are critical. For instance, while excessively low temperatures can prevent the germination of seeds (Bewley and Black 1982), very high soil surface temperatures can prevent seedling survival. Equally, temperature extremes are significant for the dynamics and distribution of many fauna, particularly insects (Mani 1968, Rubinstein 1992). Overall, the greatest concern is that rates of change in temperature may be greater than the ability of species to adapt or migrate; although this may be a lesser problem in mountain regions, where species may only have to move a few hundred meters upslope, rather than a few hundred km, as would be the case in flatter areas (Boer and de Groot 1990). Consequently, species may become extinct and, at the least, it is probable that ecotypes and genetic variation will be lost. Some species may become more abundant, however, and speciation may occur in response to new conditions (Smith and Tirpak 1989).

In addition to requirements for suitable temperature and precipitation regimes, a number of other factors limit the distribution of plant species. Among these, a suitable substrate is particularly critical. In temperate mountain regions, soils have had a relatively short evolution since the last ice age (Retzer 1974) and, even if seeds can reach new habitats whose climatic conditions are suitable, soil conditions may be inappropriate. This may be because soils have not evolved sufficiently; because their chemical or physical characteristics are unsuitable; or because they have deteriorated as a result of human activities. The latter, for instance, is the case in Berchtesgaden National Park in the Bavarian Alps, where soil has been eroded from areas whose forests have been cleared. Consequently, even if the climate improved, trees could not grow again in these locations (d'Oleire-Oltmanns 1990). Conversely, even under current climates, in areas from which trees have been cleared and where soils are appropriate, the growth of trees above the current anthropogenic timberline may be limited by fungal infections as, for instance, in the Alps (Schoenenberger, Frey and Leuenberger 1990).

In an era of climate change, the characteristics of soils would be expected to change gradually. Changes in temperature would probably lead to changes in the relative abundance of soil biota, thus affecting trophic relationships in soil food webs. Up to threshold levels, increases in temperature and available moisture would be likely to amplify the chemical and biological processes of soil development, promoting the decomposition of organic matter and thus accelerating soil formation (Whitford 1992). Changes in chemical composition would also be likely. Excessive precipitation can limit decomposition, however, and/or lead to increased erosion and downstream sedimentation (Melillo et al. 1990). Thus, estimates of average values of precipitation may not be useful in developing assessments of the effects of such changes; estimates of the intensity and amount of precipitation in extreme events may be of greater importance. Finally, changes in precipitation and temperature regimes could change the heights of water tables: a critical factor in the distribution of some species.

In some mountain ecosystems, another important ecological factor deriving from the interaction of temperature and precipitation is fire. The frequency of fires in many mountain ecosystems has been modified considerably by human actions, further complicating the projection of frequencies under new climates. Since photosynthesis is often limited by current temperature and CO_2 concentration, one can hypothesize that increases in these variables will lead to increased growth of vegetation and therefore to increased fuel loading. This problem could be exacerbated if mortality increases because trees are living in less optimal conditions and, particularly, if evapotranspiration increases (Franklin et al. 1992, Street and Semonov 1990). Over time, the distribution of certain species could be significantly changed as a result of new fire frequencies; as has happened as a result of human actions, for instance in the Rocky Mountains (Daubenmire 1943).

In addition to temperature, precipitation, soil moisture and type, and fire frequency, there are other physical constraints on the ability of organisms to disperse in response to changing climates and survive in their new environments:

a. changes in the frequency of other disturbances, such as avalanches, heavy snowfalls, major storms, floods, and droughts (Franklin et al. 1992);
b. changes in the depth and duration of snow-cover and in the length of the snow-free (growing) season. These are vital factors in the distribution of mountain flora and fauna (Ellenberg 1988. Holten and Carey 1992);
c. changes in cloud cover, which could alter the sunlight available for photosynthesis and also have other effects, such as changing rates of snow melt;
d. the availability of potential habitat. This is a major issue for species which would have to move to higher altitudes in response to a warmer climate, since mountain peaks are smaller than their bases. Not only is there a smaller area in each successive elevation zone, but potential habitats might not be available for species currently restricted to the tops of mountains (Peters 1992);
e. the availability of migration corridors. This is a crucial issue for species in the complex topography of mountains, and is exacerbated by the east-west orientation of many chains (e.g., Alps, Pyrenees, Himalaya).

Both of the last two constraints could be ameliorated or exacerbated by human actions. For instance, while corridors for migration could be kept open by appropriate land use management practices and policies, the expansion of agricultural land use to higher altitudes could decrease possibilities for dispersal (Street and Semonov 1990, World Resources Institute 1990).

The ability of organisms to disperse also depends on their own characteristics and their interactions with other organisms. A species' ability to disperse depends on its reproductive capability, its dispersal strategies and, for animals, its mobility (Gadgil 1971). Paleo-climatic studies suggest that few forest tree species would be able to disperse as fast as the projected changes in climate (Davis and Zabinski 1992, Roberts 1989). In addition, every species interacts with others in a wide range of relationships, to which must be added the multifarious intentional and unintentional human actions which can limit or assist species dispersal.

Individuals of a species not only have to be able to disperse successfully, they also have to become established in large enough numbers to reproduce and persist in their new environment, where they may encounter new competitors, predators, pests, or pathogens against which they have few, if any, defences; a situation which may have parallels in the introduction of exotic species by man (Mooney and Drake 1986, Vitousek 1988). Furthermore, obligate species may become unavailable because of responses to different components of climate change. Harte et al. (1992) cite the example of the subalpine plant *Delphinium nelsonii*, which is pollinated by broad-tailed hummingbirds. While the timing of the birds' migration is determined by photoperiod, the annual growth and development of the plant is a function of temperature and snowmelt. If the latter changed, the hummingbird might not arrive at the right stage in the plant's annual life-cycle to pollinate it, thus potentially leading to the latter's extinction.

A further suite of factors to consider are the differences in the life-history strategies of the organisms that compose any ecosystem (Rubinstein 1992). For instance, many insects and other small organisms, including microorganisms, have generation times much shorter than the plants and animals they utilize as sources of food. This means they could adapt to new climatic conditions more quickly, leading to increased pressure on "host" organisms (Franklin et al. 1992). In addition, the mortality rates of many insects are affected by temperature (Bale 1991), so that population sizes might be changed directly. This is likely to be of major importance for many phytophagous insect species and of particular relevance to the long-lived trees of many mountain forests, which tolerate a current climate that is far from optimal for regeneration and growth and therefore could be especially sensitive to the direct and indirect effects of climate change. Yet such trees could also benefit from climate change: a number of recent studies suggest that the growth rates of trees in high-altitude forests have increased in recent decades because of higher summer temperatures, the most important determinant of tree growth in these environments (Innes 1991).

The considerations of this section lead to three general conclusions. First, a "negative" response, such as local extinction, to changing environmental conditions is generally quicker than a "positive" response, such as colonization of new habitat (Smith and Tirpak 1989). Second, many of today's assemblages of organisms (communities, ecosystems, etc.) will not exist under future climates. This understanding derives particularly from theories of dynamic biogeography that suggest, as species respond in individualistic ways to changing environmental conditions, both plant and animal communities change continuously over time (Brubaker 1989, Hengeveld 1990, Sprugel 1991). These theories are based on a large number of paleo-ecological studies of a wide range of species (Birks 1989, Coope 1979, Davis 1983, Graham 1986, Van Devender and Spaulding 1979). Third, certain characteristics of species are likely to make them particularly sensitive to changes in climate. These include those which are at the edge of their range; geographically localized; genetically impoverished; poor dispersers; slow reproducers; localized and annual; highly specialized; or migratory. Many mountain species fall into a number of these categories; and many are relicts, having been isolated by past changes in climate (McNeely 1990, Street and Semonov 1990).

Approaches to the Assessment of Ecological Responses to Climate Change

There are clearly many difficulties in starting to assess the potential distribution of mountain flora and fauna in response to changing climates. Even with incomplete understanding, however, it is important for such research to be undertaken as an input to policy processes relating to the management of protected areas and other resources, and also to define future topics of research. The approaches described in this section principally refer to case studies for the future of the Alps. Comparable studies are beginning in many of the mountain National Parks and National Forests of the USA (e.g., Halpin 1993, Key and Marnell 1990). It is also likely and desirable that similar studies are planned or underway in other mountain regions where adequate data sets are available to permit the methods described.

Cartographic Approaches

Cartographic approaches are based on the assumption of optimal climatic zones mentioned above. The simplest method begins with maps of existing assemblages of species (e.g., plant species as described on vegetation maps). First, the spatial relationships between these assemblages and specific climatic variables are defined. Then, scenarios are used to determine possible future distributions of these variables. Finally, these are used to define the resulting new locations of the assemblages, taking other site factors into account. Such a study has been started for the Alps (Beniston and Price 1991, Ozenda and

Borel 1991). Given the fact that today's animal and plant communities are likely to disassemble in response to a changing climate, however, this type of method can be, at the best, exploratory and illustrative (Boer and de Groot 1990).

More realistic cartographic approaches start from the current distributions of individual species (rather than species assemblages), from which possible changes in response to changes in one or more climatic variables are assessed. One method uses physical and bioclimatic assumptions (e.g., the adiabatic lapse rate and species-area curves) to define new climatic zones. This circumvents the need for detailed information on the spatial distribution of climatic variables — which is unavailable for many mountain regions. Such a region is Nevada's Great Basin, where this approach has been used to examine potential changes for animal species, assuming that a warming of 3°C would cause potential habitats to shift upward by 500 m. The study suggested that numbers of mammal species would decrease most, followed by butterflies and resident birds (Murphy and Weiss 1992).

A second method, developed in Norway, uses a simple model that correlates the presence of plant species in 5 km (horizontal) x 100 m (vertical) grid cells with January and July mean temperatures and mean annual precipitation. The model has been used to predict shifts in the distribution of species in response to a 2°C increase in July and a 4°C increase in January temperatures. Initial conclusions are that most alpine plants will retreat upwards and some will be threatened, either by loss of habitat at high altitudes or of suitable microclimates, or through competition, especially from species moving uphill (Holten and Carey 1992). This work is being continued through monitoring and experimentation.

This single-species approach can be made more realistic, and therefore more complex, by incorporating a range of climatic variables, together with actual climatic data sets, and geographic information systems (GIS). In the Alps, bird atlases are being used, in conjunction with the development of climate scenarios, to investigate possible future distributions of sensitive bird species. A comparable study for the plant species of the Alps will be possible once the projected Flora of the Alps is completed, and statistical correlations are made between climatological variables and the distributional data contained in the Flora (Beniston and Price 1991).

MECHANISTIC APPROACHES

Mechanistic approaches use computer-aided modelling to determine the likely composition of future ecosystems in response to changing environmental conditions. The models, however, cannot provide information about possible future distributions of species in space. For the Alps, a first attempt to assess the potential effects of changes in climate used a forest stand simulation model, incorporating the results of seedling experiments to assess the concurrent effects of CO_2 enrichment. The results of model runs, each for 1,000 years, suggest that deciduous trees would invade the current montane and subalpine belts, resulting particularly in a reduction of the dominant conifer species. Given favorable seedbed conditions, however, conifers could expand beyond their present upper limits into the current krummholz and alpine zones (Kienast 1991). While these results are interesting, plausible, and useful for suggesting future research, one should note the exploratory nature of this approach. It is based on a mixture of empirical data and arbitrary rules derived from highly simplified representations of the complex processes of forest ecosystems and, furthermore, on the questionable assumption that the responses of seedlings to CO_2 enrichment are applicable to adult trees.

FURTHER APPROACHES

Two studies are currently starting to provide more realistic assessments of the future vegetation cover of the Alps. One of these will develop climate scenarios for the Alps, based on GCM outputs, and incorporate these into new simulation models of subalpine forest ecosystems. These models, including primary producers, decomposers, and dominant herbivores, will be more realistic than those used for previous studies (Fischlin 1991). A second study will link the mechanistic and cartographic approaches for both forest and alpine vegetation. In a first stage, a number of modelling and statistical approaches will be combined to provide statistical information about likely patterns of succession in plant communities, using vegetation, soil, climate, and topographic data. These outputs will then be introduced into a GIS in order to produce maps of possible future vegetation covers in response to climate change and other disturbances, including insect infestations and fire (Kienast and Brzeziecki 1992).

Implications for the Management of Protected Mountain Areas

The discussions above may appear to provide more problems than answers. Yet there is a considerable wealth of knowledge that is relevant for developing policies for the management of protected mountain areas, both for mountain regions in particular, of which the references cited above provide a very preliminary synthesis — far more in-depth compilation and synthesis is needed

— and for the conservation of biodiversity and protected areas in general (McNeely 1990, Peters and Lovejoy 1992, Wilson 1988). Yet, in defining management policies for protected areas, it must be clear what is to be protected, and why: species, biodiversity, or societal benefits (e.g., landscapes, stable watersheds). The following paragraphs attempt to provide some suggestions in these three directions, any of which may, of course, be either complementary or exclusive.

The ecology of a species is critical in determining the possibilities of maintaining populations that include a genetic variation that is adequate for the species' indefinite survival. Each species requires a particular set of interacting species and environmental conditions, including sufficient habitat. Thus, for instance, small invertebrates tend to require very different management strategies than large mammals (Haslett 1993b). The preservation of individual species in an era of climate change may require the maintenance of corridors for migration, active introduction to new potential habitats or, in the most extreme case, creation of appropriate habitats. Given the costs of the latter approaches, their scientific and political complexities, and competing demands for resources, it seems unlikely that great attention will be given to preserving individual species - although this may be an unintended result of legislation in certain countries, such as the Endangered Species Act in the USA.

In many cases, the most realistic method for preserving individual species may be within initiatives to maintain biodiversity, however it is defined and valued (Solbrig 1991, Wilson 1988). In this respect, not only number of species must be considered; the maintenance of functional groups (guilds) of organisms is also an essential criterion. One feature of protected mountain areas that may be of particular benefit for maintaining biodiversity is that they tend to cover a wide range of altitudes. Thus, if appropriate habitats can change fast enough, or can be created with the help of human intervention, it may be possible to maintain higher levels of biodiversity than in flatter areas (McNeely 1990). Conversely, because the area of habitat within each elevational zone tends to decrease with altitude, it may be difficult to preserve adequately large populations for long-term survival. While methodologies to design optimal reserve systems for maintaining biodiversity exist (Margules 1988), these assume unchanging environmental conditions and will therefore have to be modified to take climatic changes into account — once adequately detailed information becomes available. Research such as that presently beginning in the Alps and Norway may be of great importance in developing such new methodologies. Nevertheless, it must be realized that the establishment of protected areas is rarely based on such objective criteria; political decisions are usually determinant.

Given the individualistic responses of species to environmental change, it may only be possible to maintain ecosystems typical of the late twentieth century through considerable human manipulation, using techniques such as prescribed burning, artificial fertilization/insemination, and restoration ecology. Nevertheless, it is difficult to reproduce ecosystems in new environments; and more difficult to introduce and maintain component populations of animals than of plants (Jordan 1988).

Habitat mosaics of mountain areas are characteristically extremely complicated at a wide range of spatial scales, and this heterogeneity has a direct bearing on the structure of the ecological communities (Haslett 1993a). Thus, in order to maintain biodiversity, it is essential to maximize not only the area and altitudinal range of protected areas, but also the heterogeneity of their topography and of the associated sets of conditions and resources (e.g., soils, microclimates). In forested areas, individuals of each tree species should be represented by as wide a range of age classes as possible. Particularly in developing countries, however, these rules may be difficult to implement, as growing populations are likely to want to use land, previously unsuitable for agriculture, to produce crops in the new climatic regime. In industrialized countries, the possible expansion of agriculture, as climate changes, are already being assessed (Carter et al. 1991). Such land use problems also apply to the establishment of migration corridors between protected areas; in any case, it is uncertain whether enough corridors could be created (Graham 1988). One implication of these issues is that local people must be involved in defining and implementing management policies for protected mountain areas.

As well as preserving valued species and biodiversity, protected mountain areas are important for providing other public goods to human populations, and policies will have to evolve to reflect the changing importance of these different goods. In an era of climate change, the preservation of stable watersheds, a valuable role fulfilled by many protected mountain areas, may become even more critical. As discussed above, changes in climate may lead to considerably increased mortality of the vegetation on which human populations have traditionally relied to regulate the quality and quantity of water flows. Such problems may be further exacerbated if, as appears possible, episodes of extreme precipitation increase in number. Thus, just as policies for managing mountain forests originally reserved particularly to ensure long-term supplies of wood had to change as other societal functions became more important (Price 1990b), policies for managing protected mountain areas may have to find a new balance between "traditional conservation" objectives, such as the maintenance of biodiversity, and other functions such as the maintenance of an adequate cover of vegetation in watersheds. Compounding the challenges of defining new management strategies for protected mountain areas will be other changes in demands, especially for recreation and tourism, some of which are also likely to derive from climate change (Price 1990a).

Climate change is a likely response of the Earth's systems to human activities, and will result in fundamental changes in the Earth's ecosystems. As mountain ecosystems are likely to be particularly sensitive to climate change, and have a world-wide distribution, it is vital that their biological and physical components be monitored to provide both an indication of climate change and its effects and inputs to the definition and implementation of management policies. This applies especially to areas where intensive research has been undertaken in the past. With greater recognition being given to the interdependence of all of the Earth's systems — atmospheric, biological, and societal — policies for managing protected mountain areas will have to be flexible and reflect the growing societal demands on the new ecosystems which our descendants will find in the mountains of the twenty-first century.

Acknowledgements

An earlier version of this chapter was prepared for the "Parks, Peaks, and People" workshop organized in Hawaii Volcanoes National Park in October 1991 by the Environment and Policy Institute of the East-West Center (Honolulu, Hawaii). Atelier Temenos (Paris, France) provided partial support for the first author's contribution to the paper. We would also like to thank Andreas Fischlin, Felix Kienast, and Christian Koerner for providing unpublished research documents, and David Peterson for his contributions during and after the meeting in Hawaii.

REFERENCES

Andresen, S. and J. Wettestad. 1992. "International Resource Cooperation and the Greenhouse Problem." *Global Environmental Change: Human and Policy Dimensions* 2:277-291.

Bale, J.S. 1991. "Insects at Low Temperatures: a Predictable Relationship?" *Functional Ecology* 5:291-298.

Barry, R.G. 1986. "Mountain Climate Data for Long-term Ecological Research." In *Proceedings, International Symposium on the Qinghai-Xizang Plateau and Mountain Meteorology*, 170-187.

―――――. 1990. "Changes in Mountain Climate and Glacio-Hydrological Responses." *Mountain Research and Development* 10:161-170.

―――――. 1992a. "Mountain Climatology and Past and Potential Future Climatic Changes in Mountain Regions: a Review." *Mountain Research and Development* 12:71-86.

———. 1992b. *Mountain Weather and Climate*, 2 ed. New York: Methuen.
Beniston, M. and M.F. Price. 1991. "Climate Scenarios for the Alpine Region: a Collaborative Effort Between ICALPE and ProClim." *Environmental Conservation* 18:360-363.
Bewley, J.D. and M. Black. 1982. *Physiology and Biochemistry of Seeds in Relation to Germination*, vol. 2. Berlin: Springer.
Billings, W.D. 1974a. "Adaptation and Origins of Alpine Plants." *Arctic and Alpine Research* 6:129-142.
———. 1974b. "Arctic and Alpine Vegetation: Plant Adaptations to Cold Summer Climates." In *Arctic and Alpine Environments*, edited by J.D. Ives and R.G. Barry, 403-443. London: Methuen.
Birks, H.J.B. 1989. "Holocene Isochrone Maps and Patterns of Tree-spreading in the British Isles." *Journal of Biogeography* 16:503-540.
Boer, M.M. and R.S. de Groot. 1990. "Introduction, Findings and Recommendations of the LICC Conference." In *Landscape-Ecological Impact of Climatic Change*, edited by M.M. Boer and R.S. De Groot, 1-80. Amsterdam: IOS Press.
Broecker, W.S. 1987. "Unpleasant Surprises in the Greenhouse?" *Nature* 326:123-126.
Brubaker, L.B. 1989. "Vegetation History and Anticipating Future Vegetation Change." In *Ecosystem Management for Parks and Wilderness*, edited by J.K. Agee and D.R. Johnson, 41-61. Seattle: University of Washington Press.
Carter, T.R. et al. 1991. "Climatic Change and Future Agroclimatic Potential in Europe." *International Journal of Climatology* 11:251-269.
Coope, G.R. 1979. "Late-Cenozoic Fossil Coleoptera: Evolution, Biogeography, and Ecology." *Annual Review of Ecology* 10:247-267.
Curtis, P. et al. 1990. "The Effects of Elevated Atmospheric CO_2 on Belowground Processes in C_3 and C_4 Estuarine Marsh Communities." *Ecology* 71:2001-2006.
Cusbach, U. and R. Cess. 1990. "Processes and Modelling." In *Climate Change: the IPCC Scientific Assessment*, edited by J.T. Houghton et al., 75-98. Cambridge: University Press.
Dansgaard, W. et al. 1989. "The Abrupt Termination of the Younger Dryas Climate Event." *Nature* 339:532-533.
Daubenmire, R.F. 1943. "Vegetational Zonation in the Rocky Mountains." *Botanical Review* 9:325-393.
Davis, M.B. 1983. "Holocene Vegetational History of the Eastern United States." In *Late-Quaternary Environments of the United States*, vol. 2:

"The Holocene," edited by H.E. Wright, 166-181. Minneapolis: University of Minnesota Press.

Davis, M.B. and C. Zabinski. 1992. "Changes in Geographical Range Resulting from Greenhouse Warming - Effects on Biodiversity in Forests." In *Global Warming and Biological Diversity*, edited by R.L. Peters and T.J. Lovejoy, 297-308. New Haven: Yale University Press.

d'Oleire-Oltmanns, W. 1990. "The Interactions of Patchiness, Land Cover Type and Animal Distribution: an Evolution in Time and Space." In *Proceedings, Resource Technology* 90:369-375. Bethesda: American Society for Photogrammetry and Remote Sensing.

Eamus, D. and P.G. Jarvis. 1989. "The Direct Effects of Increase in the Global Atmospheric CO_2 Concentration on Natural and Commercial Temperate Trees and Forests." *Advances in Ecological Research* 19:1-55.

Ellenberg, H. 1988. *Vegetation Ecology of Central Europe*. Cambridge: Cambridge University Press.

Fanta, J. 1992. "Possible Impact of Climatic Change on Forested Landscapes in Central Europe: a Review." *Catena (supplement)* 22: 133-151.

Fischlin, A. 1991. "Workstation-Assisted Ecological Modeling and Simulation and the Impact of Climate Change on Ecosystems in an Alpine Region." Research Project paper, Bern: Swiss National Science Foundation.

Folland, C.K. et al. 1990. "Observed Climate Variations and Change." In *Climate Change: the IPCC Scientific Assessment*, edited by J.T. Houghton et al., 195-242. Cambridge: Cambridge University Press.

―――――. 1992. "Observed Climate Variability and Change." In *Climate Change 1992*, edited by J.T. Houghton et al., 135-170. Cambridge: Cambridge University Press.

Franklin, J.F. et al. 1992. "Effects of Global Climatic Change on Forests on Northwestern North America." In *Global Warming and Biological Diversity*, edited by R.L. Peters and T.J. Lovejoy, 244-257. New Haven: Yale University Press.

Gadgil, M. 1971. "Dispersal: Population Consequences and Evolution." *Ecology* 52:253-261.

Gale, J. 1986. "Carbon Dioxide Enhancement of Tree Growth at High Elevations." *Science* 231:859-860.

Gates, W.L. et al. 1992. "Climate Modelling, Climate Prediction and Model Validation." In *Climate Change 1992*, edited by J.T. Houghton et al., 97-134. Cambridge: Cambridge University Press.

Giorgi, F. 1990. "Simulation of Regional Climate Using a Limited Area Model Nested in a General Circulation Model." *Journal of Climate* 3:941-963.

Giorgi, F. et al. 1990. "Use of a Limited Area Model Nested in a General Circulation Model for Regional Climate Simulation over Europe." *Journal*

of Geophysical Research Atmospheres 95D11: 8413-8431.
Gleick, J. 1987. *Chaos: Making a New Science.* London: Cardinal.
Graham, R.W. 1986. "Response of Mammalian Communities to Environmental Changes During the Late Quaternary." In *Community Ecology*, edited by J. Diamond and T.J. Case, 300-313. New York: Harper and Row.
—————. 1988. "The Role of Climate Change in the Design of Biological Reserves: the Paleoecological Perspective for Conservation Biology." *Conservation Biology* 2:392.
Halpin, P.N. 1992. "GIS Analysis of the Potential Impacts of Climate Change on Mountain Ecosystems and Protected Areas." In *GIS and Mountain Environments*, edited by M.F. Price and D.I. Heywood, London: Taylor and Francis.
Harte, J. et al. 1992. "The Nature and Consequences of Indirect Linkages Between Climate Change and Biological Diversity." In *Global Warming and Biological Diversity*, edited by R.L. Peters and T.J. Lovejoy, 325-343. New Haven: Yale University Press.
Haslett, J.R. 1993a. "Complicated Habitat Mosaics and Insect Community Structure on Mountains." *Proceedings of the Royal Society B*: in press.
—————. 1993b. "Protection of Invertebrates in the Hohe Tauern National Park." *Wissenchaftliche Mitteilungen aus dem Nationalpark Hohe Tauern* 1: in press.
Hengeveld, R. 1990. "Theories on Species Responses to Variable Climates." In *Landscape-ecological Impact of Climatic Change*, edited by M.M. Boer and R.S. De Groot, 274-289. Amsterdam: IOS Press.
Holdridge, J.F. 1964. *Life Zone Ecology.* San Jose, Costa Rica: Tropical Science Center.
Holten, J.I. and P.D. Carey. 1992. *Responses of Climate Change on Natural Terrestrial Ecosystems in Norway.* Forskningsrapport 29. Trondheim: Norwegian Institute for Nature Research.
Houghton, J.T. et al., (eds.). 1990. *Climate Change: the IPCC Scientific Assessment.* Cambridge: Cambridge University Press.
—————. 1992. *Climate Change 1992.* Cambridge: Cambridge University Press.
Huntley, B. and T. Webb, (eds.). 1988. *Vegetation History.* Dordrecht: Kluwer.
Innes, J.L. 1991. "High-altitude and High-latitude Tree Growth in Relation to Past, Present and Future Global Climate Change." *The Holocene* 1:168-173.
Jamieson, D. 1988. "Grappling for a Glimpse of the Future." In *Societal Responses to Regional Climatic Change*, edited by M.H. Glantz, 73-93. Boulder: Westview.
IPCC Working Group III. 1990. *Formulation of Response Strategies.* Geneva:

World Meteorological Organization/United Nations Environment Programme.
Jaeger, J. and H.L. Ferguson. (eds.). 1991. *Climate Change: Science, Impacts and Policy*. Cambridge: Cambridge University Press.
Jordan, W.R. 1988. "Ecological restoration." In *Biodiversity*, edited by E.O. Wilson, 311-316. Washington DC: National Academy Press.
Katz, R.W. 1988. "Statistics of Climate Change: Implications for Scenario Development." In *Societal Responses to Regional Climatic Change*, edited by M.H. Glantz, 95-112. Boulder: Westview.
Key, C.H. and L.F. Marnell. 1990. *Global Change Operations and Conceptual Research Plan for Glacier National Park Biogeographic Area*. West Glacier: Glacier National Park.
Kienast, F. 1991. "Simulated Effects of Increasing Atmospheric CO_2 and Changing Climate on the Successional Characteristics of Alpine Forest Ecosystems." *Landscape Ecology* 5:225-238.
Kienast, F. and B. Brzeziecki. 1992. "Potential Temporal and Spatial Responses of Forest Communities to Climate Change: Application of Two Simulation Models for Ecological Risk Assessment." *Swiss Climate Abstracts Special Issue: International Conference on Mountain Environments in Changing Climates*: 36-37. Bern: ProClim.
Kienast, F. and R.J. Luxmoore. 1988. "Tree-ring Analysis and Conifer Growth Responses to Increased Atmospheric CO_2 Levels." *Oecologia* 76:487-495.
Klug-Puempel, B. 1989. "Phytomasse and Nettoproduktion naturnaher und anthropogen beeinflusster alpiner Pflanzengesellschaften in den Hohe Tauern." In *Struktur und Funktion von Graslandoekosystemen im Nationalpark Hohe Tauern*, edited by A. Cernusca, 331-355. Innsbruck: Wagner.
Koerner, C. 1992a. "Impact of Atmospheric Changes on High Altitude Vegetation." *Swiss Climate Abstracts Special Issue: International Conference on Mountain Environments in Changing Climates*: 38. Bern: ProClim.
—————. 1992b. "Response of Alpine Vegetation to Global Climate Change." *Catena (supplement)* 22:85-96.
Kotlyakov, V.M. et al. 1991. "Climate Change and Glacier Fluctuation in the Southern Mountains of the USSR During the Last 1,000 Years." *Mountain Research and Development* 11:1-12.
LaMarche, V.C. et al. 1984. "Increasing Atmospheric Carbon Dioxide: Tree-ring Evidence for Growth Enhancement in Natural Vegetation." *Science* 225:1019-1021.
Luckman, B.H. 1990. "Mountain Areas and Global Change: a View from the

Canadian Rockies." *Mountain Research and Development* 10:183-195.
Mani, M.S. 1968. *Ecology and Biogeography of High Altitude Insects.* The Hague: Junk.
Margules, C.R. et al. 1988. "Selecting Networks of Reserves to Maximize Biological Diversity." *Biological Conservation* 43:63-76.
McNeely, J.A. 1990. "Climate Change and Biological Diversity: Policy Implications." In *Landscape-ecological Impact of Climatic Change*, edited by M.M. Boer and R.S. De Groot, 406-429. Amsterdam: IOS Press.
Melillo, J. et al. 1990. "Effects on Ecosystems." In *Climate Change: the IPCC Scientific Assessment*, edited by J.T. Houghton et al., 287-318. Cambridge: Cambridge University Press.
Mitchell, J.F.B. et al. 1990. "Equilibrium Climate Change." In *Climate Change: the IPCC Scientific Assessment*, edited by J.T. Houghton et al., 139-173. Cambridge: Cambridge University Press.
Mooney, H.A. and J.A. Drake. (eds.). 1986. *Ecology of Biological Invasions of North America and Hawaii.* New York: Springer.
Murphy, D.D. and S.B. Weiss. 1992. "Effects of Climate Change on Biological Diversity in Western North America: Species Losses and Mechanisms." In *Global Warming and Biological Diversity*, edited by R.L. Peters and T.J. Lovejoy, 355-368. New Haven: Yale University Press.
O'Neill, E.G. et al. 1987. "Elevated Atmospheric CO_2 Effects on Seedling Growth, Nutrient Uptake and Rhizosphere Bacterial Population of *Liriodendron tulipifera*." *Plant and Soil* 104:3-11.
Ozenda, P. 1988. *Die Vegetation der Alpen.* Stuttgart: Fischer.
Ozenda, P. and J.L. Borel. 1991. *Les Consequences Ecologiques Possibles des Changements Climatiques dans l'arc Alpin.* Le Bourget-du-Lac: International Centre for Alpine Environments.
Peters, R.L. 1992. "Conservation of Biological Diversity in the Face of Climate Change." In *Global Warming and Biological Diversity*, edited by R.L. Peters and T.J. Lovejoy, 15-30. New Haven: Yale University Press.
Peters, R.L. and T.J. Lovejoy. (eds.). 1992. *Global Warming and Biological Diversity.* New Haven: Yale University Press.
Peterson, D.L. et al. 1990. "Growth Trends of Whitebark Pine and Lodgepole Pine in a Subalpine Sierra Nevada Forest, California, USA." *Arctic and Alpine Research* 22:233-243.
Price, M.F. 1990a. "The Sustainable Future of Mountain Communities: Resources and Tourism in the Context of Climate Variability and Change." Paper, International Coordinating Council of the UNESCO Man and the Biosphere Programme.
———. 1990b. "Temperate Mountain Forests: Common-pool Resources with Changing, Multiple Outputs for Changing Communities." *Natural*

Resources Journal 30:685-707.
ProClim, 1992. *Swiss Climate Abstracts Special Issue: International Conference on Mountain Environments in Changing Climates*. Bern: ProClim.
Retzer, J.L. 1974. "Alpine Soils." In *Arctic and Alpine Environments*, edited by J.D. Ives and R.G. Barry, 771-802. London: Methuen.
Roberts, L. 1989. "How Fast Can Trees Migrate?" *Science* 243:735-737.
Rubinstein, D.I. 1992. "The Greenhouse Effect and Changes in Animal Behavior: Effects on Social Structure and Life-History Strategies." In *Global Warming and Biological Diversity*, edited by R.L. Peters and T.J. Lovejoy, 180-192. New Haven: Yale University Press.
Rupke, J. and M.M. Boer. (eds.). 1989."Landscape Ecological Impact of Climatic Change on Alpine Regions, with Emphasis on the Alps." Report prepared for European Conference on Landscape Ecological Impact of Climatic Change, Lunteren. Wageningen, Utrecht and Amsterdam: Agricultural University of Wageningen and Universities of Utrecht and Amsterdam.
Schneider, S.H. 1989a. *Global Warming: Are We Entering the Greenhouse Century?* San Francisco: Sierra Club.
——————— 1989b. "The Greenhouse Effect: Science and Policy." *Science* 243:771-781.
Schneider, S.H. and R. Londer. 1984. *The Coevolution of Climate and Life*. San Francisco: Sierra Club.
Schoenenberger, W., W. Frey and F. Leuenberger. 1990. "Oekologie und Technik der Aufforstung im Gebirge - Anregungen fuer die Praxis." *Bericht* 325. Birmensdorf: EAFV.
Shine, K.P. et al. 1990. "Radiative Forcing of Climate." In *Climate Change: the IPCC Scientific Assessment*, edited by J.T. Houghton et al., 45-74. Cambridge: Cambridge University Press.
Slaymaker, O. 1990. "Climate Change and Erosion Processes in Mountain Regions of Western Canada." *Mountain Research and Development* 10:171-182.
Smith, J.B. and D. Tirpak. 1989. *The Potential Effects of Global Climate Change on the United States*. Report EPA-230-05-89-050. Washington DC: US Environmental Protection Agency.
Solbrig, O.T. 1991. "Biodiversity: Scientific Issues and Collaborative Research Proposals." *MAB Digest* 9. Paris: UNESCO.
Sprugel, D.G. 1991. "Disturbance, Equilibrium, and Environmental Variability: What is 'Natural' Vegetation in a Changing Environment?" *Biological Conservation* 58:1-18.
Strain, B.R. and J.D. Cure. (eds.). 1985. "Direct Effects of Increasing Carbon Dioxide on Vegetation." Report DOE/ER 0238. Washington DC: Office

of Energy Research, US Department of Energy.
Street, R.B. and S.M. Semenov. (eds.). 1990. "Natural Terrestrial Ecosystems." In *Climate Change: the IPCC Impacts Assessment*, edited by W.J.McG. Tegart et al., 3/1-3/44. Canberra: Australian Government Publishing Service.
Tegart, W.J.McG. et al. (eds.). 1990. *Climate Change: the IPCC Impacts Assessment*. Canberra: Australian Government Publishing Service.
Van Devender, T.R. and W.G. Spaulding. 1979, "Development of Vegetation and Climate in the Southwestern United States." *Science* 204:701-710.
Vitousek, P.M. 1988. "Diversity and Biological Invasion of Oceanic Islands." In *Biodiversity*, edited by E.O. Wilson, 181-189. Washington DC: National Academy Press.
Watson R.T., et al. 1990. "Greenhouse Gases and Aerosols." In *Climate Change: the IPCC Scientific Assessment*, edited by J.T. Houghton et al., 1-44. Cambridge: Cambridge University Press.
Whitford, W.G. 1992. "Effects of Climate Change on Soil Biotic Communities and Soil Processes." In *Global Warming and Biological Diversity*, edited by R.L. Peters and T.J. Lovejoy, 124-136. New Haven: Yale University Press.
Wigley, T.M.L. and T.P. Barnett. 1990. "Detection of the Greenhouse Effect in the Observations." In *Climate Change: the IPCC Scientific Assessment*, edited by J.T. Houghton et al., 243-259. Cambridge: Cambridge University Press.
Wilson, E.O. (ed.). 1988. *Biodiversity*. Washington DC: National Academy Press.
Woodward, F.I. 1992. "A Review of the Effects of Climate on Vegetation: Ranges, Competition, and Composition." In *Global Warming and Biological Diversity*, edited by R.L. Peters and T.J. Lovejoy, 105-123. New Haven: Yale University Press.
World Meteorological Organization, 1989. *The Changing Atmosphere: Conference Proceedings*. Report 710. Geneva: WMO.
World Resources Institute, 1990. *World Resources 1990-91*. Oxford: Oxford University Press.

CHAPTER 5

Hazards and Disaster in Mountain Environments: Problems in the Geography of Risk

KENNETH HEWITT

Introduction

RISK IN THE MOUNTAIN CONTEXT

The geography of risk involves the description and evaluation of two sets of phenomena. First, there are those of the actual incidence and distribution of damage to human societies. Here, studies have tended to focus upon sudden, short-lived or more extreme bouts of damage, and damaging events affecting communities, regions and states. Other fields usually deal with "chronic" or longer-term risks of, for example, disease, crime, or environmental deterioration. Problems of that sort specially associated with high mountains include those of hypoxia and goitre (Baker 1978; Goldstein et al. 1983). I will concentrate upon the short-lived events, but recognising the distinction arises mainly from the history of investigation and professional specialisation. The problems are not separate in practice nor causation, as is made clear by the second set of phenomena.

These concern the contexts and broader explanation of how risks arise. They include continuing conditions of everyday life and developments that tend to decide whether, to whom and with what intensity, damages may occur. They are important both for the interpretation of risk and in identifying strategies that will mitigate or prevent damage. Included are matters directly concerned with given hazards, such as flood control works, seismic building standards, or emergency measures. Risk always depends upon the environmental and social context, however, and what is normally discussed in terms of material life, culture, and political organisation.

It is in this sense especially that we may speak of a *human ecology of risk*, and identify it with the general concerns of human geography (Burton et al. 1968). Hazards studies have developed, however, largely as an "applied" or problem-oriented geography. They ask questions of general geography largely from the baleful perspective of human tragedy and failed projects; how the continuing patterns of human ecology and geography relate to their role in moments of collective stress and devastation.

Hazards research in mountain areas has also looked mainly at short-lived damaging events, especially those originating in natural processes such as destructive avalanches and earthquakes, natural dams, or killing frosts. Much that has been written about hazards in mountains of late has been identified with, but possibly misled by, the notion of "the crisis in the mountains" (Eckholm 1975; Ives and Messerli 1981; Nilsson and Pitt 1991; Pitt 1978). Recent publications question this purported crisis or the form it is taking, for example in the Himalaya (Ives and Messerli 1989; Thompson et al. 1986).

To return to the general phenomena of damaging events, three more or less independent sets of factors must be considered, each with particular relations to mountain risks.

HAZARDS

These identify the processes or conditions that may initiate and are often the main, immediate causes of damage. They include natural agents such as flood or landslide, artificial ones such as toxic chemical spills, and compound hazards as in photochemical smogs. Avalanches are one of the unique hazards of mountain environments. Other natural hazards such as earthquake, rockfalls and vulcanism are more common or severe in them. A few social hazards are concentrated in the world's high mountain areas; for example risks associated with guerilla and counter-insurgency warfare, large dams, and deforestation-induced mass movements. Most natural and virtually all social hazards in the mountains are not peculiar to them, however, though their incidence reflects peculiarities of this setting.

HUMAN VULNERABILITY

Whether and how the above hazards result in damage, and at which places, depends upon the presence of human communities, their property and activities. The distribution and forms of *damage* reflect patterns of vulnerability in society. Disaster is often portrayed as "indiscriminate", death or survival a matter of luck. Careful investigation shows, rather, discriminate patterns of harm as a function of social geography, land uses, and built environments. Moreover, if damage is initiated by a hazardous agent, secondary and derived effects due to human conditions bring other, sometimes the main damages. Fire damage after earthquake, famine after drought or social upheaval, generally reflect living conditions, failures of social organisation, and, often, political and moral irresponsibility. Thus they depend primarily upon social or cultural factors of the communities involved.

Intervening Factors

The scale and scope of damages does not just hinge upon the impact of a damaging agent upon a vulnerable community. Whether and with what severity an earthquake or a forest fire, a dam-burst flood, or radioactive fallout, will harm human settlements in an area depends, sometimes decisively, upon other conditions. Flood dangers vary not only with the scale and frequency of flooding, but the geometry of valley sections and shorelines, the erodibility or stability of bank material, terraces and slopes reached by the waters, settlement patterns and the particular state or activities of people at the time of the flood.

In a given disaster or type of hazard, these "intervening factors" may appear to be incidental rather than fundamental aspects of risk. Looking at risk in terms of particular habitats, however, or at the range of risks in a region, they assume a prevailing and basic role. In mountains, damaging events involving the broadest range of hazards and social context are made more severe because of some common intervening factors. The universal problems of communication and access in mountain disasters is an obvious consequence of rugged terrain and extremes of weather common to them. There is a wide range of other recurring problems associated with steep slopes, heavy cloud or snow cover; exposure of the injured and homeless to cold, altitude and high winds.

In damage description and especially the geography of risk, each of the three sets of conditions and many phenomena within each, has its own distinct role. They appear as more or less "independent variables". Damage reflects, as it were, the locations and the moments when their overlap is fatal. The devastation that occurs in a particular place or region, represents only a small fraction of the area over which, for example, avalanches or strong seismic motions occur. Elsewhere they may even operate with greater intensity but cause little or no harm.

This seems a truism yet most risk research until recently, and efforts at hazard reduction, have assumed a severity and geography of risk based primarily upon hazard agents. The mechanisms, magnitude, and frequency of hazards have dominated the mainstream of work in the field (Hewitt 1983). That articulates with, and reinforces other, determinist frameworks of interpretation that have prevailed in mountain studies. Later we will consider alternative notions of risk, but first let me review the evidence of the incidence of damaging events and conditions of risk in mountain lands.

Damaging Events Associated with Natural Hazards

Natural hazards have received the greatest attention, and are often taken to be definitive of risk in mountain environments. A good overview is Price (1981). They are a significant part of mountain risk, and their prominence in the hazards literature warrants treating them first, if it also allows us to show the limitations and excesses of an approach based mainly upon them.

Certain "catastrophic" geophysical events, associated with mountains or magnified in these environments, give rise to singular devastation (Table 1). Most reflect the more extreme processes relating to geotectonic and topoclimatic conditions, but also climatic extremes and glacierisation, especially high relief and the rugged terrain (Barry 1981; Eisbacher and Clague 1984; Gardener 1989; Tufnell 1984; Voight 1978). Climatic and hydrologic processes tend to have the greatest impacts through the exaggerating effects of high altitude, high relief, steep slopes and large variability over time and space (Hewitt 1972; Price 1981).

Such disasters involve intrinsically interesting geophysical processes. Fortunately, however, the majority of such events have not led to disaster (Cruden 1976; Hewitt 1988b). If typical of high mountain environments generally, in any given place or region they tend to be rare and uncertain events. Few societies see the value of major investments in combating them, and only do so where large engineering structures or megaprojects, and sometimes dense urban settlements, are involved. The risks from these catastrophic events do become increasingly serious as more extensive and costly developments spread into the high mountains. These hazards pose severe and perhaps unacceptable risks for all-weather transport and communications, large dams, winter and summer resort areas, military installations and growing concentrations of population that go with them (Aegeter and Messerli 1983; Chavez 1989; Hewitt 1989). In all such developments, however, risk involves more than the understanding and location of possible natural extremes. The 1963 Vaiont Dam landslide in the Italian Alps, for instance, raised questions of the role of the project in triggering the slide, of poor planning and design. The arch dam

TABLE 1. EXAMPLES OF CATASTROPHIC EARTH SURFACE PROCESSES WHOSE INCIDENCE AND SCALE ARE UNIQUELY DEPENDENT UPON MOUNTAIN CLIMA-GEOMORPHIC ENVIRONMENTS, WITH SOME EXAMPLES OF DISASTERS THEY HAVE INVOLVED.

Catastrophic Phenomena	Disaster Events
1) Rockslides	Elm, Swiss Alps, 1881 Frank, Canadian Rockies, 1906 Vaoint, Italian Alps, 1963
2) Mud and Debris flows	Mayunmarca, Peruvian Andes, 1974 Karakoram, Pakistan, 1980 European Alps, 1987 Huanuco Province, Peru, 1989
3) Debris Torrents	Coast Range, British Columbia, 1983 Rio Colorado, Chilean Andes, 1987
4) (Snow and Ice) Avalanches	Steven's Pass, Cascade range. U.S.A., 1910 Austro-Italian Alps, war front, 1916 Swiss Alps, 1985 Korak, Pakistan Himalaya, 1989 Hakkari, Turkey, 1989 Western Iran, 1990
5) Earthquake triggered mass movements	Hebgen Lake, Montana, 1959 Huascaran, Peruvian Andes, 1970 Pattan, Pakistan Himalaya, 1974 Campagna, Italian Appenines, 1980 Mt. Ontake, Japan, 1984 Sharora, Tajikistan, Pamir, 1989
6) Vulcanism triggered mass movements	Mt. Tokachi, Japan, 1925

Ruapehu, New Zealand, 1969
Villarica, Chilean Andes, 1971
Mt. St. Helens, Cascade Range, U.S.A., 1980
Nevado del Ruiz volcano, Columbia, 1985

7) Weather triggered mass movements from volcanoes
Mt. Kelut, Indonesia, 1966
Mt. Semeru, Java, 1981

8) Natural dams and dam-break floods
   i) Landslide dams
   Indus Gorge, Western Himalaya, 1841
   Lake Rinihue, Chilean Andes, 1960
   Zerafshan, Pamirs, 1963
   Ecuadorean Andes, 1987

   ii) Glacier dams
   Gietroz Gl., Swiss Alps, 1818
   Chong Khumdan Gl. Karakoram, 1926, 1929
   Rio Plomo, Argentine Andes, 1930's
   'Ape Lake', British Columbia, 1981

   iii) Moraine dams
   Khumbu, Nepal Himalaya, 1985

   iv) Avalanche dams
   Santa R., Peruvian Andes, 1962

   v) Vegetation dams
   New Guinea Highlands, 1970

   vi) Artificial dam failures
   Buffalo Creek, Appalachians, U.S.A., 1972
   Teton Dam, Idaho, U.S.A., 1976
   Arandas, Mexico, 1980
   Java, 1989
   Shanxi Province, China, 1989

Major references:
1) Heim, 1932; ed. Voight, 1978; Eisbacher and Clague, 1985;
2) eds. Brunsden and Prior, 1984; Naef et.al. 1989;
3) Carson and Bovis, 1989; Pena and Klohn 1989;

4) IAHS, 1965; Price, 1981; ed. Voight, op.cit.
5) Hewitt, 1978; Keefer, 1984; Alexander, 1981;
6, 7) eds. Sheets and Grayson, 1979; Watt et.al. 1983, es. Okuda, et.al. 1983;
8) ed. Young, 1986; eds. Starosolsky and Melder, 1989; Richardson, 1968; Lliboutry et al. 1977; Hewitt, 1982; Tufnell, 1984; Costa, 1985; Costa and Schuster, 1988; Schroder, 1989; Vuichard and Zimmermann, 1987.

itself was little harmed though it had to be written off. The enormous death toll (c. 2500 persons) and devastation, were due to the flood wave propagated over it and on down the Piave valley (Mueller 1968; Selli, 1964).

Meanwhile, a global overview requires a sense of the relation of particular hazards to the distribution of actual damaging events. Table 2 summarises natural disasters by mountain region, based upon news reports, with a cut-off at events involving at least 10 or 50 injuries, or $1 million damage. The criteria are somewhat arbitrary, the information prone to the many limitations of news reportage. It does offer a useful first approximation to the geography of natural disaster in mountains.

The inventory points to the overwhelming roles of earthquakes and floods. The importance of landslides is under-represented here because much, sometimes most of the damage in earthquakes and floods, is due to slope failures triggered by them (Keefer 1984). Various hazards not normally identified with mountain areas occur in or near them. The hazards of mountainous coastlines may be mentioned. Settlements here can be at unusual risk from coastal hazards such as tsunamis and storm surges, partly because of shoreline topography, partly through the premium on low angle areas for settlement, and the occupying of the shores of sheltered inlets (Hewitt 1981). The worst damages have occurred in association with nearby seismic sources, as evidenced in the Alaska, 1964 and Chile, 1960 earthquakes (David and Karzulovic 1963). Large landslides may also set up giant waves that sweep the shores of bays and coasts with potentially disastrous effects for communities there (Miller 1960; Weischet 1963). Forest fires also present special problems in mountains, due to high winds or valley wind systems, the greater incidence of severe lightning activity and vulcanism, the way so many surviving mature forests are in remoter mountain areas and may be identified with fire determined or "fire climax" ecology.

Most natural hazards and disasters of mountain lands reflect features of the mountain environment. Less clear from risk defined by hazard, is how and why mountain habitats and human settlement in them suffer different degrees and forms of harm. The most frequent and costly of all natural agents of disaster in mountain regions, earthquake hazards, will serve to develop this point.

The Role of Intervening Factors and Vulnerability in Natural Hazards: The Case of Earthquake Hazard

Earthquakes are concentrated in and around mountains and initiate the most frequent and destructive of natural disasters in them. In addition to the association of most seismicity with orogenic zones, their relative importance must also be attributed to the great area over which strong and destructive motions occur in larger earthquakes. They may involve tens, hundreds and even thousands of square kilometres in Shallow or Intermediate earthquakes of higher Richter magnitudes, and even for Deep foci of the highest magnitude. Most other hazards occur in much more confined spaces as with large landslides or tornadoes, or are channelled, like riverine floods, in well-defined paths. Nevertheless, whether and where seismic shaking causes damage depends critically upon aspects of the surface environment and human settlement. Indeed, seismic parameters themselves are poor predictors of the forms, scale or location of damage.

A global survey comprising the 243 most destructive earthquakes reported for the 41 years, January 1950 to December 31st, 1990, will help identify conditions repeatedly associated with disasters (Hewitt 1978, 1981, 1983). These data are certainly incomplete, but such reports as are available in the seismological and disasters literatures, supplemented with contemporary news reports, allow a preliminary "actuarial" view. Twelve parameters are singled out as having widespread significance; three derived from locational correlates, and nine repeatedly mentioned in the sources (Table 2). In each case it was asked if critical variables such as slope instability, severe weather, habitat or societal change were reported as involved in major damages. Conditions or changes that are of general interest to the study and the problems of mountain lands were repeatedly identified as correlates of damage.

The most common attribute identifies whether damage occurred partly or wholly in a region of high relief. Evidently all but a few earthquake disasters do. It may be noted, however, that some of the most destructive examples, or the greatest damages in some of these cases, occur in areas of low relief. Earthquake disasters occurring wholly outside the mountains are, nonetheless, rare.

Since seismic events and orogenic belts are now seen as interdependent this relation is usually taken for granted, and other aspects of the mountain environment and mountain settlement treated as incidental or accidental aspects of risk. This is a mistake. Even a cursory survey of damages shows their close association with habitat features, and the geography and history of human society in the mountains. Two of the most common correlates of these disasters have no obvious relation to seismology or orogeny; the predominance of damages in mountain foot settlements, and the association with semi-arid to subhumid climates.

During surveys of a range of earthquake damage zones in the Eastern Mediterranean and Southwest Asia, I was struck by the frequency with which the worst damages were in cities, towns and villages in mountain foot and intermontane basin areas instead of the high mountains or steep-slope areas that had originally attracted my attention to this hazard. Looking at the location of severe and concentrated damages, or the place from which the disaster was named in the inventory, it was found that these included mountain foot settings in nearly all cases, and the worst damages in most. Damages occurred elsewhere, including in the more rugged mountain interiors. Mountain foot damage is a dominant feature of the vast majority of all earthquake disasters. In some regions with the greatest frequency of these disasters, for example, Iran, Japan, southern California, they are of overriding importance. Clearly, a major reason why mountain foot settings predominate in damage relates to the fact that, in most regions, much greater numbers of people, property and settlements are located here. This also points up the importance of mountain studies not mainly thinking in terms of the areas of highest relief, elevation and ruggedness.

More surprising is to find that, although mountains are so often associated with higher humidity, and although there is no causal relation between climate and seismicity, the great majority of earthquake disaster zones occur in places whose climate is semi-arid or sub-humid, usually with a pronounced dry season. An exceptional number, in comparison to seismicity, land area and human populations, occur in "Mediterranean" and "sub-Mediterranean" regimes (Hewitt 1981). I suggest the relationship reflects major historic patterns of human settlement and exploitation, readily exemplified by the Mediterranean lands. If this sounds like another environmentalist interpretation, however, it leads to a necessary loosening of that.

A variant of this role of mountain foot settlement, of which the "Mediterranean" lands again provide many examples, is the concentration of damage along mountain coastlines (Category 6). This applies to about a third of all the disasters, or about the same number as those in which rugged, mountain interior areas suffer substantial damages (Category 8).

The significance of mountain foot, dryland and mountain coastline settlements, is further emphasised in the fourth most frequently identified correlate of damage. It involves the cases in which there is rapid social and

TABLE 2. RANKING OF SOME DAMAGE CORRELATES OF EARTHQUAKE DISASTERS, FOR THE 243 MOST DAMAGING EVENTS REPORTED JANUARY 1, 1950 TO DECEMBER 31, 1990.[1]

Rank	Damage-associated attribute[2]	n
1	"Mountain Land"	236
2	Piedmont/intermontaine basin	183
3	"Dry Land" Moisture deficit Seasonal (145) Moisture deficit Perennial (28)	173
4	"Development" and social change stresses	143
5	Landsliding/slope instability	106
6	Coastal mountain settlements	73
7	"Susceptible" regolith	72
8	Mountainous interior settlements	68
9	Severe weather/exposure	42
10	Tsunami damages	26
11	Damming/dam bursts	20
12	Fires	12

Notes

[1] The examples are counted only where reports indicate substantial damages associated with the attribute. In many cases, however, the information relates to a verbal report, rather than a careful survey and must, in any case, be considered incomplete for all attributes except 1, 2 and 3, which are derived from cartographic location.

[2] Attributes:
1. Mountain land: damages occur partly or wholly in areas with local relief exceeding 1000 m.
2. Piedmont/intermontane basin: substantial and often most damages in settlements located in mountain foot, foothills or intermontane basin sites.
3. "Dryland" relation: where the regional climate of the damage zone has an arid to subhumid climate, with a seasonal or perennial moisture deficit, and specifically with a Budyko-Lettau Dryness Ratio of 1 or greater (Hewitt 1982).
4. "Development" stresses: where recent and on-going changes in settlement, economic activity and habitat are prominent features of the damaged area, and cited as causes of vulnerability in reports.
5,7. "Microseismic" responses: slope and earth surface materials that tend

to be unstable under seismic shaking, resulting in substantial damages.
6. Coastal settlements: where substantial or all damages reported in mountainous coastline settlements.
8. Mountain interior: where substantial damages reported in high relief and steep slope areas.
9. Severe weather: where substantial damage or human casualties and hardship reported from weather conditions and exposure following the earthquakes.
10. Tsunami damage: substantial damages to coastal settlements from seismic water waves.
11. Damming/dam bursts: reports of devastation due to flooding induced by earthquake-triggered mass movements and dam-break floods.
12. Fires: fire damages reported following earthquakes. Some of the most devastating urban earthquakes disasters have involved mass fires, but they are relatively rare in this set.

habitat change in the area of damage, and where observers attribute actual damages to that. It is here, especially, that the "crisis in the mountains" becomes integral to the risk of disasters.

Among the other categories, numbers 5, 8, 9 and 11 are associated with prevalent attributes of mountain habitats acting as intervening factors. The phenomenon of "susceptible soils" refers to situations where the foundations of structures lose strength, and break up, often due to liquefaction in areas of high water tables. Again, this is not only a problem of soil mechanics, but of the incidence of such superficial materials and the incentives for human communities to build on them. The complex depositional, topographic, and groundwater conditions of mountain foot, intermontane basin, and mountainous coastline settlement, are intimately involved with this problem. Almost invariably, damages are reported to relatively new structures and projects. Many are built in other respects to aseismic standards, but located on alluvial fans, stream terraces and flood plain areas, dry lake beds, and shoreline areas, often with the aid of artificial fill (Hewitt 1984).

Severe weather and exposure of victims are mainly associated with damages in mountainous interiors and higher elevations. They reflect problems of communication because rescue teams are unable to reach victims for extended periods. The western Himalayan disaster at Pattan in December 1974, and the Italian Campagna earthquake of November 1980, exemplify these problems and how they are magnified by winter conditions in the mountains (Hewitt 1976).

The evidence does not allow us to say what actual amounts and proportions of damage may be attributed to these factors, only that they are widely and crucially associated with the disaster events. Where detailed surveys of damage and damaging processes exist, however, the intervening variables of mountain habitats and patterns of human vulnerability appear even more crucial. That was already abundantly clear from the descriptions and maps of damage intensity for the 1906 California earthquake. These record remarkable, almost state-wide patterns of destruction and survival side by side, relating to the complex interaction of variable surface topography, materials, vegetation cover, land uses, and construction, more clearly than to distance from an epicentre or the much-remarked tectonic effects (Carnegie Institute 1908-10). That is in addition to the special role of building quality, siting, density and uses in the most concentrated damages due to the great fire in San Francisco itself (Reed 1906). Although seismic considerations still dominate the field, the so-called microseismic factors of surface conditions, and building design are now integral parts of risk surveys in that state and its municipalities (Palm 1990; Theil 1987). They are rarely so elsewhere, and yet the evidence points to their equally decisive role in virtually all earthquake disasters (Ebert 1988; Geipel 1982,1989, Gutierrez de MacGregor 1989; Hewitt 1976; Oliver-Smith and Hansen 1987).

The seismic performance of built structures is the main factor in material damage and casualties. Behind the infinitely complex details of structures exposed to these disasters around the world, however, their location, design, maintenance and protection are uniquely dependent upon the social and land use geography of the communities involved, in turn reflecting their economic organisation and development. All buildings also depend upon or are rendered insecure by the contingent conditions of habitat and society. Where seismic design and planning consideration have been the subject of concerted efforts, as in Japan and parts of Greece over recent decades, they help explain why there are relatively fewer or less damaging events than their exposure to large earthquakes would indicate.

The microseismic geophysical properties of surface materials, slopes, water tables and vegetation cover, add significantly to our understanding of damage patterns, and are clearly of profound importance in revealing the role of the mountain and piedmont habitats in the mosaic of risk. But even with that information, one could never predict actual losses without knowing the social and material geography of the exposed communities. "Seismological dominance" in earthquake risk is, however, typical of research and management strategies for all of the natural hazards in mountains. It exemplifies the "geophysicalism" or a "hazard determinism", which diverts attention from the elements of vulnerability and intervening variables associated with the human ecology of risks. In general, socio-economic conditions that are widespread and often of over-riding significance in damage and disasters, are ignored or treated as merely peculiar to particular cases. Yet these are matters of decisive importance in disasters, and of singular interest to those of us who study mountain environments. In large measure, they govern the actual geography of risk. Were we to examine any of the other natural hazards, avalanches or floods, landslides or severe weather hazards, the same style of work and reasoning would apply. One would find the overt or assumed determinism of risk by "the hazard", while actual damage and risk patterns show that to be only part, not necessarily the main part, of the explanation of what and who suffer damage or survive (Bode 1989). Before looking further at that, we must ask about other forms of risk.

The Big Risks: War and Other Armed Violence

If earthquake is the largest of the natural agents triggering disasters in the mountains, armed violence appears to be the principal social or "man-made" one. Armed violence is normally treated in other literatures, as are, say, crime, unemployment and drug abuse. The dominant concerns of military-political or geostrategic studies do not exactly view war as a disaster, though it is full of risk. Apart from certain obvious artificialities in these divisions, however, there are strong reasons to argue for its inclusion here. In particular, there is the way the weapons, the wars and other uses of armed force in the twentieth century increasingly have caused harm to non-combatants, settlements and habitats (Craig and Egan 1979; Elliot 1972; Hewitt 1983, 1987; Lifton 1971; Timmerman et al. 1991).

Mountain wars, so often originating outside the mountain regions and waged with more or less indifference to their well-being if not actually against mountain peoples, tend to be especially destructive of their communities and habitat. Moreover, though a war may last for years and comprise a struggle between enduring political units, the harm to people and places mainly occurs in sudden bouts of severe devastation. This may be as armies or the battlefronts pass through, in bombing raids, punitive and plundering actions, enforced conscription of menfolk, or scorched earth campaigns and environmental warfare (Branfman 1972, Lewallen 1971, MacLean 1987, Rooper 1987, Westing 1984). Thus, from the point of view of those at risk, and the form in which damages occur, the "disasters of war" tend to resemble those involving natural or technological hazards.

A preliminary assessment may be made by examining the incidence of conflicts in mountainous countries and regions. Again, "mountain regions" will be taken to comprise any areas with local relief exceeding 1,000 m or nations such as Peru or Afghanistan, that are largely mountainous. In the latest year, 1991, armed conflicts involving regular state forces were recognised in at least 34 countries (Regehr 1991:14-15). A third were taking place mainly in mountain areas, and nearly all involved them to some extent (Table 3). The only full scale international event, the Iraqi invasion of Kuwait and subsequent "Desert Storm" operation may not appear to involve mountains, but a low-lying tract of desert at the head of the Persian Gulf. Yet, the bombing in northern Iraq, and consequences of the war involve some of the worst impacts on mountain lands and peoples in any recent conflict. Much of the plume of smoke and toxics from the 600 or so oil wells set on fire in Kuwait drifted eastwards over the Zagros Mountains, drastically cutting the received sunlight, and polluting the land. "Black snow" is reported from Hindukush and Western Himalaya (Climate Institute 1991). The plight of the Kurdish victims of Iraqi military forces, continues to be violent (Johnson et al. 1991; UNDRO News 1991; Timmerman et al. 1991).

TABLE 3. ARMED CONFLICTS GOING ON IN 1991, BY STATE IDENTIFYING THOSE INVOLVING MOUNTAIN LANDS (AFTER REGEHR, 1991).

Region	All Conflicts	Involving Mountain Lands	Wholly in Mountains	Duration 10+ Years
Americas	5	5	5	
Europe	2	1	1	1
Africa	10	6	3	9
S. & S.W. Asia*	8	8	6	7
S. & S.E. Asia	9	9	7	9
TOTAL	34	29	22	31

*Region from Middle East to Indus Valley

The India-Pakistan border skirmishes, mainly in the Karakorum, are the only other strictly "international" conflict, although in such cases as East Timor, and Lebanon, regular forces present are considered invaders. The remaining conflicts are struggles between central government forces and regional, ethnic, or politically dissident groups. So often, the latter are residents of the mountains, have sought refuge there or are using the terrain to outwit government forces.

Sivard estimates that 90 percent of deaths in this year's wars were to civilians and, for the 1980's that three-quarters of all war-related victims were civilians (Sivard 1991:20). It is, perhaps, of even greater note that 30 of the 33 mountain region wars have been going on for ten years or more.

The picture at the outset of the 1990's, may be extended using the inventories of twentieth century wars compiled by Small and Singer (1982). These indicate that armed conflicts involving state forces and mountain lands are a recurrent, indeed, a permanent feature of this century (Table 4). These are only indicators. Some of the wars involved mountain areas to a limited degree. Others were fought entirely within them, or strictly against mountain people. The Second World War involved as many mountain regions and probably resulted in as much devastation to their environments and death to their peoples, as in all the other wars put together. The violence stretched from the mountainous islands of the Western Pacific to the mountains of Sicily and North Africa, and from those of Norway to East and South West Africa. Because it was a "world war", its many mountain campaigns, the countless mountain towns and villages bombed and strafed or wrecked in the land campaigns, seem to have got lost in the larger view of the conflict.

TABLE 4. ARMED CONFLICTS BY STATE INVOLVING MOUNTAIN LANDS, 1900-1980 (AFTER SMALL AND SINGER, 1982).

	Conflicts	Years of War
Wars with over 1000 battle deaths.		
1) Interstate and Colonial or Imperial Wars	33	c. 133
2) Civil wars	42	c. 111
Wars with less than 1000 battle deaths.	88	c. 182
TOTAL MOUNTAIN LAND WARS	163	426

The severity of war risks and their mitigation are far more intractable problems than most other hazards. The ravages of war commonly affect or threaten much if not all parts of a country at the same time. That limits or precludes the quick infusion of assistance from surrounding areas, as happens with most disasters. This is partly why a common result of warfare is uprooting of populations and a refugee crisis as the victims of war go themselves to places of safety and life support.

Again, the main instrument of rescue and relief in disasters, even when international relief efforts are involved, is usually the state military forces. In wartime these are either not available or, often enough, the cause of the disaster rather than a means to alleviate it. In mountain regions, modern states have rarely developed an equivalent system to the civil defence and emergency measures organisations of urban-industrial areas. It seems unlikely such arrangements for the self-defence of mountain peoples in war, would be politically acceptable in most countries, although a model for it is, perhaps, implicit in Switzerland's civil defence system. In any case, the consequences of the lack of protection or relief has been to greatly magnify the scale and scope of wartime tragedies in the mountains, even where that was not the goal of the warfare.

Enforced Uprooting, "Pacification," and Genocide

The destructive consequences and accompaniments of war for the inhabitants of mountain areas are not confined to the direct impact of warfare. Often it is violence rather than climatic or other natural and demographic problems, that lead to destructive land uses, social breakdown, and famine. Perhaps the largest of the tragedies stemming from this relationship is the "geographical calamity" of forcible uprooting. It is evidenced in the vast numbers of forced migrants, refugees, and displaced folk in camps, urban slums, squatter settlements or other "holding areas" of the various regions of violence. A great many of these folk are mountain peoples.

The millions of war refugees in camps from Sudan to Somalia and from Kurdistan to the Indian Himalaya are largely mountain folk. One estimate, in 1988, of war refugees in and around Afghanistan was 7.8 million, of whom 5.6 million had fled to havens in Iran, Pakistan, and Soviet Central Asia (Brogan 1990). There may have been as many as 1 million killed and many times that number permanently maimed. A majority of these folk came from mountain towns, villages and farmsteads of the Hindukush. Most of the refugees are in valley and foothill settlements or camps of adjacent areas, often bringing social upheaval, violence and environmental devastation there too.

The most devastating consequences have come from the use of modern weaponry to destroy villages, irrigation systems, orchards, roads and bridges; resulting in both enormous civilian casualties and laying waste of the habitat and resource base. The story is similar to the better-known "ecocidal" and social impacts of the Indo-China War, a substantial part of which involved mountainous regions (Lewallen 1971, Westing 1976). It is, of course, the opposite of a common view of the mountains as "refuges" from the misfortunes and powers of history. It reflects how modern surveillance and mobility, the weapons and the sheer scale of military force available, can render the mountains uninhabitable for any but warring groups. Even without B-52 raids and helicopter gunships or biocides and napalm bombs, well-equipped ground forces can cause massive damage to mountain lands and life.

The wars referred to above do not include countless, and often far more focused and destructive uses of armed force against or affecting mountain peoples and habitats. These include other agendas, carried out by armed forces under the cloak of war measures. They involve policing and punitive expeditions, acts of military occupation, weapons testing and military training activities by home forces and violence in the name of economic development or "the national interest". A great many of the victims of violence in the so-called "Arc of Crisis", from the Horn of Africa to the Western Himalaya are in fact mountain peoples caught up in civil and regional conflicts, guerrilla wars, or state actions underwritten by "Cold War" and hegemonic strategies. Asprey's (1975) comprehensive history of guerrilla wars and strikes, refers to dozens of examples in mountain lands. The war/rebellion against British colonial rule by the Mau-Mau in Kenya, and EOKA in Cyprus in the 1950's are examples of such warfare in the mountains.

Colonial and counterinsurgency warfare has included experiments with and the use of the most modern weaponry, including the machine gun, poison gas and napalm. The use of modern fire power and weapons of mass devastation against people armed with spears or bows and arrows has much to do with the scale of the disasters caused by armed violence in the mountains. Air power has been used in countless bombings of defenceless villages begun by the colonial forces of Italy and France in North Africa before the First World War, and by Britain in Iran and on the North West Frontier of India during that war and, many other places, between the world wars (S.I.P.R.I. 1971, Kidron and Smith 1983). Today, bombing raids are standard fare for all state forces in their troubles with mountain areas.

The most extreme but by no means uncommon uses of armed violence warrant the term "genocide" (Kuiper 1981). The genocidal expulsions and massacres of the Armenians of Turkey and Persia in the First World War were, among other things, a calamity for a mainly mountain people (Permanent Peoples' Tribunal 1985). It removed perhaps 1.8 million inhabitants, more than half by killings and death from privation, dwarfing the casualties in many battles as usually understood, and most natural disasters. But there are numerous other threatened destructions of mountain peoples at this moment. They include continuing uses of regular military forces against the Kurds, a mountain people, in Iran, Iraq, and Turkey (Chaliand, 1980); by China in Tibet and by Indonesia in East Timor (Amnesty International, 1985). Many of John

Bodley's "Victims of Progress" are indigenous mountain peoples, used for forced labour, exterminated or uprooted under the guise of national security measures (Bodley 1975). Such is reported from the Chittagong Hills of Bangladesh, mountain areas of the Philippines and New Guinea, from East Africa, the east slopes of the Andes, and Central America, to name a few (Amnesty International 1984, Minority Rights Group 1989, Rowley 1966, Survival International 1984, Timm 1991, Turnbull 1972, Tobias 1986, Wirsing 1984). In the long view these are continuations of the global pattern of mountain wars, adventures and colonisation set by European powers, their heirs and settlers over the past several centuries. Throughout the Americas, North, East and Southern Africa, the Southeast Asian mainland and mountainous islands, Australasia and Siberia, untold numbers of indigenous mountain peoples have been victims of exotic diseases, superior fire power, deliberate extermination, enslavement and so-called "development" (Crosby 1986, Drinnon 1984).

The "developed nation" mountains have their problems of war-related violence too. If the impacts of nuclear and other weapons testing have been most severe in certain ocean islands and large desert areas, in the United States and the erstwhile Soviet Union they include massive explosions near, and fallout in mountain regions. The Rocky Mountain Arsenal in Colorado and Dyshtym in the Urals are notorious for radioactive contamination from weapons programmes. Semipalatinsk, near the main Kazakhstan nuclear testing grounds, is said to have exceptionally high levels of cancers, genetic disease, and infant mortality explicable only from excessive radiation exposure (Regehr 1991). We have not heard the story from the Altai and Tien Shan, which lie downwind of the test grounds and form the most likely areas of concentrated fallout or rainout.

Resource interests also intrude increasingly into the use of armed force in the mountains, notably where minerals and timber, water and power supplies, or trade routes are involved. The desire to capture or control strategic water supplies in the headwaters of "life-giving" rivers, is beginning to involve a host of potentially or actually lethal actions from the headwaters of the Nile, to the glaciers of the Karakorum, and most seriously in the Middle East (Starr and Stoll 1986; Starr 1991). But let us turn to another extraordinary "war" over another "resource" that comes from the high mountains.

"Green Mines" and "White Plagues"

In terms of expenditures and public outcry, for North Americans at least, it seems the outstanding late-twentieth century "hazard" involving mountain regions concerns two lucrative and deadly items in international drug trafficking, cocaine and heroin. The raw plant materials come entirely from a few mountain areas. Nearly all the poppies in the illicit opium/heroin trade are, or until recently were grown in a narrow belt of mountains stretching between the Anatolian plateau and the rugged mountains of Laos. Nearly all the coca leaves, from which cocaine and its rapidly spreading derivative "crack" are made, grow in the equatorial Andes. In the 1980's and 1990's, the largest suppliers and most notorious of these areas were identified as the "Golden Triangle" and "Golden Crescent" of Southeast and Southwest Asia respectively, and the "White Triangle" of Andean South America. A substantial part of the illegal trade in marijuana also involves high mountain areas of Latin America and Eurasia.

Ecologically these are "montane" crops. The Coca Belt, concentrated in the *montana* of Peru and the *yungas* of Bolivia, belongs to the high *selva* (rain forest) or "eyebrows of the jungle" between the Amazon lowlands and crests of the Andes (Morales 1989). The opium farmers of northern Laos clear fields from forested slopes below the rugged Annamite mountain chain (Westermeyer 1982). Swidden is the traditional form of agriculture. Cultivation is in the hands of mountain "peasant" families who, for the most part, have grown the white poppy or the coca plant for centuries and even millennia (Gade 1979, Kennedy 1985, Scott 1969, Rubin 1875). The main reason why these distinctive ethnobotanical regions and their diverse peoples are seen together, however, turns upon their role in the international drug trade.

In fact, knowledgeable observers tend to argue that, where they are grown, coca and the poppy, far from being "hazards", are traditionally sanctioned crops of choice (McKinnon 1983, Morales 1989). They provide one of the few options for economic advancement and even, of survival, for these folk. The human tragedy of the "white plagues" occur through addiction on the streets of, especially, North American and Western European cities. There are risks from this traffic in the mountains and for the growers, of course. Pressures to overexpand production bring ecological and social damage. Violent rivalries over the spoils spread into the source areas. There is "boom and bust" as in all such international commodity trade. The "bust" hits hardest while the "boom" is least, for the farmer. Violence termed "narcoterrorism", has cut a path of blood and fear from the main cities of Colombia, Peru, and Bolivia to the mountain villages and fields. Drug profits underwrite the armies and control by "Drug Lords" and factions in the Golden Triangle, and have helped fund the arms used to fight the war against the government in Afghanistan (Encyclopedia Britannica Yearbook 1989:243, Evans 1989, MacNicol 1983). There is a backlash of violence from the centres of power and the countries where the white-plague has its greatest rewards, its worst casualties and political fallout. "The war on drugs" of the U.S. Government has a budget approaching $2 billion a year. While conspicuously unsuccessful in stemming the tide of drugs entering and being used in North America, it is being carried to the fields and processing sites within the high mountains. There are "search and destroy" missions, using American as well as local military forces and herbicidal sprays, and stories of disastrous consequences for mountain peasants and the habitat (Collett 1989, Brogan 1989:466-477).

Highland-Lowland Interaction and the Risks of Development

The drug "hazard" and the wars, make clear how the most serious risks in the mountains depend largely upon developments and influences from outside them. The idea of "Highland-Lowland Interaction" suggests a framework for recognising these relations (Allan 1985). But it has been used to highlight environmental abuses in the mountains that may affect the more heavily populated lowlands; for instance where watershed damages increase flooding and sediment yields downstream. The so-called "Himalayan-Ganga Problem" has been seen in this sense, despite the burden of evidence that adverse environmental, social and violent impacts, including those leading to watershed abuses, have moved from the lowlands into the Himalaya (Allan 1986, Ives and Ives 1987, Tobias 1986). The drug trade or refugee camps in Sudan or Pakistan, have been interpreted in a similar fashion. The plains lands or lowland countries are seen mainly as refuges for those dispossessed and impoverished by events in the mountains, rather than both being victims of initiatives that begin in the "cities of the plains" generally, and national or international struggles.

Similar geographies of influence and interaction are relevant to other hazards, including natural ones. The avalanche hazard for skiers or all-weather roads is the more obvious of growing cases of risk linking mountains and lowland people. Actually, most of the deforested or "overgrazed" hillslopes identified with accelerated erosion relate to more or less recent economic and social change. The disastrous floods and mass movements in Thailand in November, 1988 and the Philippines in November, 1991, though triggered by intense rainstorms, have been blamed on logging of hillslopes, mostly said to be illegal. Some believe this has been exaggerated or mistaken, identifying the greater risks of increased mass movements and flooding with "cleared land" (Hamilton 1991, *infra*). That was the case in the disaster in the Pakistan Himalaya in 1974 which, though triggered by an earthquake, appeared to me primarily a "deforestation" or "development" disaster. Logging and penetration of the timber merchants was combined with clearing of more and steeper hillsides, with less well-made terracing, larger goat herds to produce meat for markets. Perhaps the main cause of death to people and animals, was a dearth of building materials for local housing. Failure to replace old, rotted timbers, the spread of homes built with rubble and mud, applied to most structures that collapsed on their occupants. Photography from early in the century showed much more old growth, heavy forest cover and more timber in built structures (Hewitt 1976). In any area where once extensive, especially mature forest is logged, that is invariably accompanied by drastic socio-economic changes for the resident populations, changes that may or may not be directly linked to the timber trade itself. It is but one ingredient, if a striking indicator of the overriding fact that the impacts of hazards and disaster are closely associated with rapid social, economic and habitat change.

Increasingly, the argument is heard that the drug and the illegal timber trades are just one manifestation of the failures or illusions of economic development and assistance in the so-called Third World. That applies not only to the hill farmers, but to governments, businesses and large landowners. Their enormous debt-load, in particular, has created a "no-win" situation, if they follow legal, let alone liberal economic practices (Hancock 1989). Not only in war and social hazards, but virtually all natural disasters, one finds that vulnerability and most of the victims in disasters relate to the same pattern of uneven or no "development"; of increasing "underdevelopment" in the presence of massive economic transformation through mechanised resource extraction, megaprojects, urbanisation, burgeoning state intervention or violence and the penetration of international markets, foreign technologies and development "aid". Mountain habitats and peoples can be made unusually vulnerable by such conditions of "development". A dissenting but growing view of hazards and disaster, would see risk as significantly or largely due to those conditions rather than the mountain habitat or indigenous practices (Hewitt 1983, 1988a, Wilkman and Timberlake 1984).

Technocracy in the Mountains: Determinism and Stereotyping

This survey of some of the more widely studied and severe risks in the mountains points to a primary role of human land uses, settlement and other activities as deciding whether, where and to whom damage occurs. At most, spontaneous or natural processes and technological "accident" decide the timing and, to some extent, the severity of harm. A great impediment to elaborating such a socially based view of risk, however, lies in the dominant views of mountain *and* hazards research. These reflect four mutually reinforcing, but dubious constructions of the problem-field.

First, risk and damage are treated as essentially a function of "the hazard"—of the avalanche, the fallout, drug production, addiction, or transport "accident". Most discussion of the geography of risk, rather than using the distribution of damages as the "actuarial space" of risk, treat the objective distribution of geophysical and other hazard agents as the defining map of risk (Ebert 1988, Waltham 1978, Whitton 1980). Such geophysicalism also fits the dominant view of mountains and their people, whether in the older environmentalism of Peattie (1936), or the more recent "geoecological" interpretations (Hewitt 1988).

Second, where recognized, human vulnerability is seen to depend upon "objective" official-type measures, notably of population, per capita and other general measures of "wealth", technology or "stage" of economic development. These, too, favor essentially determinist frameworks of the neo-malthusian, social darwinist or economic historicist schools of thought. They are social constructions of crisis and well-being that hold sway in the classrooms, media and political rhetoric of urban-industrial societies, and that underwrite the dominant views of material life in modern research. In hazards work, they appear as prevailing assumptions or arguments in most disaster reports from mountain lands, especially of the Third World, and in the work of institutions specialising in risk research or emergencies in the West (Burton et al. 1978, Grima et al. 1989, Mather and Sdasyuk 1992, Starosolsky and Medler 1989). A majority of writings published in journals containing articles on mountains reflect the same perspective.

Such explanations depend ultimately upon faith in a "hidden hand" that guides or statistically decides the outcome of countless, infinitely complex events. Human agency appears, at best, as unconscious, an ignorant or helpless accomplice. This proves to be especially easy with remoter mountain lands and cultures. Whether treated critically or romantically they commonly emerge as prisoners of an overwhelming environment, backward in economy; archaic, conservative, and superstitious in culture; having a geography but no history, incapable of effectively adapting to their setting or knowing their own way to improvement.

The terms most often used are of *over*-something, - overpopulation, overcultivation, overgrazing, - or of *un*, - and *under*-something, - unstable, underdeveloped, unsustainable. This implies an *un*defined standard that is "normal" or "desirable", - actually unspoken assumptions about the way of life of those who establish and promote these dominant views. Along with this goes a preference for mechanical models and images of the problem-field. The construction of risk in the mountains is discussed mostly in terms of "stability" and "instability", transferring notions of natural processes and engineering structures to societal conditions. Rightly, such approaches are accused of "scientism", which employs the language and concepts of sciences in a metaphorical way rather than the rigorous logical and empirical analyses of the fields they imitate (Thompson et al. 1986, Waddell 1983).

Third, risk and disaster tend to be defined and the questions posed in, as it were, a strictly "vertical" sense: as a relation between a damaging agent and those it may harm. The condition of a group of people is defined in terms of an equation between their numbers or attributes and their immediate resources and habitat. Indeed, it is the essential structure of argument throughout environmentalist, neo-malthusian and the other determinist frameworks. In particular, it ignores the two senses in which "horizontal" relations might come into play, - both those of other factors of risk in the mountains, such as the "intervening variables" noted earlier, and the play of influences from outside.

Fourth, mountain studies are preoccupied with the high alpine zone and most rugged areas, the most spectacular views or processes. These, or the "elemental alpine events", are often treated as somehow most definitive of high mountain environments. Again it is a construction placed on the problem-field by city folk or outsiders to the mountains. While the bulk of mountain peoples live on the relatively flatter areas and lower elevations in their region, few or none live in the higher alpine areas. Most who visit them do so in relation to demands and timetables set elsewhere. The case of earthquake risks discussed above amply illustrates the weakness of this restrictive "alpinist" vision of the mountain environment and peoples. Meanwhile, the lower, gentler and less remote parts not only relax some or most of the more severe "alpine" constraints, but introduce much more of the varied and complex cultures or developments that characterise the history and human geography of mountain lands and their involvement with a wider world (c.f. Clark 1949, Braudel 1972, LeRoy Ladurie 1979).

However, these four elements of today's dominant view of hazards in the mountains, are fully symptomatic of the abstracted, gender-blind, class-blind, secular and amoral, mechanistic and technocratic style of work that prevails in international "Big Science" and the preoccupations of agencies and publics in the wealthier and more powerful centres (Hewitt 1983, 1988). They not only display the Enlightment desire to generalise and command "rational" interpretation by reducing everything to a common language and set of concepts. They are repeatedly beguiled by the most "advanced" or fashionable concepts, the worries or "fast-breaking" technologies in their own places of origin, and a belief these define and alone can solve "problems" elsewhere.

There would be little point in drawing attention to this, if, in certain contexts, these approaches had not displayed power and competence. Essentially, the problem is one of what happens when they are applied to places and people more or less removed from their origins in the metropolitan centres, and to problems of society rather than technical projects. Then they display a mixture of cultural hubris and profound ignorance of conditions and concerns in other areas. The greatest threat to such technocratic expertise is cultural understanding, and a genuine empiricism which allows the place or phenomena or people of interest to define what is important. But we are robustly protected from such threats. The dominant view of hazards and the world's mountains invariably goes hand in hand with expertise in one discipline or management field associated with risk. Not speaking the language or knowing the history and culture of those at risk is normal. Often enough, "experts" are unwilling or "too busy" to make more than a cursory survey of the areas involved. This is notably the case of the expertise deployed by many national and international aid, relief and development agencies. They thus become the major promoters of abstracted and deterministic notions of how risks arise, are indifferent to socio-cultural and political understanding. It has been suggested they are more deeply moved by the latest technologies, the "buzz-words" in the most powerful institutions, and in constructing images of potency and expertise for public relations purposes (George 1990).

This approach contrasts with a small but growing number of works that look in some depth at risk or disaster in particular mountain communities, and after close, fairly long-term involvement of the researcher with the places and people concerned. Although often, from academic and other centres in the West, each comes to define risks and loss from or with the aid of the perspective of the persons and culture at risk. In addition to coming to terms with the interpersonal, historic and cultural context, they present us with a very different sense of the problem from the dominant views of mountain lands and hazards or development. Among other things they show how harm associated with natural hazards is *not* uniquely explained by, nor mainly dependent upon the geophysical processes that initiate damage (Geipel 1982, 1989; Hewitt, F. 1989, 1991; Oliver-Smith 1985; Waddell 1977). They show how those conditions and actions that actually may decide vulnerability to and damage in disaster are often unrelated either to adaptation to the environmental risks concerned or to the specifics of the mountain habitat (Ladurie 1979). Rather, they involve social and economic expectations and activities, usually undergoing drastic change through outside influences. Responses to disaster also depend largely upon continuing circumstances rather than specifically emergency responses. Meanwhile, if not before disaster, then immediately after, outside influences tend to increase sharply, often magnifying the amount of harm to many victims, in spite of assistance and reconstruction (Geipel 1982,1989, Oliver-Smith 1985). There is a growing recognition that small mountain societies, like some others, may have developed basically as hazard-minimising "security" systems of material life, and that modernisation tends to destroy this protection (Ken MacDonald, personal communication). These are developments, however, outside the dominant view and raising issues beyond the scope of this review.

REFERENCES

Alexander, D. 1981. "Preliminary Assessment of Landslides Resulting from the Earthquake of 23rd November 1980 in Southern Italy." *Disasters* 5:376-383.

Allan, N.J.R. 1985. "Highland-Lowland Interaction Systems: Hindukush-Himalaya." In *Integrated Mountain Development*, edited by T. V. Singh and J. Kaur, 239-256. New Delhi: Himalayan Books.

——————. 1986. "Accessibility and Attitudinal Zonation Models in Mountains." *Mountain Research and Development* 6:185-194, 205-206.

——————. 1987. "Impact of Afghan Refugees on the Vegetation Resources of Pakistan's Hindukush-Himalaya." *Mountain Research and Development* 7:200-204.

Allan, N.J.R. et al. (eds.). 1988. *Human Impact on Mountains*. Totowa, N.J: Rowman and Littlefield

Amnesty International. 1985. *East Timor: Violations of Human Rights*. London: A.I. Publications.

——————— 1986. *Unlawful Killings and Torture in the Chittagong Hill Tracts*. London.

Asprey, R. 1975. *War in the Shadows: The Guerilla in History*. 2 vols. Garden City, NJ: Doubleday.

Baker, P.T. 1978. *The Biology of High Altitude Peoples*. Cambridge: Cambridge University Press.

Bodley, J.H. 1975. *Victims of Progress*. Menlo Park, California: Benjamin/Cummings.

Bode, B. 1989. *No Bells to Toll: Destruction and Creation in the Andes*. New York: Charles Scribners.

Branfman, R. 1972. *Voices from the Plain of Jars, Life Under an Air War*. New York: Harper and Row.

Braudel, F. 1972. *The Mediterranean and the Mediterranean World in the Age of Philip II*. 2 vols. trans. Sian Reynolds. New York: Harper and Row.

Brunsden, D. and D.B. Prior. (eds.). 1984. *Slope Instability*. New York: Wiley.

Brogan, P. 1989. *The Fighting Never Stopped: A Comprehensive Guide to World Conflict Since 1945*. New York: Random House.

Burton, I. et al. 1978. *The Environment as Hazard*. New York: Oxford University Press.

Carnegie Institute. 1908-1910. *The California Earthquake of April 18, 1906.* Washington D.C.: California State Earthquake Investigation Commission.
Carson, M.A. and M.J. Bovis 1989. "Slope Processes." In *Quaternary Geology of Canada and Greenland*, edited by J. R. Fulton. Ottawa: Geological Survey of Canada.
Chaliand, G. (ed.). 1980. *People Without a Country: the Kurds and Kurdistan.* Translated by Michael Passis. London: Zed Press.
Clark, A.H. 1949. *The Invasion of New Zealand by People, Plants and Animals: the South Island.* New Brunswick, N.J.: Rutgers University Press.
Clarke, J.I. et al. 1989. *Population and Disaster.* Oxford: Basil Blackwell.
Collett, M. 1989. *The Cocaine Connection: Drug Trafficking and Inter-American Relations.* New York: Foreign Policy Associates, Headline Series.
Costa, J.E. 1985. "Floods From Dam Failures." United States Geological Survey. Open-File Report 85-560. Denver, Department of the Interior.
Costa, J.E. and R.L. Schuster. 1985. "The Formations and Failure of Natural Dams." *Geological Society of America Bulletin* 100:1054-1068.
Craig, D. and M. Egan. 1979. *Extreme Situations: Literature and Crisis from the Great War to the Atom Bomb.* London: Macmillan.
Crosby, A.W. 1986. *Ecological Imperialism. The Biological Expansion of Europe, 900-1900.* Cambridge: Cambridge University Press.
Cruden, D. 1985. "Rockslope Movements in the Canadian Cordillera." *Canadian Geotechnical Journal* 22:528-40.
Davis, S.N. and I. Darzulovic. 1963. "Landslides at Lago Rinihue, Chile." *Bulletin Seismological Society of America* 53:1403-1414.
Drinnon, R. 1980. *Facing West: The Metaphysics of Indian-hating and Empire-building.* New York: New American Library.
Eisbacher, G.H. and J. Clague. 1985. "Destructive Mass Movements in High Mountains." Paper 84/16. Ottawa: Geological Survey of Canada.
Ebert, C.H.V. 1988. *Disasters: Violence of Nature and Threats by Man.* Dubuque: Kendall/Hunt.
Evans, R. 1989. "The Death Industry; World Drug Economies." *Geographical Magazine* 61:5, 10-14.
Gardner, J.S. 1989. "High Magnitude Geomorphic Events in the Canadian Rocky Mountains." *Geomorphologica Studia* 23.
Geipel, R. 1982. *Disaster and Reconstruction: The Friuli (Italy) Earthquakes of 1976.* Trans. P. Wagner, London: Allen and Unwin
—————. 1989. *Friuli: Ten Years after the Earthquake of 6 May 1976.* In *Population and Disaster*, edited by J.I. Clark et al. London: Basil Blackwell.

George, S. 1990. *Ill Fares the Land*. New York: Penguin.
Goldstein, M.C. et al. 1983. "High Altitude Hypoxia, Culture, and Human Fecundity/Fertility: A Comparative Study." *American Anthropology* 85: 28-49.
Groetzbach, E.F. 1988. "High Mountains as Human Habitat." In *Human Impact on Mountains*, edited by N. J. R. Allan et al., 24-35. Totowa NJ: Rowman and Littlefield.
Hamilton, L.S. 1991. "The Philippine Storm Disaster and Logging: The Wrong Villain?" *World Mountain Newsletter* 4 December, 11.
Heim, A. 1932. *Bergsturz und Menschenleben*. Zuerich: Fretz and Wasmuth.
Hewitt, F. 1989. "Woman's Work, Woman's Place: The Gendered Life World of a High Mountain Community in Northern Pakistan." *Mountain Research and Development* 9:335-352.
————. 1991. "Women in the Landscape: A Karakoram Village Before Development." Doctoral Thesis, University of Waterloo, Canada.
Hewitt, K. 1972. "The Mountain Environment and Geomorphic Processes." In *Mountain Geomorphology*, edited by O. Slaymaker and McPherson, 17-34. Vancouver B.C.: Tantalus Press.
————. 1976. "Earthquake Hazards in the Mountains." *Natural History* 85:30-37.
————. 1981. "Settlement and Change in "Basal Zone Ecotones." An Interpretation of the Geography of Earthquake Risk." In *Social and Economic Aspects of Earthquakes*, edited by B.G. Jones and M. Tomazevic, 15-41. Ithaca, New York: National Science Foundation (U.S.) and Cornell University.
————. 1982. "Natural Dams and Outburst Floods of the Karakoram Himalaya." In *Hydrological Aspects of High Mountain Areas*, edited by J. Glen, 138:259-269. Washington D.C.: International Association of Scientific Hydrology.
————. (ed.). 1983. *Interpretations of Calamity, from the Viewpoint of Human Ecology*. London: Allen and Unwin.
————. 1983. "Seismic Risk and Mountain Environments: Aspects of the Role of Surface Conditions." *Mountain Research and Development* 3:27-44.
————. 1988. "The Study of Mountain Lands and Peoples; A Critical Overview." In *Human Impact on Mountains*, edited by N.J.R. Allan et al., 6-23. Totowa, NJ: Rowman and Littlefield.
————. 1988. "Catastrophic Landslide Deposits in the Karakoram Himalaya." *Science* 242, October, 64-67.
————. 1989. "Hazards to Water Resources Development in High

Mountains: The Himalayan Sources of the Indus." In *Hydrology of Disasters*, edited by O. Starosolsky and O. M. Medler, 294-312. London: James and James.

IAHS. 1966. *Proceedings: Symposium on Scientific Aspects of Snow and Ice Avalanches*. Publication 69. International Association of Scientific Hydrology. Geneva.

Ives, J.D. and P. Ives. 1987. "The Himalaya-Ganges Problem." *Mountain Research and Development* 7:1-344.

Ives, J.D. and B. Messerli. 1981. "Natural Hazards Mapping in Nepal." *Mountain Research and Development* 1:223-230.

——————. 1989. *The Himalayan Dilemma: Reconciling Development and Conservation*. London: Routledge.

Johnson, D.W. et al. 1991. "Airborne Observations of the Physical and Chemical Characteristics of the Kuwait Oil Smoke Plume." *Nature* 353:617-621.

Keefer, D.K. 1984. "Landslides Caused by Earthquakes." *Geological Society of America Bulletin* 95:406-421.

Kennedy, J. 1985. "Coca Exotica: The Illustrated Story of Cocaine." Madison: Farliegh Dickinson University Press.

Kidron M., and D. Smith. 1983. *The War Atlas: Armed Conflict - Armed Peace*. London: Pan Books.

Kuiper, L. 1981. *Genocide: Its Political Use in the Twentieth Century*. Harmondsworth: Penguin Books.

LeRoy, Ladurie, E. 1979. *Montaillou: The Promised Land of Error*. New York: Vintage.

Lewallen, J. 1971. *Ecology of Devastation: Indochina*. Baltimore: Penguin Books.

Lliboutry, L. et al. 1977. "Glaciological Problems Set by the Control of Dangerous Lakes in Cordillera Blanea, Peru." *Journal of Glaciology* 18:1.

MacLean, J. 1987. *Prolonging the Agony: The Human Cost of Low Intensity Warfare in El Salvador*. London: El Salvador Committee for Human Rights.

Mather, J. R. and G.V. Sdasyuk. (eds.). 1992. *Global Change: Geographical Approaches*. Tucson: University of Arizona Press.

McCoy, A.W. 1972. *The Politics of Heroin in Southeast Asia*. New York: Harper and Row.

McKinnon, J. 1983. "A Highlander's Geography of the Highlands: Mythology, Process, and Fact." *Mountain Research and Development* 3:313-317.

McNicoll, A. 1983. *Drug Trafficking: A North-South Perspective*. Ottawa: North-South Institute.

Minority Rights Group. (ed.). 1989. *World Directory of Minorities.* Chicago: St. James Press.

Monge, C.M. and C.C. Monge. 1966. *High Altitude Diseases, Mechanisms and Management.* Springfield: Charles Thomas.

Mueller, L. 1968. "New Considerations on the Vaiont Slide." *Rock Mechanics and Engineering Geology* 6:1-91.

Naef, F. et al. 1989. "Morphological Changes in the Swiss Alps Resulting From the 1987 Summer Storms." In *Hydrology of Disasters*, edited by O. Starosolszky and O. M. Melder, 36-42. London: James and James.

Nilsson, S. and D. Pitt. 1991. *Mountain World in Danger: Climate Change in the Forests and Mountains of Europe.* London: Earthscan.

Okuda, S. et al. (eds.). 1983. "Extreme Landforming Events." *Zeitschrift fuer Geomorphologie.* Supplemental volume 46.

Oliver-Smith, A. 1986. *The Martyred City: Death and Rebirth in the Andes.* Albuquerque: University of New Mexico Press.

Palm, R. 1990. *Natural Hazards: An Integrative Framework for Research and Planning.* Baltimore: Johns Hopkins University Press.

Pena, H. and W. Klohn. 1989. "Non-meteorological Flood Disasters in Chile". In *Hydrology of Disasters*, edited by O. Staroslszky and O. M. Melder. London: James and James.

Permanent People's Tribunal. 1985. *A Crime of Silence: The Armenian Genocide.* London: Zed Books.

Pitt, D.C. (ed.). 1978. *Society and Environment: The Crisis in the Mountains.* Working Papers in Comparative Sociology no.8. University of Auckland.

Price, L.W. 1981. *Mountains and Man: A Study of Process and Environment.* Berkeley: University of California Press.

Reed, S.A. 1906. *The San Francisco Conflagration of April, 1906: Special Report.* New York: National Board of Fire Underwriters.

Regehr, E. 1991. "A Pattern of War." *Ploughshares Monitor* 12:13-16. Waterloo: Institute of Peace and Conflict Studies.

Richardson, D. 1968. "Glacier Outburst Floods in the Pacific Northwest." Professional Paper 600-D, 79-86. Reston: U.S. Geological Survey.

Rooper, P. 1987. *A Fragile Victory: A Nicaraguan Community at War.* London: Weidenfeld and Nicolson.

Rowley, C.D.F. 1966. *The New Guinea Villager: The Impact of Colonial Rule on Primitive Society and Economy.* New York: Frederick A. Praeger.

Schroder, J.F. Jnr. 1989. "Hazards of the Himalaya." *American Scientist* 77:565-573.

Sheets P.D. and D.K. Grayson. (eds.). 1979. *Volcanic Activity and Human Ecology.* New York: Academic Press.

Sivard, R.L. 1991. *World Military and Social Expenditures, 1991.* Washington, D.C.: World Priorities.
Small, M. and J.D. Singer. 1982. *Resort to Arms: International and Civil Wars, 1816-1980.* Beverly Hills: Sage.
Starosolszky, O. and O.M. Melder. 1989. *Hydrology of Disasters: Proceedings of the Technical Conference in Geneva, November 1988.* World Meteorological Organisation. London: James and James.
Stockholm International Peace Research Institute. (eds.). 1976. *Chemical and Biological Warfare.* Stockholm: Almqvist and Wiksellm.
—————. 1976. *Ecological Consequences of the Second Indo-China War.* Stockholm: Almqvist and Wiksellm.
Survival International. 1984. "Genocide in Bangladesh." *Survival International Review* Number 43, London.
Theil, C.C. 1987. "Microzonation: An Approach to Seismic Land Use Planning." In *A Review of Earthquake Research Applications in the National Earthquake Hazards Reduction Program, 1977-1987.* Proceedings of Conference no. 41. Open File Report 88-13A. Reston: U.S. Geological Survey.
Timm, R.W. 1991. "The Adivasis of Bangladesh." *Minority Rights Group Report.* London.
Thompson, M. et al. 1986. *Uncertainty on a Himalayan Scale.* London: Milton Ash Editions.
Tufnell, L. 1984. *Glacier Hazards.* London: Longmans.
Turnbull, C.M. 1972. *The Mountain People.* New York: Simon and Schuster.
UNDRO News. 1991. *Gulf Crisis: Start-up Phase of the Regional Humanitarian Plan for Action.* January/February, 4-9.
Voight, B. (ed.). 1978. *Rockslides and Avalanches: Vol. I, Natural Phenomena.* Elsevier, Amsterdam.
Vuichard, D. and M. Zimmermann. 1987. "The 1985 Catastrophic Drainage of a Moraine-Dammed Lake, Khumbu Himal, Nepal: Cause and Consequences." *Mountain Research and Development* 7:91-110.
Waltham, I. 1978. *Catastrophe: The Violent Earth.* London: Macmillan.
Watt, R.B. Jnr. et al. 1983. "Eruption-Triggered Avalanche, Flood, and Lahar at Mount St. Helens - Effects of Winter Snowpack." *Science* 221:1394-6.
Weischet, W. 1963. "The Distribution of Damage Caused by the Earthquake in Valdovia in Relation to the Forms of Terrain." *Bulletin Seismological Society of America* 5:1259-1262, 1237-1257.
Westermeyer, J. 1982. *Poppies, Pipes and People: Opium and its Use in Laos.* Berkeley: University of California Press.
Westing, A.H. (ed.). 1984. *Environmental Warfare: A Technical, Legal and*

Policy Appraisal. Stockholm International Peace Research Institute. London: Taylor and Francis.

White, G.F. (ed.). 1974. *Natural Hazards: Local, National, Global.* New York: Oxford University Press.

Whittow, J. 1980. *Disasters: The Anatomy of Environmental Hazards.* New York: Penguin.

Wirsing, R.G. 1981. *The Baluchis and Pathans.* London: Minority Rights Group.

Young, G. (ed.). 1985. *Techniques For Prediction of Runoff From Glacierised Areas.* Publication 149. Washington D.C.: International Association Scientific Hydrology.

Plate 1: Intact montane forest and forest land degraded by grazing in the north Caucasus.

Plate 2: Meteorological instruments to intercept additional water capture of horizontal or occult precipitation in Andean cloud forest.

Plate 3: A landslip after five years of logging in Oregon, U.S.A.

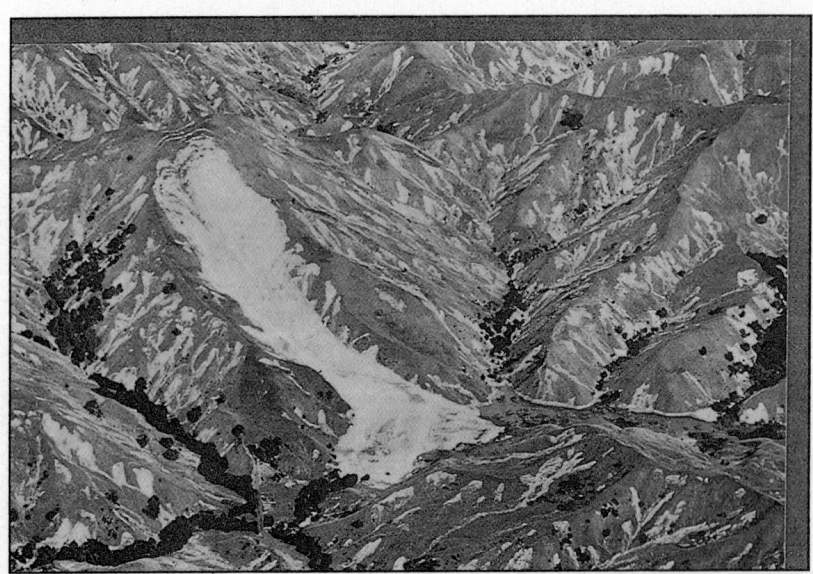

Plate 4: Cyclone Bola in New Zealand in 1988 created thousands of small landslips and a few major slope failures.

Plate 5: Road related slope failures in the Venezuelan Andes.

Plate 6: Production zones in highland Paucartambo. Maize and quinoa are cultivated at the lowest level, with barley and improved varieties of potatoes in the intermediate level, and native potatoes and ulluco at the highest elevation.

Plate 7: Peasants separating ulluco tubers in categories for seed, consumption, sale and animal feed.

Plate 8: Mixed cropping of Andean lupine in the foreground, with transplanted quinoa topping young maize plants.

Plate 9: Bighorn sheep habitat on a mine site with quality forage land adjacent to escape terrain of bench walls sculpted from the reclaimed pit.

Plate 10: Bighorn sheep nursery herd of sheep moving to mineral licks over a benched pit wall.

Plate 11: A nursery herd of bighorn sheep on reclaimed range.

Plate 12: Bighorn sheep crossing a mine haul road.

CHAPTER 6

Havens on High? The Fate of Biodiversity in Mountain Agriculture

KARL S. ZIMMERER

Introduction

Contradictory assessments on the state of native-crop loss have been offered in recent studies (Brush 1986, 1989, Wilkes 1989). The recently growing debate contrasts sharply with notable unanimity in the prognosis of a "genetic wipe-out" which had been delivered during the two decades since several scientists and agronomic institutions first expressed concern for the fate of agricultural biodiversity. If later and less convinced researchers were to detect the cries of a Cassandra in Jack Harlan's 1972 clarion call, his opinion regarding the completeness of loss in native-crop cultivars and their genetic constituents echoed widely at that time. Only slightly earlier and in a landmark volume, O. H. Frankel had warned that "primitive cultivars...are a vanished or vanishing asset" (Frankel 1970: 474). Many current analyses of agricultural biodiversity continue to paint a picture of cultivar loss so complete that it stretches in an even and uninterrupted fashion across the broad canvas that is framed by both diverse crops and geographic regions (Wilkes 1989). Other recent inquiries, on the other hand, have challenged the assumed evenness of native-crop extinction and drawn attention to certain regions of mountain agriculture as possible havens for crop-genetic resources.

In the contrasting view, cultivar loss is depicted as uneven and complexly patterned rather than uniformly complete (Brush 1986, 1989). To illustrate the unevenness in that process, Stephen Brush highlights differences associated with crop type and world geographic region in a comparison between cultivar loss in the potato and rice complexes found in South America and Southeast Asia, respectively. Brush concludes that the montane agricultural systems in the two world regions, but not the lowland ones, continue to contain substantial native-crop cultivation. Yet the degree to which the montane agricultural systems in each region actually produce the native-crop cultivars differs notably. Brush estimates that the loss of native potatoes in Andean Peru has occurred at roughly one-half the rate indicated by indigenous rice cultivars in the Philippines (Brush 1986: 162). That contrast is shaped by national and regional economic factors, local socioeconomic conditions (the production, consumption, and exchange of each crop), and the crops' biological properties. Brush's wide-ranging comparison suggests that the future examination of *different* native crops found *within* a region would permit greater specificity in assessing the various contingencies underlaying the fate of agricultural biodiversity.

Multiple contingent conditions mold the spatial and temporal unevenness increasingly evident in the change and deterioration of environmental resources (Ives and Messerli 1989). Although philosophical discussions in human geography and other social sciences have emphasized the importance of contingency in examining complex social questions (Sayer 1984), little research on human-environment relations and ecological degradation has sought to specify the contingencies embedded in environmental modification. The present study focuses on three sets of contingent conditions that shape cultivar loss or conversely cultivar maintenance. First, in examining contingent peasant-economic conditions, inquiry centers on the allocation of land, labor, and other agricultural resources by agricultural households. Secondly, the study considers variation in the importance of native crops to local people. Thirdly, the analysis of contingencies examines the spatial patterning of cultivar distribution insofar as it forms the template of agricultural biodiversity on which agricultural change occurs. Cultivar loss and maintenance shaped through the three sets of contingencies are examined with respect to four native crops—potatoes (*Solanum spp.*), maize (*Zea mays* L.), ulluco (*Ullucus tuberosus* Lozano), and quinoa (*Chenopodium quinoa* Willd.)—cultivated in a highland region of Peru's southern sierra. Potatoes and maize are major crops in the region while ulluco and quinoa are secondary ones. (It should be noted that the biogeographical meaning of "native," as is used here, refers unavoidably to a historically based definition. I use "native" to mean present prior to European conquest.)

Contingencies in the local peasant economy and society as well as in crop biogeography are found to differentiate the processes of cultivar loss and cultivar maintenance among the four native crops. Changing availability of labor in peasant household economies particularly impinges in different ways on each of the crops examined. Access to land and capital for agricultural production are also important. Social contingencies stemming from dietary importance and culinary esteem likewise differ notably among species and contribute unequally to the forces whereby peasant agriculturalists resist abandoning certain native crops more than others. Variation in the spatial patterning of native cultivars also acts as a crucial contingency in either cultivar loss or cultivar maintenance. Reflecting the complexity manifested among the interacting contingencies examined in the following case study, the role of mountains as havens for agricultural resources is seen to vary according to local-scale attributes of the crops, their production, and their consumption.

Agricultural Biodiversity in Tropical and Subtropical Mountains

Agriculture in the montane tropics and sub-tropics has long been renowned for the exceptional biological diversity contained within native crops (Sauer 1950, Vavilov 1951). Heterogeneous physical and biological growing environments, the long duration and early development of agriculture, and complex cultural histories favored extensive intraspecific divergence within the scores of crop species that evolved in numerous mountain ranges. Mountain peasants currently produce thousands of diverse native cultivars belonging to several dozen major food plants (Harlan 1975b). Cultivators in the East African Highlands, the Greater Himalayas, and the ranges of Southeast Asia continue to produce a wide spectrum of agricultural biodiversity. Notwithstanding that phenomenon, the majority of native-crop biodiversity in mountain agriculture persists in the tropical Andes. The well-known environmental complexity of agricultural habitats in the montane tropics supports the maintenance of biologically diverse crops (Harlan 1975a, Troll 1966). Persistent agricultural biodiversity in the mountainous tropics hinges also on the social landscapes in those settings.

Peasants predominate in the tropical mountain societies of Third World countries. Contrary to the scenarios posited by a range of neoclassical and Marxist economic perspectives (Schultz 1964, Lenin 1976), peasants in economically underdeveloped countries have not disappeared as a result of tumultuous economic change such as has occurred during the late twentieth century. In Latin America, for instance, the size of the peasantry is estimated to have increased by 43.6 percent between 1950 and 1980 while the number of smallfarmer households, most of them peasants, grew from 4.1 to 7.9 million (de Janvry et al. 1989). Mountainous regions in Latin America undoubtedly have supported a disproportionately high share of that demographic increase. Two fundamental attributes in the persistent peasant economy are that the household serves as the basic unit managing land, labor, and capital and that the household produces agricultural goods for both use and for sale (Blaikie 1985). The pair of perhaps obvious properties characterizing the household economies of peasant farmers are useful in evaluating the types of agricultural change that might be expected to impinge on the production of native crops.

A shortage of land has usually been fingered as the proximate culprit in cultivar loss, whether in mountainous regions or other environments. Several decades ago, Carl Sauer highlighted the spatial constraint as the primary cause of cultivar loss: "Meanwhile, the extension of commercial agriculture is causing a rapid extinction of the primitive domestic forms" (Sauer 1938:769). Plucknett and his colleagues adopted a similar explanation in averring that "The adoption of high-yielding varieties over broad areas has resulted in subsistence farmers abandoning their traditional varieties that were rich in genetic diversity" (Plucknett et al. 1983:163). More recently, evidence pointing to the incomplete areal expansion of commercial agriculture and so-called improved varieties has served as a key element in Brush's (1986, 1989) arguments for the uneven course of cultivar loss. Yet, by itself, the lack of spatial constraints does not assure the maintenance of diverse-cultivar agriculture. The allocation of labor and capital in the peasant economy particularly needs to be examined as both necessary conditions for native-crop production and elements in which change might bring about cultivar loss.

Through considering cultivar loss in a local peasant-economic context, the contingent links of land, labor, and capital underpinning native-crop production can be assessed most completely. The peasant economy framework emphasizes that conditions necessary for diverse-cultivar production are likely to be contingent on how the peasant household organizes both subsistence and non-subsistence economic activities. Expansion and intensification of commercial activities without the abandonment of diverse-cultivar production for subsistence (household consumption) has provided the empirical substance for Brush's claims countering the "genetic wipe-out" scenario and signalling that native crop diversity is often maintained during economic change in peasant societies (Brush 1986, 1989). Nonetheless, maintaining native-crop cultivars in production is not simply a mechanical function of either constraints or enabling which arise from the available factors of production controlled by peasant households. Instead, in deciding whether or not to maintain native-crop production, peasant cultivators imbue different forms of subsistence production with unequal value.

Differences in the social values of various native crops add other contingent conditions necessary to explain unevenness in the rate of cultivar loss. Social esteem takes into account culinary, ritual, and symbolic usefulness. Ethnobotanical evidence indicates how native crops differ in the utility that they offer to cultivators (Gade 1975, Sauer 1950) and thus suggests that such differences would differentiate the resolve of cultivators to continue production. The present study reveals the inequality of social values which are attributed to each of the native crops. The study finds that the abandonment of native crops cannot be ascribed to the penetration of attitudes and values entrained in a diffusing wave of cultural "modernization" (*pace* Wilkes 1989). Quite to the contrary, the four native crops under study were found to be highly esteemed by peasant cultivators.

Terminology describing the fate of native crops needs to be clarified before proceeding further. The disappearance of cultivars belonging to native crops at a local or regional geographical scale is most precisely described as the process of "cultivar loss." In an effort to define the lexicon of environmental change as clearly as possible and thereby aid in understanding such modifications (Ives and Messerli 1989), it is helpful to distinguish cultivar loss from the more general phenomenon of "genetic erosion." Although evocative and widely recognized, the term genetic erosion has been applied to a broad array of processes involving "...the loss of genes from a gene pool due to the elimination of populations" (Plucknett et al., 1987). (A similarly expansive definition has identified genetic erosion as "...the gradual persistent loss of plant genetic resources..." [Wilkes 1989:18]). Hence genetic erosion as currently used refers to a wide variety of biological changes including the loss of genetic material as a result of storage (Frankel and Bennett 1970), breeding procedures (Harlan 1972), and agricultural change in peasant societies (Hawkes 1983). Cultivar loss, on the other hand, may be seen as most accurately referring to the local disappearance of native-crop types.

Cultivar loss is also preferable to *genetic erosion* in the present study due to a pair of specific connotations often attributed to the latter term. First, genetic erosion frequently is equated with the extinction of native crop cultivars, a magnitude of biological change which cannot be assumed solely on the basis of loss from local or regional agricultural systems. (The basic regional biogeography of cultivars belonging to almost all native crops remains so inadequately understood that the overall significance of change at a local scale cannot be estimated.) Secondly, the term genetic erosion implies biological change at the genetic level whereas the loss of cultivars might or might not involve that sort of modification. Like the evident lacunae in biogeographical knowledge, the population genetics of native crops are so little known that gene-level effects accompanying the loss of indigenous cultivars have not been accurately deduced. The present study therefore does not claim to evaluate genetic erosion but rather focuses solely on cultivar loss.

The following sections of the present study discuss findings on four human and physical geographic foundations necessary for understanding the unevenness of cultivar loss in societies of mountain peasants: 1) the evolution of diversity at the cultivar level within the crop species; 2) the production, diversity, and distribution of cultivars within the region; 3) agriculturalists' reasons for cultivating the crop and for not abandoning it; and 4) proximate changes in the peasant economy which have resulted in cultivar loss. Through comparing the biogeographic and human geographic attributes of native crops in a changing system of peasant agriculture, several immediate contingencies responsible for the uneven loss of cultivars in the suite of four crops (potatoes, maize, ulluco, quinoa) are analyzed in the concluding section.

Study Area and Methodology: The Southern Peruvian Sierra

The Paucartambo region in the southern Peruvian sierra evidences the agricultural biodiversity and peasant forms of production found in many tropical mountain areas (Fig. 1). Approximately fifty kilometers from Cuzco, Paucartambo occupies a segment in the eastern Andes which separate the semi-arid central portion of the mountain range from the humid lowlands stretching eastward across the Amazon Basin. Steep ecological gradients along elevational and latitudinal transects in Paucartambo and in other eastern Andean regions favored the early domestication and cultivation of several native crop species as well as their marked evolutionary divergence during subsequent agricultural history (Sauer 1950, Vavilov 1951). Contemporary agricultural production and the cultivation of native crops in the study area is carried out by roughly 20,000 Quechua-speaking peasants. The principal social unit organizing that agriculture is the household although peasant communities and other supra-household groups are also important in shaping certain land-use activities (Brush and Guillet 1985, Orlove and Custred 1980).

The majority of peasant households in Paucartambo practice diversified agro-pastoralism, an economic strategy that cultural ecologists have referred to as "generalized" or "compact" (Rhoades and Thompson 1975 and Brush 1976, respectively). Agricultural production in the region is based on the combination of several native crops, including potatoes, maize, ulluco and quinoa, and other species such as wheat, barley, and fava beans which were introduced to the Andes by the Spaniards during the fifteenth century. Most agricultural households in Paucartambo cultivate between five and twelve fields during a single growing season. The fields are dispersed between the lowest sites in the canyon bottoms (2700-2900 m) and ones located on the high-elevation paleorelief surface at 3900-4100 m. All agricultural fields in the region can be seen as

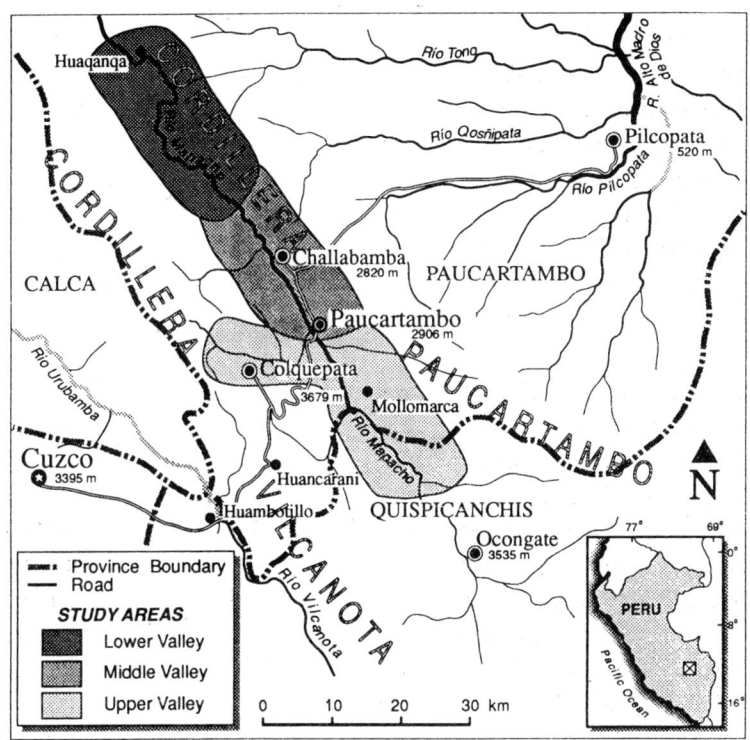

Figure 1: Paucartambo Highlands of Peru

belonging to one of four distinct production systems, each distinguished by different physical environments, crops, techniques and technologies, and social relations of production (Mayer 1985, Zimmerer 1991b). Maize and quinoa are restricted to the "valley" system, or *kheshuar*, below 3500 m (Plate 6). Ulluco and native potato cultivars, on the other hand, predominate in high-elevation "hill" agriculture, known locally as the *loma* (roughly 3800-4050 m).

Field research for the present study relied on a combination of methodologies. Participant-observer ethnography between March 1986 and August 1987 and during July and August 1990 was focused on the socioeconomic and cultural practices associated with producing each of the four crops under study in the region's peasant agriculture. Two-page and three-page interviews about those practices were completed with significant numbers of agricultural households across the region. The sample consisted of sixty households who produced native potatoes and forty-five each among ones growing maize, ulluco, and quinoa. Informal interviews in the form of oral histories were elicited from agriculturalists who had discontinued producing one or more of the four native crops. In addition, fields containing the quartet of crops were sampled in order to approximate the spatial patterning of cultivars. The relative abundance and frequency of different cultivar types in fields and in areas within Paucartambo were estimated. Collections of cultivars belonging to the four crops were identified by expert systematists and by the author using published taxonomies and identification guides.

Cultivar Loss versus Cultivar Maintenance

POTATOES

Potatoes are the premier crop for Andean peoples. Seven distinct cultivated species possess latitudinal ranges that reach between northern Bolivia and central Peru and therefore include the Paucartambo region (Hawkes 1978). Several thousand cultivars in the subspecies *S. tuberosum* subsp. *andigenum* Juz. et Buk. make up the majority of the region's native potatoes (Huamán 1986). If that subspecies is considered along with the species *S. stenotomum* Juz. et Buk., *S* x *chaucha* Juz. et Buk., and *S. goniocalyx* Juz. et Buk, at least ninety percent of the cultivar total is accounted for. Cultivation practices undertaken by Paucartambo agriculturalists divide the native-potato crop into two distinct taxonomic groups. The first contains the highly diverse species *S. tuberosum* subsp. *andigenum*, *S. stenotomum*, *S* x *chaucha*, and *S. goniocalyx* while the second group consists solely of the species *S. phureja* Juz. et Buk. (Table 1).

Cultivars belonging to the first group of native-potato species are referred to as "boiling potatoes" (*wayk'u papa*). The boiling potatoes are cultivated in mixtures within fields that are located in high-elevation "hill" agriculture. Boiling-potato parcels circumscribe the largest portion of cultivars in the region's native-potato crop. A total of 79 distinct cultivars and a mean value of 20.1 cultivars per field were ascertained from the random sampling of 225 plants in each of twenty-eight fields containing mixtures of boiling potatoes (Zimmerer 1991a). Slightly over one-half the 79 cultivars belong to the subset of boiling potatoes that exhibit localized, or endemic, distribution patterns. The limited areal ranges evident in the cultivars with locally endemic distribution were due principally to peasant farmers' practice of rarely obtaining seed for boiling potatoes from sources other than the household itself. Limited exchange thus precluded dispersal. Moreover, even when peasant farmers resorted to

TABLE 1. PROXIMATE CONDITIONS SHAPING CULTIVAR LOSS IN PAUCARTAMBO.

Crop	Elevational Range (m)	Economic Constraints	Social Usefulness	Spatial Patterning of Cultivars
boiling potatoes (*S. tuberosum* subsp. *andigenum* *S. stenotomum* *S.* x *chaucha* *S. goniocalyx*)	3800-4050	low (land/capital)	high (culinary, gift-giving, symbolic)	local/specialized
precocious potatoes *S. phureja*	3000-3400	high (labor)	medium (culinary)	local/specialized
"big-seed" maize *Z. mays*	2700-2900	high (labor)	high (culinary, ritual, gift-giving)	local/specialized
"medium-seed" "small-seed" maize *Z. mays*	2700-3500	low	high (culinary, ritual, gift-giving)	widespread/generalized
ulluco *Ullucus tuberosus*	3600-4000	medium (land)	medium (culinary, symbolic?)	widespread/generalized
quinoa *Chenopodium quinoa*	2850-3500	medium (labor)	medium (culinary, symbolic?)	widespread/generalized

seed-exchange networks, the areal extent of the transfers was geographically limited.

Peasant inhabitants in Paucartambo greatly prize boiling potatoes for their culinary qualities. Chief among the favorable attributes is high dry-matter content or mealiness (*hak'u*). Strong preference for mealy potatoes leads agriculturalists in the region to esteem boiling potatoes more highly than the improved varieties which contain more water and less dry-matter. That bias in peasant palates is apparently widespread throughout highland Peru (Brush 1986). Culinary preferences also contribute to the prestige accorded the boiling potatoes for their use as gifts and as a form of payment for workers at harvest. In addition to culinary superiority, one primary reason for the maintenance of boiling-potato cultivars is their symbolic importance in the "everyday" practices through which Quechua peasants reproduce their ethnic group identity (Zimmerer 1991b). Ideally at least, to cultivate native boiling potatoes is a sign of being Quechua. It is notable that when cultivars of the group are sold, as they occasionally are in regional markets, the mixtures are less diverse than those occurring in fields designated strictly for subsistence.

Individual boiling potato types are not being replaced by improved potato varieties through simple variety-for-cultivar substitution. Instead, cultivar loss in the boiling potatoes is more likely to occur where the fields containing mixtures of those types are abandoned or replaced with another production system involving improved varieties. Yet, despite considerable expansion in the area planted with the improved potato varieties, little cultivar loss appears to have taken place among the boiling potatoes. In fact, a comparison of cultivars sampled in the agricultural season 1986-87 with those collected during the 1930s and '40s has revealed the continued presence of 87 percent of the locally recognized types noted in the early collections (Zimmerer 1991c). Although much cultivation at elevations between 3700 and 3800 m in the region has been converted to the production of improved varieties, the number and size of fields planted with boiling potatoes in yet higher elevations have apparently been sufficient to underpin the maintenance of agricultural biodiversity in the region's boiling potatoes.

The persistence of boiling potatoes offers a notable contrast to the cultivar loss in the species *S. phureja*, the second taxonomic group of native potatoes included in the present study. Maturing within less than four months yet without the capacity to keep dormancy, the species requires nearly year-round cultivation. Its distribution is restricted to humid, intermediate-elevation eastern Andean valleys between Venezuela and northern Bolivia (Hawkes 1978). In Paucartambo, the precocious potato species does not extend beyond the humid climates in the area surrounding Waqanqa in the lower Mapacho valley (Fig. 1). At least five *S. phureja* cultivars furnished a substantial supply of soup potatoes in local diets as recently as twenty years ago. Today only a few inhabitants in Waqanqa produce the *S. phureja* cultivars. Decline in the maintenance of the precocious potatoes can be attributed to a singular condition in their production, namely the extended and augmented requirement for periodic labor inputs (Zimmerer 1991c).

Considerable expenditures on labor at frequent intervals are required to produce the precocious potatoes. Because the *S. phureja* cultivars must be planted at least twice and in some cases three times annually, the need for labor is staggered throughout the calendar year. For peasant households, the timing of labor demand for the precocious potatoes has increasingly conflicted with requirements for other economic activities which have grown in importance.

Expansion in the area of improved potatoes planted during the dry season, which constitute the production system known as the "early planting," particularly has led to recurring, seasonal shortages in households' capacity to allocate labor for *S. phureja* agriculture. The more frequent incidence of short-term labor migration by the area's inhabitants has also exacerbated the seasonal scarcity of labor and the pressure to cease producing the precocious potatoes. Cultivar loss in the crop has not been strongly resisted by peasant farmers who value them only moderately as constituents in the local diet. Containing relatively little dry matter and used mostly for soups rather than boiling alone, the precocious potatoes were easily replaced with improved varieties according to inhabitants in the region.

In summary, cultivar maintenance along with cultivar loss are apparent in the large native-potato crop cultivated in southern Peru's Paucartambo region. Although the area planted with boiling potatoes (*S. tuberosum* subsp. *andigenum*, *S. stenotomum*, *S* x *chaucha*, and *S. goniocalyx*) has been reduced, the great number of diverse cultivars belonging to that group has not declined significantly. In contrast, the production of precocious potatoes (*S. phureja*) has dropped precipitously and it is likely that at least one-half of the cultivar stock has disappeared from the region. Cultivar loss in *S. phureja* has been brought about through seasonal shortages of labor in the economies of peasant households which undermined their capacity to allocate workers for field tasks at crucial periods.

MAIZE

Peruvian maize displays a greater diversity of morphological forms than that cultivated in any other country (Grobman et al. 1961). Although current evidence points to Mesoamerica as the area where maize was domesticated (Iltis 1976), the crop had been brought to South America at least as early as 2000 B.C. (Zevallos et al. 1982). The maize crop subsequently underwent remarkable evolutionary divergence due to combined geographic isolation and selection pressures—both ecological and cultural—for specialized adaptation. Much intraspecific variation accumulated in the environmentally diverse Andean mountains where numerous, ethnically complex groups of early agriculturalists guided evolution in highland maize. Over time, the Andean portion of Peru came to contain no less than 33 of the 42 major maize races (supra-cultivar groups) occurring within the country's borders. Specialized adaptations to diverse field environments and cultural uses were fundamental in maintaining the high level of biological differentiation which separated the many maize races and their constituent cultivars.

The maize crop in the Paucartambo region represents a significant fraction of the country's total. The field sample revealed that 12 of the 33 races found in the Peruvian Andes are represented in the region (Zimmerer 1991c). The region's 11 races can be divided further into a total of 27 cultivars. Unlike the ecologically rich cultivar mixtures cultivated in boiling-potato fields, only a small number of maize cultivars occupy each parcel (mean 2.9 cultivars/field). Instead, much diversity in the maize crop is maintained through the close and nearly exclusive correspondence between cultivar type and field system. The field systems consist of three temporally distinct plantings referred to as the "small seed," "medium seed," and "large seed." Cultivars are matched to a particular planting on the basis of maturation period. In an ecological sense, each field planting comprises a temporal niche which supports a distinct group of either fast-maturing cultivars ("small seed"), ones with intermediate-length maturation periods ("medium seed"), or those that require the longest periods to mature ("large seed").

Commercialization plays a greater role in the production strategies for the Paucartambo maize crop than for the region's native potatoes. Maize fields intended to produce for marketing, however, contain little cultivar diversity. One cultivar, the "yellow" or "eight-row" type, is found in much of the commercial maize growing in the region. That cultivar is purchased by home-style breweries in Cuzco which manufacture the locally popular maize beer. Comprising part of the "small-seed" or late planting, the "yellow" maize is often planted alone in fields in order to limit outcrossing and resultant kernel mixtures. Notwithstanding the importance of commercial maize production to peasant households, that cultivation makes up a minor portion of the region's maize crop. Maize cultivars used for subsistence are maintained in each of the three field plantings. Cultivar maintenance therefore depends on the desire and capacity of agricultural households to allocate labor according to the staggered calendars characteristic of the planting system. The maturation period for the plantings varies from five to ten months although, regardless of the crop's duration in the field, significant labor is needed for the major cultivation tasks. Annual labor requirements for cultivation in sixty-seven maize fields in Paucartambo averages at the considerable amount of approximately 121 person-days/hectare (Zimmerer 1991c).

Cultivar maintenance in the maize crop benefits from the variety and importance of quotidian uses which take in culinary preparations, ritual and ceremony, and gift-giving. The major culinary uses include boiling, parching, beer-making, and gruel, each of which specifies certain local types (Zimmerer 1991b). The diversity of maize preparations in the household diet thus encourages peasant farmers to continue producing many cultivars. In addition, several well-defined maize types are highly prized for ritual and ceremony in which maize is the most important crop in the Andes (Murra 1960). Certain other cultivars are prized for gift-giving. Cultivars with the shortest maturation periods, for instance, supply corn-on-the-cob for eagerly awaiting celebrants during the Carnaval season. Maintaining maize cultivars thus involves a variety of economic, sociocultural, and ecological functions similar to those underpinning native-potato production. Yet, notwithstanding the multiple rationales for maintaining diverse maize types, some peasant households have begun to lessen the number of cultivars in production.

Incipient cultivar loss is resulting from the significant reduction in the area devoted to maize cultivation in the lower-valley section of Paucartambo. Like cultivar loss in precocious potatoes, the loss is not occurring through the replacement of native types by improved ones but rather through the conversion of field systems. The system of field plantings related to maturation period serves to steer the direction of cultivar loss (Table 1). Many peasant farmers in the lower valley have reduced the number of field plantings from three to two or sometimes even one. Most often, they have ceased cultivating the "large-seed" or early planting, the assemblage of several slow-maturing cultivars that requires a growing season of at least eight months (September-June). Labor shortages besetting households both early in the growing season and during its finale have forced them to cease cultivating that group of cultivars. The lack of labor available to peasant farmers has accompanied the cultivators' greatly increased involvement in producing the commercialized, dry-season planting of improved potatoes. Although some field sites that had once supported the slow-maturing, "large-seed" maize planting now contain the recently introduced potatoes, the succession of field types must not be confused with the underlying proximate cause for change. The seasonally acute shortage of labor in the household economy has contributed significantly to the decline of cultivars belonging to the early planting of maize in Paucartambo.

ULLUCO

Ulluco (*Ullucus tuberosus*) is the second most important tuber crop in most Andean regions. Its latitudinal range stretches from northwestern Argentina to Colombia and Venezuela while the elevational extent is delimited roughly by the contours at 2,000 and 4,000 m (León 1964, Sauer 1950). Despite the economic importance of ulluco, few efforts have been made to describe intraspecific variation in the crop or unravel its evolutionary history. In one attempt, the ulluco crop was estimated to contain a greater variety of morphological types than any of the other so-called secondary tuber crops in southern Peru's Vilcanota Valley (Gade 1975). Substantial morphological diversity apparent in ulluco has long presented an evolutionary puzzle due to the species' supposed lack of sexual recombination and hence its assumed inability to develop botanical seed. Recent research, however, has revealed periodic sexual recombination and the set of viable seed, albeit at a low frequency (Rousi et al. 1989).

Ulluco is widely cultivated throughout the area of "hill" agriculture in Paucartambo at elevations higher than 3800-3900 m and also in fields at intermediate elevations in the so-called "oxen-area" production system (Table 1, Plate 6). In addition to the crop's well-defined spatial habitat, ulluco occupies a highly specific temporal niche in the rotation pattern commonly scheduled for fields in the "hill" and "oxen-area" systems, namely the second year in the rotation sequence. Because ulluco requires only low-moderate amounts of soil nutrients (León 1964), it is well-suited to the slightly depleted soils found in second-year parcels. The cultivar composition of most ulluco fields, even those intended for marketing, is mixed (Plate 7), although the majority of parcels are planted with just two types. The sample from twenty ulluco fields in Paucartambo yielded 4 cultivars, each of which also demonstrated significant morphological variation within the cultivar group. All cultivars were found to be distributed across a wide area, unlike the localized, endemic distributions exhibited by native potatoes.

The fate of cultivars in the ulluco crops differs considerably from those of maize insofar as cultivar maintenance in ulluco is reinforced but slightly due to the crop's planting calendar and its cultural uses. In much of Paucartambo, the ulluco crop is divided into a tripartite planting schedule comprised of the "early planting," "big planting," and "late planting" (*ñawpaq tarpuy, hatun tarpuy, qhepa tarpuy,* respectively). Yet, unlike the distinct plantings in maize which are matched with distinct cultivar groups, staggered cropping periods in the ulluco crop are not related in an exclusive fashion to particular cultivar groups. Peasant inhabitants in the region utilize ulluco in an impressive array of culinary preparations, including plain boiling (*wayk'u*), mashed (*wakta, sakta*), slivered in soups (*lisas uchu*), and freeze-dried (*lingli*). Only the last in the list of culinary uses, however, entails widespread preference on the part of local people for a specific cultivar within the ulluco crop. Because peasant farmers imbue ulluco with less social and cultural value than native potatoes and maize, the resistance to cultivar loss might be less.

Despite possible cultivar loss in the ulluco crop in Paucartambo, little has occurred. Cultivar maintenance in the region's *Ullucus tuberosus* cannot be attributed to the absence of change in the crop's production. The major change in ulluco cultivation in Paucartambo has been that the extent of production has shrunk by at least one-third during the past two decades. Reduction in the area planted with ulluco has been brought about principally through the rapid expansion of barley cultivation under an ingenious and exploitive farming system based on contracts with the Cuzco factory of a national beer company. Peasant farmers incorporate barley into the second year of the rotation sequence for fields in the lower portion of "hill" agriculture and for ones throughout the "oxen area." Those spatial and temporal coordinates are exactly the same as the ones marking ulluco cultivation. Yet, notwithstanding the diminished production area, ulluco cultivars have not disappeared from Paucartambo. Because the cultivars are distributed widely and in a generalized fashion within the region, little cultivar loss in the ulluco crop has occurred. In the case of ulluco, the biogeographical contingency evidenced in spatial patterns has been critical in shaping cultivar maintenance.

QUINOA

A so-called pseudocereal, the grain chenopod quinoa (*Chenopodium quinoa*) is the most diverse of several domesticated species belonging to the genus *Chenopodium*. Latitudinal and elevational ranges in the quinoa crop resemble those of the tuber-bearing ulluco insofar as the seed crop is cultivated at elevations between 2,000 and 4,000 m in Andean habitats connecting northwestern Argentina and central Colombia. Quinoa, however, extends further westward across the transverse gradient due to its greater drought tolerance (León 1964). The species is estimated to contain over 100 cultivars, which are divided into two groups. Cultivars of one group occupy fields located in the major Andean valleys between 2400 m and 3600 m while those in the other are found in high-elevation habitats, most notably on the intermontane plateau or Altiplano of southern Peru and north-central Bolivia. (Aguirre and Tapia 1982).

In Paucartambo, the quinoa crop is comprised solely of cultivars belonging to the first set, the "valley quinoas" (*quinoas de valle*). Most quinoa cultivated in the region is confined to the "valley" production system along with maize at elevations less than 3550 m although some quinoa is found in slightly higher fields (Table 1). Quinoa is cultivated exclusively through intercropping, most often with maize but also with legume crops (Plate 8). A few intercropped fields at slightly higher elevations contain quinoa interspersed within fields of oca and potatoes. Farmers' rationales for combining quinoa in fields with other crops center chiefly on the protection afforded the chenopod against bird predators and wind, two hazards that regularly threaten to damage its cultivation. Intercropping also serves to reduce quinoa's otherwise heavy demand for soil nutrients through dispersing the location of plants within the parcel.

Quinoa is cultivated as the minor partner of intercropped parcels where it is planted in either linear "throats" (*kunka*) perpendicular to the rows containing the main field crop or in areas within the field where the primary crop has not germinated (*pank'e*). Rarely do peasant farmers in Paucartambo utilize more than two kilograms of seed in planting a quinoa field. Nonetheless, agricultural biodiversity in the crop is moderate. Between one and three cultivars characterize the quinoa mixture in most parcels and a total of 4 cultivars are found in the region. Quinoa cultivars do not evince specialized biogeographical distributions within Paucartambo but instead are uniformly widespread. Because the region's quinoa crop is little commercialized and restricted to relatively low elevations, agriculturalists have differed from those residing in other regions in the southern Peruvian sierra inasmuch as the Paucartambo cultivators have not adopted improved quinoa types. The continuation of quinoa cultivation is rooted in the crop's usefulness for culinary and other social purposes, although that usefulness does not specify individual cultivars. Quinoa is most often prepared as a hearty soup with potatoes and hot pepper (*quinoa uchu*). It also is toasted (*fatasqa*), fermented into a "beer" (*quinoa aqha*), made into a thick beverage with milk and sometimes cheese (*pesk'ay*), and used as a potherb (*howcha*). Important non-culinary uses of quinoa include the firing of stems to yield lime-rich ash that can be molded into small rounded balls (*llipta*) suitable for chewing with coca leaves and the use of the stems in weaving upright collapsible bins (*thaq'e*) for crop storage. Rather than maintain diverse quinoa cultivars in order to meet distinct purposes, Paucartambo agriculturalists continue cultivating the many types as a matter of custom that cannot be readily assigned functional attributes. It is possible that maintaining diverse quinoa cultivars fits with symbolic reproduction among peasant farmers in a way similar to that which occurs in the native-potato crop (Zimmerer 1991b).

One important function for quinoa cultivation in general, rather than for specific cultivars, deals with the social organization of labor. In maize parcels where quinoa is intercropped in rows oriented perpendicularly to the main crop, the quinoa "throats" aid owners in organizing laborers during field work. Quinoa rows are used as markers to delimit work areas in the field—essentially areal quotas—for each laborer. Spatial marking with quinoa is a crucial aid when large work teams undertake any one of several labor intensive tasks involved in maize production such as planting, mounding, and harvest. In the large work groups, the pace of laboring and the guarantee of its completion depend as much or more on the inducement of drudgery-relieving competition among workers than on direct monitoring and oversight by the owner. Quinoa's function as a delineator of work spaces thus complements the above-mentioned ecological benefits in motivating Paucartambo peasant farmers to plant it in mixtures with other crops rather than in entire fields.

Cultivar loss in quinoa has not occurred despite the inception of significant changes in its production. Fewer cultivators plant the crop now than in the past. Households who have ceased cultivating quinoa claim that the shortage of labor has played a key role in deciding to discontinue production. Labor shortages appear to undermine quinoa cultivation due to a pair of production characteristics. First, when quinoa is sown to fill gaps within fields, the young quinoa plants are tended initially in a nursery and then transplanted to the main field. The intensiveness of those steps in particular requires that quinoa receive considerable labor for continued production or, if not, be dropped from the roster of the household's crops. Secondly, during recent years certain households have found it increasingly difficult to recruit large numbers of laborers, thus diminishing the need to plant quinoa for marking field sections. Continued quinoa cultivation will also depend on the changes within maize production. As an intercropped species, the contingencies controlling the cultivation of *Chenopodium quinoa* are entwined inextricably with the companion crop. That quinoa cultivars have not been lost despite the decrease in production indicates the prominence of the same biogeographical contingency which buffers cultivar loss in the ulluco crop, namely the widespread patterning of occurrence.

Conclusion

CONTINGENCIES AND THE CONSERVATION OF
AGRICULTURAL BIODIVERSITY

The tropical-montane Paucartambo region in Peru's southern sierra represents a haven for agricultural biodiversity despite various forms of economic change. That inhabitants there continue to cultivate native crops coincides with macro-scale accounts of geographical unevenness in cultivar loss and cultivar maintenance (Brush 1986, 1989). Contingent socioeconomic, cultural, and economic conditions in the lives of the region's peasant households shape either the maintenance or the loss of native-crop cultivars. Although the prominence attained by each contingency varies among the major native crops examined in the present study (potatoes, maize, ulluco, and quinoa), the contingent conditions themselves can be seen to form both ones that direct agricultural change and other, resource-specific ones that contour the resulting environmental modification. Agricultural change has been produced through the resolution of altered proximate conditions in the peasant economy and resistant social forces. The cultivar loss or cultivar maintenance set in motion by agricultural change hinges on the spatial patterning of cultivars.

Changes in the capacity of peasant households to allocate land, labor, and capital impact differently on cultivar loss in the four crops studied. Seasonally acute labor shortages are precipitating cultivar loss in two crop groups, precocious potatoes belonging to the species *S. phureja* and slow-maturing maize types. Both sets of cultivars were once thoroughly embedded in widespread and complex temporal strategies undertaken by peasant households and designed to stagger labor demands and provision foodstuffs for local consumption. During the past two decades, the availability of labor to most households has declined due to increased involvement in non-subsistence economic activities, especially commercial crop production.

The importance of native crops to local inhabitants also differentiates the patterning of cultivar loss and maintenance. Although each of the four native crops studied are generally relished by peasant farmers inhabiting the Paucartambo countryside, the cultivators imbue different crops with unequal social value. The widely shared differences in taste correspond closely to the major cases of cultivar loss and maintenance in the region. Disappearing cultivars of the precocious potato *S. phureja* and the group of slow-maturing, big-seed maize types are thought to be not as useful or necessary as the other sets of cultivars within each of the two crops. Employed in soup-making, the precocious potatoes are considered little better for culinary purposes than the improved potato varieties which have much increased in cultivation recently. Slow-maturing maize cultivars likewise are considered expendable from a culinary viewpoint because other still-common maize types are equally valued in various dishes.

Crucial biogeographical contingencies in the process of cultivar loss and maintenance are the spatial patterns inscribed by native-crop cultivars. Whether agricultural change such as the reduced area devoted to native-crop cultivation actually induces cultivar loss depends on the regional distribution of taxa. Cultivars with localized or ecologically specialized distribution patterns are most likely to be lost. The two main instances of impending cultivar loss in Paucartambo—precocious potato cultivars and slow-maturing maize types—involve crop taxa that possess biogeographic ranges restricted to a small portion of the region. Restricted ranges, however, do not necessarily imply that crop cultivars are imperiled. Many boiling potatoes, for instance, are distributed as endemics within the region yet due to the minor impact of agricultural change on their production thus far those cultivars persist in production. Widespread or ecologically generalized distribution patterns buffer native crops against cultivar loss. The regionally cosmopolitan distributions demonstrated by ulluco and quinoa cultivars, for example, have allowed the cultivated area of both crops to be reduced without incurring the disappearance of cultivars.

Contingencies in the local production and consumption of each crop combine to shape distinct patterns of cultivar loss. On one hand, precocious potatoes and slow-maturing maize—the two cultivar groups most exposed to loss—evince localized distribution patterns, are characterized as vulnerable to labor constraints in the changing peasant economy, and are less valued than other native-crop types for their utility in household subsistence. On the other hand and a conspicuous contrast, boiling potatoes furnish little evidence of impending cultivar loss. Despite localized distribution patterns, the crop displays neither of the other chief contingencies impinging on precocious potatoes and slow-maturing maize. Ulluco and quinoa demonstrate contingent conditions which characterize the suite of secondary crops. Highly specific spatial and temporal parameters such as rotation sequences and intercropping frame the continued cultivation of both crops.

Persistent cultivation of biologically diverse native crops in tropical montane agriculture counters the assessments of many specialists in crop conservation who have continued to assert that diverse native cultivars can only be maintained through collection and storage in *ex situ* conservation (Frankel 1970; Frankel and Hawkes 1975; Hawkes 1972). Based on an alleged "genetic wipe-out," national and international agricultural institutions have relied exclusively on *ex situ* programs in their efforts to conserve agricultural biodiversity. Yet the present study demonstrates key contingencies that permit peasant agricultural systems in mountain regions to continue serving as living havens for the diversity in many native crops. Acknowledging the uneven persistence of native-crop production, a handful of researchers have suggested the development of combined *ex situ* and "in-place," or *in situ*, programs for crop conservation (Altieri and Merrick 1987, Brush 1989). The arguments for the combined approach highlight the multiple ecological and social advantages of *in situ* conservation while at the same time insisting that the continued cultivation of native crops needs to take place without hindering the social and economic goals of local peoples. Conservation *in situ*, it is argued, would best be based on local-scale, grassroots forms of social organization.

Assessing thoroughly the contingent social and environmental conditions in regional societies that underpin native-crop production will be necessary in order to examine the feasibility of local grassroots *in situ* conservation programs. Such programs will be particularly essential so that conservation programs can be envisioned in such a way that economic development is not to be stymied. The present study indicates that the functioning of montane agricultural systems as living havens of native-crop production depends on an intricate web of crop-specific contingencies involving not only national policies and market structures but also local economic, social, and biogeographic conditions. Clearly the role of mountain regions as viable havens for agricultural biodiversity is not without conditional parameters. The question remains whether the thorough knowledge of contingent conditions impacting on native-crop survival can be effectively incorporated into viable development strategies for local peoples.

Acknowledgements

Fieldwork for the present study was completed between March 1986 and August 1987 and during July and August 1990. Field study during the first period was undertaken with financial support from the Fulbright Foundation, the National Science Foundation, and the Joint Committee on Latin American Studies of the Social Science Research Council and American Council of Learned Societies with funds provided by the Andrew W. Mellon Foundation. During the second period, field research was supported by a travel grant from the Cyril B. Nave Foundation of the University of Wisconsin—Madison. Financial support from the Graduate School Research Committee at the University of Wisconsin—Madison enabled the analysis and write up of parts of the research. I am grateful to Leonidas Concha for his assistance in the field and to the many peasant farmers in Paucartambo who cooperated with the study and contributed to its dual objective based on conservation and development.

REFERENCES

Aguirre, L. and M.E. Tapia. 1982. "Estudio Sobre Quinoas de Valle." In Tercer *Congreso Internacional de Cultivos Andinos*, 55-61. La Paz: Instituto Boliviano de Tecnología Agropecuaria.

Altieri, M.A. and L.C. Merrick. 1987. "In Situ Conservation of Crop Genetic Resources Through Maintenance of Traditional Farming Systems." *Economic Botany* 41:86-96.

Blaikie, Piers. 1985. *The Political Economy of Soil Erosion in Developing Countries*. Harlow, Essex: Longman Scientific and Technical.

Brush, Stephen B. 1976. "Man's Use of an Andean Ecosystem." *Human Ecology* 4:147-166.

——————. 1986. "Genetic Diversity and Conservation in Traditional Farming Systems." *Journal of Ethnobiology* 6:157-167.

——————. 1989. "Rethinking Crop Genetic Resource Conservation." *Conservation Biology* 3:1-11.

Brush, Stephen B., H.J. Carney and Z. Huamán. 1981. "Dynamics of Andean Potato Agriculture." *Economic Botany* 35:70-88.

Brush, Stephen B. and D.W. Guillet. 1985. "Small-scale Agro-pastoral Production in the Central Andes." *Mountain Research and Development* 5:19-30.

de Janvry A., E. Sadoulet and L. Wilcox Young. 1989. "Land and Labour in Latin American Agriculture from the 1950s to the 1980s." *The Journal of Peasant Studies* 16:393-424.

Frankel, O.H. 1970. "Genetic Conservation in Perspective." In *Genetic Resources in Plants: Their Exploration and Conservation*, edited by O.H. Frankel and E. Bennett, 469-490. Oxford: Blackwell Scientific.

Frankel, O.H. and E. Bennett. 1970. "Genetic Resources—Introduction." In *Genetic Resources in Plants: Their Exploration and Conservation*, edited by O.H. Frankel and E. Bennett, 7-18. Oxford: Blackwell Scientific.

Frankel, O.H. and J.G. Hawkes. 1975. "Genetic Resources — the Past Ten Years and the Next." In *Crop Genetic Resources for Today and Tomorrow*, edited by O.H. Frankel and J.G. Hawkes, 1-11. Cambridge: Cambridge University Press.

Gade, D.W. 1975. *Plants, Man and the Land in the Vilcanota Valley of Peru*. The Hague: Dr. W. Junk B.V.

Grobman, A., W. Salhuana and R. Sevilla. 1961. *Races of Maize in Peru: Their Origins, Evolution, and Classification*. Washington, D. C.: National Academy of Sciences and National Research Council.

Harlan, Jack R. 1972. "Genetics of Disaster." *Journal of Environmental Quality* 1:212-215.

———. 1975a. "Our vanishing genetic resources." *Science* 188:618-621.

———. 1975b. *Crops and Man*. Madison: American Society of Agronomy and Crop Science Society of America.

Hawkes, J.G. 1978. "Biosystematics of the Potato." In *The Potato Crop*, edited by P.M. Harris, 15-69. London: Chapman and Hall.

———. 1983. *The Diversity of Crop Plants*. Cambridge: Harvard University Press.

Huamán, Z. 1986. "Conservación de recursos genéticos de papa en el CIP " *CIP Circular* 14:1-6.

Iltis, H.H. 1983. "From Teosinte to Maize: The Catastrophic Sexual Transmutation." *Science* 222:886-894.

Ives, J.D. and B. Messerli. 1989. *The Himalayan Dilemna: Reconciling Development and Conservation*. London: Routledge.

Lenin, V. 1976. *The Agrarian Question and the Critics of Marx*. Moscow: Progress Publishers.

León, J. 1964. *Plantas Alimenticias Andinas*. Lima: Instituto Interamericano de ciencias agricolas zona andina.

Mayer, E. 1985. "Production Zones." In *Andean Ecology and Civilization*, edited by S. Masuda, I Shimada and C. Morris. Tokyo: University of Tokyo Press.

Murra, J.V. 1960. "Rite and Crop in the Inca State." In *Culture in History:*

Essays in Honor of Paul Radin, edited by S. Diamond. New York: Columbia University Press.

Orlove, B.S. and G. Custred. 1980. *Land and Power in Latin America: Agrarian Economies and Social Processes in the Andes.* New York: Holmes and Meier Publishing.

Plucknett, D.L. et. al. 1983. "Crop Germplasm Conservation and Developing Countries." *Science* 220:163-169.

———. 1987. *Gene Banks and the World's Food.* Princeton: Princeton University Press.

Rhoades, R.E. and S.I. Thompson. 1975. "Adaptive Strategies in Alpine Environments: Beyond Ecological Particularism." *American Ethnologist* 2:535-551.

Rousi, A. et. al. 1989. "Morphological Variation Among Clones of Ulluco (Ullucus tuberosus, Basellaceae) Collected in Southern Peru." *Economic Botany* 43:58-72.

Sauer, C.O. 1938. "Theme of Plant and Animal Destruction in Economic History." *Journal of Farm Economics* 20:765-775.

———. 1950. "Cultivated Plants of South and Central America." In *Handbook of South American Indians,* Vol VI, edited by J. Steward, 487-543. Washington, D. C.: U. S. Government Printing Office.

Sayer, A. 1984. *Method in Social Science: A Realist Approach.* London: Hutchinson.

Schultz, T.W. 1964. *Transforming Traditional Agriculture.* New Haven: Yale University Press.

Troll, C. 1966. "The Cordilleras of the Tropical Americas: Aspects of Climatic, Phytogeographical and Agrarian Ecology." In *Geo-ecology of the Mountainous Regions of the Tropical Americas,* edited by C. Troll, 15-56. Bonn: Ferd Dummlers.

Vavilov, N.I. 1951. "The Origin, Variation, Immunity, and Breeding of Cultivated Plants." *Chronica Botanica* 13:1-364.

Wilkes, G. 1989. "Germplasm Preservation: Objectives and Needs." In *Biotic Diversity and Germplasm Preservation, Global Imperatives,* edited by L. Knutson and A.K. Stoner, 13-42. Dordrecht: Kluwer.

Zevallos, C.M., W.C. Galinat, D.W. Lathrop, E.R. Leng, J.G. Marcos and K. Klumpp, K. 1977. "The San Pablo Corn Kernel and its Friends." *Science* 196:385-389.

Zimmerer, K.S. 1991a. "The Regional Biogeography of Native Potato Cultivars in Highland Peru." *Journal of Biogeography* 18:165-178.

———. 1991b. "Maintaining Diversity in Potato and Maize Fields of the Peruvian Andes." *Journal of Ethnobiology*

Zimmerer, K.S. 1991c. "Labor Shortages and the Decline of Crop Diversity in the Southern Peruvian Sierra." *The Geographical Review.* 81:

Zimmerer, K.S.s 1992. "Land-use Modification and Labor Shortage Impacts on the Loss of Native Crop Diversity in the Andean Highlands." In *Sustainable Mountain Agriculture: Perspectives and Issues,* vol. 2, edited by N.S. Jodha et al., 413-422. New Delhi: Oxford and IBH.

CHAPTER 7

Reclamation of a Mountain Coal Mine: Designing Habitat for Bighorn Sheep

NORMA BETH MACCALLUM
VALERIUS GEIST

Introduction

The creation of steep walls during mining and road building, and the inadvertent exposure of mineral seeps, has attracted mountain sheep in several localities in North America (Elliot 1984, Geist 1971a, Morgantini and Worbets 1988, Morgantini and Bruns 1988). Steep, tall rock walls, be they man-made or natural are vital to the security strategies of sheep. Mineral seeps provide vital metabolic salt, essential during spring and summer, are the metabolically most active periods in the annual cycle of sheep. Such may have been the factors that attract bighorn sheep in the Canadian Rocky Mountains to open pit mines. This translates into an opportunity to rehabilitate open pit mines into permanent bighorn sheep habitat.

In 1985, Cardinal River Coals Ltd. (CRC) commissioned a wildlife study in response to the voluntary occupation of their mineral surface lease by bighorn sheep. This open pit coal mine is situated in the foothills of Alberta on the east slope of the Canadian Rocky Mountains. Mining operations began in 1969 and reclamation in 1971. By the time the study was begun in the fall of 1985, approximately 200 bighorn sheep were using the mining area despite the continuing activities of mining, plant operations, and the presence of rail and road transportation. We describe the circumstances under which bighorn sheep voluntarily occupied an active coal mine, we document the seasonal and spatial use patterns of the sheep about the mine, their health and population characteristics, and finally discuss the changes made to the reclamation plans in order to design the final landscape so as to be suitable for bighorn sheep.

Open Pit Mining

Before discussing the occupation of a coal mine by bighorn sheep it is necessary to understand the type of mining at the Cardinal River Coals Ltd. area. This is a truck shovel operation. Shovels with 15 and 30 m^3 cubic yard bucket capacity are employed in conjunction with 100 and 170 tonne trucks to mine multiple open pits.

The recoverable coal is found in the upper beds of the Luscar Formation, which is a 457 m thick non-marine sequence of interbedded soft gray sandstones, dark gray shales and coal seams of the Cretaceous age. The seam being mined is locally known as the Jewel seam and is between 10 - 14 m thick. The seam is highly folded and contains minor faulting. This folding process results in concentrations of coal at the bottom of the folds known as "pods". These "pods" of coal can range up to 60 m high on the fold axes. Open pit mining occurs where the folding process and long term erosion have exposed the coal relatively close to the earth's surface. As a result of this folding process, mining from the surface is not continuous but highly localized, depending on the depth of the underlying coal. Open pits therefore, are often disjunct being interconnected by roads cutting through undisturbed habitat where the original vegetation and soils are left intact.

THE STUDY AREA

Cardinal River Coals Ltd. is situated in west central Alberta at the former town site of Luscar at 53° 04' north latitude and 117° 24' west longitude. The study area is defined by CRC's Mineral Surface Lease #5972 comprising 2845 ha and is bisected by Highway (HWY) 40. As of December 31, 1986, a total of 43.9% or 1250 ha of the mine surface lease had been disturbed, of which 504 ha were in some stage of reclamation (Acott et al. 1987).

BIOPHYSICAL CHARACTERISTICS

The study area is located within the subalpine eco-region (Strong and Leggat 1981) and is typified by rolling topography and steep slopes of uplifted Mesozoic shales and sandstones. Elevation ranges from 1680 m to 1860 m.

The study area is located just below timber line at the eastern edge of the Rocky Mountains on the northeast flank of the Nikanassin range. This range extends 30 km to the northwest and 27 km to the southeast of Luscar and presents a considerable barrier to the easterly flow of Pacific air (Root 1976). Luscar Mountain, located immediately to the southeast of the study area attains an elevation of just over 2600 m. Prior to mining, the study area was almost entirely forested with a closed canopy spruce/fir forest. Forested areas are dominated by hybrid white x Engelmann spruce (*Picea glauca* x *engelmannii*), lodgepole pine (*Pinus contorta*), fir (*Abies lasiocarpa*) and black spruce (*Picea mariana*). Aspen (*Populus tremuloides*) and balsam poplar (*Populus balsamifera*) occur on exposed, warm, south-facing slopes. Most coniferous timber within the lease is not suitable for commercial sale. Soils of the study area are generally orthic gray luvisols on fine textured materials or eluviated brunisols on coarser textured parent materials.

CLIMATE

Cardinal River Coals Ltd. is located in an area of Cordilleran climate characterized by cold winters and cool summers (Strong and Leggat 1981). During the winter months, air that moves eastward over the Rockies periodically descends and warms adiabatically, creating the Chinooks and high temperatures that are characteristic of this area (Root 1976). Rapid removal of snow cover and desiccation of vegetation are consequences of the Chinook.

Meterological data collected at CRC from 1977 to 1987 indicate that the mean daily temperature averaged 2.4°C per year. Total precipitation for this same period averaged 744 mm per annum, 70% of which fell from May to September.

High winds are common, being strongest near timber line. Between October 1985 and March, 1986, 40 days of winds over 80 kph were recorded at the CRC security gate in the valley bottom at elevation 1753 m. This is similar to the three year average calculated from 1986 to 1988.

RECLAMATION

The reclamation process at Cardinal River Coals Ltd. begins with stripping the topsoil and upper layers of the regolith prior to mining. These materials are stockpiled for future use. Once the dumping and recontouring of an exhausted pit is accomplished, regolith material is replaced over the whole surface to a depth of 15 cm. Topsoil is placed only on locations selected for reforestation to a depth of 30 cm. A grass-legume mixture is then seeded directly onto the regolith by using a helicopter or hydroseeder (Acott 1986a). The resulting forage crop is composed of varying amounts of the following species: Durar Hard Fescue (*Festuca ovina* var. *duriuscula*, Arctic Red Fescue (*Festuca rubra*), Ruebens Canada Bluegrass (*Poa compressa*), Kentucky Bluegrass (*Poa pratensis*), Streambank Wheatgrass (*Agropyron riparium*), Kay Orchardgrass (*Dactylis glomerata*), Smooth Bromegrass (*Bromus inermis*), Rambler Alfalfa (*Medicago* spp.), Aurora Alsike Clover (*Trifolium hybridum*), Sainfoin (*Onobrychis viciifolia*), Oxley Cicer Milkvetch (*Astragalus cicer*) and Sweet Clover (*Melilotus* spp.)

Reforestation with woody species is carried out on the "topsoil islands" after a nurse crop of sweet clover has been established. The following species are planted: Engelmann Spruce (*Picea engelmannii*), Lodgepole Pine (*Pinus contorta*), Green Alder (*Alnus crispa*), Swamp Birch (*Betula pumila*), Balsam Poplar (*Populus balsamifera*), Willow (*Salix* spp.), Canadian Buffaloberry (*Shepherdia canadensis*), Wolfwillow (*Eleaegnus commutata*), Wood Rose (*Rosa woodsii*) and Black Elderberry (*Sambucus melanocarpa*).

Bighorn Sheep Habitat Requirements

The common feature of bighorn distribution in North America is the presence of rocky escape terrain (Plate 9) in proximity to quality forage (Wishart 1978:166). The bighorn's anti-predator strategy involves visual detection of predators at distance and response by running to cliffs or cliff-like terrain. A long field of view unobstructed by trees or other visual impediments is therefore essential for a successful anti-predator strategy. Radio telemetry monitoring of ewes in southern Alberta showed significantly higher heart rates when these sheep were traversing forests as compared with movement on open slopes or fields (MacArthur et al. 1979).

Bighorn sheep are thus limited to foraging areas that are near to escape terrain. Most sheep use of foraging areas occurs within 0.8 km of escape terrain (Van Dyke et al. 1983:6). Stemp (1983:117) demonstrated that heart rate of ewes increased exponentially with distance from cliffs and that sheep were almost never sighted beyond 300 m from cliffs despite the presence of excellent forage and steep hills. They were never sighted beyond 500 m of cliffs.

Grasses and sedges are the preferred foods of bighorns (Stelfox 1976). Forbs and, to a lesser extent, shrubs are also used seasonally. Mineral licks are sought out in the spring by rams and ewes (Plate 10). Weeks and Kirkpatrick (1976) postulated that white-tailed deer needed sodium in spring to compensate for an elevated intake of water and potassium. Jones and Hanson (1985:97, 120) indicate that licks used exclusively by bighorns were rich in calcium and magnesium, and that sulphur salts were used to synthesis the sulphur bearing amino acids so essential to the growth of connective tissues, hair, hooves and horn.

The other important habitat needs of bighorns are thermal cover (provided by elevation, rock outcroppings and vegetation), rutting and lambing areas. In the southern parts of their range, water may be limiting. Bighorns may make long migrations between seasonal ranges. Rams may have up to 6 ranges and ewes up to 4 (Geist 1971b:63). Knowledge of the location of seasonal ranges is passed onto lambs and young rams as a learned tradition.

RECLAMATION PLANS AND STANDARDS

Prior to 1963 there were no reclamation standards in the province of Alberta. In 1963, the combination of public concern about industrial development and the increased rate of industrial disturbance resulted in the Surface Reclamation Act of 1963 (Bratton 1987). This Act was concerned primarily with cleanup and recontouring the land and dealt with the reclamation of well sites, pipelines, battery sites, mines and quarries. In 1973, the Land Surface Conservation and Reclamation Act was passed. It provided for the planning of developments so that adverse impacts would be minimized and ensured that reclamation plans, prior to construction, were completed. This change of attitude was further emphasized by the passing of the Regulated Coal Surface Operations Regulations in 1974, which stated that land reclamation should become an integral part of mine planning and development. A major statement on reclamation objectives was made in the Coal Development Policy (Alberta Government 1976:7) states:

> The primary objective in land reclamation is to ensure that the mined or disturbed land will be returned to a state which will support plant and animal life or be otherwise productive or useful to man at least to the degree before it was disturbed.

Cardinal River Coals Ltd. began reclamation in 1971 and by the end of 1978, 198 ha of disturbed area had been revegetated (Hardy 1981). Initial reclamation efforts used a variety of strategies and operated under two objectives:

1. To stabilize the soil surface against erosion.
2. To establish a productive and self-sustaining big game wildlife habitat.

By 1979, CRC had commissioned a study (Wallis and Wershler 1979) to develop specific guidelines for reclaiming disturbed areas to bighorn sheep, mule deer, elk, and moose habitat. Reclamation objectives were refined (Acott 1983) to include:

1. A final landscape of 40% tree cover / 60% open grazing area. Under the assumption that wildlife would utilize the edge of the natural forest surrounding the mining disturbance, the amount of cover required would be correspondingly reduced.
2. Forage varieties established in the open areas would be chosen on the basis of availability, hardiness and nutritional value to wildlife.
3. Trees and shrubs planted on reforested areas would provide concealment, thermal protection, and sight line interruption in addition to providing nutritious browse.
4. Travel corridors would be developed to encourage wildlife utilization of the entire reclaimed area.

By 1986, one year after initiation of the bighorn study, the emphasis on reclamation of disturbed areas was placed on bighorn habitat (Acott 1986a).

CRC also took an opportunity to diversify its primary land use objective by reclaiming an exhausted pit as a lake to be used as a sport fishery. Approval by the government to go ahead with development of the lake was given in 1981.

Seasonal and Spatial Distribution of Bighorn Sheep

POPULATION SIZE

The number of sheep observed on the Cardinal River Coals Ltd. mine site varied seasonally during the year of observation. The maximum numbers occurred during the fall of 1985 and early winter of 1986. Fewer sheep were observed on the mine site during the late winter and spring while the fewest occurred during the months of June, July and the first half of August.

The highest one-day count for the year occurred on 8 October 1985 when 175 sheep (83 ewes, 45 lambs, 5 female yearlings, 3 male yearlings, 6 Class I rams, 24 Class II rams, 8 Class III rams and 1 Class IV ram) were observed. Population characteristics derived from daily census counts do not account for known mortality unless specified.

Seasonal Movements

During the field study, several important dates were noted regarding sheep movements on and off the mine site (Table 1). These dates were used to construct home range occupation patterns of the nursery herd and the Class II, III and IV rams.

TABLE 1. MOVEMENTS OF BIGHORN SHEEP ON AND OFF THE CARDINAL RIVER COALS LTD., MINE SITE BETWEEN SEPTEMBER 17, 1985 AND SEPTEMBER 1, 1986.

Date	Sheep Movement
October 18, 1985	- ram band moves from C-baseline to benches and slopes adjacent HWY 40
October 23, 1985	- large rams leave CRC
November 7, 1985	- rams begin to congregate on 50-A-1/2 dump (ewe pre-rut range) (Figure 2)
November 15, 1985	- large rams from off the mine site join the nursery herd on the rut range
November 19, 1985	- 3 class IV rams from off the mine site join the rut
November 20, 1985	- first day mounting was observed
December 1-7, 1985	- peak of rutting activity
December 23, 1985	- last day more than 1 ewe was observed being followed and mounted by rams
December 29, 1985	- first day large rams were seen grouped together on the rut range (50-A-1/2)
January 18, 1986	- last day mounting of an old ewe (RH) was observed

February 5, 1986	- first day the adult rams were observed segregated from the nursery herd on the subalpine meadow
February 18, 1986	- least number of sheep (31) on CRCb observed during the winter/spring of 1986 (January - May, inclusive)
February 26, 1986	- approximately half the nursery herd returns to CRC
May 15, 1986	- the ewe "MHL" was observed leaving nursery herd for ranges west of CRC. First day ewe "MHM" was not observed with nursery herd
May 28, 1986	- first lambs of year sighted
May 28, 1986	- a group of 12 yearlings and 3 ewes leave CRC via Luscar Creek
June 4, 1986	- large group of ewes were sighted using 50-A-3 as a mineral lick. Also the 5 ewes and lambs from 51-B-2 moved west across and off the mine site
June 25, 1986	- 95% of new lambs sighted on or near to CRC in June and early July were observed by this date (Figure 7)
August 11, 1986	- beginning of fall congregation of ewes onto CRC
August 22, 1986	- establishment of most of the nursery herd (134) on mine site for the pre-rut
September 1, 1986	- beginning of fall congregation of rams (8) onto the mine site

Four major movements for the nursery herd were identified as:
1. movement onto the study area in late summer and early fall
2. movement to winter range in late winter
3. movement to lambing sites in mid-May
4. movement into alpine drainages adjacent to CRC during the summer months

Four major movements for the Class II, III and IV rams were identified as:

1. movement onto the study area in late summer and early fall
2. movement to the ewe pre-rut range for the rut
3. movement to winter range in early winter
4. movement into the alpine ranges in late May and early June

The nursery herd had already congregated on the mine site when the study began on 17 September 1985, where it remained for the rut and early winter season. In mid-February, the herd left CRC in response to a severe storm event that deposited 16.2 cm of snow over three days (14-16 February) and was accompanied by -30°C temperatures. When the sheep returned, approximately half the nursery herd remained offsite, presumably to winter on traditional ranges. The portion of the herd that returned continued to use essentially the same ranges for the late winter and spring at CRC as they had for the pre-rut, rut and early winter.

In mid-May, individual ewes began to leave CRC in search of lambing areas. Most lambing occurred off the mine site with the exception of six ewes, which lambed on the highest and steepest pit wall. A portion of the nursery herd regrouped after lambing on the alpine meadows along Luscar Creek (Plate 11). These meadows were located immediately above an unreclaimed pit which had been dug at timber line. During June the ewes made extensive use of this pit as a mineral lick. Virtually no grazing took place on the mine site during this time.

The number of lambs sighted on and adjacent to CRC during lambing and early summer rose to a maximum of 36 by 10 July. Then numbers dropped as the nursery herd moved higher into the headwaters of the Gregg River and West Jarvis Creek Drainages. Few sheep were observed on CRC during July. However, on 11 August, one hundred sheep were observed on the mine site. Sheep numbers fluctuated until 22 August, after which time consistently high numbers of sheep were observed on CRC.

The pre-rut, or fall congregation of adult rams onto CRC, had already taken place when the study began on 17 September 1985. Rams remained segregated from the nursery herd until mid October. They then moved onto the pre-rut range early in November, joining the ewes for the rut. The peak of the rut occurred during the second week of December 1985. In mid-January the adult rams segregated from the ewes, leaving them on the rut range. The rams occupied a south-facing subalpine grassland that was centrally located on the mine site. They alternately used this slope and the reclaimed south-facing slopes above HWY 40 throughout the winter and spring until they began to leave CRC in late May. During the summer months of June, July, and August,

Reclamation of a Mountain Coal Mine 161

small groups of rams were observed travelling between various alpine ranges. Only the occasional individual or small group was observed on CRC. The adult rams returned to CRC for the fall of 1986, after 1 September and before 29 September. This fall congregation was apparently later than other years when rams were sighted by CRC personnel on the mine site during the last week of August.

When the four seasonal movements for the nursery herd and the four seasonal movements for the adult rams were combined, six seasonal home ranges were identified. (A seasonal home range is an area to which an animal confines itself between two seasonal migrations and which it occupies at the same time in successive years (Geist 1971b:74). These were:

PRE-RUT. 17 September 1985, to 14 November 1985.
This is the period when adult rams and ewes congregate on CRC and occupy separate ranges. The nursery herd began to return to CRC on 11 August, and were well established by 22 August. The adult rams returned later, sometime after 1 September 1986. In most years they have been reported on the mine site the last week in August.

RUT. 15 November 1985, to 18 January 1986.
The rut was defined as the period when rams and oestrous ewes were observed together. Most rutting activity was over in December. The last breeding was seen on 18 January 1986, when one old ewe was observed being mounted.

WINTER. 19 January 1986, to 14 February 1986.
This was the period when the adult rams left the ewes on the rut range and wintered separately on south-facing slopes also located on CRC.

SPRING. 15 February 1986, to 27 May 1986.
This period was defined by half the nursery herd leaving CRC and wintering presumably on traditional range. Movement off the mine site was precipitated by a major storm event with only half the herd returning. Reduction in use of CRC by the nursery herd during the late winter and early spring has been observed in subsequent years.

LAMBING. 28 May 1986, to 30 June 1986
Lambing was defined from the first day when lambs of the year were sighted; lambing probably occurred a few days earlier. This period includes lambing, isolation of new lambs and ewes and the regrouping of ewes in the alpine meadows adjacent to CRC. At this time the ewes were

using a pit situated at timber line as a mineral lick. Adult rams were not present on CRC during this period but were seen sporadically in the alpine during this time.

SUMMER. 1 July 1986, to 10 August 1986

This period was defined by the nursery herd movement higher into the headwaters of alpine drainages, presumably utilizing the new forage available as snow melted at higher elevations.

Of the 11,933 individual bighorn observations made between 17 September 1985, and 10 August 1986, 73% were lambs, ewes, or yearlings of either sex, 5% were of Class I rams and 22% were of Class II, III and IV rams (Table 2). Sheep were concentrated on the study area from the pre-rut through to the beginning of lambing in the spring, a period of 254 days.

Variation of Population Size Within Seasons

Using the maximum count method, the maximum number of bighorn sheep (193) on CRC occurred in the pre-rut (Table 3). Numbers fluctuated slightly just before the rut as several large rams left CRC, presumably to rut elsewhere. Also, there was some fluctuation of the numbers of ewes present on CRC at this time as several left apparently to rut elsewhere. During the rut, several large rams from offsite joined the CRC herd. Numbers of Class IV rams were the highest that were observed for the whole year (7) at this time. The maximum number of sheep using CRC during the early winter after the rut (168) was only slightly lower than during the pre-rut (193), especially if one accounts for known mortality that occurred during the fall (12) after the maximum one day count of 175 on 8 October 1985.

Nursery herd numbers dropped sharply in mid-February when approximately half the animals left to winter, presumably, on traditional range. From 4 March 1986, to 22 May 1986, total numbers of sheep on the mine were markedly consistent showing only a small decline in numbers (4 March = 89, 22 May = 72). After this date, total numbers dropped as ewes left for lambing sites and rams dispersed into the alpine. Until this time, the total numbers of Class II, III and IV rams had been remarkably consistent throughout the year with the exception of the rut. Between 9 June and 7 July, wide fluctuations of numbers of sheep (from 0 to 76) were observed on the mine, reflecting the nursery herds' periodic visits for minerals. The fewest numbers of sheep observed at CRC during the year occurred between 9 July and 6 August (minimum 0, maximum 24). Sheep at this time were to be found high in adjacent alpine drainages. Fluctuating and increasing numbers of sheep were then observed at CRC from 8 August to 22 August when large numbers of the nursery herd (total 134) appeared to have returned for the pre-rut. The first adult rams (8) appeared on 1 September 1986, for the pre-rut.

TABLE 3. MAXIMUM COUNT OF BIGHORN SHEEP PRESENT AT CARDINAL RIVER COALS LTD., FOR EACH SEASONAL HOME RANGE BETWEEN SEPTEMBER 17, 1985 AND AUGUST 10, 1986. NUMBERS ARE NOT CORRECTED FOR KNOWN MORTALITY.

Class	Pre-rut	Rut	Winter	Spring	Lambing	Summer
LAMB	47	42	39	19	11	24
EWE	83	74	70	48	37	35
FY	7	8	5	1	11	6
MY	8	6	5	6	8	7
I	8	10	11	8	4	3
II	28	25	25	24	17	9
III	9	9	8	10	9	2
IV	3	7	5	4	2	0
Total	193	181	168	120	99	86
#counts	23	26	14	38	20	17
Highest one day count	175	166	159	101	57	76
Date	Sep 17 to Nov 14	Nov 15 to Jan 18	Jan 19 to Feb 14	Feb 15 to May 27	May 28 to June 30	July 1 to Aug 10

Note: data are compiled for each activity period from the computer file called obsed.

FY = female yearling
MY = male yearling
I = Class I ram
II = Class II ram
III = Class III ram
IV = Class IV ram

Spatial Distribution of Bighorn Sheep

Two-thirds of all sheep observations (11,933) for the year occurred on about 1.3/km^2 of reclaimed grasslands adjacent to the alpine zone and the south-facing slopes by HWY 40, and on the centrally located subalpine meadow. These areas represented the most heavily used ranges in the pre-rut, rut, winter, and spring seasons particularly by the nursery herd. The remaining one third of sheep use was scattered over 7.8/km^2 of the mine site for a total use area of 9.1/km^2.

Approximately one third of the observations for the nursery herd (n=9,349) for the year 1985/86 were made within 32 ha of the reclaimed grasslands adjacent to the alpine zone. Another one third of observations were made within an additional 32 ha of the same grassland and within 50 ha of the south slopes and valley bottom adjacent to HWY 40. This means that two thirds of the nursery herd use was concentrated on 113 ha of reclaimed range (approximately 1 km^2). The last one third were scattered over 696 ha of the lease. The total area used by the nursery herd for grazing, security, mineral licks or travelling within the lease boundaries was 810 ha.

Rams were more widely scattered than the nursery herd. Of 2,584 observations made of the Class II, III and IV rams, one third occurred on 65 hectares of the reclaimed grasslands adjacent to the alpine zone, the south-facing subalpine meadow, and the reclaimed grasslands on the south-facing slopes above HWY 40. An additional one third of observations were scattered over 113 ha located on the reclaimed grasslands adjacent to the alpine zone, on the slopes adjacent to HWY 40, and on a topsoil stockpile located on the C-baseline. The last one third of observations were located on 696 ha of the lease. The total area used by the Class II, III and IV rams was 874 ha.

It is thus apparent that the most important area used by the sheep on the study area is the reclaimed grassland adjacent to the alpine zone. It was reclaimed in 1977, 1978, and 1979, and was used for grazing by the nursery herd during the pre-rut, rut, winter, and spring seasons. Rams congregated here to rut, during which time the high walls of the adjacent pit were used heavily by ewes escaping rams and by rams attending receptive females. The benched walls of this pit served as escape sites, bedding areas, and in May and June, the seeps from the walls were used as mineral licks by the nursery group that used the Luscar Creek valley immediately west of the lease. This daily movement was interpreted as a response to the need for minerals, as virtually no grazing took place on the mine at this season.

The sheep also made moderate to heavy use of the south-facing subalpine meadow that is centrally located on the study area. This area was used primarily by rams during the winter and spring period when they had segregated from the nursery herd. Heaviest use of this hill was on the NW corner which lies adjacent to a benched pit wall. This slope and pit wall were used by the nursery herd chiefly as a travel route connecting the reclaimed grasslands located next to the alpine zone with the HWY 40 area.

The nursery herd used the south-facing slopes and valley bottoms adjacent to HWY 40 heavily during the pre-rut and winter, while the rams used this area heavily in the winter and spring. This area was seeded in 1976. The east wall of the nearby open pit was used as escape terrain by the sheep. In May of 1985, and 1986, 6 and 5 ewes, respectively, lambed on this wall. In 1986, these lambing sites were within a few hundred meters of an active dump site. Most lambing, however, took place off the study area in the alpine zone.

Moderate use of the large bench and slopes of a dump also located adjacent to HWY 40 was made by the nursery herd during the pre-rut. This dump was reclaimed in 1972 and 1979/80.

Rams also used a topsoil dump heavily during the pre-rut. A power line located here was reclaimed in 1978; the topsoil island was reclaimed in 1983. Rams have been observed here by mine personnel since 1980.

As some or all of the sheep use areas off the study area for late winter, spring, lambing and summer range, the above figures do not represent the complete home range occupied by the CRC herd, but rather the area used by them when they are on the mine site.

Population Characteristics

"Individual and population quality appears to be a function of how well individuals grow, which in turn is determined by the nutritional regime of the pregnant and lactating females" (Geist 1971b:281). Population quality is therefore related to body and horn size, age at sexual maturation, behavioral vigor, life expectancy, reproductive success, and survival rates of the young. Factors such as parasitism, harassment, and predation cause an animal to expend energy that otherwise could be used for growth, reproduction, or maintenance (Festa-Bianchet 1987; Stemp 1983). Body size, horn size, lungworm loads, nutritional quality of forage, harassment, and predation as factors affecting population quality are discussed below.

Body Size

"The most common indices of general animal condition are measures of body size, usually body weight, or measures of body-fat reserves" (Bailey 1984:318). Weight has been used as a useful index of the recent nutritional status of ruminants (Thorne et al. 1979:74). Body weight used in conjunction with a linear body measure (such as total length) can provide an index that is better related to physical condition than that provided by body weight alone (Bailey 1984:319).

Mean live weights for the 25 ewes measured at CRC was 73.34 kg, mean heart girth was 101.58 cm, and total length averaged 152.56 cm (Table 4). Most data published for body measurements focus on the spring or summer period when sheep would be in poorer body condition than in the fall when the CRC data were collected. Direct comparisons are not possible as body weights would be near maximum in the fall after the summer feeding period. Mean weights for ewes four years or older from Alberta populations (Table 5) vary from 72.1 kg measured in Waterton during April and May 1973 to 70.3 kg in Sheep River and 65.8 kg in Jasper measured at various times of the year (Blood et al. 1970). Weights of 20 "adult" ewes measured in June and July of 1975 and 1976 at Cadomin (Kosinski 1977) averaged 57.65 kg, which is significantly different from the CRC mean weight of 73.34 kg (t=6.73 df=36 $P<0.0001$) measured two to three months later. Jorgenson and Wishart (1984) calculated summer (June, July and August) growth rates in older ewes on Ram Mountain to be linear. Linear growth rates of 0.17, 0.18 and 0.19 kg/day for 3, 4 and 5 year old ewes respectively, were calculated. Using 0.19 kg and multiplying by 60 (days), the average weight of Cadomin sheep (mostly Redcap range residents) by the first of September would be 69.05 kg, still considerably less than the CRC sheep, but not significantly different (t=1.84 df=36 $P>0.05$). A direct comparison, however, would necessitate data being collected during the same time period on sheep from both sites.

Weights of ewes four years and older from Ram Mountain, Alberta, were made available by J. Jorgenson (Alberta Fish and Wildlife) for use in this study. Live sheep were measured in September and October between the years 1978 and 1989. The average weight was 68.09 kg, significantly less (t=2.79 df=44 $P<0.0078$) than the CRC sheep average weight of 73.3 kg.

The weights of CRC sheep in the fall are similar to those of ewes in Waterton measured in the spring, but are greater than those recorded for Jasper ewes taken at various times throughout the year. Bighorns of southern Alberta attain a larger size than those of northern Alberta (Blood et al. 1970). Wishart (1969) attributed these differences to an optimum combination of climate, soil and vegetation present in southern Alberta. Weights of the CRC ewes in fall are likely to be at the high end for sheep in Alberta.

SKULL CHARACTERS

Skull characters are good indicators of population quality, mean values measured for the CRC sheep (Table 6) for lower molar length (83.2 mm) occiput - frontal length (121.1) and naso-cranial length (199.8) were similar to those for ewes from populations in the northern Rockies in Alberta (82.4, 121.2, and 198.2 mm respectively). The upper molar length of the CRC ewes (83.2 mm) was less than that for southern (85.2 mm) and greater than that for northern (81.9 mm) populations. Basisphenoid crown height for the CRC

TABLE 4. WEIGHTS (KG) AND BODY MEASUREMENTS (CM) FROM EWES GREATER THAN 4 YEARS TAKEN DURING THE CARDINAL RIVER COALS LTD., NON-TROPHY HUNT SEPTEMBER 10 TO OCTOBER 31, 1985 AND SEPTEMBER 28 TO OCTOBER 16, 1987.

Measurement	n	Mean	Range	SD
whole weight	25	73.3	58.5 - 85.7	6.7
gutted weight	18	52.7	41.3 - 62.1	5.2
heart girth	25	101.6	91.5 -108.0	3.8
total length	25	152.6	133.0 -174.0	10.2
tail length	25	13.1	7.0 - 18.0	3.6
neck circumference	15	35.3	31.5 - 41.0	2.8
hindfoot length	17	41.0	38.5 - 44.0	1.5

whole weight	=	weighed immediately after having being killed using a Salter 400 lb spring scale and net
gutted weight	=	weighed after being gutted and before bring skinned
heart girth	=	measured around the circumference of the body immediately behind the forelegs
total length	=	measured along the dorsal contour from the tip of the nose to the tip of the tail vertebrae with the animal fully extended
tail length	=	measured from the base of the tail to the tip of the tail vertebrae
neck circumference	=	measured around the circumference of the neck immediately below the head
hindfoot	=	measured from the joint of the hock to the tip of the nail

TABLE 5. WEIGHTS OF EWES FROM VARIOUS LOCATIONS AND DATES IN ALBERTA.

Location	Date	n	Age	Weight	Range	Source
Waterton	April/May	65	>4	72.1	54.4-90.7	Blood et al. 1970
Sheep R	all year	24	>4	70.3	65.3-82.5	Blood et al. 1970
Jasper	all year	12	>4	65.8	53.1-82.5	Blood et al. 1970
Cadomin	June/July	20	adult	57.6	43.1-69.9	Kosinkski 1976
Ram Mtn	Sept/Oct	21	>4	68.1	53.6-78.0	Jorgenson 1978-1989

sheep (82.8 mm) was less than both southern (92.9) and northern (88.1) populations.

POPULATION CHARACTERISTICS

Management of a population of any big game species requires knowledge of productivity, mortality, and numbers or density (Gilbert 1978:297). These measures are generally estimated due to the expense and difficulty in obtaining actual values.

Using figures corrected for known mortality and the maximum count method, the maximum numbers of bighorn sheep on the study area during the pre-rut was: 198 (47 lambs, 88 ewes, 7 female yearlings, 8 male yearlings, 8 Class I rams, 28 Class II rams, 9 Class III rams and 3 Class IV rams). It should be noted that mortality does not affect the counts of seasons other than the pre-rut (unless mortality is carried over into the next season). Population ratios calculated from these data for the pre-rut (17 September to 14 November 1985) are as follows:

lamb:100 ewes (ewes 2.5 years and older)	53:100
lamb:100 ewes and female yearlings	49:100
yearling:100 ewes (ewes 2.5 years and older)	17:100
yearling:100 sheep (rams & ewes 2.5+ years)	11:100
yearling male:yearling female	53:47
Class I, II, III & IV rams:ewes (2.5+ years)	35:65

TABLE 6. SKULL, ROSTRAL AND CRANIAL MEASUREMENTS (MM) OF BIGHORN EWES 3 YEARS AND OLDER FROM CARDINAL RIVER COALS LTD., MINE SITE 1981 TO 1986.

Measurement	n	Mean	Range	SD
Upper molar length	18	83.2	76.6 - 89.0	2.86
Lower molar length	13	82.8	77.0 - 88.0	3.28
Basisphenoid-crown height	18	82.8	74.0 - 93.1	5.43
Occiput-frontal length	18	121.1	111.5 - 125.0	3.20
Naso-cranial length	14	199.8	1860. - 229.2	10.33

definition of skull measurements:

L   Upper molar (length) series or upper tooth row = greatest alveolar length of combined upper molars and premolars.

M   Lower molar (length) series or lower tooth row = greatest alveolar length of combined molars and premolars.

W   Basisphenoid-crown height = greatest distance between the highest point of the crown between the horn cores, and the point on the basisphenoid near its junction with the presphenoid.

X   Occiput-frontal length = least distance between the superior lip of the foramen magnum and the centre of the frontals in line with the two frontal foramina.

Z   Naso-cranial length = least distance between the midline of the anterior end of the nasals and the depression of the parieta parietals in adult males or to the parietal crest in female and juveniles.

During the fall of 1986, a maximum of 32 yearlings were counted in 11 counts indicating that 68% of the 47 lambs counted during the fall of 1985 survived their first year.

Lungworm Loads

Infection of bighorn sheep by nematode parasites, *Protostrongylus stilesi* and *P. rushi*, has been related to reduced efficiency of the immune system (Festa-Bianchet 1987) and has been associated with epizootic events of pneumonia-related die-offs. Although the term "lungworm pneumonia complex" is used to describe these events, there has been little evidence in the literature for a direct causative relationship between the presence of increased amounts of lungworm and outbreaks of pneumonia (Foreyt and Jessup 1982, Spraker et al. 1984, Onderka and Wishart 1984, Samson et al. 1987). Some evidence has been presented to indicate that in some circumstances lungworm infection in bighorn sheep acts as a predisposing factor to bacterial pneumonia (Forrester and Senger 1964; Spraker and Hibler 1982). Other stress factors that reduce the immunity or resistance level of individual sheep, and thus making a population susceptible to epidemic disease include: loss or deterioration of range, inclement weather, crowding, deep snow, poor nutrition, and parasite levels (Spraker and Hibler 1982; Schwantje 1986). Pneumonia die-offs in sheep with many etiological agents has been recently termed "respiratory disease complex of bighorn sheep" (Onderka and Wishart 1984). Another manifestation of long term low level stress condition is the presence of contagious ecthyma in sheep (Lance 1980). The rate of lungworm larval output in a population can be detected by the number of first stage larvae shed per gram (LPG) of dry feces (Uhazy et al. 1973). These authors suggest that when large numbers of samples can be obtained from a herd, a useful index to the proportion of heavily infected animals in that herd may be obtained. They suggested LPG counts of greater than 1400 represent heavy output.

Larval output from the CRC sheep rose during each month during the fall of 1985 and peaked in December after which a decline occurred. Larval output during the summer months May to September were very low compared to the winter months.

A one way analysis of variance was performed on the transformed $\log(x+1)$ LPG data for the twelve months and it was found that there was a significant difference between the 12 means ($F=46.36$ $P<0.05$). A two sample-t test performed on transformed LPG values for ewes 2 years and older and rams 3 years and older indicates that there was a significance difference between the means in winter ($t=-2.23$ $df=70$ $P<0.03$) but not in summer. The means of the transformed LPG data were higher in winter for the rams than for the ewes (Table 7). Seasonal variation in the numbers of larvae per gram of dry feces in bighorn sheep has been described by other authors (Uhazy et al. 1973, Festa-Bianchet 1987, Jorgenson and Wishart 1983). LPG data for the CRC bighorns showed seasonal variation between winter and summer months as well. The highest rate of larval output (>1400 LPG) for the year occurred in December and January (60% and 36% respectively). High larval output during the summer months was virtually nonexistent. High larval output (>1400 LPG) in rams greater than 3 years occurred in the fall and early winter months. No heavy output in rams was noted between March and September. High levels of larval output in ewes peaked in December, declined, then showed a secondary peak in March and April.

The CRC herd displayed high rates of larval output during the rut and early winter period. Despite these levels, there has been no outward manifestation of pneumonia to indicate that multiple stressors are reducing the resistance of the herd to disease. It is possible that the stress of the rut on rams in the fall and the stress of late winter on the ewes is reflected in the heavy (>1400 LPG) larval output during these times of the year.

A comparison of LPG from faecal samples collected from bighorns on the Redcap range (data made available from K. Smith, Alberta Fish and Wildlife Division) and from those on CRC for the month of March 1986, shows a significant difference (t=3.02 df=29 P<0.05). The LPG levels from Redcap sheep are much higher (n=21, x=1499.1, S=1155.6, range=54-3744) than those from CRC sheep (n=26, x=673, S=540, range=36-2380).

DIET

Fifty per cent by weight of rumen material consisted of grass. Timothy (*Phleum pratense*), wheatgrass (*Agropyron* spp.), bluegrass (*Poa* spp.) and fescue (*Festuca* spp.) were the most common species identified and consisted of 43 per cent of grass material. It is likely that most of the bluegrass, fescue and wheatgrass represent the agronomic species present on the mine site. Only a trace of a "native" species, foxtail barley (*Hordeum jubatum*), was present, representing 1.4 per cent of the grass component. Fifty-five per cent of grass material was unidentified.

Legumes comprised 28 per cent of the rumen contents by weight. Cicer milkvetch (*Astragalus cicer*) pods made up 27 per cent of the legumes while another 27 per cent consisted of cicer milkvetch leaves, clover (*Trifolium* spp.) and alfalfa (*Medicago* spp.). The remaining 46% of the legumes were unidentifiable as to genus. Small amounts of forbs (7%), roots (5%) and moss

TABLE 7. TRANSFORMED LOG (x+1) LPG VALUES FOR EWES (> 2 YEARS) AND RAMS (> 3 YEARS) FOR THE WINTER AND SUMMER MONTHS 1985 TO 1986.

Summer (May - September 1986)

	Transformed Larval Counts			LPG	
n	Mean	SD	Min.	Max.	Mean
Ewes 64	1.594	0.804	0.000	2.952	140.4
Rams 32	1.496	0.832	0.000	3.066	111.8

Winter (October 1985 - April 1986)

	Transformed Larval Counts			LPG	
n	Mean	SD	Min.	Max.	Mean
Ewes 90	2.8253	0.4959	1.3010	4.1533	1195
Rams 40	3.0482	0.5388	1.5682	4.2595	2155

were found in the rumen samples. Willow (*Salix* spp.) leaves, birch (*Betula* spp.) leaves and woody stems (3%) comprised the remainder of identifiable material. Six per cent of the total contents of the rumens were unidentifiable.

Agronomic species comprised 37 per cent of the identifiable contents of the 10 rumens collected at CRC 17 September - 31 October 1985. Much of the grass and legume material was identifiable only as inflorescence, stem or leaf parts. If the assumption was made that most of this material was composed of agronomic species (most of what is present on CRC), then agronomic grasses and legumes would make up about 76 per cent of the bighorn's diet during these two months.

Microhistological analysis results were grouped into grass, sedge, forb, shrub and tree categories (Table 8). Grass and sedge genera comprised 67 per cent and 7 per cent of the annual diet of bighorn sheep using the mine site, while forbs comprised 15 per cent, shrubs 5 per cent and coniferous trees 6 per cent. Grasses were highest from October to December (82-92%) and lowest in June and July (31 and 37%). Sedge consumption on the other hand was highest in June and July (31% and 28%, respectively). The sheep, during these two months, were grazing not on the study area but in the alpine region adjacent to the mine site; this is where pellets were collected during June and July. Use of shrub material was highest in April (29%), June (20%), and July (23%). Forb components of the diet were highest in May (22%), August (22%), and September (31%). Heavy use of *Pinus* and *Picea* was made in February (19%) and April (23%).

HUMAN ACTIVITY AND SHEEP RESPONSE

Bighorn sheep at CRC moved freely through the mineral surface lease despite the continued activity in coal mining. Sheep frequently walked along and crossed haul roads (Plate 12). They commonly walked across the top of the "superpipe", a landfill constructed above HWY 40 for the passage of the large haulage trucks. Bighorn ewes were observed bedded with their lambs on the active haul road below 51-B-3 pit. On one occasion a 170 tonne haul truck loaded with rock on a down hill grade was observed stopping to let sheep cross. Sheep commonly bedded and walked along the banks adjacent to the active haul roads. Only one sheep was killed at CRC to date by mining activity. It was a ram in rut who ran off a bank onto the haul road and was killed by a large haulage vehicle.

On several occasions sheep were observed during mine blasting to determine their behavioral response. Older sheep commonly exhibited no appreciable outward reaction while younger sheep infrequently would startle and run a short distance before settling down. A mixed herd of 88 sheep (24 lambs, 38 ewes, 2 female yearling, 6 male I, 13 male II, 2 male III and 3 male IV) responded as a unit to a blast from the neighboring Gregg River Resources (GRR) mine. The sheep grazed calmly on the west side of 50-A-2 dump on CRC when suddenly they leaped as a unit into full flight for no apparent reason. A few seconds later, the sound of a blast from the GRR pit (0.8 km away) was heard. Consultation with my personnel revealed that the seam which GRR was blasting was the same as the one on which the sheep had been grazing. It seemed likely that the sheep either felt the ground shake prior to the sound arriving or reacted to the plume of dust from the blast. They ran only a short distance (15 to 30 m) away from the source of the blast, then stopped and resumed grazing. On 6 January 1986, a mixed herd of 76 grazing sheep located on the large bench south of HWY 40 and west of superpipe responded to the blast from a nearby pit located on the north side of HWY 40 by temporarily bunching together.

The most extreme panic reaction displayed by the sheep was to a helicopter that appeared suddenly from the Gregg River situated 153 m below the dump on which a portion of the nursery herd was grazing. The sheep responded by running in full panic flight to the first nearby bench and then milling excitedly around and over each other - jumping, bumping and crashing into other sheep. They continued for a few minutes after the departure of the helicopter and were bedded 18 minutes after the arrival of the helicopter.

TABLE 8. PER CENT COMPOSITION OF FORAGE INGESTED BY BIGHORN SHEEP AT CARDINAL RIVER LTD., OCTOBER 1985 TO SEPTEMBER 1986 AS MEASURED BY MICROHISTOLOGICAL ANALYSIS.

Month	Grass	Sedge	Forb	Shrub	Tree
Oct.	82	6	10	2	0
Nov	88	3	9	0	0
Dec	92	1	7	0	0
Jan	64	7	15	1	13
Feb	61	5	15	0	19
Mar	76	0	14	1	9
Apr	66	0	5	6	23
May	66	4	22	4	4
Jun	31	31	18	20	0
Jul	37	28	13	23	0
Aug	74	2	22	1	1
Sep	70	0	25	5	0
Year	67	7	15	5	6

Note:

Grass general include: *Agropyron, Agrostis, Bromus, Elymus, Festuca, Koeleria, Phleum*, and *Poa*.

Forb genera include: *Artemisia, Astragalus-Oxytropis*, Boraginaceae, Compositae, *Descurainia, Draba, Melilotus-Medicago* (likely includes *Trifolium*).

Shrub genera include: *Juniperus, Salix, Shepherdia, Symphoricarpos* and an unidentified shrub.

Tree genera include: *Picea* and *Pinus*.
Identification by: The Composition Analysis Lab, Colorado State University.

In 1984, the Alberta Fish and Wildlife Division instituted a non-trophy hunt on a portion of the CRC mineral surface lease. This hunt was opened due to the concern that sheep were moving onto the mine site early in the fall and staying through the winter, thus predisposing them to a high rate of lungworm infection (Wishart et al. 1980, Boag and Wishart 1982). Another concern was overuse of the available winter range. At that time approximately 108 ha of reclaimed grassland and 7 ha of a south-facing subalpine meadow was used intensively during the late fall and early winter months. The sheep foraged more widely over the mine site during the other seasons. The purposes of the hunt were:

1. To reduce the number of animals in the herd (about 200 sheep).
2. To use hunting as a temporary measure to move animals off the mine site (primarily 50-A-2) early in the fall, thus preserving forage for use later in the winter.

Hunting of the animals on the mine site caused the sheep not to abandon the site but to move farther north into the active area of the mine which was off limits to hunters. On 4 October 1985, a nursery group of 18 animals, which had been shot at the previous day on the hunt area, showed up on an area of the mine where they had not been observed previously. This was the only time that members of the nursery herd were observed in this location during the fall of 1985. This type of response (movement precipitated by hunting followed by return to preferred range in a few days) was typical throughout the hunting season. Hunt days were only on Tuesdays (primitive weapons) and Thursdays (shotgun) of each week for the duration of the season. In the fall of 1985, poor weather hindered the archery hunters and by the end of the season, shotgun hunters were the only persons taking advantage of the hunt. The sheep, therefore, would have almost a week to reestablish preferred grazing patterns. The sheep did not leave the mine site to occupy the neighboring WMU438 where trophy and non-trophy hunting were permitted. Hunter success in WMU438 is one of the highest in Alberta (pers. comm. K. Smith AFWD) indicating that hunting pressure is also high.

Other forms of human activity around the sheep at CRC were minimal. Once a reclaimed area is established, little human activity occurs except for the occasional crew in the summer carrying on with fertilizing, tree planting, etc. Most sheep occupied the alpine in summer thereby minimizing the chance of such interactions even less. Random human recreational activities, such as all terrain vehicle use, hiking, or cross country skiing, do not occur on the mining lease.

Predation

Many instances of coyotes either rushing sheep or passing close to them were observed during the study. One incident of a lamb escaping from a coyote onto a nearby high wall was observed; another incident involved a wounded ewe that had isolated herself from the herd and was obviously dying. Even when she was very weak and bedded most of the time, a coyote, which had been staying in her vicinity, appeared unwilling to approach the ewe as long as she was able to stand and face the coyote. Coyotes are, apparently, not significant predators of sheep in this locality.

Wolves are present in the area surrounding the mine site, and tracks were occasionally seen on the north boundary of the mine. With the exception of a lone wolf sighted in 1986 on the 50-A-1 reclamation, no wolves were observed on the main winter ranges within the mine boundary.

Grizzly bears are commonly seen on the mine in spring and fall, but no bear predation of sheep was found. Eagles have been seen immediately adjacent to the mine sites. Cougar sign was not seen on the winter sheep range and, although cougars exist in the area surrounding the mine, the extent of cougar predation on the CRC sheep is not known. This study was not designed to assess predation on sheep, nevertheless, it appears that the sheep, while on the mine site, experienced minimal predation.

Other Wildlife

Mule deer were common on the mine site, feeding in the grasslands adjacent to tree cover or moving through open areas, while using each available island of trees. The maximum count of mule deer between 17 September and 31 December 1985, was: 16 (5 does, 5 fawns, 6 bucks). No elk were sighted in 1985 and 1986, although the habitat is suitable and in recent years, a small herd of cows and calves have consistently have been sighted using a reclaimed grassland during the winter. This south-facing slope is grazed by bighorn sheep, mule deer and elk at various times of the year. Other examples of elk habituating to activities on mine sites are on mines in the Elk Valley of British Columbia and at the Chevron Pittsburgh and Midway Coal Mining Company's Edna mine near Steamboat Springs, Colorado (Arscott 1989). No moose were sighted during the surveys. An artifact of open pit mining in mountainous terrain is that the recoverable coal is not continuous, thereby not all of the surface is disturbed by mining activity. On the CRC mine, there are large areas of mature, coniferous forest that remains scattered throughout the reclaimed grasslands. These patches of forest serve as escape and thermal cover for ungulates and facilitate use of reclaimed areas by species such as mule deer and elk.

Sightings of other animals included red fox near timber line, hoary marmot and golden-mantled ground squirrel denning in the talus slopes of pits adjacent to reclaimed grasslands and red squirrel in the undisturbed subalpine forest. In later years, porcupine and wolverine tracks were also sighted on the mine site. The most common small mammal on reclaimed grasslands was the deer mouse that occurred in high densities. Bird sightings were summarized in the Alberta Bird Record (MacCallum 1986a, 1986b, and 1986c).

Bighorn Sheep Habitat Attributes of a Coal Mine

Wildlife populations are controlled by a combination of welfare and decimating factors and environmental processes that alter environments. Habitat requirements of wildlife have been described as welfare factors by Leopold (1933:25). Habitat can be defined as the arrangement of food, water and cover and the availability of other requirements such as mineral licks. A lack of welfare factors limits populations while the presence of decimating factors (hunting, predation, disease, parasites, accidents) depress populations (Bailey 1984:201). Here the CRC mine site is examined for the habitat requirements of bighorn sheep.

ESCAPE TERRAIN

It is generally agreed that the presence and distribution of escape terrain limits habitat use by bighorn sheep (Van Dyke et al. 1983:6, Tilton and Willard 1982). Various descriptions of escape terrain are in the literature. Tilton and Willard (1982) noted that sheep on winter range avoided areas having a slope steepness of 11-35 per cent (6°-19°) which were located away from cliffs and rugged terrain and preferred areas with a slope steepness greater than 80 per cent (39°). Thorne et al. (1979:52) described escape cover ranging from sagebrush-covered slopes of approximately 100 per cent (45°) to sheer rock cliffs as much as 270 m high. Size and steepness of escape terrain did not seem to be as important as did the proximity of escape terrain to other sites used by sheep for various activities. Van Dyke et al. (1983:6) described escape terrain as comprising of cliffs at least 8 m high and 200 m long. Stemp (1983:119) commented that on Ram Mountain, Alberta, the proximity of escape terrain to areas used by sheep appeared to be more important than the character of escape terrain. Three meter high cliffs amid steep talus slopes seemed perfectly adequate at Ram Mountain; although he did comment that selection for larger, more extensive cliffs would be expected by bighorns under moderate or heavy predation.

The reclaimed landscape at CRC resembles a series of plateaus with more or less flat tops surrounded by slope angles of varying degrees. Slope angles vary from 45° (cliff-like habitat with no reclamation of pit walls), to 33° (the "natural angle of repose" achieved after dumping of rock and overburden) to 27° (slopes which have been graded and reclaimed to vegetation cover). The "plateaus" are separated by valley-like depressions which the sheep must negotiate as they travel through the mine site. Two distinct travel routes were noted to be used by sheep when they moved north through the mineral surface lease. Associated with some "plateaus" are south-facing slopes used for foraging, such as the slopes above HWY 40 and the centrally located subalpine meadow.

In addition to the use of steep slopes and high walls for travel corridors, high walls were used for lambing, for mineral sources (specifically seeps in the pit nearest alpine during June, and mine waste when exposed anytime), and for bedding or as escape terrain. Animals that were sick or wounded segregated themselves from the herd and remained on grassy slopes immediately adjacent to high walls. Walls and steep slopes that were observed to be used for any of these purposes were described as "escape terrain" (Table 9). The locations of designated "escape terrain" were plotted on a separate computer file and this was used to calculate the distance that each sheep or group of sheep was observed from the nearest unit of escape terrain.

Rather than assigning distance categories for analyzing escape terrain information (Morgantini and Hudson 1981, Tilton and Willard 1982), data for distance from escape terrain were ranked and divided into quartiles. A total of 1,213 groups of sheep comprising 11,933 individuals were observed between 17 September 1985, and 10 August 1986. Twenty-five per cent of group observations were made between 0 and 40 m of escape terrain; 50 per cent of group observations were made between 0 and 160 m; 75 per cent group observations were made between 0 and 290 m; and 100 per cent of sheep observations were made between 0 and 705 m of escape terrain (Table 10). If the distance from escape terrain calculation weights the group by the number of individuals within the group, the resulting distances are farther than if the distance to the center of the group is reported. Distances would then be reported as follows: 25 per cent of individuals in groups within 115 m; 50 per cent within 235 m; 75 per cent within 360 m and 100 per cent within 705 m. It is most common, however, to report the distance to the center of the group of sheep.

Sheep use of the study area during June, July, and most of August, was focused on use of the pit nearest alpine as a source of minerals. As other activities occurred on the mine site only sporadically; distance from escape terrain for this season would reflect the concentration around this particular pit. The months represented by lambing and summer were therefore excluded from a comparison of distance from escape terrain for groups of sheep during the pre-rut, rut, winter and spring periods. A Chi-square test was used to test the hypothesis that there was no difference in distance from escape terrain during the occupation of the pre-rut, rut, winter and spring home ranges. Results show there was no difference in distance from escape terrain between the pre-rut and rut. There was a significant difference between the pre-rut and the winter (X^2=55.11 df=3 P<0.05) and the pre-rut and spring (X^2=38.52 df=3 P<0.05). Sheep were closer to escape terrain in the pre-rut and rut than in the winter and spring.

MINERAL LICKS

The attraction of bighorn sheep to mineral licks is well documented (Festa-Bianchet 1987:164, Geist 1971b:271); it was clearly evident at CRC. Sheep were observed licking at bare spots on the winter range (50-A-2), on haul roads, and on HWY 40 at various times throughout the year, but this activity was most pronounced in June when the ewes used water seeps located on the east wall of 50-A-3 and the exposed coal/sandstone of the southwest corner of the 50-A-3 pit as a mineral source. Part of the nursery herd at this time was located in the alpine areas of Luscar Creek. They used the lick in 50-A-3 pit almost daily, but returned to the alpine areas for grazing. Early in June, ewes came alone, leaving their lambs temporarily with the nursery group; later in June, ewes brought their lambs with them. As many as 56 sheep at one time have been observed using the 50-A-3 pit during this period. In June, sheep were seen in the 50-A-3 pit during 13 out of 17 days when systematic counts were made.

Soil samples were collected at 5 lick sites on the study area on 5 July 1986. Lick sites Nos. 1 - 4 were located where sheep had been observed licking in the spring of 1986; lick site No. 5 was located where mule deer had been observed licking. Samples from lick sites No. 1 and 2 were taken from exposed coal or sandstone while the sample from lick site No. 3 was taken from the residue that remains after the coal has been "cleaned". This watery sludge is dumped into open pits and covered by 1 m of overburden. Sheep appeared equally attracted to this waste material as they were to water seeps on exposed coal seams. The sample from lick site No. 4 was taken from a road bank adjacent to a haul road and the sample from No. 5 was taken from a wet depression on overburden. One sample from each site was collected from the top 5 cm of the lick surface. Samples were sent to the Provincial Soil and Feed Testing Laboratory in Edmonton for analysis of total elements.

TABLE 9. DESCRIPTION OF ESCAPE TERRAIN USED BY BIGHORN SHEEP AT CARDINAL RIVER COALS LTD., MINE SITE 1985 TO 1986.

Site	Length (m)	Height (m)	Slope (degrees)	Material	Bench # & Width (m)	Use
50-A-3 e. wall	696	81	39-42	rock	4 (7.2)	R M T E W
s. wall	590	84-105	31	rock	5-6 (4.8-9.6)	T R E
w. wall	384	66	32-35	talus	3 (16.8-96.0)	E T
n. wall	590	53	39	rock	3-4 (4.8-9.6)	E B R T
50-A-3 n. dump & n. slope	360	53	38	talus	none	B T
50-B-3 s. & w. dumps	600	121	37	talus & mine waste	3 (19.2-23.0)	T M
e. wall	346	76	39	rock	3 (4.8)	T B
n. dump	312	73	22	talus	2 (12.0)	T
51-B-2 e. wall	1046	205	45	rock	8 (4.8-24)	L E W T
s. wall	576	95	21	talus	none	T
w. wall	614	95	23	talus	none	T
north	259	38	26	rock	2 (4.8-24)	E B T
51-B-3	586	(being developed)		rock	several	future T E
C Base	768	62-108	35-36	rock/talus	0-2 (4.8)	E T
C Base (central)	1584	64-99	34-44	rock	0-4 (4.8)	T E
C Base	370	23	20	rock	2 (4.8)	T

R = rut, M = minerals, T = travel, e = escape, w = wounded, B = bedded, L = lambing

Note: benches on the 50-A-3 west wall and the 51-B-2 east wall are partly vegetated.

TABLE 10. DISTANCE FROM ESCAPE TERRAIN (M) FOR BIGHORN SHEEP (ALL CLASSES AND ACTIVITIES INCLUDED) ON THE CARDINAL RIVER COALS LTD., MINE SITE DURING THE PRE-RUT, RUT, WINTER, SPRING, LAMBING AND SUMMER FOR THE YEAR 1985 TO 1986.

	Measures of Location					
	Min.	Q1	Median	Q3	Max.	(n)
Pre-rut	0	60	165	290	590	195
Rut	0	35	175	320	680	339
Winter	0	95	190	285	630	213
Spring	0	115	210	300	705	276
Lambing	0	0	20	130	500	128
Summer	0	0	0	25	275	62
Year	0	40	160	290	705	1213

Samples were weakly to moderately alkaline (Table 11), as was also reported by Salter (undated) from 5 natural lick sites used by feral horses in the Alberta foothills west of Sundre. Levels of P, Na, K, Ca and Mg at the CRC lick sites were much higher than levels reported by Salter.

The lower values of sodium and sulphur at CRC overlapped the highest levels of these elements reported by Stockstad et al. (1953) for natural licks used by goat, elk, deer, and moose in western Montana. Calcium levels at CRC were similar, but magnesium and potassium levels at CRC were much higher than those reported by Stockstad et al. (1953). Upper levels of calcium at CRC overlapped with lower levels at licks reported to be used by mountain goats (Hebert and Cowan 1971), but sodium levels at CRC were much higher.

LAMBING SITES

During the latter part of May, 1986, individual ewes were sighted leaving the nursery herd and moving off the mine site into the alpine zone for lambing. Six ewes, however, lambed on the 51-B-2 wall within 150 m of active rock dumping. The first lambs of the year were observed here on 28 May 1986. The ewes and lambs remained within the vicinity of this pit, utilizing forage adjacent to the east and north walls until June 4, 1986, when they moved west across and off the mine site. The 51-B-2 east wall is the steepest and highest pit wall utilized by the sheep on the mine site (Table 9).

Vegetation Cover Types

Vegetation cover of CRC's mineral surface lease representing the area surveyed for sheep (21.6 km^2) was delineated into 5 types on the 1:4,800 base map: coniferous, meadow (native grass and shrubland), reclaimed grasslands, non-vegetated, open pit and water. Cover types were digitized and a program called "area-tot" (Faculty of Environmental Design, Computer Department) was run with the base map "veg.brief.map" to calculate areas of vegetation polygons. Area calculations were planimetric and did not account for the steep terrain. The area of vegetation types that occur on slopes (all except water) are therefore underestimated.

Coniferous forest comprised the largest percentage of cover type - 9.84 km^2 (46%) on the mine site followed by open pits - 3.18 km^2 (15%) and similar amounts of reclaimed grasslands - 3.03 km^2 (14%) and unreclaimed regolith - 3.11 km^2 (14%). Lesser amounts of subalpine grass and shrub meadows - 2.28 km^2 (11%) and water - 0.13 km^2 (1%) comprised the rest of the area. Mining activity at CRC has changed the landscape from primarily subalpine spruce/fir forest to that of an open landscape of grass/legume grasslands interspersed with unreclaimed open pits, regolith and islands of the original coniferous cover.

To calculate the number of sheep observations in each vegetation polygon, a "points-in-poly" program was run. Seventy per cent of all sheep observations during the year occurred in reclaimed grasslands (Table 12). Use of these areas fell off to 8 per cent in June and July when the sheep were grazing in the alpine off the study area. Conversely, the highest percentage of observations associated with the open pits occurred in these two months (36% and 67%). This reflects the use of the open pits as mineral licks during this time period. Use of the subalpine grass and shrub meadows was highest during the winter, spring and lambing seasons (February through to June) when the adult rams segregated from the nursery herd and concentrated on the south-facing slope in the center of the mine site.

Sheep use was limited to 9.1 km^2 of the study area of which there was about 2.1 km^2 of range that was grazed by the sheep at various seasons. Eighty-two per cent of this area was composed of reclaimed sites. The remaining range was composed of subalpine grasslands or meadows that had developed after tree cover removal.

Biomass Production on Reclaimed Grasslands and Subalpine Meadows

Estimates of total above ground biomass for the reclaimed grasslands as measured during late July and early August, 1986, showed them to be highly productive (x=4,190 kg/ha, n=62, range=240-19,360 kg/ha) (Table 13). Jacques

TABLE 11. PH, ELECTRICAL CONDUCTIVITY AND MINERAL ANALYSIS (PPM) OF SOIL SAMPLES COLLECTED FROM LICK SITES ON COAL, OVERBURDEN AND MINE WASTE AT CARDINAL RIVER COALS LTD., ON JULY 7, 1986.

Site	pH	E.C. (Sm)	Total N (%)	P	K	S	Total C (%)
1	9.1	0.02	0.92	4500	11900	2800	43.4
2	9.2	0.03	0.22	1800	14600	800	12.5
3	8.8	0.21	0.70	3500	10200	3300	29.4
4	9.0	0.06	0.46	3700	12500	2200	15.8
5	10.2	0.04	0.65	3500	8100	2000	30.2

Site	Cu	Zn	Mg	Se (ppb)	Na	Ca
1	14.1	26.2	1900	795	8580	5800
2	43.8	91.3	7600	816	6940	7700
3	25.1	25.5	2300	1430	4950	4900
4	37.2	46.9	3900	1572	6470	8000
5	21.8	22.1	5400	1139	3380	6700

Site description:
1 = exposed coal on SW corner of 50-A-3 pit
2 = edge of large puddle on haul road at hunters gate 50-A-3
3 = mine waste dumped on W slopes 50-B-3 pit

4 = road bank on haul road 50-B-3 pit
5 = edge of permanent wet depression in overburden in valley N of 50-A- 2 dump

Note: Bighorn sheep were observed licking at site numbers 1 through 4. Mule deer were observed licking at site number 5.

TABLE 12. PERCENTAGE OF SIGHTINGS OF BIGHORN SHEEP IN VARIOUS COVER TYPES AT CARDINAL RIVER COALS LTD., DURING THE YEAR 1985 TO 1986.

Month	Conifer	Reclaim	Pits	Meadow	Regolith	n
Sep	0	72	7	3	18	645
Oct	2	76	2	10	10	1708
Nov	0.1	87	2	10	0.6	1651
Dec	1	83	4	11	1	1440
Jan	1	80	5	9	4	1709
Feb	8	45	3	36	8	1322
Mar	4	69	2	25	1	1016
Apr	2	60	9	26	3	649
May	0	76	2	17	5	1034
Jun	5	8	36	23	28	507
Jul	0	8	67	17	8	184
Aug	0	61	13	4	22	708
Year	2	70	6	15	7	12573

n = number of sheep observations

(1980:124) described similar high above ground productivity values on certain native ranges in the foothills of southwestern Alberta. The total above ground biomass as measured on a south-facing slope comprised of native grasses and forbs was less (x=1,700 kg/ha, range=1,360-2,040 kg/ha, n=2) than that for the reclaimed grasslands.

It was noted that the clip plot size of .25 m^2 may not have been appropriate for the variety of microhabitats found on the reclaimed areas. A plot size of .5 m^2 may include this variation. It is recommended that should further work involving biomass production be conducted, a test of plot sizes be carried out prior to clipping.

CRUDE PROTEIN

The per cent crude protein values as measured by faecal nitrogen for the CRC herd began to decrease in October 1985, (11.60%) to reach an annual low during the winter months of November 1985, through to March 1986. Winter values fluctuated between 7.84 per cent and 9.77 per cent. Crude protein values began to increase in April (11.74%) and May (14.07%) of 1986, to reach an annual high of 20.9 per cent during the month of June. Values decreased slightly in July (17.93%) and more noticeably during August (11.62%) and September (12.25%).

The overall annual cycle of crude protein for CRC is similar to that of Ram Mountain (Jorgenson and Wishart 1986:48). Spring greenup as expressed by crude protein in April and May was later at CRC than at Ram Mountain for the years 1980, 1981, 1982 and 1983. Crude protein values for April and May, 1986, at CRC however, were similar to those at Ram Mountain for the years of 1984 and 1985. The summer peak of 20.9% at CRC was less than the summer peak at Ram Mountain during the years 1980 to 1983 but higher than those at Ram Mountain for the years 1984 and 1985. This suggests that weather patterns influencing the growing season are largely responsible for the variation in crude protein values from year to year. Per cent crude protein values for CRC seem to be similar to those published for the Ram mountain herd (1980 - 1985) for the months of October, November, December, January and February.

Crude protein values as measured by faecal nitrogen seem to be similar at CRC and Ram Mountain despite the fact that the CRC sheep are grazing agronomic species in the fall, winter and early spring while the Ram Mountain sheep are using native species year round.

Design Criteria for Bighorn Sheep Habitat Restoration

The formulation of specific design criteria to encourage the return of wildlife has been a deficiency in current reclamation plans in the United States and Canada. Few examples exist where specific design criteria have been developed. When this is done, the rehabilitation of wildlife habitats is more likely to succeed (see Viert 1989:213).

TOPOGRAPHIC RESTORATION

Sheep were not observed farther than 705 m from escape terrain and 75 per cent of sheep groups were not observed beyond 288 m (MacCallum 1991). Forage areas should not be farther than 300 m from escape terrain. Size of escape terrain used by sheep seems to be a function of the size of the herd and the amount of adjacent grasslands. For a nursery herd of 140 sheep, grasslands must be 40-60 ha in size to accommodate that number in fall. A group of 40 rams can use relatively small pieces of habitat (7 ha or larger) scattered throughout an area with appropriate escape terrain.

TABLE 13. TOTAL ABOVE GROUND BIOMASS (KG/HA), AREA, AND ELEVATION FOR THE RECLAIMED AREAS AND SUBALPINE MEADOWS USED BY BIGHORN SHEEP FOR GRAZING AT CARDINAL RIVER COALS LTD., BIOMASS WAS MEASURED DURING LATE JULY AND EARLY AUGUST OF 1986.

Location	mean (kg/ha)	range (kg/ha)	area (ha)	elevation (m)	n
50-A-1	5908	1,400-19,360	42	1812-1847	16
50-A-2	2780	240-6,280	18	1801-1824	8
50-A-3	1773	640-3,080	6	1803-1839	6
51-B dump	4276	1,200-10,880	41	1707-1737	10
51-B slope	5067	1,560-15,000	16	1661-1696	6
lower slopes beside HWY40	3630	680-8,240	26	1664-1698	8
slopes adjacent 51-B-2 pit	3040	2,280-4,400	16	1707-1734	6
C-baseline	4260	1,880-6,640	5	1699-1809	2
SUBTOTAL	4190	240-19,360	170	1661-1847	62
50-A-1 meadow		(area not sampled)	4		-
50-A-3 meadow		(area not sampled)	11		-
subalpine meadow	1700	1,360-2,040	7	1766-1775	2
N wall 51-B-2 meadow		(area not sampled)	3		-
C-baseline meadow		(area not sampled)	11		
SUBTOTAL			36		
TOTAL			206		

Note: Vegetation polygons were digitized from the 1:4,800 base map and areas calculated by using the area-tot program.

Low snail densities have been reported to occur on dry grasslands (Boag and Wishart 1982). Reclamation that is to be used as bighorn winter range should be well-drained and vegetated with grass legume mixtures. Shrubs and trees should be minimized for they are favorable habitat for terrestrial gastropods. Wetland areas should not be designed into sheep foraging areas. The ideal grassland would be well-drained with little opportunity for water to pool. Increased terrestrial snail (secondary host for *Protostrongylidae* larvae) activity has been associated with extended wet weather (Forrester and Senger 1964).

REVEGETATION

Bighorn sheep select a wide variety of grasses and forbs for their normal diet. Seeding with native species is not considered here as the need to establish a vegetative cover quickly as an erosion control overrides aesthetic concerns of creating a "natural" habitat. Bighorns have done well on the agronomic species planted at Cardinal River Coals Ltd. Rumen analysis shows that the following species were eaten: timothy, wheatgrass spp., bluegrass spp., fescue, cicer milkvetch, clover spp., alfalfa spp. Planting a large variety of agronomic grasses and legumes should accommodate bighorn food needs.

SPECIAL FEATURES

Escape Terrain

Escape terrain at CRC was provided by high walls of unreclaimed pits and by large "talus" slopes that had not been graded after dumping of rock overburden. Slope angle ranged from 20-45°, length ranged from 259-1584 m and height from 23-205 m.

High walls that serve as escape terrain for major winter ranges should be steep (39-40 degrees) and possess a minimum of three and preferably more benches. Foraging areas should be available immediately adjacent to the high wall with particular emphasis on the nearest 300 m. Sheep will use escape terrain that is located above, below or beside forage areas and will move easily regardless of which way they have to run.

Lambing Walls

At CRC the wall which was consistently used by ewes in the lambing season was the steepest and highest on the mine site. It also had several wide benches which had been previously seeded from a helicopter, thus providing limited forage on the wall itself. As there was rock dumping occurring within 100 m of the lambing ewes, it appears that duplicating the physical characteristics of this wall could promote acceptance for lambing purposes. The highest and steepest walls (east wall of 51-B-2 and east wall of 50-A-3) were used for lambing and by wounded sheep seeking isolation. These walls had many benches, some of which were beginning to develop vegetative cover and were located immediately adjacent to forage areas.

Talus

Steep talus slopes were used by bighorn sheep when travelling between forage sites. Sheep also commonly bedded at the top edge of these slopes, presumably because of the field of view. Sheep travel easily over talus slopes, but these would not provide escape terrain from predators.

Rock Piles

Large rocks should be placed on areas designated for bighorn grazing. Such rocks are used by lambs for playing "king-of-the-castle" and by older sheep as bedding sites or vantage points. Rock pile height should be 1 to 4 m. They should be constructed of 1 to 3 large boulders, 1 to 4 m in diameter, surrounded by smaller rocks 1 m in diameter or less.

Mineral Licks

Mining exposes previously buried mineral sources. On CRC, high walls which were wet or had some form of seepage were used by the sheep as mineral licks particularly in June; the sheep also used the mine waste from the plant wherever it lay exposed prior to reclamation. Summer distribution of nursery groups appears to be affected by the location of mineral sources. Exposure of new mineral sources strongly attracts sheep; it should be done carefully.

ADDITIONAL BENEFITS

Development of sheep habitat provides habitat for small animals such as the hoary marmot, pika and golden-mantled ground squirrel which use rock piles and talus slopes. Birds such as the killdeer, savannah sparrow and mountain bluebird have been observed nesting on the reclaimed grasslands. Open grasslands provide hunting areas for northern harrier and kestrel. Raptors such as the Great-horned Owl have used high walls as nest sites. Reclaimed grasslands are also used by mule deer and elk for grazing. Grizzly bears, coyotes, wolves, red fox and wolverine have all been present on the reclaimed landscape. The deer mouse is the most abundant small mammal on the reclaimed grasslands where it occurs in high densities.

Bighorn Sheep Habituation and Use of Industrial Sites

Negative effects of industrial activity and mining operations on ungulates have been well documented. Kuck (1986) concluded that, without careful management, the cumulative effects of the industrial impacts of phosphate mining in Idaho would result in the reduction of elk, moose and deer populations. Stanlake et al. (1978) documented reduced elk use on lands that had been stripmined for coal and subsequently reclaimed, as compared with adjacent undisturbed habitat in southeastern British Columbia. Morgantini and Bruns (1988) described the attraction of bighorns in the Alberta foothills to man-made mineral licks associated with active and abandoned gas well sites. They concluded that this attraction left sheep more susceptible to exploitation and risks associated with toxic chemicals, crowding and range depletion. Morgantini and Worbets (1988) commented that there was general agreement that the disturbance associated with drilling new gas wells on bighorn sheep ranges can affect animal distribution and habitat use. Jorgenson (1988b) recorded range abandonment on Mt. Allan due to human activities on the ridge top, snowmobiling, helicopter flights, and avalanche blasting resulting from the Nakiska ski hill development west of Calgary, Alberta.

However, some authors also refer to the bighorn's ability to habituate to human activity (Geist 1971a) and industrial disturbance under certain circumstances. Kuck (1986) found that elk, moose, and mule deer appeared capable of adjusting to many phosphate mining activities. Stanlake et al. (1976) believed that the effect of coal exploration and exploration roads in southeastern British Columbia on animals was minimal. Morgantini and Bruns (1988) noted the bighorn sheep using active gas well sites as a mineral lick source were apparently habituated to people and vehicles in the Panther River area of Alberta. Jorgenson (1986) found that sheep were attracted to the straw bales used to pad chair lift towers at Nakiska ski hills and, as a consequence, ended up in the warmup shacks and on the ski runs. He felt this was another example of sheep being attracted by human activity and then being threatened by it.

There are also cases of sheep using terrain around active coal and limestone mines. Dall's sheep use of the Usibelli Coal Mine Inc. in Alaska has been described by Elliot (1984:139). He concluded that:

"The proximity of the (Dall sheep) wintering area to human activity and its consequential deterring effect on predators (e.g. wolves); vertical topography for bedding sites and escape routes; and the tendency for the area to be kept snow free by wind, have all served to enhance the attractiveness of the mine site to the local sheep population".

Examples of bighorn sheep that have habituated to other industrial sites in Alberta include Inland Cement at Cadomin (a limestone mine), Canada Cement LaFarge, Steele Brothers and Burnco Limestone Operations at Exshaw west of Calgary.

Monitoring Wildlife Populations for Designing End Use Reclamation Plans

Wildlife habitat reclamation involves the manipulation and management of vegetation communities and special physical features. The assessment of the success of reclamation involves direct or indirect evaluations of habitat quality. This can be done by using population-based or habitat-based assessments (Green et al. 1987).

Habitat-based assessments are easily standardized among sites, not highly time-specific and are not easily influenced by external factors. They do, however, rely on the correct identification and quantification of habitat characteristics that are essential to the use of a site by a particular species.

Population-based assessments rely on accurate census techniques, must be replicated seasonally and may be affected by cyclic population fluctuations, behavior or other external factors. They have the advantage of specifically identifying where, when and what type of habitat is utilized within a particular site by a particular species. Animals may use habitat differently between areas, therefore a population/habitat study will be more precise in identifying required habitat features.

A combination of population and habitat-based census techniques was used on Cardinal River Coals Ltd. and the neighboring Gregg River Resources for reclamation planning. As bighorn sheep and mule deer had voluntarily occupied these sites, a ground census revealed the nature of this use with respect to the habitat requirements of each animal, and how these requirements were met by the physical characteristics of the mine sites. A direct census technique also provided information on the seasonality of use by these animals. This information was combined with an overall review of habitat requirements to develop habitat design criteria for reclamation. An evaluation of the existing reclamation plan with respect to these criteria was then carried out to design the final reclaimed landscape.

By considering the behavior and habitat requirements of bighorn sheep in conjunction with the constraints of an operating coal mine at Cardinal River Coals Ltd., a unique opportunity was discovered to create bighorn sheep habitat where there was none before. The mine is located at timber line adjacent to alpine range that was occupied by bighorn sheep prior to mining activities. The mining and reclamation activities changed the landscape from a closed canopy coniferous forest to one composed of forest interspersed with reclaimed grasslands and unreclaimed pit walls. By deliberately designing the habitat requirements for selected species into this changed landscape, the mine has ensured that the area will be used by bighorn sheep and other wildlife after operations have ceased.

REFERENCES

Acott, G. B.1983. "Reclamation strategy at Cardinal River Coals Ltd." In *Reclamation of Lands Disturbed by Mining*.91-104. Proceedings of the 7th Annual British Columbia Reclamation Symposium.

——————.1986a. "Reclamation Operations at Cardinal River Coals Ltd." In Proceedings: *Alberta Reclamation Conferences 1985 and 1986*, edited by C.B. Powter, R.J. Fessenden and D.G. Walker, 249-256. Edmonton: Alberta Chapter, Canadian Land Reclamation Association.

Acott, G.B., O'Toole, M.T. and Munn, F.J. 1987. "Cardinal River Coals Ltd. Reclamation and Mining Status Report 1986." Cardinal River Coals Ltd.

Alberta Fish and Wildlife Division. Undated. "Rumen Analysis Method." Edmonton: Department of Forestry, Lands and Wildlife.

Alberta Government: 1976. "A Coal Development Policy for Alberta." Edmonton: Department of Energy and Natural Resources.

Arscott, R. L.: Letter from R. L. Arscott to B. Wishart, 13 November 1989 regarding an elk sanctuary of Chevron's Colorado Coal Mine, 1989.

Bailey, J. A. 1984. *Principles of Wildlife Management.* New York: Wiley.

Blood, D.A., D.R. Flook and W.D. Wishart. 1970. "Weights and Growth of Rocky Mountain Bighorn Sheep in Western Alberta." *Journal of Wildland Management* 34:451-455.

Bratton, D.L. 1987. "Regulatory Response to Changing Reclamation Demands." In *Proceedings of a Symposium on Reclamation Targets for the 1990's*, edited by D.B. Porter, 5-12. Edmonton: Alberta Society of Professional Biologists, Alberta Chapter/CLRA, The Canadian Society of Environmental Biologists.

Elliot, C. L. 1984 . "Wildlife and Habitat Use on Revegetated Stripmine Land in Alaska." Ph.D. dissertation. Fairbanks: University of Alaska.

Festa-Bianchet, M. 1986. "Seasonal Dispersion of Overlapping Mountain Sheep Ewe Groups." *Journal of Wildlife Management* 50:325-330.

──────────. 1987. "Individual Reproductive Success of Bighorn Sheep Ewes." Ph.D. dissertation. Calgary: University of Calgary.

Foreyt, W. J., and D. A. Jessup. 1982. "Fatal Pneumonia of Bighorn Sheep Following Association with Domestic Sheep." *Journal of Wildlife Diseases* 18:163-168.

Forrester, D. J. and C. M. Senger. 1964. "A Survey of Lungworm Infection in Bighorn Sheep of Montana." *Journal of Wildlife Management* 28:481-491.

Geist, V. 1971a. "A Behavioural Approach to the Management of Wild Ungulates." In *The Scientific Management of Animal and Plant Communities for Conservation.* 413-424. Oxford: Blackwell.

──────────. 1971b. *Mountain Sheep, A Study in Behaviour and Evolution.* Chicago: University of Chicago Press.

Gilbert, J. R. 1978. "Estimating Population Characteristics." In *Big Game of North America,* edited by J.L. Schmidt and D. L. Gilbert, 297-304. Harrisburg: Stackpole.

Green, J. E., R.E. Salter and C.E. Fooks. 1987. "Reclamation of Wildlife Habitat in the Canadian Prairie Provinces." Volume 1: "Techniques for the Creation and Enhancement of Wildlife Habitat." Edmonton: The Delta Environmental Management Group.

Hardy Associates (1978) Ltd. 1981. "Evaluation of Reclamation at the Luscar Open Pit Mine." Edmonton: Cardinal River Coals Ltd.

Hebert, D. and I. McTaggart Cowan. 1971. "Natural Dalt Licks as a Part of the Ecology of the Mountain Goat." *Canadian Journal of Zoology* 49:605-610.

Jones, R. L. and H. C. Hanson. 1985. "*Mineral licks, Geophagy, and Bigeochemistry of North American Ungulates.*" Ames: The Iowa State University Press.

Jorgenson, J. T. 1988b. "Environmental Impact of the 1988 Winter Olympics on Bighorn Sheep of Mt. Allan." *Biennial Symposium Northern Wild Sheep and Goat Council* 6:121-134.

Jorgenson J.T. and W.D. Wishart. 1986. " Ram Mountain Bighorn Sheep Project Progress Report: 1984 and 1985." Edmonton: Alberta Energy and Natural Resources, Fish and Wildlife Division.

──────────. 1983. " Ram Mountain Bighorn Sheep Project Progress Report, 1983." Edmonton: Alberta Energy and Natural Resources, Fish and Wildlife Division.

Kosinski, T. 1977. "Red Cap Sheep: Their Migrations and Management (Progress Report)." Calgary: Faculty of Environmental Design, University of Calgary.

Kuck, L. 1986. "The Impacts of Phosphate Mining on Big Game in Idaho: A Cooperative Approach to Conflict Resolution." *Transactions of the 51st North American Wildlife and Natural Resource Conference.* 90-97.

Lance, W. R. 1980. "The Implications of Contagious Ecthyma in Bighorn Sheep." *Biennial Symposium of Northern Wild Sheep and Goat Council* 2:263-269.

Leopold, A. 1933. *Game Management.* New York: Scribner.

MacArthur, R. A., R. H. Johnston and V. Geist. 1979. "Factors Influencing Heart rate in Free-ranging Bighorn Sheep: A Physiological Approach to the Study of Wildlife Harassment." *Canadian Journal Zoology* 57:2010-2021.

MacCallum, N. B. 1986a. "Fall 1985 Bird Records for the Edson Region." *Alberta Bird Record* 4:29-32.

—————. 1986b. "Winter 1986 Bird Records for the Edson Region." *Alberta Bird Record* 4:55-56.

—————. 1986c. "Spring 1986 Bird Records for the Edson Region." *Alberta Bird Record* 4:77-80.

—————. 1991. "Bighorn Sheep Use of an Open Pit Coal Mine in the Foothills of Alberta." M.E.D. thesis. Calgary: Environmental Sciences, University of Calgary.

Morgantini, L. E. and E. Burns. 1988. "Attraction of Bighorn Sheep to Wellsites and Other Man-made Mineral Licks Along the Eastern Slopes of Alberta: A Management Concern." *Biennial Symposium of the Northern Wild Sheep and Goat Council* 6:135-150.

Morgantini, L.E. and R.J. Hudson. 1981. "Sex Differential in Use of the Physical Environment by Bighorn Sheep (*Ovis canadensis*)." *Canadian Field-Naturalist* 95:69-74.

Morgantini, L.E. and B.W. Worbets. 1988. "Bighorn Sheep Use of a Gas Wellsite During Servicing and Testing: A Case Study of Impact and Mitigation." *Biennial Symposium of the Northern Wild Sheep and Goat Council* 6:159-164.

Onderka, D.K. and W.D. Wishart. 1984. "A Major Bighorn Sheep Dieoff From Pneumonia in Southern Alberta." *Biennial Symposium of the Northern Wild Sheep and Goat Council* 4:356-363.

Root, J.D. 1976. "Physical Environment of an Abandoned Strip Mine Near Cadomin, Alberta." Bulletin No. 34. Edmonton: Alberta Research Council.

Samson, J., J.C. Holmes, J.T. Jorgenson and W.D. Wishart. 1987. "Experimental Infections of Free-ranging Rocky Mountain Bighorn Sheep with Lungworms (*Protostrongylus spp.*; nematoda:Protostrongylidae)." *Journal of Wildlife Diseases* 23:396-403.

Schwantje, H.M. 1986. "A Comparative Study of Bighorn Herds in Southeastern British Columbia." *Biennial Symposium Northern Wild Sheep and*

Goat Council 5:231-252.

Smith, K. and J. Edmonds. 1989. "Bighorn Sheep Aerial Survey of Designated Winter ranges Within the Edson District of the Eastern Slopes Region, Feb. 1-5 and March 16-19, 24, 1988." Edson AB: Alberta Forestry, Lands and Wildlife, Alberta Fish and Wildlife Division.

Spraker, T. R. and C. P. Hibler. 1982. "An Overview of the Clinical Signs, Gross and Histological Lesions of the Pneumonia Complex of Bighorn Sheep." *Biennial Symposium of the Northern Wild Sheep and Goat Council* 3:163-172.

Spraker, T. R., C.P. Hibler, G.G. Schoonveld, and W.S. Adney. 1984. "Pathologic Changes and Microorganisms Found in Bighorn Sheep During a Stress-Related Die-off." *Journal of Wildlife Diseases* 20:319-327.

Stanlake, M. G., E.A. Stanlake and D.S. Eastman. 1976. "Coal Exploration Activities and Their Effect on Subalpine Winter Ranges in Southeastern British Columbia." Wildlife Management Report no. 13. Victoria BC: Fish and Wildlife Branch, Ministry of Recreation and Conservation.

Stanlake, E. A., D.S. Eastman and M.G. Stanlake. 1978. "Unglate Use of Some Recently Reclaimed Strip Mines in Southeastern British Columbia." Fish and Wildlife Report No. R-1. Victoria BC: Fish and Wildlife Branch, Ministry of Recreation and Conservation.

Stelfox, J. G.1976. "Range Ecology of Rocky Mountain Sheep in Canadian National Parks." Wildlife Report No. 39. Ottawa: Canadian Wildlife Service.

Stemp, R. E. 1983. " Heart Rate Responses of Bighorn Sheep to Environmental Factors and Harassment." M.E.D. thesis. Calgary: Environmental Sciences, University of Calgary.

Stockstad, D. S., M.S. Morris and E.C. Lory. 1953. "Chemical Characteristics of Natural Licks Used by Big Game Animals in Western Montana." *Proceedings of the North American Wildlife Conference* 18:247-258.

Strong, W. L. and K. R. Leggat.1981. "Ecoregions of Alberta." ENR Technical Report No. T/4. Edmonton: Resources Evaluation and Planning Division.

Thorne, T., G. Butler, T. Varcalli, K. Becker and S. Hayden-Wing. 1979. "The Status, Mortality and Response to Management of the Bighorn Sheep of Whiskey Mountain" Wildlife Technical Report No. 7. Cheyenne: Wyoming Game and Fish department.

Tilton, M. E. and E.E. Willard. 1982. "Winter Habitat Selection by Mountain Sheep." *Journal of Wildlife Management* 46:359-366.

Uhazy, L.S., J.C. Holmes and J.G. Stelfox. 1973. " Lungworms in the Rocky Mountain Bighorn Sheep of Western Canada," *Canadian Journal of Zoology* 51:817-824.

Van Dyke, S. 1990. "Final Report, Historical Resources Impact Assessment, Freehold and 50-A Baseline Extension ASA Permit No. 89-101." Edmonton: Cardinal River Coals Ltd.

Van Dyke, W. A., A. Sands, J. Yoakum, A. Polenz and J. Blaisdell. 1983. "Wildlife Habitats in Managed Rangelands: The Great Basin of Southeastern Oregon Bighorn Sheep." General Technical Report PNW-159. Portland: US Forest Service.

Viert, S. R. 1989. "Design of Reclamation to Encourage Fauna." In *Animals, in Primary Succession, The Role of Fauna in Reclaimed Lands*, edited by J.D. Majer, 207-222. Cambridge: Cambridge University Press.

Wallis, C. and C. Wershler. 1979. "Literature Review of Considerations for Reclaiming Lands as Wildlife Habitat." Report. Hinton AB: Cottonwood Consultants.

Weeks, H.P. and C.M. Kirkpatrick. 1976. "Adaptations of White-tailed Deer to Naturally Occuring Sodium Deficiencies." *Journal of Wildlife Management* 40:610-625.

Wishart, W.D. 1969. "Bighorns and 'Littlehorns'." *Alberta Lands, Forests and Wildlife* 12(3):4-10.

_____. 1978. "Bighorn Sheep." *Biennial Symposium of the Northern Wild Sheep and Goat Council* 3:127-142.

Wishart, W. D., J. Jorgenson and M. Hilton. 1980. "A Minor Die-off of Bighorns from Pneumonia in Southern Alberta (1978)." *Biennial Symposium of the Northern Wild Sheep and Goat Council* 2:229-247.

Part Three
MOUNTAINS AND LEISURE

CHAPTER 8

Patterns of the Development of Tourism in Mountain Communities

MARTIN F. PRICE

Introduction

In recent decades, tourism has developed rapidly in mountain regions throughout the world. This growth has led to substantial economic and social change with resulting environmental consequences, frequently unforeseen. The objective of this chapter is to trace the patterns of the development of tourism in mountain regions and the impacts on the communities which live there. The literature on this subject is large and widely scattered. Thus, the examples discussed in the paper are illustrative; the bibliography is not exhaustive, particularly since it emphasizes work published in the English language. Furthermore, the chapter only marginally discusses the environmental effects of tourism in mountain areas: a major topic which, like those considered in this chapter, has been the subject of many studies which require synthesis.

One of the principal characteristics of mountain regions, at whatever spatial or temporal scale one considers them, is their diversity: ecological, historical, cultural, linguistic, and so on. Given this diversity, one might question the validity and usefulness of a global review such as presented here. Yet, in spite of the vast range of systems into which tourism has been introduced, comparable patterns of development, impacts, and responses have occurred and are taking place, in very diverse situations. This chapter attempts to present the diversity, yet also to draw out trends and lessons which appear to have wide applicability. Following this introduction, the chapter is divided into five parts which consider: accessibility; temporal dimensions; types of tourists; changes in communities as perceived by tourists; and changes in the socio-cultural structure of tourist communities. The final section draws the conclusions together and suggests needs for future research.

A final introductory remark must be made: tourism, while widespread, is not omnipresent in the world's mountains. At any spatial scale, the degree of its development is highly variable and, over time, its importance may increase and then wane. Even in the Alps, whose economy is dominated by tourism, the economy of some communities still remains based on traditional activities. Similarly, in other well-known mountain tourist destinations, such as Nepal, large areas are not directly affected by tourism. Yet, even when tourists have not actually arrived in a mountain community, tourism's indirect effects are commonly felt, for instance through the emigration of young people, changes in markets for particular products, or the differential emphases and effects of national development policies.

Accessibility

A primary impetus to the growth of tourism in mountain areas is the introduction of new means of access. The central importance of accessibility as a factor in the evolution of the economy of mountain regions has been recognized by Allan (1984, 1985), who notes that a sufficient level of accessibility can effectively break down the traditional pattern of the altitudinal zonation of land use. Although referring particularly to agricultural land use, his model is at least as valid for the development of tourism - for instance, the construction of urban infrastructures on former summer pastures in the French and Swiss Alps can be cited as an example of apparent freedom from ecological constraints.

New means of access may include either new technologies or the improvement of existing routes. In the nineteenth century, the technologies associated with the Industrial Revolution began to open up limited numbers of mountain communities to tourism. In the first half of the century, for example, the Highlands of Scotland first became accessible by regular steamship services, and tourism began to increase, reaching greater distances into the mountains as carriage roads and railways were constructed (Butler 1985). The same factors were also key in the early development of tourism in a few communities in the Alps (Barker 1982, Bernard 1978, Groetzbach 1985a). However, this trend was not restricted to Europe, the birthplace of the Industrial Revolution; it also extended to other mountain regions, such as those of India and Sri Lanka, where the colonial British developed "hill stations" for their health and to escape from the summer heat at lower altitudes (Buehrlein 1989, Groetzbach 1985b). This represented the introduction of a new type of tourism to the mountains of the Indian sub-continent, where pilgrimage to religious centers has a long history (Kaur 1985), as it does also in the mountains of Latin America (e.g., Tyrakowski 1986).

The course of these early phases of tourism is illustrative of a trend that has continued around the world. Yet, until the middle of the twentieth century, mountain tourism was restricted to a limited number of communities which people visited for religious, aesthetic, health, or sports reasons. In the Swiss Alps, the period of growth known as the "Belle Epoque" ended with the First World War, and the number of visitors did not reach the 1910 peak again until well after the end of the Second World War in spite of the existence of the necessary transport networks (Mattig and Zeiter 1984). In the Inter-War period, the development of tourism in the Colorado Rockies depended not only on the construction of new roads, but also on the strength of the national economy and rates of car ownership (Price 1990).

In mountain regions, as elsewhere, the period since the Second World War has been marked by the growth of mass tourism. In industrialized nations, this growth was particularly associated with the construction of high-quality road networks throughout the mountains and the evolution of new technologies which led to the rapid expansion of winter sports (Bridel 1984, Hartmann 1989). In many communities with an existing tourist economy, including those where winter sports had already been important before the war, the primary season changed from summer to winter (Keller and Kneubuehl 1982). In the Alps, new ski resorts, some accessible only by cable-car, were constructed on sites previously used only in summer (Mattig and Zeiter 1984, Schwabe 1984). Similarly, in North America, New Zealand, and the Andes, new roads permitted access to ski resorts in forest and alpine areas which were previously only used extensively in summer, if at all (Hartmann 1989, Pearce 1985, Solbrig 1984). Thus, in mountains in industrialized nations, the post-war period has been characterized by an increasing densification of transport networks in the mountains. However, even when new means of access are available, expected tourism does not always result (Reichart 1988); and the growth of accessibility, and therefore tourism, has been very uneven (Barker 1982, Chapeau 1986).

In the mountains of developing countries, mass tourism started later. To some extent, this was because these mountains were far from the main sources of tourists in the industrialized nations, so that the evolution of air transport, in combination with adequate internal transport systems, was essential. However, another critical factor was, and in some cases remains, the unwillingness of governments to open up mountain regions, either because of their military significance or because of concern about likely socio-economic changes deriving from the interaction of "western" tourists and local people (Allan 1988, Baumgartner 1988, Richter 1989).

Military action, or its likelihood, remains an impediment to tourism in many mountain regions, including some for which plans have been made and facilities developed, such as Afghanistan and Ethiopia (Allan 1988, Hurni 1985). Nevertheless, once strategic considerations recede, military roads have allowed tourists to reach many previously remote areas for the first time, for instance in the Hindukush/Himalaya (Allan 1988, Eppler 1983). Roads for other non-tourist purposes, such as forestry and dam construction, also provide access to new areas; tourism may even be a secondary reason for their construction (Banskota and Upadhyay 1990, Dearden 1989, Dhakal 1990). Equally, governments construct roads and hiking trails specifically to encourage the development of tourism (Crystal 1989). Airstrips are also built principally for tourism, although the number of visitors that can arrive by air is often limited by topography and weather (Fisher 1990, Groetzbach 1989). Air travel to and within mountain nations, such as Nepal, may also be restricted by the monopoly of the national airline (Richter 1989). Furthermore, control over access to some landlocked mountain nations may be used as a political tool by their neighbors: India, for instance, has limited access to both Bhutan and Nepal.

The preceding discussion clearly underlines the importance of government policies in determining accessibility to and within mountain regions and the consequent development of tourism. In many cases, the development of tourism, linked to improvements in accessibility, is a conscious goal of government policies for mountain regions. In both industrialized and developing countries, such policies may have a number of objectives, including stemming or reversing rural depopulation, improving economic conditions for mountain people, or attracting income from tourists (Crystal 1989, Gamper 1981, Groetzbach 1985a, 1989, Gueller 1986, Kemper 1979, Stadelbauer 1986, Stevens 1992, Svalastog 1988, Swindlin 1985, Tyrakowski 1986). Yet objectives for local populations are not always achieved and tourists do not necessarily arrive in spite of planning and improved access routes. Equally, the introduction and rapid growth of tourism may inadvertently result from policies apparently unlinked to tourism, such as the opening of military roads.

Temporal Dimensions

The previous section refers to the historical aspects of mountain tourism in relation to changes in accessibility. However, two temporal aspects of mountain tourism should be considered in more detail: rates of growth and seasonality.

The rate of growth of tourism critically affects a community's ability to adapt to the many direct and indirect changes which result. In all periods and in all mountain regions, tourism has developed both slowly and quickly, with different levels of control by governments and local communities. As Butler (1980) has noted, all tourist areas go through a life cycle that may involve stagnation, rejuvenation, and/or decline. Even in mountain communities with a history of tourism reaching back into the last century, growth has not been continual. For instance, with declining demand and increasing competition in the Inter-War period, some Swiss communities whose economy had depended strongly on tourism reverted partially or wholly to agriculture (Direction du Projet MAB Pays d'Enhaut 1985, Kroener 1968). From the 1960s, they experienced a new growth of tourism and, like most Alpine resorts, slower rates of growth, if not stagnation, in the 1980s (Messerli 1989). Decline after a first growth phase has also been noted in the mountains of developing nations, such as Thailand (Dearden 1989).

There is a copious literature on the rapid, generally unrestricted growth of tourism in mountain areas (e.g., Baumgartner 1988, Bridel 1984, Eppler 1983, Gilg 1988, Gosar 1989, Hartmann 1989, Kariel and Kariel 1988, Pearce 1985, Zimmermann 1988a). However, rates of growth may also be limited by actions taken to restrict supply and demand. Both may be limited either intentionally or unintentionally, by means such as advertising and other types of information dissemination, pricing, the granting of visas and the availability of access, accommodation, and other facilities. The comparison between Nepal and Bhutan, neighboring countries with a similar range of potential attractions, is illustrative (Richter 1989). Tourism is the largest source of foreign exchange for both countries. Entry visas for Nepal are generally unrestricted, and the growth of tourism has been rapid, limited principally by transport and accommodation facilities. In contrast, both the number of entry visas and the development of facilities have been tightly controlled by the government of Bhutan. This approach provides an apparently successful means of controlling, yet maintaining, a desired rate of growth. Yet, in general, mountain tourism, like all other types of tourism, is highly susceptible to changes in demand in a competitive market. The possibility of stagnation or downturn must be considered in scenario development (Zimmermann 1988b).

The seasonality of climate is one of the most marked characteristics of mountain regions. As a result, their attractions for tourists at different times of the year vary greatly. Thus, very few communities can rely on tourism as a reliable source of year-round employment and income. This is a particular problem in ski resorts in which, because they are not based on pre-existing settlements, off-season work is limited. Such resorts have been developed not only in the mountains of industrialized nations, but also in developing nations, such as the Andes (Fuentes and Castro 1982, Solbrig 1984). Seasonality is important not only in terms of employment, but also because facilities built for tourism represent investments that must be maintained year-round and paid off (Barker 1982). Yet, as noted by Watson and Watson (1982) in regard to the Swiss Alps, tourism is an "industry of fashion," and while unexpected booms in demand are not unusual, predicted new demands, for which facilities have been constructed, do not necessarily materialize. Over time, one of the most marked trends in the Alps has been the change in relative importance of summer and winter tourism (Kariel 1989).

To conclude by referring directly to the importance of the seasonality of climate for mountain tourism, one should note two apparently disparate but linked cases. The first is the restriction of the Himalayan trekking season to the dry, non-monsoon period. The second is the length and the timing of the ski season. As shown by the relatively snow-free winters of the late 1980s in the Alps, the economy of ski resorts is very susceptible to the timing and amount of snowfall. Global climate change may affect both the timing of the monsoon and the winter weather patterns (Houghton et al. 1990, Tegart et al. 1990). Initial assessments of potential climate scenarios for Australia and Canada show that the length and timing of the skiing season are sensitive to quite small climatic changes, so that such changes could lead to considerable socio-economic disruption in communities that have invested their resources in the skiing industry (Galloway 1988, Lamothe and Périard 1988, McBoyle and Wall 1987). If global climate change is likely, as widely accepted within the scientific community, the future temporal dimensions of mountain tourism may be even more complex and difficult to predict than in the past.

Types of Tourists

Tourists visit mountain areas for diverse reasons, and many typologies, applicable to each author's study area, have been published (e.g., Coppock 1978, Kaur 1979, Singh 1989, Tyrakowski 1986). One apparently strong distinction is between local, or regional, tourists (i.e., those from the same or an adjacent country) and foreign tourists - especially, in developing countries, those who bring in hard currency. Statistics on numbers of tourists visiting mountain areas are notoriously difficult to amass. In many developing countries, only foreign visitors are counted. For instance, although the majority of tourists to Nepal are from India, they do not appear in the statistics of international visitors (Richter 1989). Other problems relate to the completeness of reporting and the aggregation of many statistics; a particular problem for assessing trends in mountain tourism since mountains comprise only part of the territory of most countries or regions in which they are situated. Only rarely, as in Austria and Switzerland, are complete statistics available at the community level, and these provide only numbers of visitors, with no information about their reasons for visiting. The typology of tourism - ethnic, environmental, cultural, historical, recreational - presented by Smith (1989) is as valid in mountain areas as elsewhere. However, three additional types should also be recognized in these areas. Historically more important than at present, but still of great significance at many resorts in the mountains of Europe and the USSR, is health tourism, relying on both climate and mineral springs. A second type is business/ congress tourism, which is an increasingly important component, especially in the Alps and the Rocky Mountains, where it allows resorts developed mainly for skiing to attract customers in the off-season. A third, novel type, which may be termed "garbage tourism," occurs in both the Andes and the Himalaya (Kutay 1989, Richter 1989). The rapid growth of trekking and mountaineering in these regions led to the accumulation of large amounts of garbage along trails and at campsites. Tourists, primarily from North America, now visit these areas specifically to remove this accumulation. There have even been expeditions to the Everest and K2, the world's highest mountains, for the same purpose. It is perhaps worth noting that Nepalese Sherpas, at least, do not necessarily regard such "pollution" as a problem (Fisher 1990).

Apart from the interest in describing trends in tourism, and perhaps projecting from these, a further reason for differentiating between types of tourist is that the social, economic, and even environmental effects of different types vary considerably. The identification of market opportunities is a central component of tourism planning (e.g., Lay 1988, Mazanec and Alkier 1985). In developing countries, governments may have specific concerns about tourists from industrialized nations. For instance, in Nepal, five types - jet-set, mountaineer, packaged trekker, individual, cultural nomad - have been described (Coppock 1978). In neighboring Bhutan, the government recognizes the likely effects of large numbers of dispersed tourists and allows only tourists of the second and third types to enter (Richter 1989). At the same time, it must be recognized that people from one country often do not share the same culture and that the values and habits of the urbanized elite often differ from those of their mountain compatriots (Groetzbach 1985b, Tyrakowski 1986).

The Real Thing?

The majority of tourists who visit mountain areas expect to see, and usually photograph, "traditional" landscapes and people and to buy "traditional" souvenirs. Yet, as Dearden (1989:209) comments in regard to trekking in the mountains of Thailand,

As the Real Thing comes into increasing contact with tourists, it becomes a little less of The Real Thing as the mixing of cultures, values and economy serves inevitably to dilute the strength of the original culture.

This pattern has taken place in mountains around the world although, as discussed below, tourism can also act as a catalyst to the renaissance of traditional activities. Changes in landscapes, the "capital" of tourism (Krippendorf 1984) are not discussed below; Allan, Knapp, and Stadel (1988), Messerli (1989), and Moser and Moser (1986) are useful recent sources.

Changes in clothing are a frequent result of the introduction of tourism in mountain areas. In developing nations, a common reason is the new availability of "western" or lowland clothing and footwear. These may be worn as status symbols, because the demands of work in tourism make the production of traditional clothing impossible, or simply because they are more suitable for mountain environments (Allan 1988, Coppock 1978, Crystal 1989, Fisher 1990). In Nepal, among the "tourist Sherpas" who form a new elite, jewellery has lost its place as a status symbol to consumer items and mountaineering equipment (Bjonness 1983, Sacherer 1981). An alternative reason for the disappearance of traditional clothing may be its sale to tourists in search of authentic souvenirs (Cohen 1979, West 1990). In this regard, another common trend in mountain tourism is that souvenirs may no longer be locally made; they may be imported from considerable distances and completely different cultures (Dearden 1989, Eppler 1983, Fisher 1990, Singh and Kaur 1986).

Nevertheless, it would be wrong to conclude that tourism necessarily leads to a loss of traditional forms of cultural expression. While Ladakhis in areas visited by tourists now may wear western clothes in summer, they still wear traditional clothes in winter when the tourists are not there (Eppler 1983). Sherpa clothing has now become accepted as the clothing of the elite in Nepal and is worn for all important occasions (Fisher 1990). In the Austrian Alps, the recognition that tourists expect to see traditional costume led the people of the village of Hermagor to design a new local costume in 1965 (Gamper 1981). Both in this village and in other mountain communities, tourism has led to a renaissance of craft-making, even though the quality may not be as high as it was before goods were manufactured primarily for the tourist market (Barker 1982, Crystal 1989, Dearden 1989, Gurung 1982, West 1990).

Another area of visible change in most mountain communities influenced by tourism concerns changes in buildings and settlement patterns. In traditional communities, these generally represent the result of many generations' appreciation of the rigors of the mountain climate, and both the design of structures and their ornamentation are characteristic of a community or region (Schwabe 1984, Stein 1974). This uniqueness is also part of the image that tourists expect. However, homogenization of housing design and ornament is typical of tourist communities, foreign styles - both rural and urban - may be imported, and noteworthy old, but repairable buildings may be allowed to deteriorate (Groetzbach 1989, Jest and Sanday 1983, Kariel and Kariel 1982, Marsh 1985). While the design of new resorts often has little, if anything, in common with those of traditional settlements, and prefabricated "typical Swiss" chalets have even been imported from Sweden to Switzerland, new houses may be constructed in traditional styles, often taking advantage of new technologies (Fisher 1990, Goering 1990, Pawson et al. 1984b, Price 1990, Stevens 1992).

In addition to everyday activities, religious institutions are usually affected by tourism (Barker 1982, Cohen 1989, Eppler 1983, Crystal 1989, Fisher 1990, Sacherer 1981). One obvious example concerns the timing and content of religious ceremonies because of the demands of, and market represented by, tourists. This can lead to tensions and a loss of meaning when, as often, priority is given to paying tourists rather than local people and pilgrims. In addition, time constraints in the new economy may lead to important festivals being shortened or moved to new times, often outside the tourist season. More seriously, religious artifacts may be sold for tourist dollars, and illegal export markets may develop, fuelled by the high prices paid for authentic cultural artifacts.

The discussion in this section leads to the conclusion that, during the tourist season, the people of many mountain tourist communities are, whether or not they are dressed in the expected costume, actors in their own homes speaking the language needed to communicate with their audience (Cohen 1989, Fisher 1990, Gamper 1981, Kariel and Kariel 1982, Sacherer 1981). Yet visible signs of acculturation (Nunez 1989), or even new costumes, are not necessarily evidence of significant societal and cultural changes, the topic of the following section.

Life in the Land of Transient Cattle

Two authors, one referring to the Himalaya, the other the Alps, note that mountain people perceive tourists in the following ways:

> (T)ourists are like so many cattle, representing highly mobile, productive, and prestigious, but perishable, forms of wealth. Like cattle, tourists give good milk, but only if they are well fed. (Fisher 1990:123)

> First the cows leave, then the guests - who should we milk now? (Krippendorf 1984: 434)

While these comments come from very different cultures, both recognize the transient nature of tourism and its economic importance. An unstated theme running through the previous section is that of the monetarization of mountain cultures which typically include extensive networks of community and mutual cooperation (Beaver and Purrington 1984, Guillet 1983, Viazzo 1989). Yet, many mountain communities were not isolated from external economies before the arrival of tourism; their inhabitants had centuries-old traditions of trading and seasonal work both along mountain trading routes and in adjacent lowlands (Allan 1985, Rowell 1980, Viazzo 1989). For instance, the introduction of tourism to Nepal provided a replacement to trading which, until the closure of the Tibetan border, had provided an essential complement to subsistence agriculture (von Fuerer-Haimendorf 1975, Stevens 1992). Nevertheless, such trading took place in a barter, rather than a monetary economy.

For tourists to the mountains of developing nations, one unwelcome sign that local people have become part of a monetary economy is begging, an activity unknown and unnecessary in cultures with a tradition of mutual aid (Coppock 1978, Dearden 1989). Theft and alcoholism, also previously unknown, may also become problems (Goering 1990, Guntern 1975, Norberg-Hodge and Page 1983, Rowell 1980). With these final comments on the face of mountain cultures which tourists see, the remainder of this section concentrates on the impacts of monetary tourist economies on local people.

New possibilities for paid employment are a key factor in a rapid transition to a monetary economy affecting patterns of work, food production and consumption and, as mentioned in the previous section, clothing, fuelled particularly by the comparatively massive amounts of money which foreign tourists are willing to spend. While this picture characterizes the mountains of developing countries in recent decades, much of it was equally valid in the mountains of Europe when tourism began there.

With regard to the growth of paid employment, two types of activities may particularly be recognized: those that traditionally were either not recompensed in cash if at all, and those that were not practised. Among the first type is the provision of food and housing, which visitors traditionally received. As a tourist economy grows, there is a change from the automatic welcome given to guests by local people in their own houses to a standard "tourist treatment" in specially-constructed rooms or buildings (Barker 1982, Cohen 1989, Crystal 1989, Dearden 1989, Eppler 1983, Gamper 1981, Groetzbach 1985a, Stevens 1992). To some extent, this may be because the resources of the community are inadequate to deal with the volume and types of demand from tourists; it may also be a conscious decision to limit interactions with tourists. Depending on the culture, food and housing may have been provided traditionally by either men or women. The demands resulting from tourism place an increasing burden on these traditional providers, who therefore have less time available for other activities.

The second type of employment includes climbing, load-carrying, guiding, activities relating to the operation and maintenance of skiing facilities, and the fabrication and sale of souvenirs (Cohen 1982, Coppock 1978, Goering 1990, Haimayer 1989, Sacherer 1981, Stevens 1993, West 1990). All of these activities tend to be seasonal and to decrease the amount of work done by men in agriculture and forestry and for the benefit of neighbours and the community. They can also obviate the need to migrate seasonally in order to relieve pressure on local resources and obtain goods or income (Fuerer-Haimendorf 1975, Viazzo 1989). As a result, there is often a considerable redistribution of activities between the sexes, demands on women increase, and seasonal workers are often hired to do the necessary tasks which would otherwise be left undone - or the lower-paid jobs which local people would prefer not to do (Baumgartner 1988, Bjonness 1983, Fisher 1990, Goering 1990, Kariel and Kariel 1982, Moser and Moser 1986, Pawson et al. 1984a, Sacherer 1981, Stevens 1992). However, these trends often lead to inadequate maintenance of agricultural and forest land, which may be implicated in decreased crop yields and the increasing instability of slopes.

Changes in the production of food may come about because tourist work comes to take precedence over agricultural work (Barker 1982, Bjonness 1983, Messerli 1989) or in direct response to the demands of tourists: for instance, vegetable cultivation in Ladakh (Singh and Kaur 1985) or increased dairy production in the Alps (Gamper 1981, Keller and Kneubuehl 1982). In developing countries, new patterns of food consumption by local people may derive either from the availability of new sources of food or because new income permits more expensive, higher-status food to be bought (Sacherer 1981, Stevens 1992). However, while food prices may well rise at a greater rate than incomes as tourism grows (Fisher 1990, Solbrig 1984), this does not always occur (Stevens 1992).

Agricultural production is also affected by increases in land prices, a particular problem in mountain areas where the best agricultural land is often also the most desirable for developing new facilities for tourism (Crystal 1989, Haefner and Guenter 1984, Kariel and Kariel 1982, Solbrig 1984). This discussion of mountain agriculture will not be taken any further; it is an exceedingly complicated issue, varying significantly at all spatial scales, affected by a wide range of government policies, and with considerably different patterns in market, command, and subsistence economies. This comment also applies to the questions of land ownership and prices. Relevant policies of governments at all levels from the local to the national develop in very diverse ways, and in communities influenced by tourism across the mountains of the world, there is an almost infinite variety of patterns of both pre- and post-tourism land and property ownership (e.g., Brugger et al. 1984, Crystal 1989, Gosar 1989, Groetzbach 1985a, Schwabe 1984, Solbrig 1984). In reference to the Swiss Alps, Messerli (1987:20) states that:

> Classical tourism of the late nineteenth and early twentieth centuries undoubtedly influenced the rural social structure, but did not fundamentally change it. However, post-war tourism represents an economic and social revolution with lasting effects on the rural community. The economic opening of a village or region, as a necessity for its continued viability, is always a social and cultural threat.

These conclusions also appear to be true for many communities in other mountain regions. The changes in employment, consumption, and other cultural patterns which have been described above often lead to strong tensions within these communities. These tensions are all intricately linked; they are briefly discussed below at three levels of interaction: family, intra-community, and external.

As noted above, the growth of tourism tends to lead to a considerable redistribution of work between the sexes, with particularly greater demands being placed on women. Since this trend may be imposed on any one of a vast variety of existing patterns, one would not expect to identify any general trends for families. Examples from communities in the Alps mention a deterioration in family life (Haimayer 1989, Kariel and Kariel 1982, Moser and Moser 1986, Préau 1984), while those from Nepal, for example, describe changes in population dynamics deriving from the availability of contraception, the seasonal absence of men, and growing secularization (Fisher 1990, Pawson et al. 1984a, Sacherer 1981). Such findings cannot be linked unequivocally to tourism. They are as likely to reflect general societal trends in industrialized and developing nations, or the interests of scientific researchers, as anything else.

While traditional mountain communities are certainly not unmarked by class differences, tourism tends to increase these and often to create new ones. Tensions may appear between the newly wealthy and those who live a more traditional lifestyle; those who earn enough income to live the desired lifestyle in the new, higher-priced system and those who cannot; those who are self-employed and the wage-earners; and long-term residents and immigrants (Bjonness 1983, Coppock 1978, Crystal 1989, Gilg 1988, Goering 1990, Messerli 1987, Moser and Moser 1986, Reiter 1977, Stevens 1992). Although such tensions can lead to political change, general trends of change are unlikely

for many reasons, including the range of political institutions, both local and larger-scale, in mountain regions and the fact that the primary political issues will vary through the different phases of tourism.
Interactions with external economies and institutions are inevitably increased by tourism. Perhaps the greatest concern is the possibility of loss of control. In economic terms, tourism does not necessarily benefit the people in whose community it takes place; much of the money spent by tourists benefits, instead, those who arrange travel and have access to the capital needed to invest in land or tourist facilities (Bjonness 1983, Crystal 1989, Goering 1990, Groetzbach 1989, Haimayer 1989, Puntenney 1990, Rodriguez 1987). The reasons for such outflows of the financial benefits include the policies of governments at all scales; the lack of local investment capital, particularly in the early stages of tourism development; unexpectedly rapid increases in prices of land, labour, and commodities; and financial overcommitments that require recourse to external sources of funding. However, there are examples of communities that have maintained a high level of economic control over the development of tourism (Moser and Moser 1986, Stevens 1992).

Conclusion

The literature reviewed in this paper permits the identification of some definite patterns relating to the development of tourism in mountain areas. However, other than recognizing the importance of accessibility and the fact that tourism in mountain areas includes diverse participants in a variety of activities and goes through many phases in any one community, no formal model can be presented. Spiral models of the development of tourism in the Alps have been proposed (Kariel 1989, Messerli 1989). However, while their form is telling in relation to the concerns over lack of control voiced in many communities, these models are primarily descriptive and do not appear suited to an understanding of the development of tourism in mountain regions in general. Acculturation does not necessarily result from the growth of tourism in mountain areas: existing institutions have been strengthened in a number of instances (Crystal 1989, Fisher 1990, Gamper 1981, Moser and Peterson 1981, Stevens 1993), and tourism has been cited as both a source of both revolution (in Afghanistan: Allan 1988) and the maintenance of cultural identity under colonial rule (in Tibet: Klieger 1990).

Mountain regions, in spite of their diversity, have a number of similarities, notably environmental constraints and marked seasonality, which do not typify many other tourist destinations, such as islands and cities, to which studies of tourism and its impacts have given far greater consideration. In spite, or perhaps because, of the lack of clear-cut conclusions, the main value of this paper may be to point out issues for further research on tourism in mountain regions. Based on a range of studies from mountain regions throughout the world, where many different types of tourism have been imposed on a wide range of pre-existing conditions and evolved at different speeds, some general trends have been identified and conclusions drawn. Whether or not these are realistic should be the object of future research - perhaps they are best regarded as hypotheses. This is particularly true because repeat or longitudinal and comparative studies are essential to understand the dynamic nature of tourism. Few such studies have been undertaken (Cohen 1989, Crystal 1990, Fisher 1990, Kariel 1989, Messerli 1989, Pawson et al. 1984a,b, Stevens 1993).

In an era of rapid socio-economic and cultural changes, tourism has come to be regarded as the only solution for the future survival of mountain communities in many parts of the world. Yet these changes are also implicated in the prospect of climatic change, so that, added to the inevitable forces of competition and government policy, mountain communities that decide to rely on tourism may be faced with two additional problems. First, the physical climate may change, resulting in new changes in demand and possibilities of benefits. Second, policies to decrease the emission of greenhouse gases may lead to substantial increases in the cost of fuel, crucially implicated in mountain tourism since accessibility is a determining factor.

In most mountain communities, the development of tourism has been characterized by rapid decisions based on far more limited information than decisions relating to other activities on which these communities have relied. Mountain people in both industrialized and developing countries recognize the need for the maintenance or recovery of control over the forces of the tourist economy (Adams 1990, Goering 1990, Kariel and Kariel 1982, Lieberherr-Gardiol and Stucki 1987, Moser and Moser 1986, Puntenney 1990). A clearer understanding of these forces is needed as a basis for future decisions about an economic sector for which long-term prognoses are remarkably difficult to make.

Acknowledgements

I would like to thank Atelier Temenos (Paris, France) for support during the preparation of this chapter, and also the many individuals who provided materials for the development of the UNESCO Man and the Biosphere project on "The sustainable future of mountain communities: Resources and tourism in the context of climate variability and change."

REFERENCES

Adams, K.M. 1990. "Cultural Commoditization in Tana Toraja, Indonesia." *Cultural Survival Quarterly* 14:31-34.
Allan, N.J.R. 1984. "Accessibility and Zonation Models of Mountains." *Journal of Himalayan Research and Development* 8:11-18.
——————. 1985. "Periodic and daily markets in highland-lowland interaction systems." In *Integrated Mountain Development*, edited by T.V. Singh and J. Kaur, 239-256. New Delhi: Himalayan Books.
——————. 1988. "Highways to the Sky: The Impact of Tourism on South Asian Mountain Culture." *Tourism Recreation Research* 13:11-16.
Allan, N.J.R., G.W. Knapp and C. Stadel (eds.). 1988. *Human Impact on Mountains*. Totowa, N.J.: Rowman and Littlefield.
Banskota, K. and M. Upadhyay. n.d. "Tourism Management and Socio-Economic Survey." Field report for the Sankhuwasabha District, Nepal.
Byers, Alton. 1990. "Makalu-Barun Conservation Project." Working Paper No. 6. Franklin, West Virginia: Woodlands Mountain Institute.
Barker, M.L. 1982. "Traditional Landscape and Mass Tourism in the Alps." *Geographical Review* 72:395-415.
Baumgartner, R. 1988. "Tourism and Socio-economic Change: The Case of Rolwaling Valley in Eastern Nepal." *Tourism Recreation Research* 13:17-26.
Baver, P.D. and B.L. Purrington (eds.). 1984. *Cultural Adaptation to Mountain Environments*. Athens: University of Georgia Press.
Bernard, P.P. 1978. *Rush to the Alps*. New York: Columbia University Press.
Bjonness, I. M. 1983. "External Economic Dependency and Changing Human Adjustment to Marginal Environment in the High Himalaya, Nepal." *Mountain Research and Development* 3:263-272.
Bridel L. 1984. "Formes et tendences de l'evolution touristique." In *Umbruch im Berggebiet*, edited by E.A. Brugger, G. Furrer, B. Messerli and P. Messerli, 203-240. Bern: Haupt.
Brugger, E.A. et al. (eds.). 1984. *Umbruch im Berggebiet*. Bern: Haupt.
Buhrlein, M. 1989. "Die Bedeutung Nuwara Eliyas als "Hill Station" im Lichte moderner Kurortklimatologie." *Erdkundliches Wissen* 97:169-207.
Butler, R.W. 1980. "The Concept of a Tourism Area Cycle of Evolution: Implications for Management of Resources." *The Canadian Geographer* 24:5-12.
——————. 1985. "Evolution of Tourism in the Scottish Highlands." *Annals of Tourism Research* 12:371-391.
Chapeau, G. 1986. "Le Tourisme et la mise en valeur des Pyrenees orientales espagnoles et andorranes." *L'Information Geographique* 1986:128-130.

Cohen, E. 1979. "The Impact of Tourism on the Hill Tribes of Northern Thailand." *Internationales Asienforum* 10:5-38.
—————. 1982. "Jungle Guides in Northern Thailand - The Dynamics of a Marginal Occupational Role." *Sociological Review* 30:234-266.
—————. 1989. "Primitive and Remote - Hill Tribe Trekking in Thailand." *Annals of Tourism Research* 16:30-61.
Coppock, R. 1978. "The Influence of Himalayan Tourism on Sherpa Culture and Habitat." *Zeitschrift fur Kulturaustausch* 3:61-68.
Crystal, E. 1989. "Tourism in Toraja (Sulawesi, Indonesia)." In *Hosts and Guests: The Anthropology of Tourism*, edited by V. Smith, 139-168. Philadelphia: University of Pennsylvania Press.
Dearden, P. 1989. "Tourism in Developing Countries: Some Observations on Trekking in the Highlands of North Thailand." In *Tourism - A Vital Force for Peace*, edited by L.J. D'Amore and J. Jafari, 207-216. Montreal: International Institute for Peace through Tourism.
Dhakal, D.N.S. 1990. "Hydropower in Bhutan: A Long-term Perspective." *Mountain Research and Development* 10:291-300.
Direction du Projet MAB Pays d'Enhaut. 1985. "Tourisme Pays d'Enhaut. Synthese partielle." Schlussbericht Schweizerisches MAB-Programm No. 15. Bern: Bundesamt fuer Umweltschutz.
Eppler, P. 1983. "Impact of Tourism on Leh and Surroundings." In *Recent Research on Ladakh*, edited by D. Kantowsky and R. Sander, 253-262. Munich: Weltforum.
Fisher, J.F. 1990. *Sherpas: Reflections on Change in Himalayan Nepal.* Los Angeles: University of California Press.
Fuentes, E.R. and M. Castro. 1982. "Problems of Resource Management and Land Use in Two Mountain Regions of Chile." In *Ecology in Practice*, edited by F. di Castri, F.W.G. Baker and M. Hadley, 315-330. Dublin: Tycooly.
Galloway, R.W. 1988. "The Potential Impact of Climate Changes on Australian Ski Fields." In *Greenhouse: Planning for Climate Change*, edited by G.I. Pearman, 428-437. East Melbourne: CSIRO.
Gamper, J.A. 1981. "Tourism in Austria - A Case Study of the Influence of Tourism on Ethnic Relations." *Annals of Tourism Research* 8:432-446.
Gilg, A.W. 1988. "Switzerland: Structural Change Within Stability." In *Tourism and Economic Development: Western European Experiences*, edited by A.M. Williams and G. Shaw, 123-144. London: Belhaven.
Goering, P.G. 1990. "The Response to Tourism in Ladakh." *Cultural Survival Quarterly* 14:20-25.
Gosar, A. 1989. "Second Homes in the Alpine Region of Yugoslavia." *Mountain Research and Development* 9:165-174.

Groetzbach, E. 1985. "The Bavarian Alps: Problems of Tourism, Agriculture, and Environment Conservation." In *Integrated Mountain Development*, edited by T.V. Singh and J. Kaur, 141-155. New Delhi: Himalayan Books.

—————. 1985. "Tourismus im Indischen Westhimalaya - Entwicklung und Raueumliche Struktur." In *Beitraege zur Fremdenverkehrsgeographie*, edited by J. Steinbach, 27-47. Eichstaett: Fachgebiet Geographie der Katholischen Universitaet Eichstaett.

—————. 1989. "Mountain Tourism in North Pakistan - Tourist Regions and Problems of Further Development." *Tourism and Recreation Research* 14:69-73.

Goeller, P. 1986. *Regional Development Policy in Swiss Mountain Areas*. Wintherthur: KODIS.

Guillet, David. 1983. "Toward a Cultural Ecology of Mountains: The Central Andes and the Himalaya Compared." *Current Anthropology* 24:561-574.

Guntern, G. 1975. "Changement social et consommation d'alcool dans un village de montagne." *Archives suisses de neurologie, neurochirurgie et psychiatrie* 353-411.

Gurung, Harka. 1982. "Tourism Development in Nepal." In *Social and Economic Impact of Tourism on Asian Pacific Region*, edited by D.E. Hawkins, 245-258. Tokyo: Asian Productivity Organization.

Haefner, H. and T. Gunter. 1984. "Land-use Changes and Ecological Effects in the Swiss Alps." In *The Transformation of Swiss Mountain Regions*, edited by E.A. Brugger et al., 101-124. Bern: Haupt.

Haimayer, Peter. 1989. "Glacier Skiing Areas in Austria: A Socio-Political Perspective." *Mountain Research and Development* 9:51-58.

Fuerer-Haimendorf, C. von. 1975. *Himalayan Traders*. Murray, London.

Hartmann, R. 1989. "Vom Bergbauort zur Fremdenverkehrsgemeinde: Goldgraeber- und Western-Staedte als Ausgangspunkt touristicher Entwicklungen in den Colorado Rocky Mountains." In *Forschungsperspektiven der nordamerikanischen remdenverkehrsgeographie*, edited by R. Hartmann, 125-153. Trier: Geographische Gesellschaft.

Houghton, J.T., M. Seck and A.D. Moura (eds.). 1990. *Scientific Assessment of Climate Change*. Geneva: World Meteorological Organization.

Hurni, Hans. 1985. "Management Plan: Simen Mountains National Park and Surrounding Rural Area." Addis Ababa: Wildlife Conservation Organization.

Jest, C. and J. Sanday. 1983. "The Palace of Leh in Ladakh: An Example of Himalayan Architecture in Need of Preservation." *Mountain Research and Development* 3:1-11.

Kariel, H.G. 1989. "Socio-cultural Impacts of Tourism in the Austrian Alps." *Mountain Research and Development* 9:59-70.

Kariel, H.G. and P.E. Kariel. 1982. "Socio-cultural Impacts of Tourism: An Example from the Austrian Alps." *Geografiska Annaler* B 64:1-16.

———. 1988. "Tourist Developments in the Kananaskis Valley, Alberta, Canada, and the Impact of the 1988 Winter Olympic Games." *Mountain Research and Development* 8:1-10.

Kaur, J. 1979. "Re-examining Tourist Capacity of Nainital." *Wiener Geographische Schriften* 53/54:108-114.

———. 1985. *Himalayan Pilgrimages and the New Tourism*. New Delhi: Himalayan Books.

Keller, P. and U. Kneubuehl. 1982. "Die Entwicklungsteuerung in einem Tourismusort. Schlussbericht zum MAB Projekt 4.183." Bern: Geographisches Institut, Universitaet Bern.

Kemper, R.V. 1979. "Tourism in Taos and Patzcuaro: A Comparison of Two Approaches to Regional Development." *Annals of Tourism Research* 6:91-110.

Klieger, P.C. 1990. "Close Encounters: "Intimate" Tourism in Tibet." *Cultural Survival Quarterly* 14:38-42.

Krippendorf, J. 1984. "The Capital of Tourism in Danger." In *The Transformation of Swiss Mountain Regions*, edited by E.A. Brugger et al., 427-450. Bern: Haupt.

Kroener, A. 1968. "Grindelwald: Die Entwicklung eines Bergbauerndorfes zu einem internationalen Touristenzentrum." Stuttgart: Geographisches Institut, Universitaet Stuttgart.

Kutay, K. 1989. "The New Ethic in Adventure Travel." *Buzzworm* 1:31-36.

Lamothe et Périard. 1988. "Implications of Climate Change for Downhill Skiing in Quebec." Climate Change Digest 88-03. Downsview: Atmospheric Environment Service.

Lay, J.I. 1988. "Meeting the Challenge: The Colorado Tourism Industry." *Colorado Economic Review* 1988:34-35, 47.

Lieberherr-Gardiol, F. and E. Stucki. 1987. *Sur nos monts quand la nature* Chateau d'Oex: Switzerland: CERME.

Marsh, J. 1985. "The Rocky and the Selkirk Mountains and the Swiss Connection, 1885-1914." *Annals of Tourism Research* 12:417-433.

Mattig F. and H. P. Zeiter. 1984. "Der touristiche Wachstumsprozess im MAB-Testgebiet Aletsch, seine raeumliche Auspraegung und seine Auswirkungen auf Bevaelkerung, Arbeitsmarkt und Gemeindefinanzen." Fiesch: Druck AG.

Mazanec, J.A. and W. Alkier. 1985. "Tourism Planning in Highly Developed Mountain Areas: Recommended Methodology." In *Integrated Mountain Development*, edited by T.V. Singh and J. Kaur, 275-292. New Delhi: Himalayan Books.

McBoyle, G. and G. Wall. 1987. "The Impact of CO_2-induced Warming on Downhill Skiing in the Laurentians." *Cahiers de Géographie de Québec* 31:39-50.

Messerli, P. 1987. "The Development of Tourism in the Swiss Alps: Economic, Societal, and Environmental Effects." *Mountain Research and Development* 7:13-23.

———. 1989. *Mensch und Natur im Alpinen Lebensraum: Risiken, Chancen, Perspektiven.* Bern: Haupt.

Moser, P. and W. Moser. 1986. "Reflections on the MAB-6 Obergurgl Project and Tourism in an Alpine Environment." *Mountain Research and Development* 6:101-118.

Moser, W. and J. Peterson. 1981. "Limits to Obergurgl's Growth: An Alpine Experience in Environmental Management." *Ambio* 10:68-72.

Norberg-Hodge, H. and J. Page. 1983. "Unscientific Observations." In *Recent Research on Ladakh*, edited by D. Kantowsky and R. Sander, 263-268. Munich: Weltforum.

Nunez, T. 1989. "Touristic Studies in Anthropological Perspective." In *Hosts and Guests: The Anthropology of Tourism*, edited by V. Smith, 265-274. Philadelphia: University of Pennsylvania Press.

Pawson, I.G., D.D. Stanford and V.A. Adams. 1984a. "Effects of Modernization on the Khumbu Region of Nepal: Changes in Population Structure, 1970-1982." *Mountain Research and Development* 4:73-81.

Pawson, I.G., D.D. Stanford, V.A. Adams, and M. Norbu. 1984b. "Growth of Tourism in Nepal's Everest Region: Impact of the Physical Environment and Structure of Human Settlements." *Mountain Research and Development* 4:237-246.

Pearce, D.G. 1985. "Tourism and Planning in the Southern Alps of New Zealand." In *Integrated Mountain Development*, edited by T.V. Singh and J. Kaur, 293-308. New Delhi: Himalayan Books.

Préau, P. 1984. "Le changement social dans une commune touristique de montagne: Saint-Bon-Tarentaise (Savoie)." *Revue de Géographie Alpine* 75:411-437.

Price, M.F. 1990. *Mountain Forests As Common-Property Resources: Management Policies and Their Outcomes in the Colorado Rockies and the Swiss Alps.* Forstwissenschaftliche Beitrege No. 9. Zurich: ETH Professur Forstpolitik und Forstekonomie.

Puntenney, P.J. 1990. "Defining Solutions: The Annapurna experience." *Cultural Survival Quarterly* 14:9-14.

Reichart, T. 1988. "Socio-economic Difficulties in Developing Tourism in Small Alpine Countries: The Case of Andorra." *Tourism Recreation Research* 13: 27-32.

Reiter, R.R. 1977. "The Politics of Tourism in a French Alpine Community." In *Hosts and Guests: The Anthropology of Tourism*, edited by V.L. Smith, 139-147. Philadelphia: University of Pennsylvania Press.

Richter, L.K. 1989. *The Politics of Tourism in Asia*. Honolulu: University of Hawaii Press.

Rodriguez, S. 1987. "Impact of the Ski Industry on the Rio Hondo Watershed." *Annals of Tourism Research* 14:88-103.

Rowell, G. 1980. *Many People Come, Looking, Looking*. Seattle: The Mountaineers.

Sacherer, J. 1981. "The Recent Social and Economic Impact of Tourism on a Remote Sherpa Community." In *Asian Highland Societies in Anthropological Perspective*, edited by C. von Fuerer-Haimendorf, 157-167. Atlantic Highlands, N.J.: Humanities Press.

Schwabe, E. 1984. "Development of Settlement Structures in Swiss Mountain Areas." In *The Transformation of Swiss Mountain Regions*, edited by E.A. Brugger et al., 125-143. Bern: Haupt.

Singh, T.V. 1989. *Impact of Tourism on Mountain Areas: The Kulu Valley*. New Delhi: Himalayan Books.

Singh, T.V. and J. Kaur. 1985. "In Search of Holistic Tourism for the Himalaya." In *Integrated Mountain Development*, edited by T.V. Singh and J. Kaur, 365-401. New Delhi: Himalayan Books.

―――――. 1986. "The Paradox of Mountain Tourism: Case References from the Himalaya." *Industry and Environment* 9:21-26.

Smith, V. 1989. "Introduction." In *Hosts and Guests: The Anthropology of Tourism*, edited by V. Smith, 1-17. Philadelphia: University of Pennsylvania Press.

Solbrig, O.T. 1984. "Tourism." *Mountain Research and Development* 4:181-185.

Stadelbauer, J. 1986. "Der Fremdenverkehr in Sowjet-Kaukasien: Gesamtstaatliche Bedeutung, raueumliche Strukturen und Entwicklungsprobleme." *Zeitschrift faer Wirtschaftsgeographie* 30:1-21.

Stein J.A. 1974. "Tourism and Mountain Environment." In *Final Report, International Workshop on the Development of Mountain Environment*, edited by K. Mueller-Hohenstein, 163-170. Munich: German Foundation for International Development.

Stevens, S.F. 1993. *Claiming the High Ground: Sherpas, Subsistence, and Environmental Change in the Highest Himalaya*. Berkeley: University of California Press.

Svalastog, S. 1988. "Tourism in Norway's Rural Mountain Districts Twenty-five Years After the Mountain Planning Team's Report." *Norsk Geografisk Tidsskrift* 42:103-120.

Swindlin, B. 1985. "The Effects of the Development of Tourism on the Socio-economic Structure of a Mountain Village in France: 1962-1982." *Gloucestershire Papers in Local and Rural Planning*, No. 28. Gloucester: Gloucestershire College of Arts and Technology.

Tegart, W.J. McG., G.W. Sheldon and D.C. Griffiths (eds.). 1990. *Climate Change: The IPCC Impacts Assessment*. Canberra: Australian Government Printing Service.

Tyrakowski, K. 1986. "Zur Entwicklung des einheimischen Fremdenverkehrs in Mexico, dargestellt am Beispiel des Staates Tlaxcala." *Erdkunde* 40:293-305.

Viazzo, P.P. 1989. *Upland Communities: Environment, Population and Social Structure in the Alps Since the Sixteenth Century*. Cambridge: Cambridge University Press.

Watson, A. and R.D. Watson. 1982. *The Swiss Approach and its Relevance to Scotland*. Aberdeen: Grampian Regional Council.

West, T. 1990. "Employment Generation in the Cusco Artisan Market." Washington D.C.: US Forest Service.

Zimmerman, F. 1988a. "Austria: Contrasting Tourist Seasons and Contrasting Regions." In *Tourism and Economic Development: Western European Experiences*, edited by A.M. Williams and G. Shaw, 145-161. London: Belhaven.

―――. 1988b. "Ende des Wachstums und potentieller Raeckbau des Fremdenverkehrs." In *Tagungsbericht und Wissenschaftliche Abhandlungen*, 46. Deutscher Geographentag, edited by H. Becker and W.D. Hutteroth, 384-393. Munich: Steiner.

CHAPTER 8

Outdoor Recreation and Tourism in Mountain Environments

HERBERT G. KARIEL
DIANNE L. DRAPER

Outdoor Recreation in Mountains

Roads, airstrips, and affluence have changed the mountain environments that recreationists once knew. The unspoiled splendor of mountains is being increasingly jeopardized by growing numbers of tourists and recreationists, whose presence often creates a heavier impact than is frequently anticipated, desired, or perceived. As mountain environments have become more accessible, visitors have caused considerable change in the seasonal, subsistence economies and life-styles of mountain peoples and their habitats. In altering the landscape, too, recreation has become a source of concern as well as of optimism for the future of mountain inhabitants and environments.

This chapter provides an overview and analysis of outdoor recreation and tourism in mountain environments. The highland-lowland interaction system is used to illustrate the linkages between outdoor recreationists and tourists and mountain environments and also to identify some of the effects of recreation on the local populations and their habitats. Because mountain environments are also part of a widespread outdoor tourism and recreation system and their attractions supply many of the demands of recreationists, the roles that visitors' characteristics, origin, and socioeconomic status play in establishing a demand for leisure activities in these environments are considered. Accessibility, communication improvements, and promotion levels, which link tourists and recreationists to the resource supply, are noted. As components of the supply side, destination characteristics, attractions, and image are identified as having been important to the rapid expansion of mountain tourism and recreation over the past four decades (Dearden and Sewell 1985, Nicolson 1959). Although all these facets are discussed in a generalized way, as are the impacts of recreation and tourism on mountain lands and people, we want to emphasize that each place and area differs from the general pattern in its own peculiar way. The overall pattern may appear simple but any particular situation is complex and possibly unique. We conclude that if tourism is to be developed in an area, it should be done responsibly, for local and global sustainable benefits.

The Supply Side of Mountain Recreation and Tourism

Considering the highland and the lowland as an interaction system helps explain not only why people go to the mountains and the pattern of their movement from lowland to highland, but also the effects of their diverse activities on many mountain regions. Travel to the highlands is partly a function of the attractiveness, accessibility, and image of the region being visited. Each of these elements associated with the proximity of mountains as a recreation base is considered briefly and their interrelationships are noted. As Christaller, the German geographer astutely noted:

> Tourists look for the breadth of the sea, the brightness and fresh air of the mountains, and the silence and perceptibility of a rural milieu. These stand in counterpoise for the stony, narrow, dark and noisy towns. Thus, the landscape is the most important holiday destination. ...landscapes far away from agglomerated industrial regions provide vigorous contrasts to our confinement in towns. (Christaller 1964:103,105.)

The cultural traits of local inhabitants also contribute to the attractiveness of mountain settings. Their ways of life, agricultural methods, arts, languages, settlements, religions and customs, and the architecture of the houses, help to attract visitors. If host-guest interactions are perceived to be hospitable and authentic, then attractiveness may be enhanced (Smith 1977). Ancillary goods and services, such as permanent campsites, hotels and restaurants, potable water supplies and adequate sewage systems, and modern recreation facilities usually are required to attract and service large numbers of visitors.

A destination requires not only attractiveness, but also some form of relatively easy accessibility from the outside world. Access is one of the most important factors of the highland-lowland interaction system in accounting for the numbers and types of recreationists and tourists in an area. The perceived accessibility of mountain environment destinations depends on such factors as their distance from areas of traveller origin and on the monetary or time costs incurred in reaching them, which in turn are functions of established transportation networks and technology.

Groetzbach (1985a, 1985b, 1985c), has demonstrated how peripheral mountain areas are integrated into the core areas of society that are dominated by the urban middle class. Allan (1986) extended Groetzbach's theoretical developments further by employing a model of mountain accessibility to elucidate land use changes in the modernizing mountain world. Allan also showed how linkages solidified highland-lowland interaction systems in mountain environments (1985). Allan's use (1992) of the Bjorkland-Philbrick model of host-guest interaction exemplifies the kind of highland-lowland interaction theory that is necessary to comprehend the relationships between tourists, recreationists and the host population in mountain regions.

Examples of improved accessibility resulting from the construction or upgrading of rail lines, roads, or airports are legion. They include the building of resource roads for logging and mining in many parts of the Rocky Mountains and other mountain ranges in the western United States and Canada. Access to these mountain regions has increased as a result of major undertakings such as the Going to the Sun Highway in Glacier National Park (Montana, USA) and the Trans-Canada Highway over Rogers Pass. In addition, a myriad of minor roads has been constructed into backcountry areas. Many of these roads are used year-round by a variety of vehicles, including snowmobiles. Similarly, construction of the various roads, tunnels, snow sheds, and avalanche control devices throughout the Alps has made once remote, isolated, agricultural alpine communities readily accessible to tourists and recreationists. Access from the valleys to the mountain slopes and the peaks themselves has also been facilitated by conveyances such as cableways, lifts, mountain bikes, and helicopters.

Other examples of increased accessibility are the four major highways that have been constructed across the mountain rimland of South Asia during the past twenty-five years (Allan 1986). These are the route north of Kabul, Afghanistan over the Hindukush; the Karakorum Highway, now open between Islamabad, Pakistan and Kashgar, China; the road from Srinagar out of Kashmir to Leh in Ladakh; and the road from Kathmandu, Nepal, to Lhasa in China.

Numbers of outdoor recreationists and tourists increase when airstrips are built or public transportation is improved. This can be noted at mountain protected areas adjacent to places such as Pokhara and Jomosom on the Annapurna circuit and at Lukla and Khumjung near Mount Everest. Similarly, as local transportation technology changes have made travel easier, more tourists have visited Gilgit and Skardu in northern Pakistan (Allan 1989b) or Naeba ski resort in Japan (Shirasaka 1984). Improved bus service and road conditions, such as those between Lima and Huaraz at the gateway for the Cordilleras Blanca and Huascaran National Park, Peru, have made this area more accessible to skiers and mountain climbing expeditions from Europe and North America.

Access to mountain environments can be intensified or hindered by local and national attitudes toward outdoor recreation and tourism. Large numbers of tourists visit national parks in Argentina's lake region, for example, because visitor promotion is an explicitly stated parks objective and recreation and tourism is promoted by the automobile clubs, private travel agencies, and bus companies (Solbrig 1984). While many European nations, as well as the United States, Canada, Nepal, and New Zealand actively promote tourism and outdoor recreation, other countries (in Eastern Europe, for example) have or had currency or visa restrictions that limit visitor access. Military conflicts, terrorist activities, and strong religious or cultural animosities toward foreign visitors also hinder access. The conflicts in Afghanistan, Zaire, and Uganda, and the Islamic fundamentalist presence in Pakistan have deterred foreign visitors. The varied acceptance of and hostility to foreigners in the countries bordering on the South Asian mountain rimland also has been documented (Allan 1989a).

A foreign visitor's image of a mountain environment is another important variable in understanding the demand side of the highland-lowland interaction system. Image refers to both the reputation or fame of a destination and the tourist's impression or perception built up from formal and informal information sources. The reputation of a mountain destination may be recognized by a large segment of the general population or by a subset, such as fishermen, mountain climbers, wind-surfers, or heli-skiers. Places considered to be in vogue to visit at a particular time have positive images. In Pakistan, images are developed purposely through post cards and tourist folders portraying mythical classic and stereotypical scenes of the Khyber Pass, Nanga Parbat, a bucolic spring in the Swat Valley, a polo match and saber dance at Gilgit, and the purported health, happiness, and harmony of the Hunza people (Ali and Ferras 1976). Similar mythical views exhibiting conjured folk items can be obtained for Milford Sound, Mount Cook, and Queenstown, and mounts Kilimanjaro, Fujiyama, or the Grand Teton.

Various mountain places and areas that attract tourists and recreationists are presented in Table 1. These examples are reasonably well recognized and evoke positive images for most visitors to mountain environments.

TABLE 1. EXAMPLES OF RECREATION ATTRACTIONS IN MOUNTAIN ENVIRONMENTS.

Ski resorts: Chamonix, Grenoble, La Plagne, Maribel, Flims-Laax, St. Moritz, Wengen, Zermatt, St. Anton, Seefeld, Kitzbuehel, Cortina, Sestriere, and Garmish-Partenkirchen in the Alps; Aspen, Vail, Sun Valley and Lake Placid, U.S.A.; Whistler, Canada; Gulmarg, India; San Carlos de Bariloche, Argentina; Portillo, Chile; Nozawa Onsen, Shiga Kogen and Naeba, Japan.

Archaeological sites: Machu Picchu, Peru.

Cities: Quito, Bogota, Merida, Venezuela; Banff, Canada; Mexico City, Mexico; Cuzco, Peru; Antigua and Chichicastenango, Guatemala; San Jose, Costa Rica.

Holy places, temples, and shrines: Lourdes, France; Badrinath, India; Muktinath, Nepal; Assissi, Italy; mounts Fujiama, Olympus, and Sinai; Medicine Mountain, MT, U.S.A.; the source of the Ganges; Leh, Ladakh; Banyos, Ecuador; Guadalupe, Mexico; Nakasha and Hokosha, Japan.

Spas and hot springs: Bad Reichenhall, Bad Tolz, Germany; Bad Ischl, Austria; Radium, Canada; Karlovy Vary (Carlsbad), Marianske Lazne (Marienbad), Czech Republic; Banyos, Ecuador; Hoppo Onsen and Kumanoyu, Japan.

National parks, scenic, and wildlife areas: Crater Lake, Denali, Glacier, Grand Teton, Great Smoky, Mount Rainier, Yosemite, U.S.A.; Auyuittuq, Banff, Kluane, Canada; Virunga, Zaire; Queen Elizabeth, Uganda; Snowdonia, U.K.; Hohe Tauern, Austria; Berchtesgaden, Germany; Sagarmatha (Everest), Nepal; Nahuel Huape, Los Glaciares, Argentina; Huascaran, Peru; Fiordland, Mount Cook, New Zealand.

Second home areas: Tegernsee and other parts of southern Bavaria, Germany; Bolzano, Meran, Italy; Slovenian Alps, Yugoslavia; Invermere and the Columbia River Valley, British Columbia, Canada; Queenstown, New Zealand.

Wild rivers: Salmon and Clearwater, ID, Flathead, MT, and Rogue, OR, U.S.A.; Kootenay and Kicking Horse, Canada.

Trekking areas: Annapurna circuit, Langtang Valley, and Everest region, Nepal; northern Pakistan; Rocky Mountains, Sierra Nevada, Appalachian Mountains, and Cascade Range, U.S.A.; Rocky Mountains, Canada.

Individual peaks or ranges: Matterhorn, Zugspitze, Kilimanjaro, Grossglockner, Eiger, McKinley, Robson, Tatra, Dolomites, Cordillera Blanca, Osorno Volcano, Cotopaxi, Popocatepetl, Ixtaccihuatl, Lenin, Communism, Southern Alps.

Although these places are unequal in terms of their reputations, the length of time they have been in operation, and types of clientele attracted, they are illustrative of "famous" mountain destinations. Not included are countless locally important, but less famous places.

Recreation and Tourist Demands for Mountain Environments

Because MTNPA are not equally attractive to all tourists or recreationists, the characteristics of recreationists, tourists, and their socioeconomic status need to be considered on the demand side of the highland-lowland interaction system.

Mountain destinations attract visitors who wish to view or use the area's natural environment, to actively recreate in the outdoor environment, and to experience the area's hospitality. As some mountain destinations evolved from remote, untouched discoveries to glittering resorts, the types of visitors also changed. In the Garhwal Himalaya, for example, it was first pilgrims, later Britishers, and thereafter mass pilgrims and tourists for whom shrines, climatic resorts and sanatoria, tea houses and hotels, as well as other facilities and an infrastructure were established (Singh and Kaur 1985). The transition from the Indian Himalaya being a place of fear and loathing for the plains dweller, *maidan walla*, to one of sacred and profane worship is incisively described by Bharati (1978; 1988).

Some visitors are attracted to mountain environments to experience other cultures, to participate in or be spectators at sporting events, or to indulge in "adventure travel" as some small group tours to remote places are called. Other visitors may make spiritual or religious visits or pilgrimages, or to visit friends and relatives.

Depending, in part, on their characteristics (personalities, interests, and motivations), visitors have varying degrees of an impact on their destination. Relatively small numbers of people in individual or group organized adventure travel might be elitist, are recognized as individualistic, curious, and often pompous. Their impacts on indigenous cultures and environments are usually small although their presence may initiate social and economic changes (Butz 1993). In their search for off the beaten track experiences, these travellers tend to visit an area removed from the familiar tourist haunts. At the other end of the visitor spectrum is mass tourism. These groups have an impact on all localities because they seek familiar or popular settings and expect standardization (usually European) of accommodation, food, activities, and sometimes entertainment. These visitors may annoy residents and increase their feeling of being irritated by foreigners (Cohen 1978, Doxey 1975, Hudman and Hawkins 1989, Plog 1973).

As popular mountain destinations with burgeoning facilities and favorable reputations emerge, the numbers of group travellers increases. The combination of greater accessibility, better service, and heightened popularity results in increased commercialization of host-visitor interactions. At the same time there is a separation of the social from the natural attractions that first drew the group travellers. As particular mountain areas such as MTNPA become attractive to the masses, people at one end of the social scale visit less frequently.

Visitors to mountain environments can also be classified according to their participation in different physical activities (Jackson and Schinkel 1981, McCool 1976). Activity preferences for recreational pursuits in the mountains are important for marketing and promotion efforts, for appreciation of the impacts of tourism and recreation on the landscape, and because they present a potential for conflict between and among uses and users, including visitors and local residents.

Visitors come primarily from the urban middle class of the lowlands of the developed world from Western Europe, America, and, increasingly, Japan. The linkages between origin, personal mobility, leisure time, socioeconomic status, and accessibility are vital elements in the evolution of mountain areas as tourist destinations. Often, peripheral mountain areas function not only as living space for local populations, but also to meet the recreational demands imposed by core or metropolitan areas (Danz 1978).

Complementarity of mountain environments to conditions in the lowlands and intervening opportunities offered by other competing tourist areas also help to explain why certain areas are visited and others are not (Ullman 1956). The range of attractions noted previously provides desired complementarity (Christaller 1964). Movement of visitors from the lowland urban areas to the mountain destinations will not occur unless the cost of travel (measured in time, distance, difficulty, or money) is relatively equal to that incurred in a visit to an intervening opportunity. Furthermore, accessibility is a function of personal factors as well as distance and physical connections. Thus the importance of tourist travel mode and activity preferences, of mountain environment images, of ethnocentric perceptions, and of group stereotypes of distant places becomes evident.

Jeffers' (1922) dream of frequent air service has become reality and lowland dwellers world-wide have become recreationists and tourists in mountain environments. While much of this travel is international, a strong distance-decay effect is present at all scales and the gravity model of spatial interaction applies generally. Most visitors tend to be from near-by: for example, most recreationists within Canada's Cordillera come from British Columbia and Alberta; visitors to American mountains come from the state in which the area is located; those to the High Tatra Mountains come from Slovakia; and those to San Carlos de Bariloche are from Argentina. The number and types of recreational pursuits have also increased remarkably. Initially, mountain recreational activities focused primarily on mountain hiking, hunting and fishing, mountain climbing, and skiing on unprepared slopes. Now, mountain visitors take part in mountain biking, hanggliding, off-road vehicle driving, summer glacier skiing, heli-skiing, ski boarding, free climbing, and orienteering. The increased use of commercial accommodations as well as technologically more sophisticated equipment has accompanied this wide growth in the range of mountain recreation.

Tourism and Recreation Impacts on Mountain Environments and their Inhabitants

Recreation is part of an overall development or modernization process that brings external influences to less developed areas (de Kadt 1979, De los Santos 1982). This process involves a change from traditional life-styles and leads to urbanization and development among the agro-pastoral and silvi-agricultural landscapes (Singh and Kaur 1985). In many parts of the world modernization, including tourism, has transformed many formerly rural valleys into semi-urban landscapes (Bernard 1978, Brugger et al. 1984, Groetzbach 1985, Lichtenberger 1988, Tobias 1986, Wiesmann 1986). Willingly or otherwise, mountain people are being integrated into the larger, more developed society.

Acculturation theory, which examines the interaction between hosts and guests, states that, as two cultures come into contact, each becomes more like the other (Nunez 1977). The more technologically advanced group usually gains supremacy, since the functionalist components of a society are more readily adopted than are the interpersonal ones. Hence, tools, clothing, cooking utensils, and other mass-produced items of the urbanized lowland people replace indigenously manufactured goods, including clothing. Symbolic items of the more technologically advanced culture are also borrowed. In Nepal and in northern Pakistan, for example, local villagers hiring themselves out as porters or guides take on parts of the mountain climbers' culture and display alpine clothing and equipment, such as ice axes and packs, as emblems. Porters may wear wrist watches, even if they are not always consulted, as the sun is their time-piece. Attitudes of mountain dwellers also change. "If only the mountains were flat, I could plough them," is replaced by an appreciation of mountains as mountains (Allan 1989). Similarly, as ideas of conservation creep into the vocabulary and thoughts of local mountain people, inhabitants are becoming aware of the consequences of the impacts that visitors are having on their environment.

As residents become integrated into the larger society they and their environments lose some of their uniqueness and individuality. Such a transformation has been discussed by Brugger et al. (1984) for the Swiss mountains. Tobias (1986) noticed the changes to the life-styles and cultures of less modernized people in various other parts of the world's mountain environments. An example of the shift in Ladakh's economic dependence from virtual self-sufficiency to reliance on the outside world and the replacement of traditional values by those of Western culture was presented by Norberg-Hodge and Page (1983). The way events have actually unfolded in Ladakh's response to recreation and tourism was recently discussed by Goering (1990). He describes the positive and negative effects on education, health care, and social fabric of the people in this strategically important region.

Many studies detail environmental impacts of recreation and tourism on mountain landscapes. These studies document a range of impacts from the effects on the landscape itself due to construction or enlargement of trails, roads, guest houses, hotels, ski lifts, golf courses, and other facilities, to impacts on wildlife, vegetation, soils, and air and water quality (Bayfield and Barrow 1985, Environment Committee 1978, Kariel and Kariel 1988, Kariel 1991, Price 1981, Wall and Wright 1977).

The natural environment has received heavier impacts as accessibility has become easier. The denuded slopes, litter, and pasture damage caused by trekkers and mountain climbing expeditions on Mount Everest and other Himalayan mountains is one well known example (Bishop 1988, Jefferies 1982, Socher 1976). Activities of sightseers, hikers, mountain bikers, and others who recreate in the mountains have a similar impact, although on different scales. Streams have been fished out, for example, when large numbers of recreationists have gained access to remote areas with mountain bikes.

Most mountain use impacts and conflicts occur in valley bottoms where most of the transportation routes, lodging and resort facilities, and wildlife habitat are situated. As the more adventurous visitors independently penetrate the remote highland environments, or as trails are built to accommodate increasing numbers of visitors, as at the Sunshine ski area in Banff National Park, Canada, alpine vegetation, wildlife, and other sanctuaries are disturbed.

There are also numerous studies and observations of social, cultural, and economic impacts in many different mountain environments (Allan 1988, Berreman 1986, Eppler 1983, Kariel 1989, Krippendorf 1986, Meyrat-Schlee 1983, Pawson 1984, Messerli 1989, Solbrig 1984, Singh and Kaur 1985). Examples of such changes are Obergurgl, Austria (Meleghy, Preglau, and Walter 1982, Moser and Peterson 1988) and in the Swiss Alps (Krippendorf and Mueller 1987) and several studies by the Council of Europe about tourism and recreation impacts in planning for the future of the Alps (Bernt and Ruhl 1978, Feurstein 1973, 1979). Runyan and Wu (1979) used the findings of many studies to provide an overview of tourism's complex consequences on economic activities, recreational resources, and on culture, family, and community life. Economic changes are probably the most immediate outdoor recreation impacts. They are looked upon most favorably by residents because tourism and recreation provide new sources of income and employment, and often stops out-migration. This view exists despite monetary leakages from the area and the need for increased taxes to pay for much of the community infrastructure (Eppler 1983, Singh and Kaur 1985). Other positive effects include improved living conditions through public health programs and increased food and nutritional adequacy. An improved infrastructure, increased levels of education, and increased knowledge of and interaction with the outside world are also considered beneficial.

Because prices for goods and services and land values inevitably increase, those persons not working in tourism and outdoor recreation or who are on fixed incomes tend to lose as dependency shifts from primarily agricultural pursuits, which are locally controlled, to externally determined tourism and recreation. Mountain inhabitants experience personal and interpersonal changes, including those in traditional family life, societal patterns and values, and a sense of community. These changes include residents' spending more time with guests than with their families, the improved status of women, young people being exposed to the values of visitors, an increased crime rate, a loss of the traditional meanings of festivals, ceremonies, and art forms, the sale and removal of irreplaceable artifacts, less inclination for residents to assist each other with community tasks, and increased value placed upon material possessions and money.

Unless visitors bring food and fuel from the outside, their activity also makes heavy demands on local supplies. Requirements of trekkers and expeditions in the Himalaya, Hindukush, and Karakorum ranges frequently strain inhabitants' ability to provide for themselves. The needs of more than forty expeditions trudging annually up the Baltoro glacier (Ali and Ferras 1976), and the cutting of trees for fuel on the hill stations in India, serve as examples. These and other incidents of deterioration occur when commercial aspects of catering to visitors override carrying capacities or aesthetic considerations.

Stevens (1993) cites many examples of recent change in the Everest area, including the building of new houses with Western-style windows, corrugated metal roofs, and chimneys. Water supply systems have been developed. Wealth is now more often measured in terms of equipment and money than as it was traditionally, in the size of yak and sheep herds. A variety of Western goods are found throughout the mountains, including the school bell at Khumjung, which is an old oxygen cylinder. Western areas are not immune to architectural changes brought about by tourism either. In parts of the Alps and even in Kimberley, British Columbia, Canada, Tyrolean and Bavarian house styles and decorations are copied in a conscious effort to attract visitors.

Future Directions

Whatever may be thought about the effects of outdoor recreation and tourism, they appear to be inevitable. Also, traditional cultures and lifestyles will continue to change as a result of modernization, acculturation, and other influences (Allan et al. 1988, Gurung 1982, Ives 1986). The outcome is uncertain even when two strong cultures meet, like the Inca and the Western in Peru. Despite great alterations and degradation in many areas, much has survived. Mountain inhabitants and their cultures as well as the mountains themselves still dominate the landscape. There is an inevitability of integration as well as of development, the goals of the two should be the same development "for" instead of development "of." It is necessary to channel outside visitation into mountains to enhance the quality of life and well-being of mountain inhabitants as well as to ensure the integrity of these environments. Recently established MTNPA like the Annapurna Conservation Area and the Makalu-Barun Conservation Area recognize these features and integrate mountain people and their habitat into a master plan (Taylor-Ide, *infra*).

To achieve these goals requires a reversal of past exploitative practices. Part of this reversal means freeing inhabitants from dependence on those in positions of political and economic power so that residents may achieve their self-determined goals. Such a change will require a major attitude shift on the part of lowland people, both the visitors and those in business, industry, and central governments who influence what occurs in mountain environments and among their inhabitants.

To help preserve the character of a region's communities and life-style and reduce ecological burdens, tourists and outdoor recreationists need to follow suggestions such as those made by Gruber (1983) and Bezruchka (1985) for trekking in Nepal, Maeder (1987) for touring less developed regions, and Haßlacher (1984) for visiting the Alps. These recommendations include travelling singly or in small groups, learning about the region being visited, and being considerate of the hosts. Governments and the recreation and tourism industry need to be more sensitive to the effects of large-scale activities and take concrete steps to decrease its negative impacts. Using Krippendorf's (1986) ten principles that embody the ideas of soft recreation and ecotourism would go a long way toward achieving harmonious development between people and their environment. These ideas include constructing smaller hotels, hiring local residents, drawing upon knowledge of local populations, providing for local participation in development and planning, encouraging local education, and retaining ownership of land and facilities in the hands of local residents. Even modest efforts, such as providing public transportation to the remote areas at Denali National Park in Alaska, or educating tourists and recreationists on nature walks in Obergurgl, help to bring about desired outcomes. Larger ventures, such as ecotourism, which link the growing interest in visiting natural areas with the desperate need for developing nations to conserve their resources, as well as the new direction of many European alpine clubs to stop promoting tourism, add vitality and momentum to the drive for harmonious development of the people and their environments.

To be successful, these and other changes usually require aware, considerate, and dedicated individuals to introduce the ideas and to act as catalysts (Rogers 1969). A determination on the part of academicians interested in mountain environments to consider the impacts of their own research and encourage constructive development is also required (Ives 1979).

Finding a balance between economic development and environment is advocated in *Our Common Future*, the report of the World Commission on Environment and Development (1987). Planning for mountain tourism and recreation requires appropriate consideration of the role of visitors, activity preferences, and host-guest relations, as well as an understanding of potential environmental impacts.

Mountain residents themselves also will need to retain ownership and control of hotels, other accommodations, and visitor facilities. Residents need to have an actual and effective political voice in events that influence them. They also need better knowledge on which to base their development and planning decisions. Otherwise, catering for visitor operations tends to be for short-term advantage with revenues returning to the lowlands. Experiences in communities such as Silvaplana (Reich 1979), Bonneval-sur-Arc (Letourneux 1978) and the Val d'Anniviers (Diem 1980) in the Alps, suggest that such local actions are possible. Choices are involved in balancing the advantages of tourism recreation and development with the potential endangerment of mountain environments or cultures—the very things for which tourists come (Krippendorf 1984).

If sensitive and sustainable tourism and recreation development is to take place, there is a need to acknowledge that the traditional view of the supply and demand for tourist areas is incomplete. Also required is consideration of the areas' inhabitants and physical environment. This view may be called metatourism, analogous to metaeconomics that recognizes the finite nature of the earth (Draper and Kariel 1990).

Acknowledgements

We would like to express our appreciation for constructive comments on an earlier draft to J. Christian, N. Kariel, P. Kariel, and L. Rouse, who also assisted with the bibliographic search.

REFERENCES

Ali, R. and Ferras R. 1976. "Le Tourisme au Pakistan: Potentialites et Image de Marque." *Societe Languedocienne de Geographie Bulletin* 10:313-333.

Allan, N.J.R. 1985. "Highland-Lowland Interaction Systems: Hindukush-Western Himalaya." In *Integrated Mountain Development*, edited by T.V. Singh and J. Kaur, 239-256. New Delhi: Himalayan Books.

—————. 1986. "Accessibility and Altitudinal Zonation Models of Mountains." *Mountain Research and Development* 6:185-194.

—————. 1989a. "Highways to the Sky: The Impact of Tourism on South Asian Mountain Culture." In *Impact of Tourism on the Mountain Environment*, edited by T.V. Singh, 290-304. Meerut: Research India.

—————. 1989b. "Kashgar to Islamabad: The Impact of the Karakorum Highway on Mountain Society and Habitat." *Scottish Geographical Magazine* 105:130-141.

—————. 1992. "Cultural Conflation." In *Tourism Environment: Nature, Culture, and Economy*, edited by T.V. Singh, M. Fish, V.L. Smith and L.K. Richter. New Delhi: Inter-India Publications.

Allan. N.J.R. et al. (eds.). 1988. *Human Impact on Mountains*. Totowa NJ: Rowman Littlefield.

Bayfield, N.G. and G.C. Barrow (eds.). 1985. *The Ecological Impacts of Outdoor Recreation on Mountain Areas in Europe and North America*. Recreation Ecology Research Group Report No. 9. Ashford, Kent: Department of Horticulture, Wye College.

Bernard, P.P. 1978. *Rush to the Alps: The Evolution of Vacationing in Switzerland*. East European Quarterly Monograph No. 37. Boulder, CO: East European Quarterly.

Bernt, D. and G. Ruhl. 1978. "Seminar report on pressures and regional planning problems in mountain regions, particularly in the Alps." Council of Europe, Strasbourg.

Bharati, Agehananda. 1978. "Actual and Ideal Himalayas." In *Himalayan Anthropology: the Indo-Tibetan Interface*, edited by J.F. Fisher, 77-82. The Hague: Mouton.

———. 1988. "Mountain People and Monastics in Kumaon Himalaya, India." In *Human Impact on Mountains*, edited by J.R. Allan et al. 83-95. Totowa NJ: Rowman and Littlefield.
Bishop, B.C. 1988. "A Fragile Heritage: The Mighty Himalaya." *National Geographic* 174:624-631.
Brugger, E.A. et al. (eds.). 1984. *The Transformation of Swiss Mountain Regions.* Bern: Paul Haupt.
Butz, David A. O. 1995. "True Stories, Partial Stories: A Century of Interpreting Shimshal from the Outside." In *North Pakistan: Karakorum Conquered:* edited by N.J.R. Allan. New York: St. Martin's Press.
Christaller, W. 1964. "Some Consideration of Tourist Location in Europe: The Peripheral Regions; Underdeveloped Countries; Recreational Areas." *Regional Science Association Papers* 12:95-105.
Cohen E. 1978. "Impact of Tourism on the Physical Environment." *Annals of Tourism Research* 5:215-237.
Danz, W. 1978. *The function of Alpine regions in European regional planning.* European Regional Planning Series No. 20. Strasbourg: Council of Europe.
de Kadt, E. 1979. *Tourism: Passport to Development?* Oxford: Oxford University Press.
De los Santos, J.S. 1982. "The Economic and Social Impact of Tourism Development." In *Social and Economic Impact of Tourism on Asian Pacific Region*, edited by D.E. Hawkins, 207-228, Tokyo: Asian Productivity Organization.
Dearden, P. and W.R.D. Sewell. 1985. "From Gloom to Glory and Beyond: The North American Mountain Recreation Experience." In *The Ecological Impacts of Outdoor Recreation on Mountain Areas in Europe and North America*, edited by N.G. Bayfield. and G.C. Barrow, 1-17. Recreation Ecology Research Group Report No. 9. Ashford, Kent: Department of Horticulture, Wye College.
Diem, A. 1980. "Valley Renaissance in the High Alps." *The Geographical Magazine* 52:492-497.
Doxey, G.V. 1975. "A Causation Theory of Visitor-resident Irritants, Methodology, and Research Inferences." In *The Impact of Tourism*, 195-198. Sixth Annual Conference Proceedings of the Travel Research Association, San Diego, CA.
Draper, D. and H.G. Kariel. 1990. "Metatourism: Dealing Critically with the Future of Tourism Environments." *Journal of Cultural Geography* 11:139-155.
Environment Committee Group of Experts on the Environment and Tourism. 1978. "Tourism and the Environment: A case-study of Shiga Highland, Japan." Organization for Economic Cooperation and Development, Paris.

Eppler, P. 1983. "Impact of Tourism on Leh and Surroundings." In *Recent Research on Ladakh*, edited by D. Kantousky and R.W. Sander, 253-262. Munich: Weltforum.

Feurstein, G. 1973. *Economic and Social Problems in Mountain Regions, Local and Regional Authorities in Europe*. Study No. 5, Strasbourg: Council of Europe.

————. 1979. *27 Principles for the Development of Tourism in Mountain Regions, Local and Regional Authorities in Europe*. Study No. 19. Strasbourg: Council of Europe.

Goering, P.G. 1990. "The Response to Tourism in Ladakh." *Cultural Survival Quarterly* 14:20-25.

Grosjean, G. et al. 1986. "Aesthetische Bewertung laendlischer Raeume." Schlussbericht zum Schweizerischen MAB-Programm No. 20, Bern: Department of Geography, University of Bern.

Groetzbach, Erwin F. 1985a. "Tourismus im Indischen Westhimalaya Entwicklung und raeumliche Struktur." In *Beitraege zur Fremdenverkehrsgeographie*, edited by Joseph Steinbach, 27-47. Munich: Geobuch.

————. 1985b. "Autostrassen durchbrechen die Isolation der Taeler." *Deutsche Forschungsgemeinschaft* 2:13-16.

————. 1985c. "The Bavarian Alps: Problems of Tourism, Agriculture, and Environmental Conservation." In *Integrated Mountain Development*, edited by T.V. Singh and J. Kaur, 141-155. New Delhi: Himalayan Books.

Gruber, G. 1983. "Ecological Endurance Limits of Mountain Regions and Current Dangers through Tourism." In *Deutscher Alpenverein, Himalaya Konferenz '83*, 57-67. Munich: German Alpine Club.

Gurung, H. 1982. "Tourism Development in Nepal." In *Social and Economic Impact of Tourism on Asian Pacific Region*, Symposium on Tourism Management, Kathmandu, Nepal, edited by D.E. Hawkins, 245-258. Tokyo: Asian Productivity Organization.

Haβlacher, P. 1984. *Sanfter Tourismus Virgental*. Innsbruck: Austrian Alpine Club.

Hudman, L.E. and D.E. Hawkins. 1989. *Tourism in Contemporary Society*. Englewood Cliffs, N.J.: Prentice-Hall.

Ives, J.D. 1979. "Applied High Altitude Geoecology: Can the Scientist Assist in the Preservation of the Mountains?" In *High Altitude Geoecology*, Patrick J. Webber, A Selected Symposium 12, 9-45. Boulder, CO: Westview Press.

————. 1986. "Introduction: The Future of the Earth's Mountains." In *Mountain People*, edited by M. Tobias, 3-15. Norman, OK: University of Oklahoma Press.

Jackson, E.L. and D.R. Schinkel. 1981. "Perceived Conflict Between Urban Cross-Country Skiers and Snowmobiles in Alberta." *Journal of Leisure Research* 14:47-62.
Jefferies, B.E. 1982. "Sagarmatha National Park: The Impact of Tourism in the Himalayas." *Ambio* 11:274-281.
Jeffers, L. 1922. *The Call of the Mountains.* New York: Dodd Mead.
Kariel, H.G. 1988. "Tourism and Recreation Developments in the Rocky Mountains of Canada." In *Human Impact on Mountains*, edited by N.J.R. Allan et al., 228-242. Totowa NJ: Rowman and Littlefield.
——————. 1989. "Socio-cultural Impacts of Tourism in the Austrian Alps." *Mountain Research and Development* 9:59-70.
Kariel, H.G. and P.E. Kariel. 1988. "Tourist Developments in the Kananaskis Valley Area, Alberta, Canada, and the Impact of the 1988 Winter Olympic Games." *Mountain Research and Development* 8:1-10.
Krippendorf, J. 1984. "The Capital of Tourism in Danger." In *The Transformation of Swiss Mountain Regions*, edited by E.A. Brugger et al., 427-450. Bern: Paul Haupt.
——————. 1986. *Alpsegen Alptraum: Fuer eine Tourismus-Entwicklung im Einklang mit Mensch und Natur.* Bern: Kuemmerly and Frey.
Krippendorf, Jost and Hans-reudi Mueller. 1987. *La Haut sur la Montagne: Pour un development du tourisme en harmonie evec l'homme et la nature.* Bern: Kuemmerly & Frey.
Letourneux, Andre. 1978. "Bonneval-sur-Arc lives!" *Naturopa* 30:7-10.
Lichtenberger, E. 1988. "The Succession of an Agricultural Society to a Leisure Society: The High Mountains of Europe." In *Human Impact on Mountains*, edited by N.J.R. Allan, G.W. Knapp and C. Stadel, 218-227. Totowa, NJ: Roman and Littlefield.
Maeder, U. 1987. *Vom Kolonialismus zum Tourismus - von der Freizeit zur Freiheit.* Zurich: Rotpunkt.
McCool, S..F. 1976. "Implications of Recreational Activity Aggregates for Tourism Development Policies." *Journal of Travel Research* 14:1-4.
Melaghy, Tamas, Max Preglau and Ursula Walther. 1982. "Die Entwicklung Obergurgl vom Berg-Bauerndorf zum Tourismuszentrum." Innsbrueck: Institut fuer Soziologie.
Meyrat-Schlee, E. 1983. "Werte E. und Verhalten." Schlussbericht zum Schweizerischen MAB-Programm No. 2. Bern: Department of Geography, University of Bern.
Messerli, P. 1989. *Landwirtschaft, Tourismus, und Natur.* Bern: Paul Haupt.
Moser, W. and J. Peterson. 1988. "Limits to Obergugl's Growth." In *Human Impact on Mountains*, edited by N.J.R. Allan et al., 201-212. Totowa NJ: Rowman and Littlefield.

Nicolson, M.H. 1959. *Mountain Gloom and Mountain Glory.* New York: W.W. Norton.

Norberg-Hodge, H. and J. Page. 1983. "Unscientific Observations." In *Recent Research on Ladakh*, edited by D. Kantousky and R. Sander, 263-268. Munich: Weltforum.

Nunez, T.A. 1977. "Touristic Studies in Anthropological Perspective." In *Hosts and Guests: The Anthropology of Tourism*, edited by V.L. Smith, 207-216. Philadelphia, PA: University of Pennsylvania Press.

Pawson, I.G., D.D. Stanford and V.A. Adams. 1984. "Effects of Modernization on the Khumbu region of Nepal: Changes in Population Structure, 1970-1982." *Mountain Research and Development* 6:101-118.

Pearce, D.G. 1985. "Tourism and Planning in the Southern Alps of New Zealand." In *Integrated Mountain Development*, edited by T.V. Singh and J. Kaur, 293-308. New Delhi: Himalayan Books.

Plog, S.C. 1973. "Why Destination Areas Rise and Fall in Popularity." *Cornell H.R.A. Quarterly* November: 13-16.

Price, L.W. 1981. *Mountains & Man: A Study of Process and Environment.* Berkeley, CA: University of California Press.

Reich, A. 1979. "Beitrag der Gemeinde Silvaplana zum Schutze der Engadiner Seenlandschaft." In *Landespflege in der Schweiz*, edited by G. Olschowy. Series of the Deutscher Rat fuer Landespflege 32:122-125.

Rogers, E.M. 1969. *Modernization Among Peasants.* New York: Holt. Reinhart and Winston.

Runyan, D. and C.T. Wu. 1979. "Assessing Tourism's More Complex Consequences." *Annals of Tourism Research* 6:448-463.

Shirasaka, S. 1984. "Skiing Grounds and Ski Settlements in Japan." *Geographical Review of Japan* 57:68-86.

Singh, T.V. and J. Kaur. 1985. "In Search of Holistic Tourism in the Himalaya." In *Integrated Mountain Development*, edited by T.V. Singh and J. Kaur, 365-401. New Delhi: Himalayan Books.

Smith, V.L. (ed.). 1977. *Hosts and Guests: The Anthropology of Tourism.* Philadelphia, PA: University of Pennsylvania Press.

Socher, E. 1976. "No litter please on Everest." *Geographical Magazine* 48:388.

Solbrig, O.T. (ed.). 1984. "Tourism." *Mountain Research and Development* 4:181-185.

Tobias, M. (ed.). 1986. *Mountain People.* Norman, OK: University of Oklahoma Press.

Ullman, E.L. 1956. "The Role of Transportation and the Bases for Interaction." In *Man's Role in Changing the Face of the Earth*, edited by W.L. Thomas, 862-880. Chicago: University of Chicago Press.

Wall, G. and C. Wright. 1977. "The Environmental Impact of Outdoor Recreation." Department of Geography Publication Series 11, Waterloo: University of Waterloo.

Wiesmann, U. 1986. "Wirtschaftliche, Gesellschaftliche und Raeumliche Bedeutung des Fremdenverkehrs in Grindelwald." Schluebericht No. 24 MAB Bern: Department of Geography.

World Commission on Environment and Development (Bruntland Commission) 1987. *Our Common Future*. Oxford: Oxford University Press.

CHAPTER 10

Mountains, Nations, Parks, and Conservation: A Case Study of the Mt. Everest Area

DANIEL TAYLOR-IDE

Introduction

Recognition of the aesthetic, biophysical, and cultural importance of mountain habitat and society has gained considerable momentum during the past decade (Allan 1988, Ives 1985). As a result, impressive conservation programs have been initiated in many mountainous regions of the world. Recent surveys of MTNPA, however, indicate that significant additional initiatives are needed, particularly in the Atlas range, Antarctica, the Alps, Papua New Guinea, the Hindukush, and the mountains of Burma. Concurrent with increased protection of biophysical properties is the urgent need to develop improved management systems for existing mountain parks (Byers 1992a, Thorsell and Harrison *infra*).

Unfortunately, even the best intentions to expand mountain protected area coverage in the 1990's will be confronted with major constraints. The lack of adequate funding has consistently represented a major barrier, often exacerbated by the concerned agency's inexperience in appropriate research, coordination, program strategies, planning, and publicity.

However, a more substantial block to initiating forceful action may be governmental growing reluctance to set aside limited land area in the face of recognized growing population pressure. This chapter discusses how MTNPA can do a more effective job of integration with developmental priorities - both to the long-term benefit of the people and for long-term biophysical conservation.

I document how the Woodlands Mountain Institute collaborated with

Mountains, Nations, Parks, and Conservation 239

indigenous organizations and people to establish new MTNPA in the vicinity of Mt. Everest. Following a review of each project's history, characteristics common to both are examined in an effort to provide insights of potential value to practitioners and conservation agencies elsewhere in the mountain world. This chapter does not document the management systems of these two MTNPA, but rather focuses on describing the methods by which the MTNPA were created.

WOODLANDS MOUNTAIN INSTITUTE

Since its founding in 1972, the Woodlands Mountain Institute has grown through financial contributions from individuals, private foundations, and domestic and international development agencies. Institutional expenditures in 1991 exceeded $2 million, and more than thirty U.S. and international professionals are employed on a full-time basis.

Five inter-related programs, *Mountain Learning, Leadership,Community Schools, Mount Everest Ecosystem Conservation Program*, and *Research and Development*, constitute the core services of Woodlands. The program dealt with in this chapter is The *Mount Everest Ecosystem Conservation Program*, which coordinates an international partnership that assists the governments of Nepal and the Tibet Autonomous Region of the People's Republic of China in developing adjoining MTNPA in the Mount Everest region combining conservation with a focus on community development. (Campbell, 1990c). The total area of the two MTNPA — the Makalu-Barun National Park and Conservation Area, and Qomolangma Nature Preserve — exceeds 35,000 km^2, and includes five peaks in excess of 8000 m (Everest, Lhotse, Makalu, Cho Oyu, and Shisha Pangma). These two projects share similar ecological features, wildlife, and cultures. Separate twelve-year agreements between Woodlands and both governments were signed in 1988, in which Woodlands provides coordination, funding, and technical support. The five management themes common to each project include:

(a) the integration of conservation and development objectives in environmentally sustainable, culturally viable, economically feasible ways;
(b) the conservation of the biological and cultural diversity unique to each region;
(c) the development of partnerships between local people, governments, NGOs, and the international conservation community;
(d) the use of both scientific and indigenous knowledge for management decision-making; and

(e) the designation of protected areas based on total ecosystem dynamics.

Nepal: The Makalu-Barun National Park and Conservation Area

PHYSICAL AND CULTURAL SETTING

The Makalu-Barun area covers 2,330 km² and is located in the Sankhuwasabha and Solukhumbu districts of northeastern Nepal (Figs. 1, 2). Within a north-south distance of less than 40 km, elevations range from 435 m at the Arun-Sankhuwa confluence to the 8,463 m summit of Makalu (Cronin 1979). A large precipitation variation follows this same altitudinal transect: lower elevations may receive more than 4,000 mm/yr, diminishing to less than 1000 mm/yr in the sub-alpine and alpine regions of the higher mountain summits (Khanal 1991a, 1991b; Shrestha 1989, 1990a).

Unusually diverse and distinct bioclimatic zones, ranging from tropical to nival, are found within very short distances. Reflective of this precipitation/ temperature gradient are many vegetation zones ranging from tropical *sal* forests at elevations below 1000 m; temperate zone oak/maple/magnolia forests between 2000-3000 m; fir/birch/rhododendron forests in the sub-alpine (3000-4000 m); and the herbs, grasses, and rhododendron/ juniper shrub of the alpine pastures (4000-5000 m) (Byers 1992b, Dunsmore 1988, Shrestha 1989, Stainton 1972).

The corresponding wealth of bio-physical diversity in the region is of global significance. For example, scientific investigations recorded the presence of more than 3,000 species of flowering plants, including 25 of Nepal's 30 varieties of rhododendron; 48 species of primrose; 47 species of orchid; 19 species of bamboos; 15 species of oak; 86 species of fodder trees; and 67 species of economically valuable medicinal and aromatic plants (Numata 1966, 1983, Shrestha et al. 1990, 1990b). An oak species previously unrecorded in Nepal, two bird species never before seen in Nepal (the spotted wren babbler and olive ground warbler), and fourteen other extremely rare bird species were also recorded. Wildlife include the endangered red panda, musk deer, clouded leopard, wild dog and snow leopard, in addition to more substantial populations of Himalayan black bear, wild boar, barking deer, and serow (Jackson 1990a, Jackson and Ahlborn 1987, Jackson et al. 1990, Taylor-Ide 1984).

South and west of the Barun river are other remote, high altitude valleys, including the Isuwa, Apsuwa, and Sankhuwa (Figure 2). In addition to containing one of the famous "Hidden Valleys" of Shambala mythology (Reinhard 1978), they are used for seasonal grazing, hunting and the collecting of various forest products.

Mountains, Nations, Parks, and Conservation

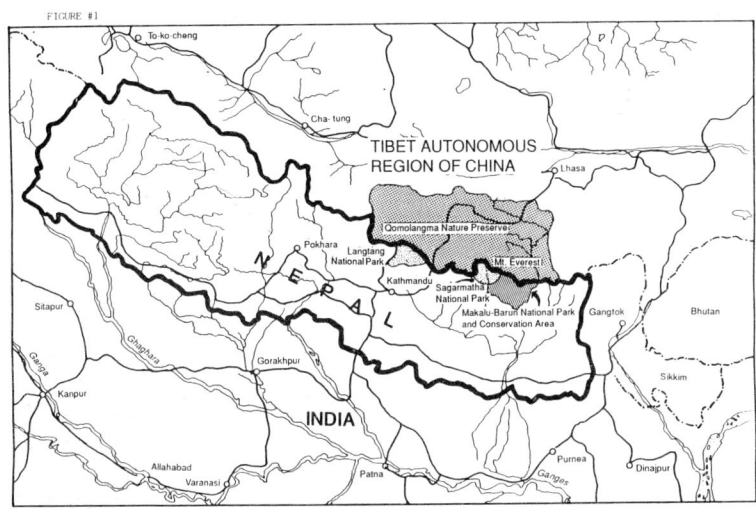

The external boundaries of India depicted in this map are neither correct nor authentic.

Figure 1: Trans-frontier protected area in the Mt. Everest Area

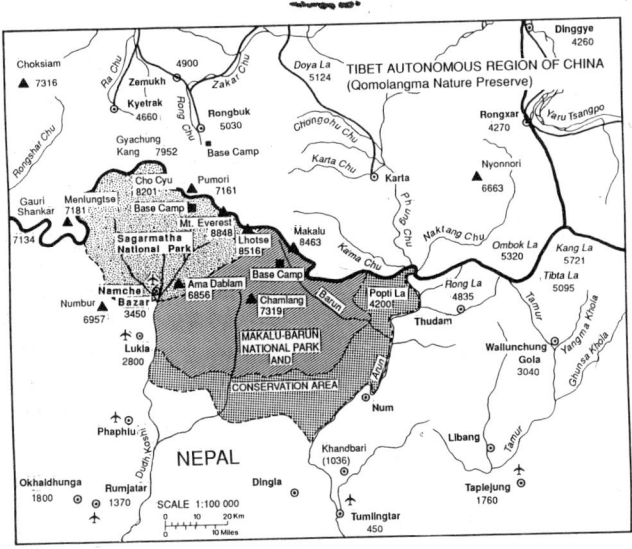

The external boundaries of India depicted in this map are neither correct nor authentic.

Figure 2: Sagarmatha-Qomolangma and Makalu-Barun Protected Areas

Surrounding this seasonally used area is a population of 32,000 people from a number of ethnic/caste groups. The majority are Rai, followed by Sherpa and Tibetan-speaking groups. More than seven different languages are spoken in the area (Nepali et al. 1990). The population is dependent primarily upon low-productivity subsistence agriculture and pastoralism, supplemented by the use of forest products, small-scale seasonal trade, and seasonal migration for labor (Chaffey 1989, Forbes 1989, Nepali and Sangam 1940). Swidden agriculture is extensively practiced. The availability of health and education facilities is extremely limited, and health conditions are poor (Nepali et al. 1990).

Contiguous to the Makalu-Barun area is the 1,148 km^2 Sagarmatha (Everest) National Park, created in 1976 as Nepal's third national park (Jeffries 1985). The 35,000 km^2 Quomolangma (Everest) Nature Reserve, established in 1989 by the Tibet Autonomous Region of China also borders the Makalu-Barun area in addition to the Sagarmatha National Park and the Langtang National Park. Together, these four contiguous MTNPA protect a vast 40,000 km^2 area surrounding the Everest massif, an area of the same approximate size as Switzerland.

Most of the valleys of the Makalu-Barun area drain into the upper reaches of the Arun River, which originates as the Pengqu River in the adjoining Qomolangma Nature Reserve in China. This river is now the site of Nepal's largest development project to date — the 403 MW Arun III hydroelectric facility with an accompanying 193 km access road, financed by the World Bank and a consortium of international donors (NEA 1990). While targeted to assist Nepal's economic and energy needs, this project will rapidly alter the biological, social, and economic life of the area (MBCP Task Force 1990). The Management Plan prepared by a task force of Nepalese specialists recommends a series of programs aimed at mitigating potential negative effects upon the environment and culture, while taking advantage of its economic opportunities for local people.

Evolution of the Makalu-Barun Conservation Project: 1983-1990

In 1983 and 1984, Nepalese and American scientists working on a WMI wildlife study in the remote Barun valley developed the proposal to create a 500 km^2 preserve that would protect the valleys and forests of the Makalu-Barun region (Taylor-Ide 1984). The proposal was presented at the International Workshop on the Management of National Parks and Protected Areas held in Kathmandu, Nepal in 1985 (Taylor-Ide and Shrestha 1985; McNeely et al.

1985), and received with interest by Nepalese policy makers. In 1988, a Nepalese Task Force was appointed by King Birendra of Nepal. Their mandate was to develop plans for protecting the area's biodiversity by developing a new model for conservation that incorporated the participation of the surrounding local people. A twelve-year agreement was signed by the Department of National Parks and Wildlife Conservation with Woodlands Mountain Institute on August 29, 1988. During the following year, the Task Force spent more than 3,000 person-days collecting primary data and interviewing local people in the project area. Funding for the project during this period was raised by WMI from private sources, international development agencies, and conservation foundations that include the Ministry of Foreign Affairs, Government of the Netherlands; the Canadian International Development Research Center (IDRC); the Swedish Agency for Research Cooperation in Developing Countries (SAREC); the International Fund for Animal Welfare; the U.S. Agency for International Development (USAID); Dr. Thomas Roush; The Needmor Foundation; the George H. Mifflin & Jane A. Mifflin Memorial Fund and other private foundations and individuals. Additional funding arrangements between the World Bank/Arun Hydroelectric Project and the MBCP are currently under consideration.

On December 20, 1990, the Task Force for the Makalu-Barun Conservation Project concluded its two-year study and submitted formal recommendations to the Government of Nepal for the immediate establishment of the Makalu-Barun National Park and Conservation Area. Proposed were a focused, integrated set of programs under the categories of park management, community development, tourism management, and scientific research. Task Force results also included twenty background reports in the project's Working Paper Publication Series, the previously mentioned four Component Plans, and the overall Management Plan for the Makalu-Barun National Park and Conservation Area that summarizes Task Force recommendations.

The Management Plan, representing one of the most detailed planning documents prepared for any protected area in Nepal, provides an important model for the establishment and management of MTNPA in Nepal and elsewhere in the mountain world. Although national parks have existed in Nepal for 17 years, protecting unique and representative natural resources and habitats, "conservation area" is a more recent protected area designation (Wells et al. 1990). The first of these, the Annapurna Conservation Area, was created in 1985 by the King Mahendra Trust for Nature Conservation to assist local people in the Annapurna region to better manage their own natural resources in the face of threats from the impact of increased population, tourism, and development. The Makalu-Barun Conservation Project combines these two approaches of strict protection and controlled use into an integrated management system that builds continuity through partnerships between local people, the private sector, and the Government of Nepal. Conservation and development are viewed as being complementary. Implementation is based upon a participatory model of land management and resource use, incorporating the experience, traditional management systems, and recommendations of local people into project policies, strategies, and actions.

Following review by Nepalese experts and the Government of Nepal, the creation of the new national park and conservation area was approved by the Cabinet of Ministers in September, 1991 and officially gazetted on 18 November 1991. Most funds necessary for implementing the project's first five-year phase were available at the time of official park gazettement. Infrastructure development (personnel hiring, headquarters establishment, small-scale community projects) commenced in late 1992.

People's Republic of China:
Qomolangma Nature Preserve, Tibet Autonomous Region

Physical and Culture Setting

Qomolangma (Mt. Everest) Nature Preserve (QNP) encompasses a 34,480 km^2 area in Shigatse Prefecture located in the southern part of the Tibet Autonomous Region of China (Figure 1). It includes all of Dingye, Tingri, Nyelam, Dingye and Kyirong countries, extending from east of the Pungchu (N. Arun) near Dinggye (4260 m) to west of Jilongzangbu (N. Trisuli) River near Kyirong (3800 m) in the west. The northern boundary roughly parallels the 29° N latitude line south of Lhasa, and the southern boundary is delimited by the international border with Nepal.

Contiguous to the Preserve are Nepal's Langtang National Park, Sagarmatha (Mt. Everest) National Park, and the Makalu-Barun National Park and Conservation Area. Two-thirds of the Arun watershed above Nepal's forthcoming 403 MW, $1 billion Arun III Hydroelectric Project is contained within QNP boundaries, a point which highlights the critical importance of promoting international dialogue on conservation and water management practices.

Contrary to popular perception, Tibet is not solely a high, cold, dry plateau. In fact, the QNP contains a tremendous diversity of landscapes and environments ranging from ice clad, 8000+ meter peaks to subtropical, densely forested valleys below 2000 m (Fleming 1989). In addition to being the location of the world's highest peaks, the juxtaposition of two major biogeographical zones within the MTNPA — the Paleoarctic and Indian-Malay — contribute to the area's high biological diversity and the presence of a number of rare and endangered species (CAS 1990a, 1990b, Schweinfurth 1957, Schweinfurth *supra*).

The biologically richest region is the Kama valley, which begins on the eastern flank of Mt. Everest and runs east for 30 km to join the Pengqu Valley. The forests at the head of the valley are among the highest in the world, with tree line as high as 4,800 m (Howard-Bury 1922). Forests that cover the five low-altitude river valleys flowing southward into Nepal provide exceptional habitat, with many Indian subcontinent species occurring in close proximity to those of the Tibetan Plateau. Among larger animals, the QNP contains the rare or endangered snow leopard, kiang (wild ass), and black-necked crane (Jackson 1991). It also supports Tibet's only populations of the Assamese macaque, as well as langur monkey, Himalayan palm civet, jungle cat, Himalayan musk deer and Himalayan tahr, and a number of small rodent and bat species (Feng et al. 1986, Wang et al. 1984).

Similar species variety characterizes QNP's plant associations. It has forests, and the Preserve also supports a great diversity of shrub and grassland communities. At least seven distinct rhododendron communities occur between elevations of 3,800 and 4,800 m; a cinquefoil sub-shrub association (*Potentilla parvifolia*) is found as high as 5,100 m; two species of buckthorn (*Hippophae*) form dense riparian groves in stream-beds above the tree-line; and juniper communities, a vegetation type that has been greatly depleted in many parts of Tibet, thrive in a nearly pristine state in some areas. Additionally, this part of the eastern Himalaya is well known for its spectacular displays of wildflowers (Polunin and Stainton 1984, Ward 1937).

The role of the High Himalaya as a meteorological barrier (Schweinfurth *supra*; Stainton 1972; Troll 1972) is particularly striking in the Preserve. The moist, southern aspects of the range are strongly affected by the South Asian monsoon and average 2000-2500 mm of rainfall per year. In contrast, regions north of the range, and thus within its imposed rainshadow, receive less than 250 mm of precipitation annually and exhibit continental, semi-arid plateau climates with characteristically xeric vegetation formations (Schweinfurth *supra*, Schweinfurth 1957, Zhang et al. 1988). In addition to the the north-south temperature and rainfall gradient, there is a similar east-west climatic trend (Chang 1981, Zhang et al. 1988).

Archaeological, historical and contemporary cultural richness also characterizes the region. It is inhabited by approximately 68,000 people of whom more then 95 percent are Tibetan nomads and farmers who maintain a low-productivity subsistence livelihood. Major crops include highland barley, winter wheat, and some potatoes. Yak, yak hybrids, sheep and goat populations totaled 182,518 animals in a 1989 survey (Coburn and Menzies 1987, Goldstein and Beall 1990, TASS 1990).

Evolution of the Qomolangma Nature Preserve: 1985-1991

During the 1970's local administrations in Tibet created two small nature preserves in the Zhangmu and Kyirong valleys. In 1985, discussions began between Chinese scientists and Woodlands Mountain Institute concerning the possibility of creating a single preserve encompassing a much larger area. The government of the Tibet Autonomous Region studied the proposal for four years, during which two field expeditions inventoried the area's biogeographical features and two international study exchanges introduced key personnel to preserve management options.

On March 18, 1989, less than four years from the date of initial discussions, the Qomolangma Nature Preserve became a reality through formal designation by the Government of the Tibet Autonomous Region. This was followed in August with the formal inauguration of the Qomolangma Nature Preserve Management Bureau in Xikeze, and the creation of a branch office in nearby Xegar. On 25 October 1989, the Working Commission of the Qomolangma Nature Preserve and Woodlands Mountain Institute signed a twelve-year cooperative agreement to provide international assistance to the Preserve (Chien 1989a, 1989b). The QNP became the first nature preserve in China to combine nature conservation and socio-economic development (Campbell 1990c).

These formal events were accompanied by a significant increase in integrated planning and applied research. Field surveys were conducted by the Chinese Academy of Sciences, the Tibet Academy of Social Sciences, the Culture Department, the Health Department, the Education Department, the Tourism Bureau, and the Environmental Protection Bureau of the Tibet Autonomous Region Government. These surveys facilitated production of the Master Plan for the Preserve area, to be formally approved in the spring of 1992. Since the creation of the QNP, the Tibet Autonomous Region Government has taken consistent and vigorous action to protect the project area. On 24 June 1989, after careful field study, the construction of a major forestry access road — the Chentang road, in the eastern Preserve — was halted. This difficult decision was made despite the fact that over 1,000 workers were engaged in the project and RMB 7 million (US$ 2 million) had already been spent. Additionally, throughout the preserve, wildlife hunting has been curtailed and new legislation to halt illegal hunting and trade in wildlife products is under preparation.

Fruitful international exchanges during 1989 and 1990 were highlighted by the 1989 participation of QNP scientists in the Makalu-Baruñ Conservation Project field workshop in Nepal and participation of a Nepalese park management specialist in workshops and field surveys in Shigatze. A Senior Advisory Committee Meeting in the United States in September, 1990, involving a study tour of national parks, national forests, wildlife refuges, and universities, brought together members of both projects.

International support for the Qomolangma Nature Preserve comes through the twelve-year cooperative agreement with WMI mentioned previously. Under this agreement, WMI provides or arranges for the provision from international sources for only 10% of project costs consisting of technical assistance, partial support for materials, vehicles, equipment, planning, implementation costs, and international exchange. The Tibet Autonomous Region Government provides the majority of support including existing scientific and technical assistance, offices and equipment, daily office expenses, personnel salaries, and most of the implementation costs. Implementation of the preserve's management is through existing governing systems with the central QNP offices working in stimulus and support roles.

The ambitious management of the QNP combines participatory resource management, local economic development, ongoing scientific research and integrated management through the use of controlled-use zonation. Within the large 34,480 km^2 region three types of management zones have been established. Seven *core zones*, representing 31 per cent of the preserve, will be strictly protected. *Buffer zones*, or scientific experiment zones, make up 20 percent of the preserve where limited human use will be permitted. Villages, farmland, prime pasturage, and other areas of economic importance are designated as *peripheral zones* in which all developmental activities are structured on a self-supporting basis. Peripheral zones will operate within appropriate environmental guidelines and will make up 49 per cent of the preserve.

Principles Common to the Establishment of the Two MTNPA

The experiences of both Nepal's Makalu-Barun National Park and Conservation Area, and China's Qomolangma Nature Preserve, reveal several common characteristics that may be applicable to efforts to protect other MTNPA. These guiding principles, however, do not constitute a step-by-step "recipe" that NGOs can follow for the establishment of new MTNPA. Differences in governments, socio-economic conditions, political climates, available technical and financial resources, and potential non-governmental partners will vary greatly between countries, and strategies must understandably be flexible, creative, and realistic.

The following points address pre-project considerations primarily although they will also be applicable during the challenges of field implementation.
1. Based upon the best available information, identify a dominant and driving rationale for MTNPA establishment.

While initial justification for MTNPA establishment may be aesthetic, biophysical or cultural, one of these reasons is usually dominant. It may be strengthened, challenged, or combined as more information about the region becomes available through initial field surveys. The experience of both projects, however, indicates that stating this justification clearly and powerfully is a *sine qua non* without which the project cannot materialize; i.e., nothing is more important than an easily acceptable statement of why the MTNPA should exist.

For example, the Makalu-Barun Conservation Project was initiated primarily to protect what was identified to be one of the most diverse, and last remaining, biological resources in Nepal. Although the area is also visually spectacular, and field studies later documented the presence of a unique cultural diversity, and later research also established its importance as a watershed for the Arun III project, the conservation momentum was primarily driven by the biological rationale.

The Qomolangma Nature Preserve was initiated with a primarily aesthetic focus: i.e., to preserve the ecosystem of the highest mountain on earth. However, whereas this grand vision was politically powerful on a global scale, the driving force for local Tibetan leaders came from an interest in promoting environmentally sound socio-economic development.

2. Establish a local support constituency

From the outset, a diversified local support base needs to be established. The experience of the case studies in China and Nepal suggests that this broad spectrum of local support is just as necessary as the traditional governmental park (or forestry) department support. Local people, scientists, country planners, tourism planners, decision makers in government, leaders of the private sector, the military — all affected sectors of leadership need to be involved. In both case studies, this involvement was facilitated through host country and international field study programs. Field visits allowed policy makers and practitioners to experience first-hand the proposed MTNPA as well as to understand better the successes and failures of MTNPA area management in other regions.

3. Establish an outside, highly credible advisory group

In both cases a special Senior Advisory Committee of distinguished international figures was established that consisted of political leaders, conservationists, scholars, and businessmen. By virtue of their individual reputations and experience, this Senior Advisory Committee provided a level of credibility to both projects that greatly augmented field work, fund-raising, and publicity endeavors in addition to the central role of project guidance. The field-based meetings (often held in the MTNPA themselves) were central to the committee's success.

Mountains, Nations, Parks, and Conservation 249

4. Establish a Task Force of host country specialists to conduct detailed assessments of the proposed MTNPA feasibility, biophysical and cultural features, and prospective management strategies; and to take the lead in project promotion

Because data on most proposed MTNPA are so limited, detailed, quantitative studies that document the biophysical, socio-economic and cultural values of the particular site are important from the management and, when implementation is dependent on external grants, fund-raising perspectives. While the benefits of reliable data from a project management perspective are self-evident, the production of quality field reports also represents tangible outputs critical to developing and maintaining credibility with international donors. As an example, the Working Paper Series, Component Plans, and final Management Plan developed by the Makalu-Barun Task Force were instrumental toward rapid international endorsement of the Nepal project, as well as the success of later fund-raising endeavors.

5. Link conservation with development in project design, incorporating the needs of local people in conservation projects.

Traditional MTNPA have excluded people, and in Nepal several cases of enforced resettlement during the 1970s resulted in a severe resentment for national parks that was felt throughout the country (Wells 1991). Increasingly, however, it is being recognized that the long-term conservation of many MTNPA will only be possible through the active participation of local people in ways which blend natural resource protection, conservation, and socioeconomic development. Tangible benefits from adhering to park regulations — e.g., prohibiting expansion of swidden cultivation into existing forests — must be immediately apparent to local people whether in the form of benefits from increased tourism, agricultural productivity, training, or employment opportunities. Both projects were designed on this principle and utilized management zones (national park, conservation area, strict nature reserve, core zone, peripheral zones, buffer zones), representing varying functions of usage, as the primary management tool. Additionally, both Makalu-Barun and World Bank/Arun III project representatives recognized the importance of combining development and conservation objectives, thus working in mutually supportive ways during the design process of each project.

6. Develop short- and long-term funding strategies and mechanisms

Following identification of the rationale for preserve establishment, seed grants from private donors constituted the primary funding source during the first several years of each of the two case studies. This flexible, private money allowed for the initiation of pilot field projects, the creation of the advisory groups, project proposals and political momentum prior to approaching international governments and conservation foundations for larger amounts of money for actual implementation.

Raising adequate funds, however, is a time-consuming and demanding activity that occupied key staff on a nearly full-time basis between 1984-1991. The strategy employed involved a process of shared and collaborative responsibility—the Institutional Director and Program Director provided direction, experience, and contacts; technical staff wrote proposals; secretarial staff provided office and document production support; and all three groups shared in editing and terminal responsibilities. Successful fund-raising strategies included a clear and powerful articulation of project purpose, sensitivity to donor priorities, a network of supporting contacts, and a well-articulated, multiple-year project strategy.

It should be noted that all five of the principles described above operated within a larger vision. The individuals involved in both projects all believed, with remarkable unanimity, in what they were doing, how they were doing it, and who they were doing it for. They represented a collection of individuals of remarkable and diverse strengths but with a trust in a common objective. Without the shared goal of protecting mountain environments and advancing mountain cultures, and the confidence that resulted from this vision, the successes achieved to date would not have been possible for either initiative.

Conclusion

I have presented a summary of significant characteristics common to the successful establishment of two new MTNPA in the Himalaya. This was initiated by a small American NGO working intimately with conservationists in Nepal and China's Tibet Autonomous Region over a period of eight years.

New challenges await both the Makalu-Barun and Qomolangma projects as, in the coming years, these models of participatory and multi-sectoral management are tested, refined, and implemented. Nevertheless, a significant first step has been made in their design and official designations. This process can and should be replicated elsewhere in the mountain world.

It is to be hoped that the insights derived from the experiences of Woodlands Mountain Institute may be of value to other NGOs, scientists, and governments attempting to preserve mountain environments world-wide. In this process, the importance of increased communications and collaboration between all entities involved — NGO, academic, development and donor agencies — cannot be overstated. In all likelihood, this building of partnerships will represent the single most critical component toward the effective establishment of new, protected mountain areas.

Acknowledgements

Alton Byers and Gabriel Campbell assisted in writing and commenting on earlier drafts of this chapter. Their assistance is gratefully appreciated.

REFERENCES

Allan, N.J.R., et al. (eds). 1988. *Human Impact on Mountains.* Totowa NJ: Rowman and Littlefield.
Byers, A.C. 1992. "Contemporary Tourist impacts on three sides of Everest." Paper presented at the IV World Congress on National Parks and Protected Areas, Caracas, Venezuela.
—————. 1992b. "Sub-Alpine forest dynamics and pllen analysis in the Upper Barun valley, Nepal." Report. Franklin WV: Woodlands Mountain Institute.
Campbell, J.G. 1990a. "Closing Speech: Community Development Workshop, Shigatze, May 10-12, 1990." Shigatze: Qomolangma Nature Preserve.
—————. 1990b. "Seminar on Community Development in Qomolangma Nature Preserve, Shigatze." Report. Franklin WV: Woodlands Mountain Institute.
—————. 1990c. "Mt. Everest Ecosystem Conservation Program." Paper presented at the 8th Meeting of Investment Priorities for Biodiversity Conservation in the Asia/Pacific Region, The World Bank, Washington, D.C. 25 September 1990.
Chaffey, P. 1989. "Livestock Survey in Northwest Sankhuwasabha." Report, Makalu-Barun Conservation Project, Kathmandu: Woodlands Mountain Institute.
Chang, D.H.S. 1981. "The Vegetation Zonation of the Tibet Plateau." *Mountain Research and Development* 1:29-48.
Chinese Academy of Sciences. 1990a. "The Mammals of Mount Qomolangma (Mt. Everest) Area in China." Beijing: Chinese Academy of Sciences.
—————.1990b. "Physical Geography of the Mt. Qomolangma (Everest) Region." Beijing: Chinese Academy of Sciences.
Chien, Chun Wuei Su. 1989a. "The Signing of an Agreement: 26 October 1989, Lhasa, Tibet Autonomous Region, China." Report. Franklin WV: Woodlands Mountain Institute.
—————.1989b. "Trip Report," February 13 to March 28, 1989. Franklin WV: Woodlands Mountain Institute.
Coburn, B. and N. Menzies. 1987. "Report on the Summer 1987 Tibet Study

Tour." Report. Franklin WV: Woodlands Mountain Institute.
Cronin, E.W. 1979. *The Arun: A Natural History of the World's Deepest Valley.* Boston: Houghton Mifflin Company.
Dunsmore, S. 1988. "Mountain Environmental Management in the Arun River Basin of Nepal." Occasional Paper No. 9, Kathmandu: International Center for Integrated Mountain Development.
Feng Zuo-jian, Gui-quan Cai and Chang-lin Zheng. 1986. *The Mammals of Tibet.* Beijing: Science Press.
Fleming, R L., Jnr. 1989. "A Natural History of the Everest Area: A Summary." Report, Makalu-Barun Conservation Project, Kathmandu: Woodlands Mountain Institute.
Forbes, A.A. 1989. "Preliminary Report on Forest Management Systems in Bung and Chheskam Panchayats." Report, Makalu-Barun Conservation Project, Kathmandu: Woodlands Mountain Institute.
Goldstein, M.C. and C.M. Beall. 1990. *Nomads of Western Tibet.* Berkeley: University of California Press.
Howard-Bury, C.K. 1922. *Mount Everest: The Reconnaissance.* London: Edward Arnold.
Ives, J.D. 1985. "The Mountain Malaise." In *Integrated Mountain Development*, edited by T.V. Singh and J. Kaur. New Delhi: Himalayan Books.
Jackson, R. 1990a. "Threatened Wildlife, Crop and Wildlife Depredation and Grazing in the Makalu-Barun Conservation Area." Report 12, Working Paper Publication Series, Makalu-Barun Conservation Project. Kathmandu: Woodlands Mountain Institute.
Jackson, R. and G. Ahlborn. 1987. "A High-Altitude Survey of the Hong Valley with Special Emphasis on Snow Leopard." Consultant Report, Kathmandu: Woodlands Mountain Institute and HMG Department of National Parks and Wild Conservation.
Jackson, R., H.S. Nepali and A.R. Sherpa. 1990. "Aspects of Wildlife Protection and Utilization in the Makalu-Barun Conservation Area." Working Publication Series, Makalu-Barun Conservation Project, Report 11, Kathmandu: Woodlands Mountain Institute.
Jeffries, M. 1985. *Sagarmatha, Mother of the Universe: The Story of Mt Everest National Park.* Auckland: Cobb/Hornwood Publications.
Khanal, N.R. 1991a. "Study of Geo-Hydrology, Land Use and Population of Makalu-Barun Conservation Project Area." Working Paper Publication Series, Makalu-Barun Conservation Project, Report 14, Kathmandu: Woodlands Mountain Institute.
————.1991b. Geo-Ecological Study of Apsuwa Watershed. Working Paper Publication Series, Makalu-Barun Conservation Project, Report 15,

Kathmandu: Woodlands Mountain Institute.

Makalu-Barun Conservation Project Task Force. 1990. *The Makalu-Barun Conservation Project Management Plan*. Kathmandu: Makalu-Barun Conservation Project.

Nepal Electricity Authority. 1990. "Arun III Hydroelectric Project: Detailed Engineering Services." Environmental and Socio-Economic Report. Vol. 1: "Main Report." Kathmandu: Government of Nepal.

Nepali, R.K. and K. Sangam. 1990. "Status of Community Needs, Resources and Development: Sankhuwasabha District." Working Paper Publication Series, Makalu-Barun Conservation Project, Report 7, Kathmandu: Woodlands Mountain Institute.

Numata, M. 1986. Vegetation and Conservation in Eastern Nepal. *Journal College of Arts and Sciences, Chiba University*. 4:559-569.

—————. 1983. "Ecological Studies in the Arun Valley, East Nepal and Mountaineering of Mt. Baruntse, 1981." Chiba: Himalayan Committee Chiba University.

Polunin, O. and A. Stainton. 1984. *Flowers of the Himalaya*. Delhi: Oxford University Press.

Reinhard, J. 1978. "Khembalung: The Hidden Valley." *Kailash* 6:5-36.

Schweinfurth, U. 1957. *Die Horizontale und Vertikale Verbreitung der Vegetation im Himalaya*. Bonn: Ferd Dummlers Verlag.

Shrestha, T.B. 1989. "Development Ecology of the Arun River Basin in Nepal." Kathmandu: International Center for Integrated Mountain Development.

—————. 1990a. "The Makalu-Barun Conservation Project in the Everest Ecosystem." Paper presented on Environment Media Seminar Toronto, Canada, March 1990.

—————. 1990b. "Scientific Research Management Plan." Kathmandu: Makalu-Barun Conservation Project.

Shrestha, T.B., P.R. Shakya and H.S. Nepali, H.S. 1990. "Scientific Report on 1989 Field Survey: General and Phyto-Ecology." Report 8, Working Paper Publication Series, Makalu-Barun Conservation Project, Kathmandu: Woodlands Mountain Institute.

Stainton, J.D.A. 1972. *Forests of Nepal*. London: John Murray.

Taylor-Ide D. 1984. "The Barun Valley Report." Project Report. Kathmandu: The King Mahendra Trust for Nature Conservation/Woodlands Mountain Institute.

Tibet Academy of Social Sciences (TASS). 1990. "General Survey of Social Science, Qomolangma Nature Preserve." Report Summary. Lhasa: TASS.

Troll, C. (ed.). 1972. *Geoecology of the High Mountain Regions of Eurasia*. Weisbaden: Franz Steiner Verlag.

Wang Zuxiang, Dehao Li and Guiquan Cai. 1984. "New Materials on Birds and

Mammals from Qomolangma Area and an Approach to the Subspecies of *Hemitragus jemlahicus.*" *Acta Biologica Plateau Sinica* 2:81-100.
Ward, F.K. 1937. *Plant Hunter's Paradise.* Reprint. Minerva Press.
Wells, M., K. Brandon and L. Hannah. 1990. "People and Parks: An Analysis of Projects Linking Protected Area Management with Local Communities." Draft report. Washington, D.C.: The World Bank.
Zhang Jing-wei, Bosheng Li, Wei-lie Chen and Jin-ting Wang. 1988. *Vegetation of Xizang (Tibet).*Beijing: Science Press.

CHAPTER 11

National Parks and Nature Reserves in Mountain Environments of the World

JIM THORSELL
JEREMY HARRISON

Introduction

Suggestions for accelerated conservation efforts in mountain regions have become increasingly frequent during the past decade. During an active period of interest in mountains at IUCN in the 1970s, Dasmann and Poore (1979) produced a set of guidelines that prescribed actions and strategies for conservation in mountain regions. One of the actions proposed was the establishment of mountain protected areas (MTNPA).

There are many reasons why protected areas are particularly applicable tools in mountain conservation strategies. Among these are:

1. Mountains often harbor many endemic and threatened species and are nature's last strongholds for others that have been extirpated in adjacent lowlands, e.g., Hawaii Volcanoes, Kinabalu, Rockies;
2. Mountain regions often harbor a wealth of human tradition and protected areas can provide a mechanism whereby the alliance between conservation and local cultures can be strengthened, e.g., Neblina, Lorentz, Sagarmatha;
3. Mountains act as focal points for those seeking aesthetic and recreational benefits and many cultures have a reverence for certain peaks considered "sacred," e.g., Tongariro, Kailas, Huangshan;
4. Mountains are fragile high energy environments where regulatory

controls over potentially disturbing human activities are often needed, e.g., Huascaran, Nanda Devi;
5. Mountains have immense downstream values in terms of soil erosion control and watershed protection and nature reserves can be an ideal measure in stabilizing upland resource use, e.g., Virunga, Apo;
6. Mountain ranges in many cases act to form the frontiers between countries and there is often value in maintaining them as lightly inhabited buffer zones, e.g., Khunjerab, Amistad; and
7. Mountains are particularly sensitive indicators of global climatic change and are ideal environments for research on the impact of global warming on species and ecosystems, e.g., High Tatras, Great Smokies.

These rationale for mountain park establishment lead to several fundamental questions: How many mountain protected areas exist? Where are they located? How well do they represent the features of each range? Where are the lacunae in the world's mountain protected area system? These questions frame the objectives of this review, which is the first inventory and classification of protected areas (MTNPA) of the world's mountain environments.

Inventory Criteria

In undertaking a global assessment of mountains that are under some form of conservation regime, it is first necessary to establish some definitions and criteria for classification. Categories of protected areas have been clearly defined by IUCN (Table 1) but definitions of what constitutes a mountain vary widely. After noting those given by Peattie (1936), Price (1981), and Gerrard (1990), and to facilitate use of the database at WCMC, we have used the following three criteria for our definition of a mountain protected area (MTNPA):

1. minimum relative relief of 1500 m
2. minimum size of 10,000 ha
3. IUCN category I-IV

Such an arbitrary definition precludes consideration of many areas locally considered mountains, e.g., Scottish Highlands, Jura, Urals, Border Ranges, as well as those areas too small or with management objectives that do not give highest priority to nature conservation. There are, of course, several thousand other protected areas in mountainous or steep slope settings that do not meet these criteria. Nevertheless, many principles and management issues discussed here will be equally applicable.

TABLE 1. CATEGORIES AND MANAGEMENT OBJECTIVES OF PROTECTED AREAS.

I. Strict Nature Reserve. To protect nature and maintain natural processes in an undisturbed state in order to have ecologically representative examples of the natural environment available for scientific study, environmental monitoring, education, and for the maintenance of genetic resources in a dynamic and evolutionary state.

II. National Park. To protect outstanding natural and scenic areas of national or international significance for scientific, educational, and recreational use. These are relatively large natural areas not materially altered by human activity where extractive resource uses are not allowed.

III. Natural Monument/Natural Landmark. To protect and preserve nationally significant natural features because of their special interest or unique characteristics. These are relatively small areas focused on protection of specific features.

IV. Managed Nature Reserve/Wildlife Sanctuary. To assure the natural conditions necessary to protect nationally significant species, groups of species, biotic communities, or physical features of the environment where these may require specific human manipulation for their perpetuation. Controlled harvesting of some resources can be permitted.

V. Protected Landscapes and Seascapes. To maintain nationally significant natural landscapes which are characteristic of the harmonious interaction of man and land while providing opportunities for public enjoyment through recreation and tourism within the normal life style and economic activity of these areas. These are mixed cultural/natural landscapes of high scenic value where traditional land uses are maintained.

VI. Resource Reserve. To protect the natural resources of the area for future use and prevent or contain development activities that could affect the resource pending the establishment of objectives which are based upon appropriate knowledge and planning. This is a 'holding' category used until a permanent classification can be determined.

VII. Anthropological Reserve/Natural Biotic Area. To allow the way of life of societies living in harmony with the environment to continue undisturbed by modern technology. This category is appropriate where resource extraction by indigenous people is conducted in a traditional manner.

VIII. Multiple Use Management Area/Managed Resource Area. To provide for the sustained production of water, timber, wildlife, pasture and tourism, with the conservation of nature primarily oriented to the support of the economic activities (although specific zones may also be designated within these areas to achieve specific conservation objectives).

Two additional categories are international labels which overlay protected areas in the above eight categories:

IX. Biosphere Reserve. To conserve for present and future use the diversity and integrity of biotic communities of plants and animals within natural ecosystems, and to safeguard the genetic diversity of species on which their continuing evolution depends. These are internationally designated sites managed for research, education and training.

X. World Heritage Site. To protect the natural features for which the area is considered to be of outstanding universal significance. This is a select list of the world's unique natural and cultural sites nominated by countries that are Party to the World Heritage Convention.

A total of 442 MTNPA in 63 countries were selected from the WCMC protected areas database on the basis of the above three criteria (Table 7). These include over 210 sites lying in biogeographical provinces with a mixed mountain biome type (Udvardy 1975), but not the great number of parks and reserves established around mountain lakes and wetlands that are either of small size or have very little vertical relief.

A similar number of sites (over 220) meeting the three criteria lie outside mixed mountain biogeographical provinces. Many of these occur on dissected high plateaus, e.g., Grand Canyon, Ethiopian Highlands, Yunnan Plateau, or on islands with the relative relief necessary but that are not normally considered MTNPA, e.g., Galapagos Islands National Park.

Finally, we recognize a limitation in the database itself. Altitude data were not available for all sites, some of which likely qualify as MTNPA. These will be added to the list as the information becomes available.

Inventory of the World's Mountain Protected Areas

The number of MTNPA in the world selected by the above criteria and grouped by biogeographical realm is given in Table 2. The total number of MTNPA is 442. All eight realms contain MTNPA although 63 per cent of the total land area is found in the MTNPA of the Nearctic Realm. The full list is provided in Table 7.

TABLE 2. INVENTORY OF THE WORLD'S MOUNTAIN PROTECTED AREAS.

Biogeographical Realm	Number	Total Area (ha)
Nearctic	96	153,804,175
Palaearctic	147	30,270,611
Afrotropical	35	10,986,512
Indomalayan	52	8,794,398
Oceania	8	3,598,032
Australia	3	2,649,148
Antarctic	11	2,086,861
Neotropical	90	30,969,739
TOTAL	442	243,159,476

According to the 1990 *UN List of National Parks and Protected Areas* (IUCN 1990), a total of 5310 protected areas are classified under IUCN Categories I - IV and cover 574 million hectares. MTNPA constitute 8% of the total number of sites and 42% of the total area. It should be noted that one site, the Greenland National Park at 97 million hectares, accounts for 40 % of this total but still it is clear that MTNPA have a higher mean size than protected areas found in lowland regions. The total size of the global MTNPA system then is approximately equivalent to that of the State of Alaska and the Province of British Colombia combined or only Alaska if Greenland National Park is excluded.

The distribution by relative relief is given in Table 3. The sites with the highest relative relief are found on the montane borders of Inner and Central Asia with South Asia: Qomolongma National Park (China) is greatest with 7415 m. difference from its high and low elevations and both other reserves that include more than 6500 m relief also are found in this mountain rimland. If the minimum relief was lowered to 1000 m the list would expand by another 200 sites.

TABLE 3. MOUNTAIN PROTECTED AREAS BY RELATIVE RELIEF.

Relative Relief (m)	Number	Area (ha)
1500-2499	259	61,371,668
2500-3499	121	134,339,155
3500-4499	34	16,866,976
4500-5499	16	22,176,319
5500-6499	8	4,607,788
6500+	4	3,797,570
TOTAL	442	243,159,476

In terms of protected area management categories, 242 mountain protected areas are Category II (National Parks), 57 are Category I, 25 are Category III and 118 are Category IV. Fully 73% of the total land area of MTNPA falls under Category II. Another 58 MTNPA in Category V were identified but have been excluded from this inventory (apart from three notable exceptions) as the level of actual protection in most cases is questionable e.g., the French pre-parks, and in many, non-existent, e.g., Morocco's Toubkal.

Inventory by Biogeographical Realm

Udvardy's (1975) eight biogeographical realms are used for the classification that identifies the 92 provinces where MTNPA are found. All MTNPA are listed below by their biogeographical province.

INDOMALAYA

Extending from the foothills of the Himalaya through to the Indonesian Archipelago, this realm consists of relatively low hills and lowlands and a large number of volcanoes. Moderate sized mountain ranges are found in the Western Ghats of India, the Tenasserim Hills in Thailand, the Annamite Range in Vietnam/Laos and a number of mountainous islands in the Philippines, Malaysia and Indonesia. The highest point is Mt. Kinabalu (4101 m) in Sabah. Most of the qualifying MTNPA are found along the volcanic arc which follows the Pacific and Australian tectonic plates with the greatest concentration found on the island of Sumatra. The total number of MTNPA in this realm is 53 with an area of 8.8 million hectares:

	Number	Area (ha)
Malabar Rainforest	3	107,767
Bengalian Rainforest	1	65,800
Indochinese Rainforest	2	340,000
Malayan Rainforest	3	556,304
Indus-Ganges Monsoon Forest	2	78,128
Burma Monsoon Forest	2	46,150
Thailandian Monsoon Forest	3	200,640
Ceylonese Monsoon Forest	1	22,380
Sumatra	13	3,982,571
Java	2	72,606
Lesser Sunda Islands	2	70,000
Sulawesi (Celebes)	4	846,000
Borneo	6	1,954,945
Philippines	5	206,617
Taiwan	3	244,490
TOTAL	52	8,794,398

AFROTROPICAL

This realm consists of all of Africa, south of the Sahara plus Madagascar and adjacent oceanic islands. The realm, like Indomalaya, has no major mountain ranges, rather, African mountains are widely separated and have been likened floristically to an archipelago of islands (Kingdon 1990).

An exception to this are the Drakensberg Mountains that rise to 3482 m. and stretch almost 1000 km through Natal and Lesotho. The total area of Afromontane vegetation including that found on high plateaux has been mapped (White 1983) and totals 715,000 km^2. Of this, 4.5% is under protected area status. Highest point is Mt. Kilimanjaro (5895 m) in Tanzania which stands 4900 m above its base. There are a total of 35 MTNPA in Africa covering 11 million hectares. One single park in Namibia accounts for 45% of this total.

	Number	Area (ha)
Malagasy Rain Forest	3	167,330
East African Woodland	4	482,723
Congo Woodland/Savanna	1	1,173,000
Miombo Woodland/Savanna	2	190,200
Malagasy Woodland/Savanna	1	48,622
Cape Sclerophyll	8	710,846
Eastern Sahel	1	163,900
Somalian	4	726,675
Namib	1	4,976,800
Ethiopian Highlands	2	265,000
Central African Highlands	4	1,708,400
East African Highlands	2	148,378
South African Highlands	2	224,638
TOTAL	35	10,986,512

WESTERN PALEARCTIC

In addition to the Atlas and Tibesti Mountains in northern Africa, the main alpine feature of this portion of the realm is the Alps. Other lesser mountain ranges in the realm are the Pyrenees, Cantabrians, the Balkan group, the Taurus, the Appenines, the Carpathians, the Jotunheim and the highlands of northern Scandinavia.

The Alps extend in a crescent of some 1000 km across seven countries from southern France to western Yugoslavia. Mont Blanc at 4807 m is the high point, rising 3800 m from its base. Of a total mountain area of 180,000 km^2 there exist only ten MTNPA in the Alps covering 4720 km^2 or 2.6% of the area. We have included three national parks in the Alps that are currently classified Category V but are in the process of becoming Category IIs in the near future (Hohe Tauern, Stelvio, Berchtesgaden). No MTNPA, by our definition, exist in the Atlas Mountains.

	Number	Area (ha)
West Eurasian Taiga	2	320,900
Icelandian	1	160,000
Middle European Forest	4	199,978
Iberian Highlands	4	120,768
Mediterranean Sclerophyll	3	117,752
Central European Highlands	10	472,086
Balkan Highlands	10	328,315
Macronesian Islands	1	13,571
Sahara	1	480,000
TOTAL	36	2,213,370

EASTERN PALEARCTIC

This part of the realm extends from the Caucasus and Altai through to the Japanese Alps. A number of lesser-known high ranges extend northward across Siberia to the Kamchatca Peninsula (Badenkov 1990). One quarter of the total MTNPA area in this realm is found within Mongolia's Great Gobi Desert National Park. WCMC's existing records record the following MTNPA.

	Number	Area (ha)
East Siberian Taiga	4	1,110,974
Altai Highlands	3	1,346,646
Caucaso-Iranian Highlands	17	1,534,747
Mongolian-Manchurian Steppe	2	304,567
Sichuan Highlands	13	756,976
Japanese Evergreen Forest	4	312,608
Manchu-Japanese Mixed Forest	6	926,715
Kamchatka	1	1,099,000
Taklimakan-Gobi Desert	4	11,340,000
Oriental Deciduous Forest	3	461,512
Iranian Desert	1	324,688
Anatolian - Iranian Desert	4	361,445
TOTAL	62	19,879,878

South/Central Palearctic

This realm contains the greatest concentration all the high mountains in the world including all the 8000 m peaks. It includes the geologically-linked ranges of the Himalaya (500,000 km^2), Hindukush, Karakorum and Pamir (57,000 km^2) and involves 7 countries. We have included the new Makalu-Barun National Park but not the Annapurna Conservation Area in Nepal, because the gazettement process for this area is not yet complete.

	Number	Area (ha)
Pamir-Karakorum-Tianshan Highlands	14	822,024
Himalaya Highlands	33	7,247,401
Hindukush Highlands	2	107,938
TOTAL	49	8,177,363

Nearctic

The North American Cordillera, extending from Alaska to Mexico along the western side of the continent, is the largest single mountainous region in the world (6 million km^2 including interior plateaux). Other areas with high relief

	Number	Area (ha)
Sitkan	10	13,889,597
Oregonian	1	371,225
Yukon Taiga	10	10,391,318
Canadian Taiga	1	476,560
Eastern Forest	1	209,160
Sonoran	3	1,364,665
Chihuahuan	2	317,936
Great Basin	1	59,308
Aleutian Islands	4	4,492,832
Alaskan Tundra	3	2,317,154
Canadian Tundra	1	2,147,110
Arctic Desert and Icecap	1	97,200,000
Rocky Mountains	40	8,914,817
Sierra-Cascade	9	1,155,571
Madrean-Cordilleran	9	496,922
TOTAL	96	153,804,175

are found in the Arctic, Greenland and southern Appalachians. The realm has 96 MTNPA covering nearly 154 million hectares (including the single 97 million hectares site in Greenland). There is a noticeably large area of MTNPA in Alaska and the Aleutian Islands.

NEOTROPICAL

Apart from a small area in Central America where five MTNPA are found and upland massifs in Brazil and Venezuela where eight sites are listed, the major feature in this realm is the Andean Cordillera. The Andes extend 7000 km. from the Paria Peninsula in Venezuela south to Tierra del Fuego across seven countries. A comprehensive environmental profile has been compiled under a MAB State of Knowledge Report on Andean Ecosystems as published in special issues of *Mountain Research and Development*. The Andes are dotted with many active volcanoes with the high point Aconcagua at 6959 m. MTNPA number 96 and cover 31 million hectares.

	Number	Area (ha)
Panamanian	1	597,000
Colombian Coastal	4	858,420
Amazonian	4	5,364,731
Serro Do Mar	2	130,000
Valdivian Forest	3	2,053,733
Chilean Nothofagus	2	1,508,232
Central American	5	509,178
Venezuelan Dry Forest	3	514,470
Venezuelan Deciduous Forest	5	492,153
Monte	1	76,000
Patagonian	2	32,720
Campos Limpos	1	3,000,000
Northern Andean	8	903,681
Colombian Montane	7	1,519,374
Yungas	5	2,021,623
Puna	7	1,616,524
Southern Andean	27	8,852,386
Greater Antillean	2	153,000
Galapagos Islands	1	766,514
TOTAL	90	30,969,739

Oceania

Being primarily in the Pacific Ocean, most mountains in this realm here are under water! The island of New Guinea, however, with peaks rising to 4884 m. in the Indonesian portion of the Central Dividing Range, has five MTNPA covering 3,484,000 million hectares. The Hawaiian Islands have three MTNPA covering 114,032 ha.

Antarctic

Although there are extensive high peaks in Antarctica in the Ellsworth Mountains (5140 m), the Trans Antarctic Mountains and on Ross Island (3794 m), there is only one MTNPA on this continent. By contrast the New Zealand Southern Alps are the most fully protected mountain range in the world with 70% of the area protected in eight MTNPA totalling 1.94 million hectares. Two other MTNPA occur as volcanoes on the North Island and total 110,044 ha. in size.

Australian

It has been wryly noted by a New Zealander that, as a continent, Australia is simply too old and worn out to have a decent mountain range. Nevertheless, three MTNPA qualify under the criteria used in this paper. The seven contiguous protected areas that comprise the Australian Alps National Parks collectively cover 62 percent of the total area of the Australian Alps (25,000 km^2). Relative relief is 1928 m, being the difference between the summit of Kosciusko 2228 m and the lowest point in the Alps park complex. All of Tasmania's major mountains are contained in the World Heritage site there, which rises to 1617 m from sea level. One park, Bellenden Ker, within the Queensland Wet Tropics World Heritage site rises from sea level to 1622 m. There also exist locally significant mountains in the Flinders and Stirling Ranges of Western Australia but they do not have the relief differentials required for inclusion in this review.

Oceanic Islands

A number of high oceanic islands (all volcanics) that have MTNPA deserve separate mention. These include Tiede on Tenerife, Hawaii Volcanoes, Galapagos, and several islands in Indonesia and the Philippines. Australia's subantarctic Heard Island would also qualify but it does not have statutory protection.

Defining the World's Mountain Heritage

INTERNATIONAL DESIGNATIONS

Twenty-five mountains or mountain regions have been considered of such exceptional importance for science and conservation that they have been inscribed on the World Heritage List. These are listed in Table 4. From this table it can be seen that natural World Heritage sites are found in most major mountain ranges of the world except Antarctica and the Alps. Others that may merit consideration for eventual nomination to this prestigious list are Kinabalu, Fuji, Santa Marta, Torres del Paine, Denali, Auyuittuq, Neblina, Kenya, K2, and a selected area in the Pamirs, Atlas, Drakensburg, and Caucasus.

TABLE 4. WORLD HERITAGE MOUNTAINS.

Name	Country
Los Glaciares NP	Argentina
Tasmanian Wilderness	Australia
Pirin NP	Bulgaria
Rocky Mountain Parks	Canada
Kluane/Wrangell/St.Elias	Canada/USA
Talamanca/Amistad	Costa Rica/Panama
Galapagos NP	Ecuador
Sangay NP	Ecuador
Simien NP	Ethiopia
Nanda Devi NP	India
Sagarmatha NP	Nepal
Te Wahi Pounamu/S W New Zealand	New Zealand
Tongariro NP	New Zealand
Rio Abiseo NP	Peru
Huascaran NP	Peru
Manu NP	Peru
Kilimanjaro NP	Tanzania
Yosemite NP	USA
Hawaii Volcanoes NP	USA
Great Smoky Mountains	USA
Olympic NP	USA
Yellowstone NP	USA
Grand Canyon NP	USA
Virunga NP	Zaire
Kahuzi - Biega NP	Zaire

The Biosphere Reserve Program of UNESCO also has recognized 67 MTNPA in the world. These are found in 26 countries. The Biosphere Reserve Programme is seen to have particular applicability to mountain environments that have resident human populations and that would be suitable sites for training and research. Biosphere Reserves differ from Category V protected areas (Protected Landscapes) in that they require a relatively large and natural core zone and are linked closely with activities carried out under UNESCO's MAB Project 6 on Mountain Ecosystems.

TRANSFRONTIER/BORDER PARKS

The perimeters of many nations often follow the crest line of mountain ranges and thus can serve to promote international cooperation in a number of ways (Thorsell 1990). Management arrangements between neighboring countries, or States as in the case of Australia, India, Canada, also can be beneficial to more effective conservation. Table 5 lists the 24 mountain transfrontier reserve "pairs" that are found between countries. A number of others have been proposed.

Discussion

Mountains are not as prominent on the conservation agenda as are tropical forests, wetlands and marine environments. As a reflection of this, *Caring for the Earth*, the successor to the World Conservation Strategy, launched in October 1991 by IUCN, UNEP and WWF, devotes 38 pages to forests, wetlands and marine issues but less than one full page to mountains. Nevertheless, mountain protected areas are one part of the solution to sustainable management of mountain regions and it is seen in this review that an extensive network of MTNPA is already in existence throughout the world.

Three questions that were posed at the beginning of this review can now be addressed, 1) how many MTNPA should exist, 2) where are the lacunae in the MTNPA system, and 3) what can be done to promote more and better managed MTNPA.

1) How many MTNPA should exist?

The short answer is that there will never be enough! This statement, of course, is not an adequate response and it would be useful to have some guidelines for assessing the adequacy and/or representativeness of the current system. This is what is referred to as "coverage".

TABLE 5. MOUNTAIN TRANSFRONTIER RESERVES (BORDER PARKS).

North America

Wrangell-St Elias (USA)	Kluane (Canada)
Glacier (USA)	Waterton Lakes (Canada)
Cathedral/Manning/Skagit/Cascade (Canada)	Pasayten, N.Cascade (USA)
Arctic (USA)	N Yukon (Canada)

Europe

Tartrzanski (Poland)	High Tatra (Czechoslovakia)
Pyrenees Occidentales (France)	Ordessa (Spain)
Vanoise (France)	Gran Paradiso (Italy)
Swiss (Switzerland)	Stelvio (Italy)
Sarek,Padjelanta,Stora Sjofallet (Sweden)	Rago (Norway)
Berchtesgaden (Germany)	Various sites in Austria

Asia

Manas (India)	Manas (Bhutan)
Khunjerab (Pakistan)	Taxkorgan (China)
Sagarmatha (Nepal)	Qomolangma (China)

Africa

Volcanoes (Rwanda), Virunga (Zaire) and Gorilla (Uganda)	Queen Elizabeth (Uganda) Nyika (Zambia)
Virunga (Zaire)	Prop. Gebel Elba (Sudan)
Nyika (Malawi)	Gebel Elba (Egypt)

Latin America

La Amistad (Costa Rica	La Amistad (Panama)
La Neblina (Venezuela)	Pico da Neblina (Brazil)
Puyehue & Vincente Perez Rosales (Chile)	Lanin & Nahuel Huapi (Argentina)
Bernado O'Higgins & Torres del Paine (Chile)	Los Glaciares (Argentina)
Sajama (Bolivia)	Lauca (Chile
Los Katios (Colombia)	Darien (Panama)

Australia
Australian Alps National Parks (NSW, SA, Victoria, ACT)

It is generally accepted by IUCN and UNEP that 10% of total territory is a good starting target for nations to aim for in their protected area systems. When this issue was discussed at the World Parks Congress in Bali in 1982, the figure used was 10 percent of each habitat (or biome) type within each country.

Species are not uniformly distributed, however, and it has been suggested (Myers 1983) that for biodiversity reasons, the global system should be biased in favour of areas with higher species richness. Based on this argument 20% of mountains in the tropics should be protected while targets in temperate zones would be 10% and 5% in high latitude boreal systems. But biodiversity is only one measure of "conservation value" and we also must take account of vulnerability, attractiveness, and fragility—all of which are well displayed in mountains.

Furthermore, as most recently noted by Shores (1991), the percentage of land in protected areas does not necessarily translate into an effective conservation system. Reserves could be in a suboptimal location, receive inadequate funding, or be poorly integrated into the regional landscape. We do not address management issues in this article but comprehension of these factors is necessary when making overall judgements on coverage.

It is not possible to provide a simple percentage figure would indicate the proportion of the earth's high mountains that have been given legal protected status. This would require an estimate of the total area of the different high mountain ranges with allowances for icecaps, dissected plateaux and certain oceanic islands.

The biogeographic realm analysis has, however, indicated that some mountain environments are much better protected than others. Certainly a disproportionately high number of parks and reserves are found in the mountain biome compared to other biomes such as temperate grasslands or lake systems (IUCN 1990).

As a generalization, using Groetzbach's (1988) Typology of High Mountain Regions (Table 6), the "Young and Relatively Sparsely Settled High Mountains" are much better protected than those grouped as "Old and Relatively Densely Settled High Mountains." This, of course, is a reflection of the options available for establishing nature reserves and, in some cases, the strength of the conservation sentiment and "will" of a country to devote areas for nature conservation.

TABLE 6. TYPOLOGY OF HIGH MOUNTAIN REGIONS FROM A HUMAN GEOGRAPHICAL PERSPECTIVE (GROETZBACH 1988).

A. *Old and Relatively Densely Settled High Mountains*

1. Largely intact traditional subsistence agriculture and a tendency toward overpopulation:
   • Population of mountain peasants.
   (Large parts of the Himalaya-Karakorum-Hindukush; Andes.)
   • A population of mountain peasants, overlain by nomads.
   (High Atlas; mountains of Southwest Asia; western parts of the Hindukush and Himalaya.)
2. Strongly declining traditional agriculture and expanding new activities (tourism, among others)
   (High mountains of Europe, especially the Alps and Pyrenees.)
3. Largely collectivized or nationalized agriculture, in parts with new activities (island-like scattered tourism)
   (High mountains of the erstwhile Soviet Union and China; parts of the Carpathians)

B. *Young and Relatively Sparsely Settled High Mountains*

In areas of European overseas colonization, with extensive market-oriented agriculture and forestry and recent tourism.
(High mountains of North America and New Zealand.)

2) Where are the lacunae in the MTNPA system?

Once the coverage question is addressed it is possible to move on to identifying specific locations that merit investigation as potential new protected areas or where existing protection can be strengthened to ensure improved coverage. It is obvious from the data above that attention needs to be given to the Atlas range, Antarctica, the Alps, Papua New Guinea, the Hindukush, and the mountains of Burma.

Apart from lacunae in the global system, inadequacies occur in the boundaries of many existing MTNPA. Many mountain parks suffer from "hole in the doughnut" design where only the higher slopes of the mountain are contained within the reserve. Vanoise in France and Mount Kenya are two classic examples where montane forests have been largely left out of the park. But valley bottoms and lower elevation forests are integral parts of mountains and design flaws that omit these habitats detract from the integrity of many reserves. Powell et al. (1990) provide an example from the Tilaran mountains in Costa Rica where migratory patterns of the resplendent Quetzal bird require additional lower elevation forest fragments to be protected if habitat requirements are to be met. Stuart (1990) has also found similar seasonal altitudinal movements of the forest mountain bird community on several African mountains with the attendant implications for MTNPA design. Critical habitat for the European brown bear remains outside the parks of the Pyrenees, and only the highland portion of Argentina's Nahuel Huapi National Park is zoned for complete protection; other examples of design flaws exist.

3) What can be done to promote more and better managed MTNPA?

This subject exceeds the scope of this review but there are five areas where conservation efforts need attention. The recommendations listed below sustain the proposals considered by the World Congress on National Parks and Protected Areas being in February 1992 in Venezuela.

a. **Information:** Improve information on the status of MTNPAs and refine the definition of the global MTNPA network. This review has provided an initial list and WCMC/IUCN are also publishing the *Directory of Nature Reserves in the Himalaya and Central Asia* (Green 1991). The possibility of protected areas directories for other mountain regions is also being considered.

b. **The System:** Promote the establishment of more MTNPA and boundary modifications to existing areas. Perhaps the best mechanism would be to undertake regional reviews on each major mountain range using the model that has been applied in the tropical Andes by Saavedra and Freese (1986). Countries can also be encouraged to consider international status and participation in international programmes for selected MTNPA. The question of protected areas in the mountains of Antarctica needs special attention because of their fragility and their significance to long-term effects on global climate.

c. **Cooperation:** Foster regional cooperation in MTNPA management. Border parks, twinning programmes, staff exchange and regional workshops are various tools that can be used to strengthen professionalism and cross-border cooperation. Perhaps the prospect of a MTNPA Network with its own newsletter could be investigated.

d. Science: Strengthen the application of science to MTNPA management. As UNEP (1980) and others have emphasized, mountains, particularly those found in tropical zones, are not nearly as well-researched as they should be. For example, many MTNPAs do not have basic species inventories or vegetation maps. Alliances between MTNPA managers and scientists need to be improved with the objectives of making managers more science-oriented and making scientists more management-oriented.

e. Social Issues: Integrate social concerns as a basic element in MTNPA management. Most MTNPA have resident human populations and/or are used on a seasonal basis by pastoralists or tourists. People as well as peaks and parks, are inseparable. A whole range of social/economic/political factors lie behind all of the four actions above and in most cases are the ones that require the greatest attention. The biosphere reserve *approach* is one that encapsulates these concerns and one which should be applied in all MTNPA.

TABLE 7. INVENTORY OF MOUNTAIN PROTECTED AREAS (MTNPA)
(Protected areas of over 10,000ha, Category I-IV, Relative relief > 1500).

	IUCN Category	Relative relief(m)	Size (ha)
Afghanistan			
Ajar Valley WR	IV	1800	40,000
Pamir-i-Buzurg WS	IV	2853	67,938
Antarctic Treaty Territory			
Barwick Valley SSSI	I	1500	29,120
Argentina			
Calilegua NP	II	2710	76,000
Lago Puelo NP	II	2900	14,220
Lanin NP	II	3174	200,870
Lanin NaR	IV	3174	178,130
Los Alerces NP	II	1880	186,730
Los Alerces NaR	IV	1880	76,270

Los Andes SciR	IV	1894	1,440,000
Los Glaciares NP	II	3300	450,000
Los Glaciares NaR	IV	3300	150,000
Nahuel Huapi NP	II	2854	475,781
Nahuel Huapi NaR	IV	2854	282,219
Perito Francisco P. Moreno NaR	IV	1870	29,900
Perito Moreno NP	II	1870	85,100
Santa Ana NatR	IV	1600	18,500

Australia
Australian Alps NP	II	1917	1,536,800
Bellenden Ker NP	II	1657	31,000
Tasmania Wilderness World Heritage Site	II	1617	1,081,348

Austria
Hohe Tauern NP	II	2698	25,000

Bhutan
Dungsum WR	IV	1600	18,000
Jigme Dorji WS	IV	2554	790,495
Royal Manas NP	II	2110	65,800

Bolivia
Amboro NP	II	1529	180,000
Eduardo Avaroa NaR	IV	1502	714,000
Isiboro Secure NP	II	3300	1,100,000
Sajama NFR	IV	2430	153,570
Sajama NP	II	2042	29,940
Ulla Ulla NaR	IV	2800	250,000

Brazil
Pico da Neblina NP	II	2914	2,200,000
Itatiaia NP	II	1971	30,000
Serra da Bocaina NP	II	2132	100,000

Brunei Darussalam
Batu Apoi (Conservation Forest) FoR	IV	1750	46,210

Bulgaria
Pirin NP	II	1915	27,400
Vitosha NP	II	1560	26,547

National Parks and Nature Reserves 275

Canada

Atlin Park PP	II	1817	271,138
Auyuittuq NP	II	2100	2,147,110
Banff NP	II	2245	664,109
Cathedral PP	II	2062	33,272
Garibaldi PP	II	2000	21,290
Glacier NP	II	2535	134,939
Hamber PP	II	2290	24,518
Jasper NP	II	2689	1,087,800
Kluane NP	II	5350	2,201,500
Kootenay NP	II	2352	137,788
Kwadacha Wilderness P	II	2000	167,540
Manning PP	II	1829	65,863
Mount Edziza PP	II	2784	131,928
Mount Assiniboine PP	II	1789	39,052
Mount Revelstoke NP	II	2150	26,263
Mount Robson PP	II	3040	219,829
Nahanni NP	II	2400	476,560
Peter Lougheed PP	II	1815	50,142
Siffleur WA	II	1953	41,214
Spatsizi Plateau Wilderness Area PP	II	1525	675,024
Strathcona PP	II	2200	201,003
Tweedsmuir PP	II	2339	981,120
Waterton Lakes NP	II	1644	52,597
Wells Gray PP	II	1500	527,305
White Goat WA	II	1880	44,457
Willmore Wilderness Park	I	1698	459,673
Yoho NP	II	2526	131,313

Chile

Alberto de Agostini NP	II	2438	1,460,000
Bernardo O'Higgins NP	II	3600	3,525,901
Conguillio NP	II	2324	60,832
Hornopiren NP	II	1670	48,232
Isla Magdalena NP	II	1660	157,640
Laguna San Rafael NP	II	4058	1,742,000
Laguna del Laja NP	II	2500	11,600
Las Vicunas NR	IV	2200	209,131
Lauca NP	II	2210	137,883
Llanquihue NR	IV	2600	33,972
Los Flamencos NR	IV	1900	70.000

Malalcahuello NR	IV	2500	28,910
Puyehue NP	II	2136	107,000
Queulat NP	II	2035	154,093
Rio Clarillo NR	IV	2900	10,185
Rio de Los Cipreses NR	IV	4000	38,582
Torres del Paine NP	II	2146	181,414
Vicente Perez Rosales NP	II	3454	226,305
Villarrica NP	II	3026	61,000
Villarrica NaR	IV	2340	60,005
Volcan Isluga NP	II	2500	174,744

China

A Er Jin Shan (Arjin Mountains) NR	IV	4625	4,512,000
Bayanbulak NR	IV	2370	100,000
Cangshan Erhai NR	IV	2297	70,000
Changbai Mountains NR	IV	1971	190,582
Daxue Mountain NR	IV	1500	15,787
Erhai Lake NR	IV	2184	24,976
Fengtongzai NR	IV	2900	40,000
Huanglongsi NR	IV	1800	40,000
Lake of Heaven NR	IV	3000	38,069
Mabian Dafengding NR	IV	3000	30,000
Medog NR	IV	7156	62,620
Meigudafengding NR	IV	3800	16,000
Mount Tomur NR	IV	2095	100,000
Qomolangma NR	IV	7415	3,500,000
Schrenk Spruce NR	IV	2500	28,000
Tangjia River NR	IV	2600	28,000
Taxkorgan NR	IV	5611	1,500,000
Tongbiguan NR	IV	1500	34,160
Urumqi Geological NR	IV	4945	200,000
Wanglang NR	IV	2583	27,700
Wolong NR	IV	5050	200,000
Wuliang Mountain NR	IV	1806	23,353
Xishuangbanna NR	IV	1880	207,000
Zayu NR	IV	2000	101,400

Colombia

Chingaza NatNP	II	3000	50,374
Cordillera de los Picachos NatNP	II	3350	286,000
El Cocuy NatNP	II	4900	306,000

National Parks and Nature Reserves

Farallones de Cali NatNP	II	3400	150,000
Las Hermosas NatNP	II	1500	125,000
Las Orquideas NatNP	II	3550	32,000
Los Nevados NatNP	II	2800	38,000
Munchique NatNP	II	2500	44,000
Nevado del Huila NatNP	II	3150	158,000
Paramillo NatNP	II	3850	460,000
Pisba NatNP	II	2000	45,000
Purace NatNP	II	2500	83,000
Sierra Nevada de Santa Marta NatNP	II	5879	383,000
Sierra de la Macarena NatNP	II	2300	630,000
Sumapaz NatNP	II	3100	154,000
Tama NatNP	II	3250	48,000

Costa Rica

Braulio Carrillo NP	II	2400	44,099
Chirripo NP	II	2599	50,150
Cordillera de Talamanca NP	II	2900	193,929

Czechoslovakia

Tatransky NP	II	1955	74,111

Denmark - Greenland

Greenland NP	II	3000	97,200,000

Dominican Republic

J. Armando Bermudez NP	II	2587	76,600
J. del Carmen Ramirez NP	II	2387	76,400

Ecuador

Cayambe-Coca ER	I	5100	403,103
Cotachi-Cayapas ER	I	4839	204,420
Cotopaxi NP	II	2700	33,393
Sangay NP	II	4340	271,925
Galapagos NP	II	1707	766,514

Egypt

Gebel Elba CA	IV	1500	480,000

Ethiopia

Bale Mountains NP	II	2837	247,100

Chew Bahr WR	IV	2500	421,200
Mago NP	II	2078	216,200
Nakfa WR	IV	1500	163,900
Simen Mountains NP	II	2530	17,900
France			
Ecrins NP	II	3303	91,800
Pyrenees Occidentales NP	II	2198	45,700
Vanoise NP	II	2602	52,839
Germany, Federal Republic of			
Berchtesgaden NP	II	2113	20,800
Iceland			
Skaftafell NP	II	1775	160,000
India			
Anamalai S	IV	2000	84,935
Dachigam NP	II	2600	14,100
Gamgul Siahbehi S	IV	2119	10,546
Govind Pashu Vihar S	IV	5097	48,104
Great Himalayan NP	II	4305	60,561
Gugamal NP	II	2110	36,180
Hemis NP	II	3430	410,000
Hirapora S	IV	2188	11,000
Karakorum S	IV	4300	180,000
Kedarnath S	IV	5908	97,524
Khangchendzonga NP	II	6757	84,950
Kishtwar NP	II	3100	31,000
Kugti S	IV	3794	33,000
Mehao S	IV	3156	28,150
Mouling NP	II	2314	48,300
Namdapha NP	II	4378	198,524
Nanda Devi NP	I	5717	63,033
Nargu S	IV	3064	24,313
Neyyar S	IV	1800	12,800
Overa-Aru S	IV	3175	42,500
Pin Valley NP	II	3332	80,736
Rupi Bhabha S	IV	4741	85,414
Sechu Tuan Nala S	IV	3522	65,532
Shenduruny S	IV	1650	10,032
Tundah S	IV	3426	41,948

Indonesia

Barisan Selatan NP	II	1964	365,000
Bromo-Tengger-Semeru NP	II	2676	57,606
Bukit Baka NR	I	1878	70,500
Bukit Gedang Seblat GR	IV	2063	48,750
Bukit Tapan NR	I	1576	66,500
Bukit Kayu Embun GR	IV	2247	106,000
Bukit Raya NR	I	2228	110,000
Dolok Surungan GR	IV	1981	23,800
Dumoga-Bone NP	II	1768	300,000
Enarotali NR	I	2250	300,000
Gumai Pasemah GR	IV	1576	45,883
Gunung Raya GR	IV	1932	39,500
Gunung Gede Pangrango NP	II	2019	15,000
Gunung Lorentz NR	I	4884	2,150,000
Gunung Rinjani National Park	II	3426	40,000
Gunung Leuser NP	II	3466	792,675
Indrapura NR	I	1800	221,136
Kerinci Seblat NP	II	3600	1,484,650
Lore Lindu NP	II	2410	231,000
Manusela NP	II	3027	189,000
Morowali NR	I	2630	225,000
Pegunungan Feruhumpenai NR	I	1518	90,000
Pegunungan Jayawijaya GR	IV	4466	800,000
Pegunungan Arfak NR	I	2720	45,000
Rawas Ulu Lakitan GR	IV	2084	213,437
Ruteng NR (Flores Is.)	I	1500	30,000
Sekundur and Langkat (S & W) GR	IV	2921	218,440
Sumatera Selatan GR	IV	1811	356,800
Sungai Kayan Sungai Mentarang NR	I	2358	1,600,000

Iran

Argan PA	IV	2188	52,800
Bazman PA	IV	2915	324,688
Bisiton (Varmangeh) WRef	I	2077	31,250
Golestan (Mohammad Reza Shah) NP	II	2030	91,895
Khaber-o-Rouchon WRef	I	2681	173,750
Kiamaky WRef	I	2847	84,400
Touran WRef	I	1681	565,000

Italy
Gran Paradiso NP	II	3261	70,000
Stelvio NP	II	3000	134,620

Japan
Bandai-Asahi NP	II	2028	187,041
Chubu-Sangaku NP	II	2790	174,323
Daisetsuzan NP	II	1990	230,894
Hakusan NP	II	2532	47,700
Joshinetsu Kogen NP	II	1742	189,062
Kirishima-Yaku NP	II	1955	54,833
Minami Arupusu (Minami Alps) NP	II	1992	35,752
Rishiri-Rebun-Sarobetsu	II	1718	21,222
Shikotsu - Toya NP	II	1843	98,332
Shiretoko NP	II	1661	38,633
Towada-Hachimantai NP	II	2041	85,409

Kenya
Aberdare NP	II	2165	76,619
Mount Elgon NP	II	1985	16,923
Mount Kenya NP	II	3599	71,759

Madagascar
Andohahela SNR	I	1836	76,020
Andringitra SNR	I	1658	31,160
Marojejy SNR	I	2047	60,150
Tsaratanana SNR	I	2176	48,622

Malawi
Nyika NP	II	2006	313,400

Malaysia
Cameron Highlands WS	IV	1930	64,953
Taman Negara NP	II	2030	434,351
Kinabalu P	II	3949	75,370
Gunung Mulu NP	II	2346	52,865

Mexico
Cofre de Perote NP	II	2282	11,700
El Triunfo BR (N)	I	1700	119,177
Iztaccihuatl-Popocatepetl NP	II	1852	25,679
La Malinche NP	II	2461	45,700

National Parks and Nature Reserves

Nevado de Colima NP	II	2339	22,200
Nevado de Toluca NP	II	1690	51,000
Papigochic Ref	IV	1800	172,400
Pico de Orizaba NP	II	3060	19,750
Pico de Tancitaro NP	II	1859	29,316
Mongolia			
Ar-Toul NP	II	1500	93,560
Great Gobi Desert NP	II	2000	5,300,000
Namibia			
Namib/Naukluft GP	II	2000	4,976,800
Nepal			
Langtang NP	II	6453	171,000
Makalu-Barun NP	II	7000	150,000
Sagarmatha NP	II	6003	114,800
Shey-Phoksundo NP	II	4883	355,500
New Zealand			
Arthur's Pass NP	II	1971	94,422
Egmont NP	II	2368	33,540
Fiordland (Takahe) NPSA	I	1700	177,252
Fiordland NP	II	2756	1,023,186
Lewis Pass ScR	IV	1549	13,737
Mount Aspiring NP	II	3033	355,518
Mount Cook NP	II	3164	69,923
Nelson Lakes NP	II	1909	96,112
Tongariro NP	II	2197	76,504
Westland NP	II	3498	117,547
Oman			
Wadi Serin/Jabal Aswad Arabian Tahr R	IV	1700	53,000
Pakistan			
Astore WS	IV	4848	41,472
Baltistan WS	IV	4012	41,457
Kargah WS	IV	2727	44,308
Khunjerab NP	II	2340	226,913
Naltar WS	IV	3974	27,206
Satpara WS	IV	1551	31,093

Panama
- Darien NP — II — 1500 — 597,000
- La Amistad IP — II — 3770 — 207,000
- Volcan Baru NP — II — 1931 — 14,000

Peru
- Calipuy NaR — IV — 2800 — 64,000
- Huascaran NP — II — 3568 — 340,000
- Manu NP — II — 3635 — 1,532,806
- Rio Abiseo NP — II — 3880 — 274,520
- Salinas y Aguada Blanca NaR — IV — 6057 — 366,936
- Yanachaga-Chemillen NP — II — 3000 — 122,000

Philippines
- Bataan NP — IV — 1800 — 23,688
- Mount Apo NP — II — 2454 — 72,814
- Mount Canlaon NP — II — 1800 — 24,558
- Mount Isarog NP — II — 1800 — 10,112
- Mounts Iglit-Baco NP — IV — 2088 — 75,445

Poland
- Tatra NP — II — 1649 — 21,164

Romania
- Retezat NP — II — 1619 — 54,400

Rwanda
- Volcans NP — II — 2107 — 15,000

South Africa
- Anysberg/Klein Swartberg MCA — IV — 1655 — 58,785
- Drakensberg State Forests — IV — 2027 — 190,000
- Giant's Castle GR — IV — 2071 — 34,638
- Groot Winterhoek MCA — IV — 1877 — 81,188
- Hawequas MCA — IV — 1895 — 115,910
- Hottentots Holland MCA — IV — 1589 — 84,936
- Langeberg East MCA — IV — 1576 — 71,300
- Langeberg West MCA — IV — 1588 — 77,096
- Matroosberg MCA — IV — 1849 — 95,256
- Sederberg MCA — IV — 1814 — 126,375

National Parks and Nature Reserves

Spain
Aigues Tortes y Lago de San Mauricio NP	II	1514	10,230
Ordesa y Monte Perdido NP	II	3066	15,608
Vinamala NGR	IV	3066	49,230
Teide NP	II	1717	13,571

Sri Lanka
Peak Wilderness S	IV	2188	22,380

Sweden
Sarek NP	II	1647	193,100
Stora Sjofallet NP	II	1635	127,800

Switzerland
Swiss NP	II	1674	16,887
Val de Bagnes NR	IV	1500	20,000

Taiwan
Ta-Wu Mountain Nature Pr	IV	2940	47,000
Taroko NP	II	3740	92,000
Yushan NP	II	3652	105,490

Tanzania
Arusha NP	II	3040	13,700
Kilimanjaro NP	II	4065	75,575
Mahale Mountain NP	II	1680	161,300
Uzungwa FoR	IV	2500	100,000

Thailand
Doi Chiang Dao WS	IV	1825	52,100
Doi Inthanon NP	II	1976	48,240
Khao Luang NP	II	1535	57,000
Mae Ping NP	II	1747	100,300
Thung Yai Naresuan WS	IV	1561	320,000

Turkey
Koprulu Kanyon NP	II	2830	36,614
Munzur NP	II	2300	42,800
Olimpos-Beydaglari NP	II	2366	69,800
Uludag NP	II	2393	11,338

U.S.A.

Absaroka-Beartooth NFW	III	1586	372,762
Alaska Peninsula NWR	IV	2714	1,417,500
Alaska Maritime NWR	IV	2857	1,440,597
Arctic NWR	IV	2758	7,714,940
Big Bend NP	II	1855	286,572
Bridger NFW	III	1525	158,841
Cabinet Mountains NFW	III	2198	38,191
Chugach NF	IV	4016	2,404,000
Crater Lake NP	II	1521	74,150
Death Valley NaM	III	3454	837,388
Denali NP	II	6034	1,911,495
Endicott River NFW	III	1754	40,540
Gates of the Arctic NaM	III	2504	2,939,689
Gates of the Mountain NFW	III	1829	11,583
Glacier Bay NP	II	4663	1,304,550
Glacier NP	II	2213	410,058
Grand Canyon NP	II	2275	493,441
Grand Teton NP	II	2271	124,140
Great Smoky Mountains NP	II	1766	209,160
Guadalupe Mountains NP	II	1676	31,364
Haleakala NP	II	3055	11,728
Hawaii Volcanoes NP	II	4170	91,960
Hell's Canyon NFW	III	1829	33,939
Henry Mountains NNL	III	2587	13,187
Holy Cross NFW	III	1526	47,223
Izembek NWR	IV	1763	129,961
Katmai NP	II	2318	1,504,774
Kenai NWR	IV	2015	797,850
Kenai Fjords NP	II	1932	271,255
Kings Canyon NP	II	4082	187,069
La Garita NFW	III	1620	43,942
Lake Clark NP	II	3108	1,068,805
Lassen Volcanic NP	II	2214	43,293
Manuka SNAR	IV	1684	10,344
Misty Fjords NaM	IV	2286	928,491
Mount Rainier NP	II	4325	95,268
Mount Evans NFW	III	1604	29,605
Mount Zirkel NFW	III	1896	57,105
North Cascades NP	II	2555	204,284
North Absaroka NFW	III	1740	142,114

National Parks and Nature Reserves 285

Olympic NP	II	2428	371,225
Rocky Mountain NP	II	2017	107,519
Russell Fiord NFW	III	2360	141,993
Saguaro NaM	III	1788	33,836
San Gorgonio NFW	III	1672	14,256
Sawtooth NFW	III	1798	87,925
Scapegoat NFW	III	2639	96,916
Sequoia NP	II	4082	163,115
Stikine-LeConte NFW	III	3055	182,128
Tetlin NWR	IV	1800	283,500
Teton NFW	III	2245	225,706
Togiak NWR	IV	1700	1,662,525
Tongass NF	IV	4663	6,708,900
Tracy Arm-Fords Terror NFW	III	2599	264,343
Washakie NFW	III	1982	278,073
West Elk NFW	III	1548	78,730
Wrangell-St Elias NP	II	5489	3,382,014
Yellowstone NP	II	1753	899,139
Yosemite NP	II	3327	308,273
Yukon Charley Rivers NaPr	III	1781	915,000
Zion NP	II	1524	59,308

Eurasian Republics

Armenia

Dilizhanskiy Z	I	2000	24,232
Khosrovskiy Z	I	1700	29,680
Sevan NP	II	1675	150,000
Shikaokhskiy Z	I	1500	18,000

Azerbaydzhan

Zakatal'skiy Z	I	3000	23,843

Georgia

Akhmetskiy Z	I	1700	16,297
Kintrishskiy Z	I	2150	13,893
Lagodekhskiy Z	I	2700	17,818
Tbilisskiy NP	II	3242	19,410

Kazakhstan

Aksu-Dzhabagly Z	I	3000	75,094

Alma-Atinskiy Z	I	4551	73,342
Markakol'skiy Z	I	2205	75,040

Kirghizstan

Ala-Archa NP	II	3276	19,400
Issyk-Kul'skiy Z	I	3322	18,999
Narynskiy Z	I	3531	18,260
Sary-Chelekskiy Z	I	3290	23,868

Russia

Altaiskiy Z	I	2600	881,238
Barguzinskiy Z	I	2600	263,200
Baykal'skiy Z	I	1673	165,724
Kabardino-Balkarskiy Z	I	2800	74,099
Kavkazskiy Z	I	3360	263,277
Kronotskiy Z	I	3528	1,099,000
Pribaikalskiy NP	II	1673	412,750
Sayano-Shushenskiy Z	I	1765	390,368
Severo-Osetinskiy Z	I	3338	28,999
Sikhote-Alinskiy Z	I	1600	347,052
Sokhondinskiy Z	I	1808	211,007
Teberdinskiy Z	I	2500	84,996
Zabaikalskiy NP	II	1673	269,300

Tajikistan

Ramit Z	I	2019	16,168

Turkmenistan

Kopetdagskiy Z	I	1835	49,793
Kugitangskiy Z	I	2137	27,100

Ukraine

Karpatskiy NP	II	1700	50,303

Uzbekistan

Chatkal'skiy Z	I	2890	35,686
Gissarskiy Z (Kyzylsuyskiy/ Mirakinskiy)	I	1879	87,538
Zaaminskiy Z	I	2900	15,600

Uganda

Kidepo Valley NP	II	1850	134,400
Pian-Upe GR	IV	2068	231,400

Venezuela			
Canaima NP	II	2360	3,000,000
El Avila NP	II	2765	85,192
El Tama NP	II	3009	139,000
Guaramacal NP	II	1700	21,000
Henri Pittier NP	II	2435	107,800
Mochima NP	II	1500	94,935
Perija NP	II	3320	295,288
Serrania de la Neblina NP	II	2941	1,360,000
Sierra Nevada NP	II	4400	276,446
Yacambu NP	II	1700	14,580
Yurubi NP	II	1500	23,670
Vietnam			
Chu Yang Sinh NR	IV	1605	20,000
Yugoslavia			
Durmitor NP	II	1984	33,000
Galicica NP	II	1582	22,750
Kopaonik NP	II	1917	11,800
Mavrovo NP	II	1800	73,088
Pelister NP	II	1701	12,500
Sutjeska NP	II	1686	17,250
Tara NP	II	2089	19,175
Triglav NP	II	2664	84,805
Zaire			
Kahuzi-Biega NP	II	2600	600,000
Upemba NP	II	1600	1,173,000
Virunga NP	II	4321	780,000
Zimbabwe			
Inyanga NP	II	1712	28,900

Finally, a closing thought that relates to the fifth recommendation is the observation by Groetzbach (1988) on the future of high mountain regions. He predicts an increasing attention to the tourism/recreation function of mountains primarily for seasonal use by populations from large cities *outside* the mountain realms. This functional change has already come about in the high mountains of developed countries but it is also in the initial stages in others such as the

South American Andes, the High Atlas, the Elburz and the Himalaya-Hindukush. In the same volume, Allan (1988) notes that the 1000 bed four-star hotel in Lhasa is but one indication of the modernization of mountain areas and rapid increase in their accessibility and use by lowlanders. The MTNPA "movement" needs to assess the implications of this trend and to channel it in a direction that will lead to increased efforts in protecting the world's mountain heritage.

Acknowledgements

An earlier version of this review was presented at the "International Consultation on Protected Areas in Mountain Environments" held at Volcanoes National Park on the Island of Hawaii in October 1991. We are grateful to the participants at that meeting for their assistance in refining the list and for providing additional data. Thanks are also due to our colleagues Michael Green and Jeff McNeely for their comments.

REFERENCES

Allan, N.J.R. et al. (eds.). 1988. *Human Impact on Mountains*. Rowman and Littlefield, New Jersey.
Badenkov, Y.P. 1990. "Sustainable Development of the Mountain Regions of the USSR." *Mountain Research and Development* 10:129-139.
Dasmann, R.F. and D. Poore. 1979. *Ecological Guidelines for Balanced Land Use, Conservation, and Development in High Mountains*. IUCN/WWF/UNEP Gland, Switzerland.
Gerrard, A.J. 1990. *Mountain Environments*. London: Belhaven Press.
Green, M.J.B. 1991. *Nature Reserves of the Himalaya and the Mountains of Central Asia*. Cambridge: IUCN/WCMC.
Groetzbach, E.F. 1988. "High Mountains as Human Habitat." In *Human Impacts on Mountains*, edited by N.J.R. Allan et al., 24-35. Totowa NJ: Rowman and Littlefield.
IUCN. 1990. *UN List of National Parks and Protected Areas*. Gland: IUCN.
IUCN/UNEP/WWF. 1991. *Caring For the Earth*. Gland.
Kingdon, J. 1990. *Island Africa*. London: Collins.
Myers, N. 1983. "A Priority Ranking Strategy for Threatened Species?" *Environmentalist* 3:97-120.
Peattie, R. 1936. *Mountain Geography*. New York: Greenwood Press.
Powell, G.V.N. R. and Bjork. 1990. "A Study for the Design of Viable Montane Reserves in Middle America." Report Washington D.C.: RARE.
Price, L.W. 1981. *Mountains and Man*. Berkeley: University of California

Press.

Saavedra, C. and C. Freese. 1986. "Priodidades Biologicas de Conservacion en Los Andes Tropicales." In *Conservado el Patrimonio Natural de la Region Neotropical*, 31-36. Gland, Switzerland: IUCN

Shores, J.N. 1991. "Where in the World is Biodiversity? Background Report prepared for Biodiversity Strategy and Action Plan." Gland, Switzerland: WRI/UNEP/IUCN.

Stuart, S.N. 1992. "The Zoogeography of the Montane Forest Avifauna of Eastern Tanzania." Gland, Switzerland: IUCN.

Thorsell, J.W. (ed.). 1991. *Parks on the Borderline: Experience in Transfrontier Conservation*. Gland, Switzerland: IUCN.

Udvardy, M.D.F. 1975. "A Classification of the Biogeographical Provinces of the World." Occasional Paper 18. Gland, Switzerland: IUCN.

White, F. 1983. *Vegetation Map of Africa*. Paris: UNESCO/AETFAT/UNSO.

Index

Accessibility 200
Action Plan for the Human Environment 5
Actuarial space 119
Adiabatic lapse rate 86
Adirondack Mountains 50
Adventure travel 225
Allan, Nigel J.R. 3-4; 8, 18, 223, 227
Alpine xvii
Alpine Areas Workshop 10
Alpinist' vision 120
Alps xviii
Aletch 11
Altiplano xviii
Amazon Basin 52
Antarctic 266
Apa Tanis 41
Apel, Heino 11
Arc of Crisis 114
Area-tot 182
Armitage 40
Arscott 176
Assam Himalaya 35
Anthropo-geographie 6

Bailey 37
Baker, Paul 13
Bandyopadhyay 18
Barry 76
Bastille, La and Pool 52
Beall, Cynthia 13
Berchtesgaden National Park 82
Bernard 51
Bharati, Agehananda 14, 225
Bhutan (ohsawa) 35, 43
Biodiversity xix
Biogeographical Realm 260
Biomass Production 182
Biophysicalist model 17-18
Bishop, Peter 14
Biosphere Project-6 xv
Biosphere Reserve 258
Blache, Vidal de la 6
Black Snow 111
Blackie 61
Blaikie xv, 15
Blanchard 6
Boiling potatoes 136, 138
Bookfield 15
Brandis, Sir Dietrich 40
Braudel 6
Bruijnzeel 10, 61-62
Brunham 13
Brush 130, 132, 134, 137, 145, 147
Bunnell 9
Burley 40

Caloric obsession 13
Carson 53
Cartécologique du **Nepal** 33

Castri 10
Catrographic Approaches 85-86
Changing Atmosphere 73
Cheng 40
Chipko 51
Chi-square 179
Christaller 221
Climatically dry valleys 30, 37-39, 43
Closed forests 62
Colloqia 9
Cooling 40
Comparative Geography of High Mountains 8
Comparative Cultural Geography 7
Commission on Mountain Geoecology 7
Conference on the Human Environment xv
Conference on the "Changing Atmosphere" 73
Cultivar loss 133, 139, 143-45

Davos 11
Dendrograms 18
d'Enhaut, Pays 11
Deforestation 50
Degenhardt, Bodo 16
Determinism 118
Deterministic 11
"Desert Storm" operation 111
Diaries of Lundlow and Sheriff 34
Dibang system 37
diCastri 10
Dobremez 45
Dombois 61
Douglass 60
Durand Line 19

Earth Summit 19
Earthquake Hazard 105
East of Bhutan 35

Eastern Palearctic 263
Eco-doomsters xvii
Eckholm 50
Ecology and Development on Mountains and Islands 10
Edaphic hazard 55
Eichstaett 7-8, 18
Ekologi, Lembaga 53
Ekern 52
Ellenberg, Heinz 7, 10
Elliot 189
Endangered Act in the USA 88
End Use Reclamation Plans 190
Enlightenment xvii
Environmental degradation 15
Ernst, Winkler xvi
Erosion 52
Escape Terrain 177-78, 181, 187
Ethopian Highlands 52, 62
Eurocentric 4, 14

Flatlanders 50
Folland 74, 76
Fourth World 20
Freeman, Orville xvii
Freezer-thaw cycle 33
French Centre National de la Researche Scientifique maps 33

Garbage tourism 205
GCMs 81
GCM outputs 87
Geist 161, 165
General Circulation Models 76
Genetic erosion 133
Genetic wipe out 129
Geography of risk 98
Geographical Information Centre 16, 18
Geoecology 6-7, 119
Geophysicalism 109
Geopony 42

German Foundation for Inter-national Development 11
Gilmour 15
GIS 86-87
Glacier, Sjachen 32
Glaser 10
Gleick 74
Global Climate Models 76
Global warming 75, 77
Goldstein 13
Golubets 50
Gorrie 38
Government of Bhutan 35
Greater Himalaya 3
Green Mines 115
Greenhouse gases 75
Grindelwald 11

Habitat mosaics 89
Haffner, Wilibald 8
Hamilton, Lawrence S. xix, xxi, 15, 49, 55, 59, 61
Harrison xx, 4, 18
Haslett xix
Hatley 9, 12
Heidelberg 39-40
Hengduan 3, 45
Hertz 8
Hesmer 40
Hewitt xv, xix 4-5, 8-9, 12, 18, 104, 106, 108, 110, 118-19
Highland-Lowland Interaction Systems 17
Highways to the Sky 17
Himalayan biotic environment 3
Himalayan Dilemma 50, 63
Hindukush 3
Hoehengrenzen 3
Hoehenguertel 3
Hohenstein, Klaus Mueller 7, 10
Human Environment, United Nations Conference on 4

Human Impact on Mountains 4-5, 8
Human Impact on Tundra Ecosystem 8
Humboldt, Alexander von 6

IIASA 5, 15
Imperial Eyes 14
Indomalaya 260
Indus Kohistan 32
International Institute for Applied Systems Analysis 10-11
International Union for the Conservation of Nature and National Resources xx
International Workshop on the Development on Mountain Environments 7, 10
International Workshop on Management on National Parks and Protected Areas 242
IPCC Working Group 78, 81
IUCN 4, 12
IUCN Commission on National Parks and Protected Areas xxi
Ives, Jack 10, 50, 63, 130

Juvik 52
Jentsch, Christoph 8
Jiang, Chang 37
Jodha 18
Journal of Ecology 6
Jugal Himal 33

Karakorum World Heritage Site 19
Katz 77
Kuhn, Thomas xvi
Kirby xv
Kirdon 114
Kirkpatrik 155
Kleinert's thesis of housetypes and settlements 42
Kuechler 40

Kuck 189
Kuiper 114

Lall, Johan xvi, 52
Lamb 19
Landscape ecology 7
Lenin 131
Lichtenberger 8
Lin 52
Loma 135

MAB-6 10, 12, 15
MacArthur 13, 155
MacCallum 177, 185
MacDonald 16-17
MacMohan Line 19
Mainz 7
Major Problems of Man and Environment Interaction in Mountain Ecosytems 5
Man and the Andes 13
Mass erosion 55-57; tourism 201-202; washing 52
Mechanistic Approaches 86
Mekong 37-38
Messerli 10-11, 50, 59, 63, 101, 130, 203, 206, 209-12
Microhistological analysis 172
Miehe 15, 33-34, 45
Migration corridors 89
Miklos Udvardy 4
Mikro-Makro 11
Mineral Licks 179, 188
Mohonk Mountain Conference 10
Montology: The Ecology of Mountains 11
Moser, 9, 15
Mountain Climates 74, 76-77; ecosystems 74; erosions 57; Heritage 267; Habitat and Society 4; regions 110; Tourism 202

Mountain Research and Development 4, 12
MTNPA 256

Nakao, Sasuke 34-35
Nanda 35
Narcoterrorism 116
Negative response 85
Neo-colonialism 17
Neotropical 265
New York Times 9
Nomethetic approach 11
Northern Thailand 43
Numata, M. 35

Obergurgl 9, 11, 14, 16
Oceanic islands 266
Ohsawa 35
O'Loughlin 56
Outdoor Recreation 220, 229
Oxen-area Production System 142

Pacification 113
Parsons 4
Peattie 4
Pereira 52
Peruvian Sierra 134
Peterson 9
Pinus 40
Pip-crake 33
Pitt 10
Phytophagous insect species 84
Pohle 8
Points-in-poly program 182
Polyandry xviii
Polygynandry xviii
Price xix, 12, 101, 201, 207
ProClim 78
Protective role of mountain forests 49
Purrington xvii

Qomolangma Nature Preserve 246-48
Quinoa 143-45, 147

Randschwelle 30
Ratzel, Friedrich 3-6, 8
Ratzel/Troll model 17
Reclamation objectives 157
Recreationists 222, 227
Revegetation 187
Rhoades 18
Rimland 12
Robbins 40
Rock Piles 188
Reiger, Hans-Christoph 10

Saarbrucken 8
Sagarmatha National Park xx, 19
Salani 51
Salween 37-38
Santisuk, T. 40
Santisuk's monograph 43
Sauer, Carl 132
Sawyer 40
Schmidt-Vogt 41-42, 45
Schneider, Erwin 34, 74
Scientistical xvi
Schweinfurth, Ulrich xix, 15, 27, 32, 37-40, 42-43
Sediment (damage) 56-57
Sediment load 63
Sedimentation 57
Selva 116
Sharp and Sharp 51, 67
Shores 270
Shpak 51
Shukla 51
Sichuan Province 38
Skull Characters 166
Small and Singer 112
Smitinand 40
Sopher, David 18

South Asia xix
Southeast Asian Peninsula 39
Species dispersal 84
Splash erosion 53
Stability 11
Stadtmuller 52
Staszewski xviii
Stein 40
Stemp 165
Stereotyping 118
Stevens 229
Stockholm Conference 15
Strong and Leggat 153
Surface 52
Surface Erosion 53, 62
Susceptible soils 108
Sustainability 11
Swidden-management 41
Swift 16

Talus 188
Tenga Valley 36
Terai forests 44
Territorial imperative 44
Thak Khola 33
The Appliance of the Wrong Science 12
The Indo-Tibetan Interface 14
The Myth of ShangriLa 14
Thompson 9, 12-13
Thorsell xx, 4, 18
Throne 165
Tibet 44, 244
Tibetan Plateau xviii, 42-44, 245
Timmerman 111
Toba, Lake 40
Tourism 199, 204, 206-7, 227
Tourists 222
Traditional conservation 89
Transfrontier/ Border Parks 268
Tsangpo gorge 37
Troendle 62

Troll, Carl 4-7, 15, 27, 29-31, 42, 44
Troll's Nanga Parbat map 37
Troll's vegetation map 39

Udvardy, Miklos, 4, 260
Uhlig 4, 7
Ulluco 141-42, 147
UN Conference on Environment and Development 73
UN Conference on Human Experiment 4-5
UN Environment Programme xv
Uncertainty on a Himalayan Scale 15
UNEP 5
UNESCO MAB-6 xvi, 11, 15
UNESCO's Man and the Biosphere Project-6 9
UNESCO/UNEP/PAO 52
United Nations 4
United Nations Environment Programme 5
Upper Burma 40

Velley-chambers 35
Vegetation map 27, 29-32, 34
1957 vegetation map 42
Vegetation Map Construction 41
Vegetation map of Namcha Barwa 37
Vegetation map of China 38, 43
Vegetation map of Himalayas 39, 44
Vegetation map of Tibet 39, 43
Vegetation Map of Xizang (Tibet) 38-39

Vegetation mapping by analogy 42, 44
Vegetationsgeographische Untersuchungen im Dhaulagiri- und Annapurna-Himalaya 33
Veyret 4, 6
Vogt, Schmidt 15, 33
Vose 51

War and Other Armed Violence 110
Warburton 9
Waterstone xv
Watson 75
Weeks 155
Weilie, Chen 36, 39, 43
Werner 40, 43
White Plagues 115-16
Wiersum 53
Wigley 74
Wisner xv
Woodlands Mountain Institute 238
World Data Center xx
World Heritage Site 258
World Resources Institute 84

Yangtsekiang 38

Zeballos 139
Zhang 38
Zimmerer 136, 138, 140, 144, 203
Zurick 16
Zwerman and Richard 50